FILMMAKERS SERIES
edited by
ANTHONY SLIDE

SCARECROW PRESS, INC.

Published in the United States of America
by Scarecrow Press, Inc.
4720 Boston Way
Lanham, Maryland 20706

4 Pleydell Gardens, Folkestone
Kent CT20 2DN, England

British Library Cataloguing in Publication Information Available

Library of Congress Cataloging-in-Publication Data

Salwolke, Scott, 1964–
The films of Michael Powell and the Archers / Scott Salwolke.
p. cm.— (Filmakers series ; no. 52)
Filmography: p.
Includes bibliographical references and index.
1. Powell, Michael. 2. Pressburger, Emeric. 3. Archer Films—
History. I. Title. II. Series.
PN1998.3.P69S26 1997
791.43'0233'092—dc20   96–44286   CIP

ISBN 0-8108-3183-X (cloth : alk. paper)

Manufactured in the United States of America.

The Films of Michael Powell and the Archers

Scott Salwolke

Filmmakers Series, No. 52

The Scarecrow Press, Inc.
Lanham, Md., & London
1997

To Mom,
who died too soon and who deserved more

Contents

Introduction

It is hard to imagine that just two decades ago, Michael Powell and Emeric Pressburger seemed destined to be just footnotes in film histories. They were the Archers, one of cinema's most successful collaborations, having produced sixteen films over a fifteen-year span. Their films were often breathtaking to watch, particularly those produced in Technicolor, and often commercially successful, in both their native England and the United States, but the critics were sometimes less than kind. The British critics, though conceding that they were master technicians, thought that they were too out of the ordinary. What was the purpose of turning the comic figure of Colonel Blimp into the central figure of a film in the midst of the war, what perversion lay behind a character pouring glue into young women's hair, and why was so much blood needed for the conclusion of a ballet film? When they parted ways in 1956, there was no public outcry, only a deathly silence, similar to what had greeted their last few films. If possible, Powell's career only went downhill, particularly after the release of the infamous *Peeping Tom*. It seemed to end his career in the minds of many, and he became like Clive Candy in *The Life and Death of Colonel Blimp*, a sympathetic figure out of step with the times.

For all of the critical indifference that the Archers engendered, they had always had a few supporters, whose voices began to be heard. Raymond Durgnat was among the first to praise Powell's work, but even he first assumed a pseudonym with which to do it. The French had also discovered Powell, in particular singling out *Peeping Tom* for attention, but it wouldn't be until the seventies that revivals of his films increased interest in his films, first in England, then in the United States. Kevin Gough Yates produced two of these revivals and conducted an extensive interview with Powell for both. This was followed by Ian Christie's first book on the Archers, to be succeeded by another, and later by an adaptation of their script *The Life and Death of Colonel Blimp*. Powell's greatest proponents, however, turned out to be two American film directors, Martin Scorsese and Francis Ford Coppola. He developed a long-lasting friendship with the first, while also working at Coppola's studio for a time as an artist in residence. He became the grand old man of the English cinema, eventually moving to the United States to take a position at Dartmouth College, where he began work on his sweeping two-volume autobiography. Where once Powell's name had been pariah, he was now considered by many to be England's greatest director, and certainly his body of work strengthens this argument. Unfortunately, all of this attention ignored Powell's longtime collaborator and the second half of the Archers, Emeric Pressburger.

If the moniker of the Archers served to unite the two men's contributions, it was often taken for granted that Powell was the director and Pressburger simply the writer, albeit an extremely talented one. Even as Powell's reputation was being resurrected, Pressburger remained lost in the shadows, partly out of his own reticence but also because many critics misconstrued the whole concept of the Archers. Powell was an extremely talented director, whose work before and after Pressburger remains of tremendous interest, but it was with the Hungarian emigré that he created most of his masterpieces. If Pressburger had been subtracted from the equation, Powell's work surely would not have reached such heights and challenged viewers so much.

Powell and Pressburger were men of divergent backgrounds but with similar passions. Powell was introduced to the cinema relatively late in life, and like many Englishmen he found little to appreciate in the British cinema. His influences would be the Americans and the Germans, and he would gain his experience with an American unit in France. Whereas Powell

admired the German film industry, Pressburger gained his education in it. Thus, while most British filmmakers worked in
either the literary tradition or the documentary movement, the
Archers were creating original works that examined higher ideals, such as dying for one's country or dying for one's art. Perhaps Raymond Durgnat put it best when he characterized
Powell as being "born into the wrong period. Had he, and the
cinema, and Technicolor, been born during any of the periods
celebrated in Mario Praz's 'The Romantic Agony,' he might have
been working with the cultural grain instead of against it. Ad-
mittedly his romantic-expressionistic films chime in with a
post-war English nostalgia for period exoticism."[1]

Powell's and Pressburger's partnership was born in a war,
in an atmosphere where everyone was united in a single cause:
to defeat the Germans. In the beginning, this was the objective
of the Archers, as their films attempted to identify the enemy
and the causes for which the English were fighting. Yet, even
before the war had ended, their attention had turned to the
effect the conflict would have on the English culture, champi-
oning values that other directors were ignoring. If the union of
two men is not unique to the history of cinema, Powell and
Pressburger's collaboration is perhaps unusual in that each
man seemed to retain their original roles, with Pressburger continuing to serve as writer, seldom stepping foot on the set. If
this seems to imply that Powell was indeed director of their
films, it ignores the fact that the resulting film is composed of
equal parts of each man's identity. "Produced, written and directed by Michael Powell and Emeric Pressburger" is how the
Archers identified themselves, and this is how they should be
remembered. The image of an arrow striking a target became
not only the logo for the Archers but also synonymous with
quality and originality.

The bulk of this book focuses on Powell, with the realization that most of his greatest achievements came in collaboration with Pressburger. Until recently little was known of
Pressburger's personal life, because he gave few interviews. He
was content to let his films speak for themselves. His grandson's biography adds to our knowledge, but even Kevin Mac-
Donald was not able to fill out completely the details of his
grandfather's life. Assessing Pressburger's pre-English films is
nearly impossible as only a handful are still thought to exist,

and determining his contribution on each is similarly difficult. Also, by examining Powell's career in toto, one gets a unique perspective on the English cinema, for he was there when the silent cinema was still in vogue and it ended when the English cinema, for the most part, had long passed its prime. Powell was the first to recognize this. "I live cinema. I chose the cinema when I was very young, sixteen years old, and from then on my memories virtually coincide with the history of cinema. I have worked actively in the cinema for the last forty years and I live as much in the future, since I'm profoundly dissatisfied with what has been done so far. As I have already said, I am not a director with a personal style, I am simply cinema."[2]

1

Images Are Everything

Because Michael Powell presents his life story in a two-part, 1,250-page autobiography, recounting his early life here would seem superfluous, although a brief outline of the events leading up to his film career is necessary. Michael Latham Powell was born on September 30, 1905, in Bekesbourne, a small village near Canterbury. In his autobiography he creates an evocative portrait of not just his early life, but also the countryside, which would later be the setting for one of his first masterpieces with Emeric Pressburger. When the First World War broke out, his father, a farmer, was sent to France to help grow crops for the Royal Army Service, but after the Armistice Thomas Powell failed to return. He had become infatuated with France and decided to take on the task of running a hotel in Cap Ferrat, overlooking the Riviera. The estrangement was hard for the family, with Michael visiting his father only occasionally. The elder Powell, however, was to have a tremendous impact on Michael's future career.

At the age of five, Powell was already a voracious reader, absorbing the works of Louisa May Alcott, H. G. Wells, and Rudyard Kipling. He didn't just read, he also recounted what he read, entertaining his fellow students at King's School in Canterbury with these stories, already assuming the role of "interpreter rather than an originator."[1] For a man who entitled his autobiography *A Life in Films*, his introduction to the cinema came relatively late in life and not in a manner one would expect. When he was sixteen, he came across an issue of *Pic-*

turegoer, one of the first British publications to examine the cinema. Reading it from cover to cover, he became intrigued with film, so much so that decades later he could still recall its cover, actress Ivy Close sitting on a toboggan. After absorbing the works of Charles Chaplin, D. W. Griffith, and Fritz Lang, among others, he became determined to pursue a career in film, despite the obvious risks involved.

Powell's first experience in film was not behind the camera but in front. His father, supportive if not quite understanding of his son's desire to enter film, arranged for a screen test. The test was a failure, but his father's next action was more effective. An American company was filming in Nice, and Powell senior managed to get his son an introduction. The head of the company was Rex Ingram, then one of the most recognized directors in the world, the equal of D. W. Griffith and Cecil B. DeMille. Ingram first gained fame directing Rudolph Valentino in *The Four Horsemen of the Apocalypse*, then for a series of films featuring his wife Alice Terry. Films such as *Scaramouche* and *Where the Pavement Ends* solidified his critical and commercial reputation, but he still held differences with the management of M-G-M. In 1925, he left the United States to escape the presence of Louis B. Mayer and began filming *Mare Nostrum*, the film on which Powell first found work. It was based on a novel by Vincente Blasco-Ibañez, who had also written *The Four Horsemen of the Apocalypse*. At first no one knew what to do with the eager employee, but Powell was finally placed in the stills department. It was a tremendous learning experience for Powell, as it was a lavish spectacle, "full of enormous tricks with a great theme and an international cast. It was the kind of film that gives you ideas that stay with you all your life. Ingram had an epic style. He also had the grand manner. These are things if you see them when you're young you don't forget them."[2]

Although Powell barely survived the first week of production, particularly after making a costly mistake, he would remain with Ingram's unit for his next two films, *The Magician* and *The Garden of Allah*. *Mare Nostrum* was a tale of spies and betrayal and, as would be many of Powell's own films, had a wartime setting. If this film anticipated the milieu for many of Powell's films, *The Magician* predicted a recurring motif, the power of gazing. The antagonist of the film is a magician who hypnotizes a young woman and takes her away from her lover. Unlike Jaffar in *The Thief of Bagdad*, however, the magician is not in love with the woman but needs her heart to rejuvenate a corpse. The magician's laboratory was set on the edge of a mountain, perhaps influencing the locale of *Black Narcissus*. *The Magician* would be a commercial and critical failure, but from it Powell would learn one lesson that would influence his later films, which was to "distrust, in films of imaginative power, a mixture of studio settings and location shooting."[3] Thus, twenty years later when he was to codirect a film set in India, he would film the work entirely in the studio.

The Garden of Allah, Powell's last film with Ingram, could have also served as an influence on *Black Narcissus*, with its story of a Trappist monk falling in love with a young woman. As with all three of the works Ingram directed in Europe, the film was a failure, and he was forced to disband his European unit. Not for the last time, Powell found himself out of work. *The Garden of Allah*, however, had provided him with a second career, albeit a short-lived one, for among his many duties on that film was playing the part of an English tourist, providing some comic relief. Harry Lachman, who had served as an assistant director to Ingram, initiated a series of two-reel comedies to be called *Travelaughs* starring Powell in a similar role. The format for each was to remain the same: a group of tourists bumbling through some exotic locale, such as North Africa, the setting for *Camels to Cannibals*. It's not known how many of these comedies were filmed, but the arrival of sound seemed to end this stage of Powell's career. Except for an occasional cameo in his own films, Powell would remain safely behind the camera.

Returning to England, Powell found work in the story department of British International Pictures, working alongside Alfred Hitchcock. Hitchcock had already developed into one of England's premier directors, primarily on the strength of his thriller *The Lodger*, and he was to have as great an influence on Powell as Ingram had. In fact, the men's careers would continuously intersect, even after Hitchcock had emigrated to the United States.

Hitchcock, like Powell, had begun his career not with an English company but an American one. Both men recognized the deficiencies of the English cinema and instead were stirred by imported films, particularly those from Germany. German expressionism infused both men's work, and, because each had had their apprenticeship in the silent cinema, neither would trust the spoken word, preferring instead to rely on images to convey emotions and feelings. "In my films images are everything," claimed Powell, "words are used like music to distill emotion."[4] Similarly, each man's style is characterized by the continuous movement of the camera and by their innovative use of music to heighten emotions.

Powell first worked on Hitchcock's silent film *Champagne*, for which he took the stills and out of which a friendship developed. He next worked on *The Manxman* and later contributed to the script of *Blackmail*, which midway through production was turned into England's first talking picture. In his autobiography, Powell takes credit for the film's climax, a chase through a British landmark, which inaugurated a trend in Hitchcock's films involving the use of famous locations as backdrops for his adventures. Powell, however, received no screen credit for his work, and his statement concerning the climax has never been confirmed.

For all of Hitchcock's success, there was little doubt that he was a big fish in a very small pond, for the British cinema was already in the shadow of its American counterpart. Whereas American films could recoup their costs in their own country, English films were not afforded such a luxury. In 1926, when Powell was just beginning his film career, only thirty-four films were made in Britain, accounting for 5 percent of the films released there. The disparity was not lost on the politicians. Not for the last time, Parliament attempted to remedy the situation through legislation, creating the Cinematograph Film Acts of 1927, which set a quota for British exhibitors. Theaters were required to show an established percentage of English films, starting at 5 percent in the year of the law's creation and gradually increasing to 20 percent by 1937. If the law stipulated the percentage of British films to be exhibited, however, it had no control over their quality. The result was the creation of the "quota quickie," films rarely longer than an hour and often made on the lowest possible budget. The quota quickie would be denigrated by not just film critics but also the viewing public, whose opinion of the British film industry could only get worse.

By 1930, Powell had already developed a reputation for himself, and it seemed predestined that he would become a director. With the film *Caste*, for which he adapted the script, he also gained his first exposure with his future vocation, taking over for the credited director when the latter took a day off. In each of his undertakings, Powell continued to acquaint himself with all aspects of filmmaking, working in the editing room and with the art department. He next worked on the script for *77 Park Lane*, an A-budget film that was filmed in three languages—English, French, and Spanish (a common practice in the early years of talkies)—which gave him a taste for higher quality films. At this time, the producer of *Caste*, Jerry Jackson, came to Powell with an offer to direct for Ideal Films, a company that marketed quota quickies. With some reluctance, Powell accepted the offer and thus began his directorial career.

In this early stage of Powell's career, Jackson would be among his closest collaborators, with only Emeric Pressburger arguably having a greater impact on his career. In the next five years Powell directed twenty-three films, twelve of which are still thought to be missing. Perhaps the greatest loss of these is his directorial debut, *Two Crowded Hours*. Jackson and Powell were to be paid one pound for each foot of film delivered, which meant that for a profit to be made, the film would have to be brought in considerably under budget. Undaunted, Powell began the first day on location and confidently told the crew he was satisfied with the first take. The film was to be completed in just twelve days, but even in this abbreviated schedule Powell's attention to detail was apparent. He carefully scouted the locations, determining the perfect time of day in which to film. He benefited from the experience of his two lead actors, comedian Jerry Verno and John Longden, who had gained fame for his performance in Hitchcock's *Blackmail*. His leading lady, Jane Welsh, is less well known but notable for being the first in a long line of red headed actresses whom Powell would feature in his films. If Hitchcock is remembered for his cool blond heroines, Powell is remembered for his stunning redheads: Deborah Kerr, Moira Shearer, Anna Massey, Pamela Brown, and Clare Dunne.

The comedy-thriller concerns an escaped murderer who goes after the woman who testified against him and who, in the interim, has fallen in love with the detective from the case. The detective, Harry Fielding (Longden), chases after him and is assisted by Jim (Jerry Verno), a cockney taxi driver who supplies the film with its humor. Looking back nearly fifty years later and without the benefit of a copy, Powell felt the film was full of "clever angles and quick cutting, but it was also obvious that the director meant to entertain first and foremost."[5] It was almost universally praised, despite its miniscule budget and Powell was hailed as a director, "whose future will certainly be watched with interest."[6] Even in the United States, the film was recognized as untypical fare from the British market. "Just a quota quickie, but much better than many more ambitious pictures turned out this side."[7] It was followed up by *My Friend the King*, a sequel of sorts with Verno again portraying Jim the cab driver. This time Jim is caught up in a plot to kidnap the boy king of a Ruritanian country. This film did not equal the success of the first, and Powell admitted it was "a highly improbable story."[8] He would remember it only as a failure.

The Rasp would be Powell's fourth film, following *Rynox*, and like that film, which does survive, the source is a story by mystery writer Philip MacDonald. MacDonald had been impressed with Powell's adaption of *Rynox* and would contribute to the scripts of his next four films. In *The Rasp*, a cabinet minister is found dead in his country home, the murder weapon being a rasp. Journalist Anthony Gethryn (Claude Horton) has intended to interview the politician but after finding the body, begins an investigation into the murder. The police have their own suspect, but Gethryn is able to extract a confession from the real killer. Gethryn would be MacDonald's response to Sherlock Holmes, a cerebral investigator who appears in a series of mysteries. In the book, the police even allow Gethryn a free hand in his investigation. *Kine Weekly* decried that "in tackling a murder mystery drama, in which a newspaperman is involved, Michael Powell, the director, has butted in on America's favorite theme, and this effort, although moderately good, suffers in comparison. However, the atmosphere is refreshingly English, and there remains sufficient to entertain the unsophisticated."[9] Powell was even more succinct in his appraisal, declaring that *The Rasp* "refused to become a film and remained a book."[10]

Of *The Star Reporter*, Powell reported that it was "done with great panache and a bloody good script, very good dialect-sophisticated dialect."[11] The protagonist would once more be a journalist, with Major Starr (Harold French) going undercover as the chauffeur to Lady Susan Loman (Isla Bevan). He intends to research a feature article, but in the midst of his work, he comes across a robbery in which the jewels of Lady Susan's father are stolen. His pursuit of the robber concludes on a rooftop, where the thief falls to his death. Powell's ability to overcome his budget restraints is evident in this film; for example he hired a camera for eight pounds and photographed the Queen Mary, which he incorporated into his story. Actions such as this separated Powell's work from many of the quota quickies which often were hurriedly produced with little regard to quality. The reviews of the time reflected this. Graham Greene had enjoyed *Rynox* and likewise praised *The Star Reporter*. "The passage showing the arrival of the Berengaria demonstrates a unique power of observation which promises much," he wrote. "His angles are strong, his continuity, shot by shot, direct and definite. Powell can certainly see things. One only waits now for evidence of his powers to recognize ideas."[12]

Powell's initial success with quota quickies soon allowed him and Jackson to set up their own company. Westminister Films chose as its logo Big Ben, which two years later became the symbol for Alexander Korda's more successful production company. None of the films produced by Westminister is thought to exist. *C.O.D.*, the first film produced, was another mystery, whose complex plot is detailed by a critic for the *Biograph*:

> Peter Craven, temporarily down and out, enters a West End mansion during the absence of servants and, while helping himself to refreshments, is confronted by a lovely girl, Frances, who offers to pay him to dispose of the body of her stepfather, who has just been murdered in circumstances likely to incriminate her. Peter takes the body in a trunk to the cloakroom at St. Pancras, but on his return he and Frances are annoyed to find that the body has been put in its original position in the library. Frances's cousin, Edward, arrives with a friend and sends for the police. While Frances is being cross-examined, Peter calls on a doctor, chloroforms him and going back to the house in his name, forces a confession at the point of a stethoscope from a confederate, who denounces Edward as the murderer. Peter and Edward then fight a revolver duel up to the top of the

house, from which Edward falls to his death and Peter returns
to arrange a marriage with Frances.[13]

His Lordship was one of Powell's greatest failures, even to
the point of being booed at by the audience on its premiere at
London's Dominion Theatre. The exhibitors contacted the producers in hopes of being released from their contract, while for
once critics seemed to agree with the public, stating that Jerry
Verno was "badly served with material in this queer mixture of
musical comedy, burlesque and satire."[14] Bert Gibbs (Verno), a
plumber with ties to nobility, finds himself engaged to a Russian actress, despite his already having a girlfriend. His mother is pleased with the arrangement, as are the two con men
also involved in the plot. "One of the musical numbers featured a chorus of girl reporters, dressed in horn-rimmed glasses, tailored costumes and berets, writing in enormous
notebooks, with enormous pencils, in unison to music."[15] It is
unlikely that the film could be called a precursor to *The Red
Shoes* or *The Tales of Hoffmann*, but one is reluctant to dismiss the film out of hand, considering the similar response
Peeping Tom would receive nearly thirty years later.

Little is known of *Born Lucky* except that *Picturegoer* reported that it was the "simple story of a humble girl's rise to
stage fame."[16] It was scripted by Ralph Smart, who would work
with Powell on six films, their most successful collaboration
being *The Phantom Light*. Powell would dismiss this film as "real
schmaltz."[17] For him the film's primary attraction was that it
gave him a chance to work with the art director assigned to
the project, Ian Campbell Grey. He was the first of many talented art directors with whom Powell would collaborate and, if
not for his premature death in the war, would have most likely
established a greater name for himself.

The Girl in the Crowd was the second film Powell directed
for Irving Asher, a producer best known for being the man
Korda pushed aside to allow Powell and Emeric Pressburger to
collaborate on their first film, *The Spy in Black*. Powell thought
the film was "terrible. It was a complete failure, nobody ever
saw it."[18] David Gordon (Barry Clifton) is a bookseller who
marries college student Marian (Patricia Hilliard). When Marian
gives advice on romance over the phone to David's best friend
Bob (Harold French), she finds herself the subject of his affections. After various entanglements, everyone ends up in court,

where the couple are reunited. This work was another in a series of films attempting to model themselves after the screwball comedies of Hollywood. A similarly convoluted plot highlighted *The Price of a Song*, which despite the impression given by the title is not a musical but a mystery. Arnold Grierson (Campbell Gullan), a clerk desperate for money, forces his stepdaughter to marry Nevern (Eric Maturin), a successful songwriter. Margaret (Marjorie Corbett) has little love for her husband, instead wanting to marry Michael Hardwicke (Gerald Fielding), a newspaper reporter. Grierson eventually murders Nevern in hopes that his daughter will inherit his fortune, but his crime is found out and Margaret is left free to marry Michael.

Someday was based on the novel *Young Nowheres* by I. A. R. Wylie, which had already been filmed in 1929 by First National under its original title. Powell's remake, transplanted to England, is perhaps most significant for being Esmond Knight's first film with Powell. The two would work together on seven more films over thirty-seven years, with Knight's portraying everything from the village idiot to an Indian general. Here Knight plays Curly Blake, an elevator operator who is in love with Emily (Margaret Lockwood), a young woman about to be released from the hospital. Finances have prevented the couple from marrying, but Blake hopes to surprise her by preparing a supper for her in the apartment of a tenant thought to be out. When the man returns unexpectedly, a fight ensues and Blake is arrested. Only when Emily's employer bails Blake out is the couple reunited. *Monthly Film Bulletin* thought it a "pleasant unpretentious story pleasantly told. The direction, however, lacks polish and is not convincing. It is full of good ideas insufficiently carried out; the scenes at the sea-side particularly fail in this respect."[19]

In *The Brown Wallet*, John Gillespie (Patric Knowles) learns that his business partner has embezzled their money, thus leaving him broke. In desperation he turns to a wealthy aunt, who refuses to help, but then he discovers a wallet full of money inside a taxi cab. He keeps the cash, but after his aunt is found murdered and robbed, he is accused of the crime. He is eventually acquitted when the real murderer confesses. One critic found that the "characterization is unconvincing throughout the film, and each part is overdrawn in an attempt to simulate reality."[20] Powell's opinions of his films often seemed to be influenced by their critical reception, as in the case of *A Canterbury Tale*, but here he defended a film that he characterized as a "very ingenious little thriller—too ingenious. It's funny when a thriller's too ingenious it becomes a little picture; when it's simple it's got a chance of being big. This was a beautifully worked-out thriller."[21]

The Man behind the Mask would be the last quota quickie Powell would direct, and it is most notable for being the film that introduced him to Joe Rock, the man who would produce *The Edge of the World*. The *Monthly Film Bulletin* thought that Powell should be "congratulated for having made what must be termed a good film out of very unlikely material."[22] Powell, however, would not be as tolerant, especially of the script, but he attempted to salvage the film by turning it into a "rather German type expressionistic thriller."[23] On the eve of their wedding, Nick Barclay (Hugh Williams) and June Slade (Jane Baxter) are assaulted as they are returning from a masked ball. The masked man elopes with June and steals from her father the Shield of Kahm. Lord Slade (Peter Gawthorne) suspects Nick of the robbery, and the latter is forced to track down the kidnapper. June is found, and she and Nick are finally married only to be lured, along with Lord Slade, to the home of an international criminal who had instigated the robbery. Eventually everyone is rescued, and the burglar is taken into custody. The critic for *Kine Weekly* found the film a "sensational melodrama entirely unconvincing as to plot, but holding the attention by its extremely good acting and some clever touches of production which introduce the human note. Michael Powell has done everything possible to give plausibility to the tale; he provides a clear continuity, concentrates on facial expression and detail rather than background, and is responsible for many amusing touches."[24]

2

Quota Quickies: An Important Step Down

There can be no question that Powell thought little of his work in quota quickies. In his two-volume autobiography, only twenty-five pages are devoted to this phase of his career, despite its accounting for seven years and nearly half of his films. When he did speak of quota quickies, it was often with regret, as if this period of his was wasted. By 1931, he had already cultivated a reputation for himself as a screenwriter and with hindsight he wondered whether he would not have been better off remaining at this job a while longer rather than accepting the opportunity to direct quota quickies. The occasion to direct would certainly have presented itself again and presumably with a more creditable assignment. Instead he found himself on the "wrong track" for the next five years.[1]

A second lost chance, according to Powell, was after the release of *Two Crowded Hours* and *Rynox*. He had been hailed by many critics as an important new talent and C. A. Lejeune wrote that he had become one of England's three premier directors, the other two being Alfred Hitchcock and Anthony Asquith. This success could have also transferred to a break for Powell, but instead he continued to work with producer Jerry Jackson. The results were films that he dismissed as simply "footage. Some of them were downright bad. Jerry was perfectly happy with this sort of hit-and-miss existence; but films

were my life, my art, my mistress, my religion. And I was be-
traying all of them by making potboilers."[2]

Powell's disdain for these films was often echoed by the
critics of the day and many historians since. In his book *The
Great Picture Show*, George Perry writes that the quota quickies of the "thirties may have kept people in work, but they did
little to generate enthusiasm for British films, and until the
Second World War they were, with few exceptions, notorious
for their shoddy and vapid values."[3] Indeed, some of these "potboilers" are bad, but what is surprising is that the majority of
Powell's early films remain entertaining. Unquestionably, Powell could have become a successful director had he taken either of the two paths he suggests, but it must also be
remembered that it was in these low-budget films that he received his training and through them developed the talent that
produced the later masterpieces. It also introduced him to
many of the technicians and actors who would be so crucial to
him later. Googie Withers, Esmond Knight, and John Laurie all
came from these films, as did such technicians as Alfred Junge.
Some evidence even indicates that despite his proclamations,
Powell carried some affection for these films. Thus the actors
who would star in his quota quickies often turn up in small
roles later. Jerry Verno, the star of four of his early films, plays
the doorman in *The Red Shoes*; Ian Hunter portrays a Navy
Captain in *The Battle of River Plate*; and Leslie Banks is featured in *The Small Back Room*. At times Powell even had a
conciliatory attitude to his experience in quota quickies. "These
films were so very simple. I think probably what they had and
which made people sometimes hate them and sometimes remember them was a mixture, naturally, of considerable style
in the storytelling because I came in from a very stylistic background."[4]

Rynox/Hotel Splendide

Rynox is the earliest of the Powell films to survive, the second
he directed but the third released. It is one of the films that

Lejeune thought highly of, and in fact many critics, including Graham Greene, praised it. While conceding that the story was flawed, Greene also felt it was a film "which in beautific settings, in superb photography, in dressing, in angle, in movement, in direction generally, achieves all the neatness and finish one has come to regard as the exclusive possession of Americans."[5] Such praise today seems overly demonstrative for a film which is no better nor no worse than many of the early talkies coming out of the United States at this time.

F. X. Benedik (Stewart Rome) is the head of Rynox, a company facing financial ruin and for which he is held responsible. Benedik seems unconcerned by the threat of the companies creditors or the personal threats he is receiving from Boswell Marsh, a man who accuses him of stealing a patent. Marsh, a loud, coarse man given to fits of rage, arranges for Benedik's staff to be out of the house when he arrives for a confrontation one night. Gunshots are heard and Benedik appears dead in his study, with neither Marsh nor the murder weapon to be found. Benedik's insurance money saves the company, and his son successfully takes over as president. Months later, with the murder still unsolved Tony Benedik (John Longden) is approached by a man attempting to sell a letter written by the elder Benedik. In it his father describes how he created the character of Marsh, staging his suicide so it would appear to be murder. After hastily paying back the insurance company, Tony assaults the blackmailer to retrieve the now worthless letter. When asked by the man why he went to the trouble of assaulting him, Tony casually remarks that he "wouldn't understand."

Nearly thirty years separate the release of the first of Powell's films to have been discovered and *Peeping Tom*, the film that would be the culmination of his career. Both concern a man who creates a drama in which the final act is his own suicide and that results in his son's endeavoring to excise his father's predominance over him. While Mark completes a documentary, the climax of which is his own death, Benedik creates a drama with a similar ending. Although he does not create a filmed record of the event, Benedik does leave behind a letter outlining how, as his company faced financial ruin, he carefully staged his own death by first generating his own antagonist. In both physical appearance and manner, Marsh is his complete antithesis, and he seems to relish the impunity the character provides him, loudly banging his cane on counters and intimidating shop clerks. When purchasing the murder weapon, he bullies the salesman, telling him to hurry up so that he "can get away from your face." Having arranged for the staff to be away for the night, making sure that his butler witnesses the arrival of Marsh, he disposes of the disguise into the fire. After carefully placing one gun in a tree branch he has pulled in through a window, he begins to fire another one about the room, before killing himself with the first gun. As he falls to the floor dead, the released branch hurls the gun out into the darkness. It as convoluted a death as Mark Lewis will undergo in *Peeping Tom*, racing through a carefully timed sequence of cameras to impale himself on a blade.

Rynox is a mystery, the objective of which is to determine how a man died. Once this is revealed, there is little to recommend the film, despite the convincing performances. Like many early sound films, in both England and in the United States, the effect is like that of watching a stage play, with most of the action occurring in the study or the office. Yet it is leagues above the next film available, *The Hotel Splendide*, a confused attempt at a comedy thriller. Of the four quota quickies Powell directed starring Jerry Verno, this is the only to survive, and one hopes it is not symptomatic of the series. Verno portrays Jerry Mason, a Walter Mitty type of clerk who inherits the Hotel Splendide. Imagining it to be an expensive resort, Jerry quits his job and leaves for the hotel, only to find that it is a run-down boarding house, about to go out of business. As he attempts a variety of promotions to attract business, he finds himself mixed up with a gang of jewel thieves, two undercover police officers, and a female desk clerk, whom he desperately wants to impress. The criminals are undertaking to recover a valuable jewel concealed on the grounds, but by the end they are arrested and Jerry is able to save the hotel with the reward money.

The Hotel Splendide is the film that gives credence to the myth that quota quickies were inferior. In nearly every category the film is abysmal, almost excruciating to watch, particularly in its attempts at humor. The editing only amplifies the deficient production values, with actors seemingly looking on other characters but with the matching cuts failing to conform. Most damaging of all is that the comedy falls flat, as in an extended sequence in which Verno leads one group of guests around while the female desk clerk leads another and the groups constantly stumble into one another. The film opens pleasantly enough with Mason sitting in his boss's office, imagining that he is in charge. Talking on the phone, he pretends to berate an employee, not realizing that his own supervisor has walked in behind him. He meekly leaves, but on learning of his windfall, he returns to rebuke his supervisor before boarding a train for the hotel. Many of Powell's and the Archers' protagonists start out on such a journey, with fixed expectations that are forsaken upon their arrival; *A Canterbury Tale*, *I Know Where I'm Going*, *Black Narcissus*, *They're a Weird Mob*, and *Age of Consent* are the most obvious examples. In fact, Mason falls asleep on his train ride and dreams of a magnificent hotel with many employees, but, like Joan Webster's dream in *I Know Where I'm Going*, this proves to be the antithesis of reality. There is even a unrefined attempt to choreograph movement to music as all of the characters begin to follow a black cat up the stairs, their steps timed to Gounod's "Funeral March of a Marionette," the music that later became Alfred Hitchcock's signature tune.

Night of the Party / The Fire Raisers

There is a noticeable development in Powell's next film to survive, owing to the fact that it was already his tenth film and to the involvement of Michael Balcon, who, as the head of Gaumount-British, was already garnering a reputation for quality. Powell and producer Jerry Jackson leaped at his offer of a contract for four eighty-minute films. With only a budget of 12,500 pounds for each film, the two men realized the best way to ensure a profit would be to originate their own stories. Powell immediately set to work on a story involving fire raisers, men who burn property for profit. Balcon, however, first convinced them to take on a stage play entitled *The Night of the Party*.

Only after they accepted the project did they realize they had been burdened with what Powell diplomatically characterized as a stinker. "It was a bad film from a bad script, from a very poor play and was not very successful. I don't know that it was ever produced in the theatre. It was very stagey and I couldn't make much of it."[6] The first cut of the film proved to be too short; after completion of *The Fire Raisers*, Powell and the crew returned to the production for three more days of filming, but even this did little to enhance his opinion of the finished product.

Lord Studholme (Malcom Keen) is to entertain Princess Amelia of Corsova (Muriel Aked), but most of the invited guests have some reason for resenting the powerful newspaper publisher. Princess Amelia has discovered that Studholme is working against an oil deal involving her country for his own gain, while another guest, author Adrian Chiddiatt (Ernest Thesiger), abhors Studholme for the manner in which his newspapers ridicule his books. Chiddiat also despises Studholme's secretary, Guy Kennington (Ian Hunter), believing he has helped to turn his employer against him. As the invitations are being sent out, Studholme calls on Howard Vernon (Cecil Ramage), a married man who reluctantly sells a series of letters written to him by Joan Holland, the best friend of Studholme's daughter Peggy (Jane Baxter). He uses the letters in an attempt to coerce Joan into having sex with him, seemingly not indisposed by the fact that his butler is already blackmailing him for similar indiscretions with married women. As the guests begin to arrive, Studholme discovers that Kennington has secretly married his daughter; and after a fierce row, he fires Kennington, promising to disinherit his daughter.

Despite the tension, the party begins innocuously enough with Princess Amelia suggesting a game called "murder," in which one person pretends to murder one of the guests and the rest must solve the crime. Chiddiatt welcomes the suggestion, even recruiting Joan's father, Scotland Yard Commissioner Sir John Holland (Leslie Banks), to play the detective. With the lights turned out as the "murder" is committed, Chiddiatt runs around the house firing a gun loaded with blanks, but when the lights come on it is discovered an actual murder has occurred. When Studholme is found dead in his study, shot by his own revolver, suspicion immediately falls on Kennington, whose argument with his employer is related to the police. In the ensuing trial, the defense attorney attempts to implicate Joan, but in a startling move her father takes the stand, confessing to the murder. This action infuriates the real killer, Chiddiatt, who waves a gun about as he boasts of murdering Studholme and hoping that Kennington would be put to death for the crime. After remarking that it is a "great game, murder," Chiddiatt kills himself.

Powell's aversion to the script centered on its plot, a drawing room murder mystery that offered few cinematic opportunities, particularly when it concluded in a courtroom. What salvages the film is its humor, most of which is supplied by Princess Amelia. An early predecessor to the Audrey Hepburn character in *Roman Holiday*, the princess is described by one character as a "schoolgirl on the loose" and who seems to delight in shocking people, as in her announcement that all of the best games are played in the dark. Later she is visibly disappointed when she is not considered as a suspect in the murder.

The film also contains the first evidence of the influence of German expressionism on Powell's films, which would come to infuse his work. In the darkness in which the game of murder is being played, a neon light flashes outside the window for Studholme's newspaper, a constant reminder of his influence. Mirrors, with their association with introspection and the soul, are important elements of two scenes. In the first, a gentleman, having just sold his love letters for money, looks with scorn at himself, musing that "I'm afraid poverty has brought you pretty low, my son." Later, Joan Holland, having just rebuffed Studholme's advances, watches in the mirror as he greets his daughter, and her face registers her disgust at his presence. Powell's lack of interest in the courtroom scenes anticipates his later difficulties with the climax of *A Matter of Life and Death*.

With *The Fire Raisers* Powell took his cue from the Warner Brothers films of the thirties, finding inspiration for his story in a newspaper article. Jim Bronson (Leslie Banks) is an insurance agent whose ethics are as low as his finances. Although he is willing to use blackmail and intimidation to get his way, he is reluctant to join forces with Stedding (Francis L. Sullivan), who leads a group of fire raisers. Bronson begins to romance Arden Brent (Anne Grey), whose father, an insurance underwriter, disapproves of Bronson's dubious methods. Arden and Bronson secretly marry, but her spending and his gambling losses eventually compel him to accept Stedding's offer.

The fire raisers' activities draw the attention of the under-writers forced to pay on the false claims, and they approach Twist (Laurence Anderson), a man already investigating Bronson. Twist agrees to bring in the fire raisers, provided no charges are brought against Bronson's secretary, Helen Vaughan (Carol Goodner), with whom he has fallen in love. After establishing a phony business, he contacts the fire raisers about having it destroyed, but Stedding's men are already engaged in the destruction of a cargo ship. Fearing that the men onboard would be placed too much at risk, Bronson dismisses the idea, only to learn too late that they have gone ahead with the plan anyway. Arden learns of Bronson's association with Stedding and believing he is responsible for the sailors' deaths, she leaves him. Stedding's men, having discovered Twist's identity, tie the investigator up in his building and set fire to it. Having learned of the scheme, Bronson races to the scene and, after a shootout with Stedding, unties Twist. The two men make their way to a window, but Bronson loses his footing and falls back into the fire.

The most striking feature of this film is its evocative portrait of a criminal gang when the British censors prohibited the depiction of such activities. Stedding's crew sets fire to buildings, viciously beats one man to death, attempts to murder another in a fire, and shoots at a third. The most heinous activity is their destruction of a ship with men onboard. Sitting around a wireless radio, Stedding and his men listen impassively as the sailors call out for help. Throughout the film Bronson's moral deficiency has been in evidence, from his use of blackmail to obtain clients to his browbeating of a young woman to gain access to stolen property. For all of this he is unwilling to murder. After the incident, he is haunted by the deaths, hearing a newspaper boy announcing the tragedy outside his window and noticing the headlines of the newspapers. His aversion to this action, as much as Arden's rejection of him, results in the awakening of his conscience; reminders such as this as much as Arden's departure cause him finally to reject Stedding and what he represents.

If the story with its "torn from today's headlines" approach recalls Warner Brothers films of the time, the lead character anticipates that studio's most famous icon, Humphrey Bogart. Bronson's cynical assessment of life makes him the English cousin to the world-weary detectives Bogart would portray in the forties, as does his easy manner with his secretary. There is an unspoken attraction between Bronson and Helen that is brought out in their smart dialogue. When he boasts that he has just had a stroke of luck, referring to the successful coercion of a businessman, she wonders who had the stroke. Even his response to a businessman plaintively asking whether he intends to ruin him has the quality of something uttered by Sam Spade. "I don't know, I haven't thought about it yet."

For all of his self-assurance, Bronson relinquishes his poise for passion, and Powell himself seems ill at ease at portraying a couple in love. The romantic posturing here is clumsy and curiously immature such as when the couple takes each other's hand and races across a room, smiling broadly. Yet it is the relationship that will give the film its poignancy in the end. When Arden first threatens to leave him, he pleads with her that "if you lose your faith in my love for you, I can't go on." After she leaves, she meets with Helen, who confesses to her own infatuation with Bronson. "If I loved a man, it wouldn't matter what he did." Realizing that she still loves Bronson, she attempts to call his office, just as he is rescuing Twist. As the phone rings and rings she becomes more desperate, and the film concludes with her crying "he doesn't answer, oh, God, he doesn't answer," as she seems to anticipate his death.

The Red Ensign

If *The Fire Raisers* was a step forward for Powell, its presentation was as stagebound as his work on *The Night of the Party* had been. Rarely was his camera liberated from its casing, and, for the most part, the action is restricted to interior sequences. This is not the case with Powell's next film, which is a quota quickie in length only and the first film in which even the director expressed satisfaction.

Leslie Banks was again the protagonist, starring as David Barr in *The Red Ensign*. The British shipping industry is in the midst of a depression, but Barr, the managing director of Burns/MacKinnon, intends to build a series of ships whose design will make them more cost-effective than the current ships, most of which lie anchored offshore gathering rust. The board, however, is put off by the tremendous cost of the project even though the government is expected to pass a quota bill requiring the use of more British ships. The board's chairman, Lord Dean (Frank Vosper), contends that the ships should be sold to a rival shipping magnate, Manning (Alfred Drayton), despite his flying his ships under a foreign flag and using a non-English crew. Barr is first content to build five ships, then revises it to twenty to keep the costs down on the individual ships. When the quota bill fails to pass, Lord Dean resigns and the other board members withdraw their support of Barr. Only June MacKinnon (Carol Goodner), the principal shareholder in the company, continues to back Barr, but even she turns against him on learning that he has withheld information from her. Undaunted, Barr carries on, using his own money to build the prototype.

Although Barr's finances eventually run out, he manages to convince the workers to continue on with the project; witnessing their devotion to the project, June offers to provide financial assistance. Her support of Barr evolves into an emotional involvement, causing her to break off her engagement to Lord Dean. Manning, having already attempted an uprising among Barr's workers, now engages two men to sabotage the ship, and it is blown up just as it is nearing completion. Forced to start over, Barr decides to use June's trust money, but needing Lord Dean's approval and knowing he will not receive it, he instead forges the man's signature. Manning discovers what Barr has done and thus attempts to blackmail him, but when this proves unsuccessful, he speaks to Lord Dean. Barr is arrested and sentenced to six months in prison, but public outcry supports the director's effort to reinvigorate the British shipping industry, and even Lord Dean has a change of heart. His sentence rescinded, Barr is released from prison, just as the first ship is being launched.

Even on its release *The Red Ensign* was recognized as "frankly a propaganda picture for encouragement of trade revival with Scottish shipyard for locale,"[7] but if the focus of the film was the British shipping industry, the arguments put forth also applied to the British film industry. Barr begins the project on the assumption that the quota bill will be passed, a bill similar to one then governing the film industry. It would require British shipping to use a specific number of British ships and for these ships to use a British crew, but when the bill fails to pass, it is men like Manning who look to prosper. He is willing to sail his ships under another country's flag and with a non-British crew, just as most of the films being shown in Britain were American products with little native involvement. Barr is the first character who acts as a surrogate for Powell himself, as he boasts that the "important thing was, is, that I should get my own way." If his methods are extremist, the results prove him to be a visionary, just as Powell would later fancy himself. In fact, the first shot of Barr is on a boat looking out into the distance, as if staring into the future. For Powell, however, the future at that moment was not as clear. He was still under contract to Balcon for one more film, but first he undertook a series of films featuring Ian Hunter, whose light approach was the antithesis of Banks's more intense personality. The shift in tone resulting from a change of actors would be repeated later when the Archers moved from films featuring Roger Livesey to those starring David Farrar.

Something Always Happens, Lazybones, The Love Test

If Powell's films with Balcon owed their allegiance to the Warner Brothers style of filmmaking, his next films were modeled after the screwball comedies coming out of the United States. The British cinema of the early thirties lacked an identity and it was not to develop its own genres until the end of the decade when Hitchcock's thrillers and Korda's British Empire epics began to give the English cinema its own personality. For the moment, the British directors often worked on films that appropriated their material from the more successful imports from the United States. If Powell's films here lack the pacing of the films by Howard Hawks and Leo McCarey, they remain enjoyable experiences.

In *Something Always Happens*, Peter Middleton (Ian Hunter) is a gambler on a losing streak, who remains optimistic

believing that "something always happens" to bring him luck.
Penniless, he comes across a street urchin, Billy (John Singer),
and the two join up, moving into the boarding house of a sympathetic landlady. Peter first aspires to make money by locating specific automobiles for buyers and convincing the original
owners to sell, from which he will receive a commission. While
searching for an automobile, Peter comes across Cynthia Hatch
(Nancy O'Neil), a pretty girl who he attempts to impress by
pretending the car she is looking at is his. Not only is the car
hers, but she is also the daughter of the owner of Hatch Oil.
She nevertheless goes along with the charade, pretending in
turn that she is an unemployed secretary. She persuades Peter
to go to Hatch Oil to seek employment, and, suitably motivat-
ed, he sits down that night to fashion an ambitious marketing
plan that he takes to Mr. Hatch (Peter Gawthorne). Rebuffed
by Hatch, he takes the plan to the competition, Blue Point Oil,
and is rewarded with a management position and a large salary. After paying off his many debts, he hires Cynthia as his
secretary and assigns Billy to be his doorman. Hatch initially
derides Peter's schemes, but as Blue Point stations gain on his
own, he becomes determined to eradicate his competition.
Learning of Peter's plan to purchase property adjacent to a
proposed highway, Hatch immediately buys up the land and,
in anticipation of victory, offers to Peter his most successful
stations, which he believes will become worthless after the highway opens. Upset over having lost the property in the first place
and having witnessed Cynthia talking to Hatch, Peter presumes
that she is the informant, something she angrily denies. When
the highway bill fails to pass, however, it is Hatch's property
that becomes obsolete, and, with the informant having been
discovered, Cynthia and Peter are reconciled as Blue Point becomes the more prosperous company.

 Something Always Happens is symptomatic of many thirties comedies with its portrait of a street hustler who succeeds
in business despite having no business experience. Peter boasts
that "this city is full of opportunities" and proceeds to prove
this observation right. Despite his having no experience in the
oil business, Peter sits down in one night and creates a plan
that revolutionizes the industry and is promptly rewarded with
a management position and a large bonus.

 If this action suggests that London is a city of opportunity, the opening portrays a darker side, as a young boy wanders the streets alone. Billy is introduced looking on as a group of children are playing hopscotch. When the other children are called home, Billy poignantly goes to the squares and hops as two women watch from their windows above. The one woman wonders why he does not go home, then admits that she would feed him but already has too many of her own children to support.

The stark circumstances of Billy's life are brought out in the next scene when he attempts to steal from a street vendor and is viciously beaten for his efforts. Peter emerges from the crowd to stop the man, shoving him back into the cart. As a crowd gathers Billy pulls Peter into an alley then offers him one of the apples he has stolen. The two have an immediate bond, as Peter admits that he mostly "runs too." They eventually make their way to a boarding house, where outside stands a blind beggar—further commentary on the conditions of the time. The landlady takes the pair in only when she catches sight of Billy's ragged clothing and although Peter promises to pay her back tomorrow, she replies that "tomorrow never comes." Many of these early scenes resemble Chaplin's *The Kid*, particularly a sequence in which Peter fashions a pair of pajamas for Billy from a tablecloth, carefully measuring him as if a tailor. Understandably, the action does not endear him to the landlady, although she refrains from evicting them. These scenes are unique to British cinema of the time, and many contemporary critics complained that they had little relation to the social problems of the day, which would only be addressed by the documentary movement beginning to develop.

With the introduction of Cynthia, the film undergoes an abrupt transformation, moving away from the Chaplin-inspired pathos of the opening to one of a screwball comedy as Cynthia and Peter's relationship is developed. Billy is pushed to the background, relegated to announcing the visitors to Peter's office as the focus shifts to the competition with Hatch Oil and the romance between Cynthia and Peter. Powell would have little use for broad comedy, although his next two films are also in this genre. Instead he would be most effective with humor that emerged from the characters, as when a destitute Peter attempts to impress Cynthia in a diner, while also fending off the entreaties of the management to whom he has an outstanding debt. Cynthia, who is also known to the maitre'd, motions to him not to give away her identity and adds to Peter's discomfort by ordering items for which he has no money. Eventually Peter manages to extricate himself from the situation by asking a waiter for change and conning the man out of the money, even gallantly offering him a tip. Powell experiments in this film with match cuts, in which one sequence ends with a statement that is picked up in the next sequence as if in response. His experiment with these visual and verbal puns would not be repeated until *Peeping Tom*, some twenty-five years later.

In the next film Powell directed featuring Hunter, the actor portrays a similarly destitute character, although this time one with a title. *Lazybones*, the name of the film, is also the nickname of Sir Reginald Ford, a man more content with staying in bed than with pursuing any vocation. Although Reggy has an expensive manor, but no income or savings, American Kitty McCarthy (Claire Luce) is in love with him, despite his reluctance to propose to her. On a whim Kitty has purchased an English pub, but after learning her business manager has misappropriated her savings, she realizes the pub is all she has left. Reggy's brother-in-law, Hildrebrand Pope (Michael Shepley), arrives at the manor accompanied by his wife and two plainclothes detectives. A cabinet minister, Pope is carrying with him important documents that quickly draw the attention of Michael McCarthy (Bernard Nedell), whose criminal activities are well known to the detectives. Reggy's family mistakenly pins their future on Kitty's nonexistent fortune and pressures him to propose to her. When he does finally ask for her hand, Kitty confesses to him her misfortune, something his family is unwilling to accept, because they assume it is an attempt to test his fidelity. Not particularly concerned about their opinion, Reggy elopes with Kitty and the newlyweds return to her pub to inform his family. Shocked to learn that she is indeed impoverished, the family admits to her their initial skepticism; believing Reggy had proposed to her under the same assumption, Kitty becomes angry.

In the midst of all this, McCarthy has managed to steal the documents and hide them away in a golf bag, which Kitty unwittingly takes with her when she abandons Reggy. Only with her departure does Reggy begin to take himself seriously and, determined to become self-sufficient, establishes a rest home in his mansion. Wealthy individuals are invited to the home to participate in manual labor and in the process undergo a repose. With the business a success, Reggy has the detectives bring by Michael, who despite being in custody still refuses to reveal the location of the documents. Reggy persuades Michael to contact Kitty and have her take back the golf bag, but only as she is transported in a cab does she realize that she is being returned to Reggy. She is further stunned to learn of his profession and that she has been unwittingly carrying stolen documents. The documents are retrieved but McCarthy manages to escape and as everyone else gives pursuit, Kitty and Reggy embrace.

As critics at the time pointed out, the "purely farcical moments were quite entertaining, but such an incredible story needs more pace and a lighter touch throughout."[8] Ian Christie felt in retrospect that *Lazybones* and *Something Always Happens* "provided scope for Powell's irreverent sense of humor and his determination to experiment with sudden changes of texture and tone."[9] Although the performers are engaging, only once does Powell reach the level of irreverence of a true screwball comedy. The couple arrives at the justice of the peace and, requiring a witness, attempts to convince a man off the street to help them. Played by Miles Malleson, who was later to write *Thief of Bagdad* and perform in *Peeping Tom*, the man attempts to dissuade the couple from marrying. Loath to be involved in the proceedings, he maintains his disapproval even after the couple have married. As they drive off, he offers that at least they have the option of divorce.

Powell's next film is a testament to his ability to work under the most chaotic of conditions, as filming would take only sixteen days. It too owed much to the screwball genre and in many ways the style to which Powell is conforming himself would become prominent in one of the Archers' most successful films, *I Know Where I'm Going*. The setting for *The Love Test* is a laboratory, where the current head of the lab is announcing his upcoming retirement due to an intestinal disorder (he is constantly getting hiccups). Believing that seniority makes him the logical successor, Thompson (Dave Hutcheson) is upset when Mary Lee (Judy Gunn) is announced as the prospective replacement. Vowing not to take orders from a woman, he comes up with a scheme in which one of the lab technicians will court the bookish Miss Lee to distract her from the task at hand. A reluctant John Gregg (Louis Hayward) is chosen to be her suitor, not realizing Thompson has, in fact, set him up. Despite his own inexperience with the opposite sex, Gregg manages to ask Mary out, but the pair spend their first date discussing the habitats of bees. Thompson is impatient with the progress of their date and engages the secretary from the lab, Minnie (Googie Withers), to school Gregg on romance. At the same time, Mary's neighbor is helping to transform her from a dowdy lab technician into a beautiful woman. Dressed in an evening gown, with her hair done up and wearing makeup, Mary invites Gregg out for supper, and both are surprised by the other's transformation. Their second date ends with their kissing.

Mary's new appearance catches everyone by surprise, and, on seeing her, the chief chemist goes into a hiccupping attack, resulting in his immediate resignation. With Mary assuming the role of supervisor, Thompson is forced to alter his strategy, persuading Mary that Gregg only dated her to advance his career, presenting as evidence the chart on which the progress of their dates had been kept. He also depicts Gregg as the seducer of Minnie, and an angry Mary rebuffs her unsuspecting suitor, instead taking up with Thompson. Not content with breaking up the couple, Thompson recruits the other chemists to quit working on the experiment, thus jeopardizing Mary's career. Mary momentarily forgets herself when Gregg is injured in an explosion, but, convinced that he is feigning his injury, she rejects him once more and he quits the laboratory. On returning to his home, he realizes the explosion has provided him with the answer to the experiment, and he returns to the lab after hours to work out the formula. He successfully duplicates the experiment but after leaving the formula for Mary to find, he is caught by a security guard and detained in the boiler room. The next morning the president of the company pressures Mary for results, but his more direct concern is the lack of the heat in the building (the entrapped Gregg having shut off the boilers). Thompson discovers Gregg's note and takes the formula to the president, claiming it for his own. Only Gregg's cries from the basement reveal the truth, and the entire laboratory rushes to the boiler room to free him. As the president attempts to thank Gregg for his work, he and Mary reconcile their differences and embrace.

On *The Love Test's* release, a critic for *Monthly Film Bulletin* accurately wrote that the "setting is unusual and interesting, but the development of the plot is conventional and obvious, and contains many improbabilities."[10] If the film remains something of a trifle, it is interesting for Powell's early attempts at experiment with both imagery and sound. Many of Powell's films are characterized by long tracking shots, and of his early films to survive, this is the first in which he begins to employ a moving camera, at one point panning along the length of the laboratory, revealing the various chemists to be involved in various extracurricular activities to avoid working on the needed experiment. He also attempts visual gags, such as fading from a round test tube to the similarly shaped face of the company president.

The true discovery of the film is not a technique, however, but an actress. As the president's secretary, Googie Withers's constant flirting with men and lack of respect for her employer provides much of the film's humor. Asked to coach Gregg on the fine art of kissing, she obviously revels in the work and as he nears completion of the course, Thompson pronounces that he's "improving." "You're telling me" is her breathless reply. Powell had discovered both Withers and Hutcheson in a play in London, *Nice Goings On.* He would use Withers in three more of his quota quickies then give her a prominent role in the dramas, *One of Our Aircraft Is Missing* and *The Silver Fleet.* Hutcheson, meanwhile, would turn up in a number of Powell's films, often in supporting roles. Just as John Ford had his stock company, so would the Archers, many of them actors from these early films.

The Phantom Light

The Phantom Light was the last film to be completed under the contract with Michael Balcon, and it is the most fondly remembered of Powell's early films. It contains few of the trappings of the quota quickies, again owing to Balcon's influence, and its success initiated Powell's most successful period. A critic of the time wrote that the "atmosphere is well built up and sustained, and the tension is balanced by the comic relief."[11] Sixty years later, this assessment remains apt, as Powell begins to create tension even as the credits begin to roll, with a bedraggled figure rising from the sea and entering the lighthouse. Powell constantly cuts to the rotating light as the shadows it produces pass over the occupants of the lighthouse. *The Phantom Light* applies a successful format, shaping a horror film, but inserting into the mixture a comedian, in this case Gordon Harker. Laurel and Hardy, Harold Lloyd, and Buster Keaton had all tried their hands at material such as this, and later Abbott and Costello would make a career out of it. Whereas the action often occurs in a haunted house, here the setting is a lighthouse. Even as the ambience is established Harker takes a sardonic approach to the proceedings. "He ain't normal. I mean, he has these come-and-go fits. When they come, someone goes."

Sam Higgins (Harker) arrives in a small Scottish village, where he is to take over his new post as lighthouse keeper. He is met by Alice Bright (Binnie Hale), a young woman who claims to be interested in the ghost stories surrounding the lighthouse and who wishes to visit it. He declines her request but finds it more difficult to ignore the stories surrounding the lighthouse, of attendants committing suicide or becoming deranged and of a mysterious light that appears on the hill drawing ships off course. At the harbor station, newspaper reporter Jim Pierce (Ian Hunter) is also trying to gain access to the lighthouse, but Sam remains firm, not even accepting a bribe. Sam is accompanied to the lighthouse by the local constable and Dr. Carey (Milton Rosmer), who is to examine Tom Evans (Reginald Tate), a lighthouse attendant gone insane from all that has occurred. When Carey pronounces him unfit to travel, a hesitant Sam is told to care for him. Assisting him in his work is a young man named Bob Peters (Mickey Brantford) and a giant of a man, Claff Owen (Herbert Lomas), whom Sam nicknames King Kong. Sam's night is first disturbed by the violent ravings of Evans, whom he has tied up for safe keeping, then by the arrival of Jim, who declares that his motor boat has run out of fuel. Sam reluctantly agrees to take him in, but, as they prepare to cast off the boat, Alice pops out from underneath a blanket. Although she is drenched in the process, Alice is taken in and amuses the men with a second story, this one of being an actress on the run from the police.

As fires break out in the lighthouse and doors mysteriously open, Sam grows more apprehensive, particularly after hearing Jim ask Alice to distract the others so that he can prepare
a box. Sam mistakes them for communists, particularly after
coming across them setting up a wireless. Jim admits that he
is a naval officer intent on capturing "wreckers," locals who
own insurance on the ships that have been destroyed. Alice
changes her story once more, proclaiming herself to be a Scotland Yard detective also investigating the wreckers, but by now
neither man gives much credence to her story. Using a wireless, Jim contacts the *Mary Fern*, the ship due to pass by and
whose captain is his brother. Evans, having been freed from
his bindings, attacks Jim, destroys the wireless, and locks him,
Alice, and Sam up in the room. The light from the lighthouse
goes out while another appears on shore, just as the *Mary Fern*
is about to pass through a series of rocks. Jim manages to
lower himself from the window and swim to shore, where he
rouses the locals. Sam and Alice are released by a barely conscious Claff, the victim of a severe beating, and the couple
manage to lock the saboteurs outside the lighthouse. As an
inexperienced Alice works to turn the light back on, Dr. Carey
threatens to kill Bob, forcing Sam to open the door, but not
until the *Mary Fern* has successfully navigated its way through.
Jim leads a band of men to the lighthouse, and, fearing arrest,
Dr. Carey throws himself over the side. The mystery having
been solved, Sam can only shake his head, exclaiming, "What
a night."

The Hotel Splendide had inaugurated the plot contrivance
of a character undertaking a trip, but *The Phantom Light* would
prove to be an even greater influence, anticipating much of *I
Know Where I'm Going*. Like Joan Webster, Sam arrives in a
small Scottish village, where he is first greeted by someone
speaking Gaelic. He will then be confronted by ghost stories,
just as Joan will discover the legends that have perpetuated
on the island. There is also a foreshadowing of *A Canterbury
Tale* in a reference that Harker's character makes when another character pulls a gun on him: "Here now, put that down,
this isn't Chicago." In addition there is the recurring motif in
Powell's and later the Archers' films of characters falling to
their deaths. Whether coincidence or not, this film, *Edge of the
World*, *The Thief of Bagdad*, *A Matter of Life and Death*, *Black*

Narcissus, The Red Shoes, Gone to Earth, The Tales of Hoff-mann, and *Age of Consent*, all feature characters meeting such fates, although one, Peter Carter, miraculously survives. Even more significant is the fact that for all of the bizarre occur-rences which take place, the resolution has a basis in reality. With the exception of *The Thief of Bagdad*, which he had little creative control over, Powell had little use for fantasy. Thus when he and Pressburger would produce *A Matter of Life and Death* he would insist that the events ostensibly occurring in heaven have a basis in reality.

Her Last Affaire

If *The Phantom Light* is thick with atmosphere, the films to follow begin to focus on chiaroscuro (an Italian word that Ger-man expressionists used in describing the soul). According to writer Jack C. Ellis, "while the Americans had concentrated on action and melodrama, the Germans explored the psycho-logical and pictorial. In their quest for means to objectify inner consciousness, they created a world on film that repre-sents not so much a physical reality as most of us perceive it, but the projection of a state of mind: the universe distorted and stylized to express what one might feel about it. Expres-sionism, as opposed to American realism, was the prevalent mode."[12]

Her Last Affaire is based on the play *S.O.S.* by Walter Ellis and Powell had few fond memories of the production. This makes it all the more extraordinary that the final result is so effective in creating the nightmarish situation in which the lead character finds himself. The play had first been performed in London in 1928 and is remembered most for providing Gracie Fields with her first serious role. For some inexplicable reason, a contemporary reviewer characterized the film as a "social comedy on a very old theme" then found that the "story is not redeemed by any outstanding performances by the actors and the attempts to reveal the characters' thoughts by flashes-backs are confusing rather than helpful."[13] It was not the last time Powell would be criticized for his use of effects to enhance a story.

In adapting the play, Ian Dalrymple would make one significant alteration, changing the protagonist from the father to the son, who is trying to clear not his wife's name but his father's reputation. Alan Heriot (Hugh Williams) is the successful secretary to Cabinet Minister Sir Julian Weyre (Francis L. Sullivan), but he is haunted by the death of his father, who died in prison convicted of treason. The scandal surrounding his father precludes him from marrying Weyre's daughter, Judith (Sophie Stewart). Hoping to vindicate his father's name, Alan goes away with Weyre's adulterous wife, Lady Avril (Viola Keats), believing she can provide him with the evidence he needs. After they arrive at a small country inn, Lady Avril becomes angry when she learns his true intent: to blackmail her into writing a letter telling what really transpired. She initially writes the letter, then decides to withhold it from him. Incensed, he goes downstairs and turns on the radio, in time to hear a bulletin asking of the whereabouts of a woman who has recently picked up medication that has since been discovered to be poison. Realizing it is Lady Avril the police are looking for, he goes upstairs to find her already dead. Unable to locate the letter and believing he will be implicated in her death, he sneaks out of the inn, pushing the car down the road until he can safely start it without waking anyone. The body is discovered the next morning by the maid, Effie (Googie Withers), who also comes across the letter but withholds it from the police. Alan, who has flown to Paris in hopes of establishing an alibi, is called back to London by Weyre, who takes him to the scene of the death. As Alan attempts to keep out of sight of the innkeeper, Cobb (John Laurie), and his staff, he reluctantly admits to Judith his role in Lady Avril's death.

Fearing a scandal, Weyre dissuades the police from looking for the man his wife was with, but Cobb, worried about his establishment's reputation, convinces them otherwise. Although Alan manages to escape from the inn without being recognized, he remains haunted by the death. Weyre learns that his wife died not of poisoning but as a result of her heart condition. Alan's behavior having aroused his suspicions Weyre feigns giving his daughter the tainted medicine, thus inducing Alan to admit the truth. Vowing that he will destroy Alan, Weyre has the innkeeper and the maid brought to the manor to identify him. Effie, however, produces Lady Avril's letter, which clears Alan's father, and Weyre is forced to admit that he has known of his wife's involvement all along. With both his and his father's name finally cleared, Alan is finally free to marry Judith.

The central theme of the film is the need to protect one's
reputation. Lady Avril had committed the crime for which Alan's
father was convicted, but she allowed him to be convicted in
order to save herself. Having already been established as a
deeply religious man, Cobb worries about his inn's standing,
so continues to press for an investigation, despite the death
having been of natural causes. Alan's circumstances occur because he must first clear his father's name before he can marry Judith and in desperation he threatens to destroy Lady
Avril's reputation after she has accompanied him to the inn.
Sir Julian is the most culpable, for he is aware of the father's
innocence but withheld the information to protect his wife's
name and, more important, to spare his career. A similar rationale causes him to reject the need for an investigation, being less concerned who she was with than how it would look.
"I shall get at the truth, privately, in my own way, you understand," he tells the authorities. With the discovery of her body,
Alan's goal changes from vindicating his father to protecting
himself.

If Alan is innocent of any crime, he is still morally culpable for his actions. Turning on the radio he learns of the tainted medicine, but he hesitates for a moment, even turning the
radio back on as the word "poison" is announced. He does not
race up the stairs but instead pauses at the landing as if deliberating what to do. The stairs, a recurring motif in not just
the German cinema, but also Powell's oeuvre, are bathed in
shadows as he slowly climbs them. On discovering the body,
he imagines how Judith and Sir Julian will react to his involvement; even after he escapes to Paris, these imaginings
continue to plague him. Sitting alone in his darkened hotel
room, his face lined by the shadows of the blind, he is like a
trapped animal. Cobb will later espouse that "there is still but
one authority, the still small voice of conscience," and Powell
attempts to evoke a visual approximation of this, just as the
Archers will later attempt to provide an illustration of Sammy
Rice's struggle with alcoholism in *The Small Back Room*.

Googie Withers, who so enlivened *The Love Test*, again commands our attention with her portrayal of Effie, whom one
character refers to as a child of nature, thus uniting her with
future characters in *Gone to Earth* and *Age of Consent*. She is

the antithesis of Laurie's character, who reads the Bible each night while regularly reproaching his guests for their revelry. He is especially scornful of Effie, who openly cavorts in the bar, flirting with the men. She develops an immediate attraction to Alan, and it is she who eventually saves him. On discovering Lady Avril's body, Effie behaves unexpectedly. She calmly sets down her breakfast tray and, after examining the body, glances about the room, recovering the letter Lady Avril had written. Pocketing it, she picks up the tray, returns to the door, and, letting out a scream, drops the tray to the floor, the response we had expected on her entrance. Later when Alan visits the inn with the police, she does not let on that she recognizes him and prevents her companion from giving him away. She provides the film with humor but also tension, as her actions constantly confound our expectations, adding to the suspense. She would be similarly interesting in Powell's next film to survive, which also focuses on an innocent man caught up in a compromising situation.

Crown v. Stevens

Many elements of *Her Last Affaire* anticipate the ambiance of American film noir, which like Powell's films was heavily influenced by German expressionism and often focused on innocent men caught up in situations out of their control. Alan's fear of being implicated in a woman's death could also be applied to the male character in Edgar Ulmer's *Detour. Crown v. Stevens* also tells the story of an individual caught up in circumstances that spiral out of his control. Chris Jansen (Partic Knowles) has taken a diamond out on loan to impress his girlfriend, but, when she takes the ring and runs off with another man, he is left unable to pay for it. With the loan shark, Julius Bayleck (Morris Harvey), threatening to denounce him to the police, Chris arrives at his business with neither the money nor the ring. Chris discovers that the man has been murdered, and from the shadows emerges a woman holding a gun on him. She escapes into the night, but Alan learns her identity the next morning, for she is his employer's wife. Doris Stevens (Beatrix Thomson) claims she killed the man in self-defense, but is now afraid to go to the police, concerned what not just the authorities but also her husband might think. Chris agrees not to turn her in, but relations between Doris and her husband Arthur (Frederick Piper) deteriorate, as he constrains her spending and social activities. Her life contrasts with that of her best friend, Ella Levine (Withers), whose fiance allows her unlimited spending and freedom to go out. Ella suggests that at least Doris will one day inherit her husband's money, then leaves making her promise to attend her party. That night Arthur tells her of a visit he had from the police asking about the revolver that had killed Bayleck, causing her to discard the gun off of a bridge, not realizing it has landed on a passing barge.

Chris has begun to romance a young lady named Molly Hobbs (Glennis Lorimer), but he remains haunted by his knowledge of the murder. His misgivings increase when his boss calls in sick and another employee expresses surprise, having just visited with a healthy Mr. Stevens. His health is at risk, however, for his wife has placed a sleeping tablet into his coffee and helped him to his car. As he falls asleep behind the wheel, the car's exhaust begins to fill the enclosed garage, while she waits in their home for him to die. Having become concerned by Mr. Stevens' absence, Chris stops by the house, only to be told by Doris that he has left for the night. The sound of the running engine alerts Chris to Mr. Stevens's situation, and he succeeds in freeing him from the garage. The police have also arrived on the scene, having been advised by the Stevens's maid of the missing gun. On learning of Doris's attempt on her husband's life, the police take her into custody, as she calmly confesses to the murder too. "I'll see you at the trial," she informs Chris, serenely smoking on a cigarette, then turns to the police, "or shall I have two?"

In film noir, the main antagonist is often a femme fatale, leading men to their demise, and in this film most of the women are portrayed as manipulative and evil, the exception being the girl Chris meets after the murder. The first femme fatale introduced is Mamie (Mabel Poulton), Chris's current girlfriend, who openly flirts with the men around her, then absconds with the ring he gave her, not caring that it is beyond his means. Her cruelty, however, will be overshadowed by the title character. Mrs. Stevens's first murder could indeed have been an accident and the victim is hardly above reproach, yet the murder and the fact that she is not caught seem to embolden her. She begins to chafe at her husband's restrictions, particularly after meeting up with Ella, a "gold digger," who wonders about Doris's predicament. "You could have gotten any man you wanted. What has happened to you." She realizes the only means to her salvation is the death of her husband. Having drugged his milk, Doris waits expectantly for him to drink from his glass, even as they argue over the fate of the missing gun. When the drugs begin to take effect, he barely makes his way downstairs, finally seeking the comfort of a chair to sleep in. Roused by his wife, he is assisted to the car, where she leaves him to die. She waits in her darkened home for the outcome of her crime, hiding in the shadows when someone comes to the door. She is nearly overwhelmed by a mixture of fear and anticipation as she waits and even after she is caught, she shows no remorse, calmly smoking a cigarette as she confesses to her crimes.

Some would later characterize Powell as a misogynist for his treatment of women in *Peeping Tom*, which, in fact, is a misrepresentation of that film, but although Powell would become noted for the performances of his actresses, at this point he held a chauvinistic attitude toward them. For example, in *The Phantom Light* the female character is constantly ridiculed and humiliated, even tossed into the water at one point. Powell conceded that he was tough on all actors, particularly women, sometimes not even looking on them as "women at all. They sensed this indifference and were insulted. Most women haven't got time to cultivate a sense of humor. In my first thirty films, I left behind no broken hearts, but a string of complexes."[14]

Mrs. Stevens describes Chris as a "victim of circumstances," which for the most part he is, for it is through the actions of others that he finds himself in his predicament. Yet, one wonders whether Doris is not really his unconscious agent, who frees him from his own constraints. The money lender had threatened to destroy him, just as he had intimidated Doris ("he was going to ruin my life,"). This ambiguity about what Chris had intended to do leaves us wondering whether murder may have been his mission too. Even she realizes that "we are both in the same boat," and there are other doublings, such as when Mr. Stevens lectures each of them over their financial difficulties. If Chris is haunted by the pawnbroker's death, it may be due to his own longing for it to occur.

These films, of which Powell often seemed ashamed, were his training ground. He was still developing as a director and even in *The Phantom Light* and *Crown v. Stevens*, two of his most successful films from this period, he continued to allow actors too much autonomy. The atmosphere of *Crown v. Stevens* is nearly squandered by the demonstrative performance of Davina Craig as Maggie. Yet, a certain maturity to these last few films is evident as Powell had developed into a technically proficient craftsman.

> These films were so very simple. I think probably what they had and which made people sometimes hate them and sometimes remember them was a mixture, naturally, of considerable style in the storytelling because I came in from a very stylistic background—you know, three years with a great director and all the foreign directors that came in and out of the Victoreen in those days, Germans, French, you know. I'd seen everybody work so I had clear ideas about style in films. Film storytelling, so I think this mixture of no money, cutting corners, cheese paring and style was rather unusual. But of course sometimes it was terrible and sometimes it was rather striking.[15]

The period of the quota quickie was nearing its end, for the government order that had initiated it was reaching its final year and was not to be renewed. The British film industry was certainly a much stronger one than when the act had first gone into effect, but toward what end? With the exception of the films being directed by Alfred Hitchcock and those being produced by Alexander Korda, the British cinema was still lacking an identity or a direction. Yet, in the next five years, three of England's greatest directors would rise to prominence: Carol Reed, David Lean, and Powell. World events would also play a hand in the creation of a British cinematic identity, for anticipation of the Second World War was already rising.

3

The Edge of the World

As with many of Powell's quota quickies, the inspiration for *The Edge of the World* was a newspaper article. In 1931 the residents of the island of St. Kilda were transplanted to the Scottish mainland because their island no longer supported them economically. Reading a brief account in *The Times*, Powell was intrigued by the possibilities the story offered. Later, reading Alasdair Alpin MacGregor's account of the island's evacuation, *The Last Days of St. Kilda*, Powell's interest only increased. For the next six years he worked to have a film made of the event and his failure to have it produced only intensified his sense of entrapment. In filming *The Man behind the Mask*, Powell finally convinced its producer, Joe Rock, to invest in the idea. The story, which had germinated in his mind for so long, only took him eight days to dictate. "My story was the story of a strong, hardy, independent people being driven back from the outposts to live in towns. Exhaustion of the peat beds, bad harvests and high mortality, combined with the encroachment on the main livelihood of the islanders, deep-sea fishing by steam trawlers from the mainland, were slowly wearing down the inhabitants."[1]

Even before production began, Powell suffered his first setback, one that seemed to doom the project: he was denied access to St. Kilda, which had become a sanctuary for birds and a rare species of sheep. Powell was devastated by the news, but in the end it was to be of little consequence to his film. "I had begun to analyze my story. Its appeal was a universal one. Its theme was just as vital, its story, just as timely, on any Scottish island. But it is difficult to describe what sort of wrench it was to discard everything I had painfully learnt and plan to start over again in a different setting. I didn't realize then how different. I still thought in terms of the Hebrides."[2]

As the deadline for production neared, Powell finally learned of the island of Foula, located in the Hebrides. The logistics of the production were daunting, which Powell discovered when he and two others went to scout the island. A storm stranded them on the island; although they were soon rescued, the film had already received its first publicity, as their plight had made the newspapers. This event not withstanding, the island was everything Powell desired, and, after assembling a cast and crew, many of whom had worked with him on his earlier films, he set sail for Foula. A cast and crew of twenty eventually took residence on the island, which was already inhabited by nearly a hundred people, most of whom were fishermen with little exposure to the cinema.

On the eve of production Powell addressed the cast and crew, informing them that "this is no ordinary film that we are going to make and we are no ordinary film company. Every one of you is doing several jobs. Every one of you is here because you were picked as the best person for your job. Every one is as important as any other to the success of our picture. I have worked with nearly all of you before. This is not like a studio, nor like a studio picture in the very least. We have all got to live together as well as work together and the ordinary rules do not apply."[3] This philosophy would later infuse the work of the Archers.

Just as Powell had an established view of what he expected from his crew, so too did he clearly define his own role as director. "This is why 'director' is such an accurate title. He takes the genius available to him, in the experience of an actor or the path of a storm, and directs it into the firm channel of his imagination. In this particular instance I imagined the effect I wished to create on the screen, long before I ever saw Foula. After that I had only to remain true to my conception, to snatch opportunity as it was disclosed and to present those moments as dramatically as I could, at considerable risk to my cameraman, my friends and myself."[4]

The isolated conditions, as well as the primitive surroundings of the island, understandably created many difficulties. The weather proved unpredictable, and the islanders were initially distrustful of the filmmakers, while John Laurie, who portrayed the central character, broke his leg and was unable to work for a month. The producers grew concerned about the rising costs and the inaccessibility of the production unit and soon were calling for the film to be shut down. Eventually the unit became divided into two camps, those loyal to Powell and those sympathetic to the demands of the producer. By the time production was completed, Powell ended up with 200,000 feet of film that editor Derek Twist eventually fashioned into an eighty-one minute film. Powell later credited Twist for saving his film.

The film was finally released in Britain in January 1938, but the initial critical response was lukewarm. "Storm-swept seas, rugged cliffs, craggy mountain peaks, moors and old stone cottages are admirably photographed, and have a memory of beauty and austerity. Unfortunately this is all marred by a feeble and melodramatic plot."[5] In the United States, however, the film was quickly discovered and ended the year on many ten best lists or as the choice for the top foreign film. "Mr. Powell has handled the human story with restraint; and he has recorded the bleakness, and the extraordinary dignity and beauty, of the island itself in magnificent photography which shows to what extent the camera as well as the brush can project strong feeling."[6]

Andrew Gray (Niall McGinnis) escorts a couple to Hirtha, an island that was once inhabited but is now deserted except for sea birds and sheep. Coming across a grave marker for Peter Manson (Laurie), Andrew thinks back to ten years earlier when he had lived on the island and had been engaged to Ruth Manson (Belle Chrystall). Ruth's twin brother, Robbie (Eric Berry), has recently returned from the Scottish mainland and announces not only his own engagement but also his determination to leave the island for good. Andrew and Robbie argue over the decision and decide to race up the south cliffs, something their ancestors had done to settle disputes. The next morning the two men appear before the island's council to announce their contest, but Peter is angry over his son's seeming betrayal. Andrew's father, James (Finlay Currie), is more understanding of Robbie's petition to leave, realizing that the exodus of the island's population, the government restrictions on fishing, and the competition from trawlers have made life arduous for the islanders. Although most of the council is against the hazardous trial, Peter approves and the two men are taken by boat to the base of the cliffs. During the climb, Robbie attempts to take a short cut but loses his grip and falls to his death.

Peter holds Andrew responsible for Robbie's death, forbidding him from marrying Ruth and not even allowing his name to be mentioned in his presence. After three months, Andrew reluctantly leaves the island, hoping to find work, as Robbie had, on the mainland. Robbie's prediction of the island's fortunes proves to be accurate as a poor harvest adds to the travails of the islanders. Peter, meanwhile, has discovered Ruth is pregnant with Andrew's child, but instead of condemning her, he embraces the child, relishing the role of grandfather. Unaware that he is a father, Andrew struggles to find work, his pride preventing him from taking a job on a trawler. The island's seclusion results in a life-and-death situation when the baby becomes sick with diphtheria. On the mainland, one of the many mailboats sent out from Hirtha has been discovered by a trawler, whose captain takes the letter with the news of his son to Andrew. He manages to gain passage on the ship, making his way home as the island is buffeted by gale force winds. He returns to the mainland, with Ruth and his son, who is saved by a doctor. The incident awakens Peter to the futility of the situation, and he agrees to contact the laird to obtain permission to evacuate the island. As the residents gather up their belongings, Peter goes off in search of a valuable bird's egg, but as he makes his way back up a rocky surface, his rope breaks and he falls to his death.

On its release, The Edge of the World was often characterized as a documentary, most often being compared to Robert Flaherty's Man of Aran which had been released three years previously. Powell had little use for the comparison, just as he would disavow any fondness for the genre as a whole. "I distrust documentary. Always have. I have no interest in what people tell me is the truth—how do I know it's the truth? I'd rather make up my own truth."[7] In fact, he would only direct two films in his career that can legitimately be characterized as documentaries, *An Airman's Letter to His Mother* and, ironically, his later *Return to the Edge of the World*.

A brief examination of *Man of Aran* and *The Edge of the World* delineates Powell's central differences with the movement. *Man of Aran* documents the physical travails of the people of Aran, who, like the residents of Hirtha, were primarily fisher-men. Certainly Flaherty was not a strict practitioner of photo-graphing actual events, for the activities of the islanders portrayed were often of his own staging, but, even if one takes this into account, the result is a legitimate portrait of their way of life. The lack of a narrative adds to the sense that the viewer is an observer of their struggle against nature. Flaherty concentrates on the details to which Powell only alludes, for, although the residents of Hirtha rely on fishing for their suste-nance, this detail of their daily routine is omitted. The factors contributing to the island's extinction are delineated at the council meeting, but except for one character working at his farm and complaining of a poor harvest and a brief montage of the locals shearing sheep, little of their lifestyle is shown. In-stead, Powell focuses on the internal struggles of the charac-ters, particularly Peter Manson. Toward this end, Powell constructs a story based on a conflict between men, not be-tween man and nature, and imbues it with many cinematic effects that are diametrically opposed to the philosophy of the strict documentarist.

In contrast to documentaries in the United States, which were either on the fringe of cinema or simply propaganda ex-ercises, those in England would have a profound influence on the film industry, ingratiating themselves into the philosophies of critics who equated realism with quality. If a film was not based on a literary source, then it must be mirrored on real life, especially during the war when feature films were shown side by side with documentaries. It would be against this back-drop that Powell and the Archers would create their films, and their romantic sensibilities would not find favor with many English critics. Powell's influences (like Pressburger's) were the silent films of the German cinema. "I suppose that I'm not in-terested at all in naturalism," Powell said. "The films that moved me from the very beginning, which because of my age, I'd grown up with, were borrowing from the arts and stirring our imagination so much visually that we hardly noticed the stories. You don't when the images are exciting."[8]

If the location work suggests a naturalistic setting, Powell still managed to infuse the film with chiaroscuro. Certainly its low-spirited story and fixation with death relate it to the German filmmakers of the twenties. The opening title establishes the sense of pessimism that permeates the film with the proclamation that "the slow shadow of death is falling on the outer isles of Scotland." The island of Hirtha is photographed from a distance, its silhouette shrouded in fog, as a sailboat moves into frame. The island's very name means death, and the opening sequence constantly returns to this leitmotif. A hawk is about to kill a sheep, but it is shot and killed by Mr. Graham (Michael Powell), whom Andrew is guiding to the island. The sense of bleakness continues as Andrew moves around the island, passing the ruins of buildings, now shrouded in weeds, as the wind seems to call out his name. Looking about, Andrew imagines its inhabitants passing by, ghostly images that pass through him, like something out of Fritz Lang's *Destiny*. He takes the couple to a grave marker at the top of a cliff, and its words, "Gone Over," take on an ambiguity, as Andrew will later criticize Robbie for having "gone over to the other side," in his desire to leave the island. Looking up from the marker, Andrew is startled to see the hills of Scotland, a sight he had only seen once before and which is thought to be a terrible omen. It is this sight that generates the flashback, to that first time. Ruth had been the first to see the occurrence, and, as Robbie and Andrew prepare to scale the cliffs, she realizes its significance: "You'll both be killed. I felt it when I saw the mountains and the sky and the sun went into the clouds. I'll lose you both."

In *The Edge of the World*, Powell first manifests his attraction to the Celtic culture, incorporating the mists and legends along with the population. It was to continue with *A Canterbury Tale*, *I Know Where I'm Going*, and *Gone to Earth*, three of the Archers' greatest achievements. The spectacle of the hills of Scotland predicts the tragedy to ensue, but so too do the clouds passing over the islands as the young men prepare to scale the cliffs. Moreover, as Peter falls to his death, his blind grandmother suffers a heart attack at the same time, as if perceiving the tragedy. Following their death, Peter and Ruth must go through the ritual of bidding the locals to the funeral of their loved one, their movements influenced by generations of ancestors. On the day of the funeral, the sky is gray and the island is shrouded in mist, and a light rain falls on the mourners as the casket is taken up a hill. Powell places the camera at ground level as the men pass by, the flowers in the foreground gently blowing. It is one of the first instances of Powell using music (the choir is singing "Black Angus") and visuals (the men standing about as the vicar completes his sermon, their suits soaked from the rain) to create a mood, in this case one of melancholy. The principal figures hold back, and Peter's glance toward Andrew indicates whom he holds accountable for the tragedy.

Yet, if fate anticipates the tragedy, it is man who precipitates it. Powell's ambivalent approach to Peter Manson anticipates the Archers' later characterization of Clive Candy; in fact, Peter's determination to hold onto the past unites him with the English general. Peter is alternately the aggressor and a casualty. His actions result in his son's death, because although most of the council is against the contest in which the two men participate, Peter advocates it, even when another suggests he could put an end to it. If Peter's motivation is to some extent due to his displeasure with his son, it is also because he is bound to a sense of tradition. Yet, he will take no responsibility for his involvement in the tragedy, instead blaming Andrew for all that has happened. More important, as Robbie's words of the island's demise become reality, Peter begins to emerge as a sympathetic character, representing a lifestyle no longer feasible. When Peter learns his unwed daughter is pregnant, he does not castigate her but pulls her close to him and looks on proudly once his grandson is born. Also, the audience knows that Peter will not leave the island, that in fact his destiny is tied to it. When he gives his approval to evacuate the island, he recalls the departed residents, including his son whom he is to join.

If the film is not a documentary, it remains an interesting illustration of a way of life no longer practical. Like John Ford, Powell is able to create a community that is united in work and recreation. The people of Hirtha are introduced making their way to mass, the men dressed in black suits and the woman in their finest dresses as a bell tolls in the background.

The dogs are tied up outside the church; during the sermon, which lasts an hour and fifteen minutes, Powell constantly cuts to the animals to denote the passage of time. Initially the dogs run around, full of energy and pulling at their leashes, but as time passes they grow tired and eventually fall asleep on the grass, while inside the parishioners are just as weary, nudging one another to keep awake. The birth of the baby also unites the people. As Ruth gently rocks the baby in its crib, the women look on from the hillside, each of them knitting garments for the new arrival. The factor walks among them, playing a violin, but the feeling of repose segues into one of celebration, as the priest now is shown playing dance music.

This cutting away from the central action would become symptomatic not just of Powell's work but also the Archers'. According to one critic, "The habit of cutting away from human characters at important moments to concentrate on natural phenomena of various kinds—a tree, a stone, the passing of a cloud across the sky—which make some kind of mute comment on the human action, clarify or intensify or maybe undermine and redirect the emotional content of a scene. Nature in Powell's films is never 'l'impossible theatre' in which mankind's little dramas are played out, but an active participant."[9] This approach was to culminate in *I Know Where I'm Going, Black Narcissus,* and *Gone to Earth.*

The Edge of the World resuscitated Powell's career, and it would remain part of his consciousness until his death. Soon after the film's release, Powell's account of the movie's creation was released under the title of *200,000 Feet on Foula,* but even with this Powell realized his experience with the film was not over.

> I do not think that the last word upon *The Edge of the World* will be said for many years. When a theme has beauty, integrity and a national, as well as human, importance, it is apt to last a long time, even in such a brittle and ephemeral shape as eight cans of celluloid; and when you add the spirit of an old land and its people, strong enough to influence the shaping of the theme, you have something more. In making our film many of us formed ties of sympathy and friendship that will never be broken, that are stronger than many we have had all our lives."[10]

4

Every Film Had an Organic Reason for Existing

The completion of *The Edge of the World* had been the realization of a dream for Powell, finally relieving him of the quota quickies. Unfortunately the result was not what he had imagined, for no offers of work came from any British producers. America was calling, but he was reluctant to follow the lead of Alfred Hitchcock, who had recently signed a contract with the American producer David O. Selznick. "I had always had a deep sense of place; if anything has so far come out of these pages it is the feeling that I was part of a known world. It has kept me in this country, where I was born and brought up, long after it had been made clear to me that my devotion was not reciprocated. I love England. I have mirrored England to the English in my films. They have not understood the image in the mirror."[1] Fortunately he was to find work with an English studio, but it was not a native born producer who hired him, but an emigre from Hungary who had also worked in quota quickies, as well as Hollywood. When Alexander Korda returned from the United States in 1931, he was intent on making the English cinema an international competitor. He would succeed at this with a film he had directed himself, *The Private Life of Henry VIII*, a world-wide critical and financial success. For the rest of his life, Korda attempted to equal the success of this costume drama, but more often than not he came up short. This despite the fact that he surrounded himself with some of the best talent available not just from Britain, but from Europe as a whole.

His new surroundings could have only added to Powell's expectations, but a contract did not guarantee a film and for the first few months he occupied himself with a variety of projects, none of which came to fruition. He directed an advertisement featuring Ralph Richardson and Flora Robson and was assigned to a number of projects designed to showcase Conrad Veidt, the great German star of many of the expressionist films which had so influenced Powell, but none seemed to be the ideal vehicle for him. For Powell the most promising seemed to be *Burmese Silver* and he set off on a scouting expedition to the Far East to research the project, only to learn on his return that the film had been cancelled. In its stead he was assigned to a project based on the novel by J. Storer Clouston. The title for the script Powell was handed was *A Spy in Black* and after reading the script he decided the title was the best thing about it. For Powell the picture seemed to be another misstep and he went to the producers to complain about the picture, only to find that Korda was equally critical of the script and had already brought in another writer. When Powell had first entered the room he had not even noticed the nondescript man sitting off to the side, a Hungarian named Emeric Pressburger. In a scene which would be echoed seven years later in *The Red Shoes*, Pressburger discarded the original script and fashioned a completely new one, which bore little resemblance to the novel. The bespectacled, softspoken man with the Hungarian accent began to recount his story to the gathering of filmmakers and Powell was immediately impressed. He would always pride himself on being the "teller of the tale," and he had now found the man who would supply him with the tales. From that moment on, the lives of these two men would be forever intertwined.

For all of the attention the Archers were to receive, Pressburger was something of an enigma, satisfied to work behind the scenes, while Powell directed the films and spoke to the critics. In the end it was usually Powell who received either the condemnation or the praise of critics while Pressburger's contribution was conveniently forgotten, even in the eighties when Powell's reputation was resurrected. Often it was Pressburger's own reticence to speak to writers which resulted in his own anonymity and he was content to live out his life, writing in relative obscurity and perfecting his skills as a gour-met cook. Imre Pressburger was born on December 5, 1902, in the city of Miskolc. The Hungarian city had a large population of Jews and Pressburger's father had successfully established himself as the manager of an estate. In contrast to Powell, Pressburger's introduction to film came relatively early, at the age of eight when he was taken to see a short. It had such an impact on him that decades later he could still recall the plot. If film intrigued him, the love of music possessed him, as he began to study the violin. Yet film and music were little more than passions, for engineering seemed to be in his future. He was one year away from entering a university to study this field when the first World War broke out, and by war's end, Hunga-ry would be divided into four territories, so that even though Pressburger had not moved, he'd already become an emigre. For the rest of his life, Pressburger would suffer from a sense of displacement, of being an outsider. He would eventually spend time in three other countries, with his longest sojourn being in England.

The secession of hostilities found Pressburger in, of all plac-es, Germany, where he endeavored to complete his engineering degree. The postwar difficulties of Germany made his own fi-nancial standing even more disheartening and he struggled through the first two years and would have to take time off before completing a third, relying on his music to provide an income. The death of his father caused him to briefly return to Hungary, but Germany would continue to call to him, and he returned, surviving on a variety of jobs, most of which held little interest for him. It was at this time, when his life seemed its most discouraging, that he turned to writing. His first works were met with only rejection, but one morning he opened a local paper to find one of his stories had been reprinted. He had become a professional writer, but even as he began to pursue this career, he was already looking to film. Against tre-mendous odds he managed to gain interest in one of his sce-narios with an executive at UFA, one of Germany's and Europe's, for that matter, most prestigious studios. Although the story was ultimately rejected he was given the opportunity to adapt another work, and even though this came to naught, one of his scripts had come to the notice of a young director, whose first film had been a tremendous critical success. Robert Siodmak had directed *Menschen am Sonntag*, a silent film, but was now attempting to follow it up with his initial sound film. The result would be *Abschied*, a story involving the dissolution of a young couple in a tenement building (where all of the action is set), but more significantly it is the first film for which Pressburger received a screen credit (although his name had now been altered to Emmerich Pressburger). The year was 1930. While only a handful of Powell's early films are missing, most of Pressburger's have long since disappeared and those that have survived are often difficult to find. In writing of the film, Ian Christie thought that "the importance of architectural setting for so many of Pressburger's scenarios was already evident in *Abschied*, as if topography and narrative condition each other. So too was his preoccupation with the plasticity of time in cinema to break the normal convention of temporal ellipsis in films by limiting screen time to real time is precisely to draw the audience's attention to it, and thus make the perception of time an active theme of the film."[2] Later, the Archers would often challenge their audiences even as they reminded them that what they were watching was a film. It was only one of many ways in which they would go against the precepts of the realist movement.

Pressburger was to work on seventeen films over the next six years, even more if one takes into account the fact that many films on which he worked were made in a variety of languages, a common practice at the time, but he was to develop more than just his writing skills. UFA was one of the best studios for a filmmaker to learn his craft, for writers were not only encouraged to work at their own profession, but to learn other aspects of production, such as editing, for which Pressburger even received a screen credit. If Powell grew up influenced by the German film industry, Pressburger would be educated by it, and if its prominence had faded somewhat since the introduction of sound, UFA still employed some of the finest technicians available. Pressburger seldom received a screen credit for his work, a common fate of many screenwriters, not just in Germany, but in Hollywood, and not just in the thirties, but even now. *Emil und Detektive* was one such project, with Billy Wilder receiving sole credit for the screenplay.

Of the films still thought to be lost perhaps the greatest

tragedy is *Dann Schonn*, not simply because of Pressburger's involvement, but also because it was the directorial debut of Max Ophuls. Pressburger finished out his work at UFA primarily in collaboration with director Reinhold Schunzel, working in close partnership with him on three films, all of which were operettas, a genre he would return to with Powell on *Oh Rosalinda!!* These films were often shot in playback, with the recorded music played out over the action, allowing the camera more freedom then generally permitted in the sound era and anticipating a technique the Archers would use to perfection on *The Tales of Hoffmann*, and which is now standard. Yet, if Pressburger's writing career was successful, it was not enough to overcome the events beginning to take place in Germany. Certainly he must have felt the growing anti-Semitism of the time, but it did not really hit home until the end of 1932, when his contract with UFA was not renewed, despite his talent. The reasons were obvious, but surprisingly Pressburger remained in Germany and continued to find work even as Adolph Hitler was made chancellor. Soon after, Joseph Goebbels, the German propaganda minister, warned against the employment of Jews in the film industry and by April Pressburger could no longer ignore the warnings, deciding his best opportunity was to escape to France. This was not a simple assignment due to restrictions on Jewish travel and he instead returned to Hungary, where a sympathetic police captain and aficionado of film, supplied him with a French visa. Unbelievably Pressburger returned to Germany to continue to look for work and only after he received an anonymous phone call warning him of the danger did he finally flee Germany. It was now the spring of 1933.

As many of the films on which Pressburger had worked had been released in France in French language versions with French casts, his name was already known to many in the industry. He also benefited from the large number of German emigres already at work in France, so that he was soon hired by a small company owned by fellow emigrants Erich Pommer and Seymour Nebenzal. The inferior conditions of the studio were in marked contrast to the working environment to which he had become accustomed at UFA, but the resulting film, *Incognito*, was a modest success and he soon was at work on *Une Femme au Volant*. It was at this time that Pressburger wrote the screenplay entitled *The Miracle in St. Anthony's Lane*, which, although optioned at the time, would not be made for another thirty years under the title of *A Miracle in Soho*. His inability to get the film produced became symptomatic of the difficulties he began to face for he soon found he was unable to support himself. His difficulty learning the French language only added to his discomfort and when he did find work it was often on lighthearted material such as the operettas with which he had made his reputation in Germany. Seldom would he receive a screen credit for his work and many of the projects on which he worked never even made it before the cameras. Ironically his last film assignment in France would be his most successful as he was reunited with Robert Siodmak on *La Vie Parisienne*. Based on an operetta by Jacques Offenbach, the creator of *The Tales of Hoffmann*, the story was originally set in the 1800s, but as with his adaptation of *Die Fledermaus*, Pressburger transposed the story to a contemporary setting. More importantly his work here had begun to anticipate his later style with Powell, as Ian Christie discerned.

> The fact remains that the Archers' films regularly disturbed critics with their unexpected changes of register, from comic to serious, and their ironic detachment of form from content—both attributable to Pressburger's Hungarian background and sophisticated experience scripting in Berlin and Paris. In his work with Robert Siodmak (*Abschied, La Vie Parisienne*), and Reinhold Schunzel (*Der Kleine Seitensprung, Ronny, Das Schone Abenteuer*), he learned the structural principles of ellipsis, allusion, rhyming and dramatic paradox.[3]

It was in the midst of preparing *La Vie Parisienne* that Pressburger first traveled to London and soon after its completion he made the decision to emigrate once more, this time to England. Being of Hungarian descent would seem to have been an asset at the time for Korda, England's most influential producer, often hired many relocated Europeans for his studio, particularly those of the same nationality, but neither his heritage nor his experience helped to find Pressburger employment. He busied himself with preparing shooting scripts of other screenwriters' work, detailing the sequential order of the film and determining the shots required. His big break came when he was hired to work on the film *The Challenge*, produced by

Korda's company, but with which the impresario would have little involvement. The film starred and was co-directed by Luis Trenker, a German filmmaker who had made his reputation with films centered on mountain climbing, including some featuring a young Leni Riefenstahl. *The Challenge* would be only a moderate success and when no additional work was forthcoming, Pressburger entertained ideas of moving to Hollywood. *The Challenge*, however, may have finally convinced Korda to give Pressburger a chance, for he provided him with a two week assignment in order to test his skills. Although the writer seemed to pass the test, a contract was not forthcoming for cutbacks at the studio were then in the midst of taking place. Korda admitted the only work he had for him was an adaptation that the production department couldn't come to terms with. The script was *The Spy in Black*.

The project was to serve as a vehicle for Conrad Veidt, but the original script offered the actor little opportunity. Pressburger, however, created a new character for Veidt, while also incorporating many elements from the German films for which Veidt first gained notoriety. This only served to endear the project even more to Powell, and soon the two men began to collaborate on the script, working in tandem with Veidt and the actress who was to play opposite him, Valerie Hobson. Powell had received permission to research in the Orkney Islands, where the story is set and he returned from the expedition with specific ideas in mind for the set design, which he passed on to the production designer, Vincent Korda. The filming would take over five weeks and everyone associated with the project was convinced that what had seemed to be a disaster would now become a commercial and critical success. Ironically once filming was completed, Powell and Pressburger found themselves out of work, for neither of their contracts were renewed. Powell's only contribution to the final cut was a twenty-three page letter he sent the editor offering suggestions. When the film was released it was the success they had envisioned, its box-office receipts buoyed by the fact that a U-boat had been actually sighted off the Orkney Islands. In the United States, where it was released as *U-Boat 29*, it was a similar success. "Here is as thrill-packed a motion picture as you'll see this season. Made in England, it suffers none of the faults usually associated with British product. It moves at lightning fast pace,

has been brilliantly directed and enhanced by excellent performances by Conrad Veidt and Valerie Hobson."[4]

U-boat Captain Ernst Hardt (Veidt) returns from a successful mission of destroying British transport ships, only to discover that food supplies in his own country are in short
abundance. His leave is cut short when he is sent on a secret
mission to the Orkney Islands, where the British fleet is currently engaged in training exercises and where he is to contact
a German agent who is passing herself off as a British schoolteacher. Hardt makes his way successfully onto the English
shore and contacts Frau Tiel (Hobson), who introduces him to
Lieutenant Ashington (Sebastian Shaw), a disgruntled serviceman who can provide the location of the English fleet. The plan
is to have the German navy ambush the fleet, thus neutraliz-
ing the English navy. Their plan nearly goes awry when the
real schoolteacher's fiancé arrives, but after the Reverend John
Harris (Cyril Richmond) is tied up in the basement, Hardt contacts his navy. As the German navy sails for the site, Hardt
celebrates in expectation of a massive victory, and declares
his love for Frau Tiel. She rebuffs him and after he has made
his way to his bedroom, she sneaks out of the house to meet
with Ashington. Hardt overhears their discussion and learns
that not only are they British agents, but that he has put his
own navy in jeopardy. As the military moves in to arrest him,
Hardt manages to escape wearing the clothes of the captured
pastor.

Hardt manages to make his way on board a ship on which
Joan Blacklock, the British agent who had posed as Frau Tiel,
is also a passenger. A group of German prisoners are also on
board and Hardt manages to release them and with their assistance commandeer the ship. As the British begin to pursue
them, Hardt and his men make their way out to sea, where
they hope to contact his ship. They catch sight of the U-boat,
but the men inside cannot pass up the opportunity to sink an
English freighter and fire on it, even as Hardt frantically sig-
nals them from the deck. The British pursuers arrive on the
scene and destroy the U-boat, but are too late to save the
freighter, which has begun to sink. All on board, except Hardt,
make their way onto lifeboats, but he remains behind, content
to die with his men.

In this, Pressburger's first script for Powell, one can already discern the elliptic style and attention to detail which was to make up their greatest works. Powell obviously savors the complexity of the script and the visual opportunities it offered him. Hitchcock had gained his reputation with taut, atmospheric thrillers and with his departure to the United States, it looked as if Powell would carry on his tradition. In fact one of the first scenes of the film is almost the inverse of Hitchcock's popular *The Lady Vanishes*, in which an old woman mysteriously disappears from a train, but is eventually revealed to be a British agent. In *The Spy in Black* a young schoolteacher is about to depart for Longhope to take up her new post, but the vehicle that was to transport her to the boat has broken down. Fortunately an elderly matron has stopped by for tea and offers the young woman a lift, taking her along the deserted country road, while engaging her in a conversation on her new position, as well as her upcoming marriage. Our suspicions are only aroused when Powell cuts to the front seat of the car, where the chauffeur is carefully taking notes on the conversation. The older woman feigns concern about her companion becoming cold and carefully places about her neck a scarf, then abruptly holds the cloth against the young woman's mouth as the anesthetic on it takes effect. Arriving at a cliff, the young woman is tossed into the sea, where only the timely arrival of a patrol boat saves her. This in turn alerts the British to the Germans' plan and they replace Frau Tiel with one of their own agents.

Yet, the influence on the film, as it had been for Hitchcock was Fritz Lang. The milieu is that of *Dr. Mabuse* and *Spies*, the atmospheric thrillers with which Lang had made his name and which are echoed here—in Hardt, clad in black riding his motorcycle silently into town; in the shadows which criss-cross Hardt as he hides underneath the stairwell; and when he looks out at the training mission of the British fleet, then glances downward into the skylight of the schoolhouse where the children are singing. There are also the ironies of Pressburger's screenplay, as in the motorcycle Hardt carries on board his U-boat and which is to be used for his mission. After making his way into the schoolhouse, he is forced to cart it up the staircase, then keep it with him in his cramped quarters. He makes the best of the situation by using the rear view mirror on the bike to help him shave. The film opens with Hardt entering a

German restaurant and discovering to his chagrin that most of
the items on the menu are no longer available due to the British blockade. He is particularly dismayed to learn that butter
is no longer available. On entering the schoolhouse for the first
time, he gives out an exclamation of surprise, not because he
realizes Frau Tiel is a British agent, but because her table has
a large slab of butter on it. When he later returns to his submarine he tosses to his men a chunk of butter and their delighted reaction echoes his. Finally, there is Hardt's order to
the passengers on board the ship he has taken possession of,
telling them everyone is to remain quiet. "All who disobey will
be shot," he tells them, only to have a baby begin crying. "With
one exception," he reluctantly adds.

The film looks forward to *49th Parallel*, with its portrait of
a determined, resourceful German leader and its construction
of a plot which implicates the audience in the plight of a German. When Hardt manages to commandeer a British ship and
hastens to save his U-boat, the audience cannot help but get
caught up in his race against time. The film also anticipates
the change the British people will be forced to undergo, anticipating the primary thesis of *The Life and Death of Colonel
Blimp*. It is only because of June's sympathetic treatment of
Hardt that he manages to escape and when she finds herself
to be his prisoner, she recognizes her complicity. "I forgot we
were at war. Forgot that war means that it kills every fine decent human feeling." This statement was not simply an admission of guilt, but also a warning to the British audience who
were aware that a second war with Germany was on the horizon. In fact, its success following the declaration of war was
that with the exception of an opening title which states the
year as 1917, there is little to identify it as a story set in the
First World War and not the second.

Although he was not allowed to complete the film, Powell
was not out of work long, as he was again approached by Korda to contribute to what would be Korda's final spectacle before the war, *The Thief of Bagdad*, while Pressburger began
work on the script which would eventually become *The Red
Shoes*. With the declaration of war, Powell immediately began
work on Korda's propaganda campaign, *The Lion Has Wings*
and Pressburger's script was set aside, not to be filmed until
after the war and not by Korda. Even as they were working on

their separate projects, Powell and Pressburger were intent on collaborating on a second film. A chance alliance had resulted in a successful partnership, which neither man wanted to end. Powell had discovered in Pressburger a writer whose sensibilities complemented his own. "I had always dreamt of this phenomenon: a screenwriter with the heart and mind of a novelist, who would be interested in the medium of film, and who would have wonderful ideas, which I would turn into even more wonderful images, and who would only use dialogue to make a joke or clarify the plot."[5]

The first projects they attempted to find backing for had little relevance to the events of the day, but with the formal declaration of war, they were determined to use this as the backdrop for their next story. In fact, for the next six years, their films would be tied to the calamitous event in which England was engulfed, providing them not only with material for their stories, but also with a specific objective. They were also intent on reuniting Veidt and Hobson, whose obvious screen chemistry had not been lost on them. The script for *Contraband* was completed in October and the filming took six weeks. By December of 1939, with the war only four months old, Powell and Pressburger had already completed a film set in the Second World War. It was a foretaste of the ingenuity which would come to characterize the film's of the Archers. More importantly the film was another critical and commercial success, with one critic paying Powell the ultimate tribute. "The British industry needn't worry too much about Alfred Hitchcock's disaffection and decision to make films in the Hollywoods. *Blackout* shows there is a worthy disciple of the Master in Michael Powell."[6]

A Dutch cargo ship is making its way along the English coast when it is stopped by the British navy, who are concerned that it is smuggling contraband to the enemy. The ship eventually receives clearance to continue on its journey, but Captain Anderson (Veidt) discovers that two of his passengers have stolen boarding passes and a small motorboat to get ashore. With his ship set to leave the next morning, Anderson goes off in pursuit of the couple, eventually catching up with them on a train bound for London. Although the man, Mr. Pigeon (Esmond Knight), manages to escape, Anderson remains with the young woman, Mrs. Sorensen (Hobson), only to dis-

cover that she and her companion are British agents. Anderson and Mrs. Sorensen are kidnapped by German agents and
taken to a secret hideout, where the secret message she is
transporting is discovered. Although Anderson manages to escape, he is too late to prevent the Germans from capturing Mr.
Pigeon. Not knowing where he had been held, but believing he
can identify the singer he had heard, Anderson recruits a group
of Danish waiters to help him search the various nightclubs.
Having located the singer, he makes his way to the basement
of the nightclub, as his companions create a disturbance above.
Although a German agent, Van Dyne (Raymond Lovell), is holding a gun on Mrs. Sorensen and Mr. Pigeon, Anderson manages to attain their release, escaping with them to the top floor.
As Van Dyne pursues them, gun in hand, Anderson hides
among the plaster busts being stored in the warehouse and
eventually uses one of them to knock out the German. With
the two British agents in tow, the captain makes his way back
to his ship, his activities seemingly unnoticed by the British
authorities. On the ship, however, Anderson learns that the English were indeed aware of his adventure, but by this time he
has begun to revive his relationship with Mrs. Sorensen.

Just as the previous film had been modeled after the work
of Lang, so too is his influence evident in this film, as when
Anderson is knocked unconscious and experiences his subsequent interrogation as if it is a nightmare. Yet, it is also influenced by the war which served as its backdrop. The film opens
and closes with a confrontation over life preservers, which were
mandatory for all passengers due to the constant threat of
German U-boats. As the passengers gather in the dining room
of the *Helvig*, Mrs. Sorensen's jacket is noticeably absent and
she is called before the captain. Anderson admits that on first
catching sight of her, he recognized her as trouble, but then
adds that he enjoys his women that way. Mrs. Sorensen constantly attempts to outwit Anderson, but they emerge not only
as allies, but also romantically entangled. By the film's end she
is again brought before the captain, still refusing to wear her
life preserver, but this time it is only serves as a pretense to
meet Anderson.

If the film is meant to be little more than a thriller, it remains an interesting portrait of a nation at war. The film un-
folds with the camera passing along an English harbor, where

soldiers have appropriated a seaside restaurant to serve as their headquarters. In London a street peddler sells flashlights and gas masks, while the streets are lined so that pedestrians can find their way along the darkened streets. At restaurants, gas masks are checked in just as someone would check in their hat. The blackout is in constant evidence, even providing Anderson the mechanism with which to escape the building in which he is entrapped. Turning on all of the lights attracts the attention of a Home Guard captain, who, accompanied by the police, breaks into the building to extinguish them. He boasts of his ability to navigate in the darkness of the blackout, only to run into someone, but later his navigational skills will help him locate the district in which Mrs. Sorensen is being held.

As in *The Spy in Black*, Pressburger seems to delight in creating situations where appearances are not what they seem. Anderson and his Danish companions search for a male singer only to discover the husky voice is actually that of a woman and she is performing, in of all places, The Mouse Trap. In the ensuing altercation the members of the female band race off in terror, leaving behind their legs, which we only now realize are cardboard cutouts. Equally ingenious is the climactic shootout, set in the attic of the building, which serves as a warehouse for plaster busts, many of which are of British Prime Minister Neville Chamberlain, and the bullet which strikes them becomes almost a political statement in itself. When Anderson knocks the German out with a bust, it is not of Chamberlain, but of Teddy Roosevelt. "They always said he was tough," another dig at the British leader. In the process of escaping Anderson had lost his esteemed watch which plays the Danish anthem, but after returning to his ship at the end, his escapade seemingly undetected by the British authorities, his watch is returned. The film served notice that there were German agents already entrenched in Britain, but that the resourcefulness of the British would eventually win out.

5

We Must Keep Our Freedom, We Must Fight for What We Believe In

To credit a single person with the success or failure of a film is perhaps film criticism's greatest fallacy. Even the staunchest supporters of the auteur theory must acknowledge that actors, writers, editors, and various other technicians all influence the final product. Even in this book, which singles out Michael Powell for examination, the contributions of others are acknowledged, most obviously those of Emeric Pressburger but also of the many technicians who contributed to the look of their films and the actors who influenced the presentation of the characters they created. Powell is simply the thread that runs through all of these films. In the case of *The Thief of Bagdad* and *The Lion Has Wings*, however, it would not be hard to single out one man as the auteur of these works. Alexander Korda produced both of these films at incredible odds, with Powell's contribution only one of many. The success and failure of these films ride on Korda's shoulders.

The Thief of Bagdad is the British equivalent of *Gone with the Wind*, with Korda assuming the role of David O. Selznick. Korda is said to have been seated at a banquet across from Douglas Fairbanks, when he had the idea of remaking one of the latter's silent classics, which in turn had been a reworking of the stories of the Arabian adventures. Korda realized he could not hope to compete with either Fairbanks's athleticism or the spectacle of his production but instead could offer only technical advances, Technicolor and sound. The resulting story borrowed many of the ingredients of the original (flying horses and carpets, a sleeping princess, and an evil sorcerer) but divided the central figure into two characters, the thief and Prince Ahmad (Fairbanks's alias in the original). This allowed Korda to cast in the title role Sabu, the young Indian boy then at the height of his popularity thanks to roles in *The Drum* and *Elephant Boy*. What Korda had not anticipated was that his expansive production would be disrupted by the Second World War.

Ludwig Berger was first assigned the motion picture, most likely because of his previous work in silent fantasies, but from the beginning he and Korda were often at odds. When Berger proved unwilling to resign, Korda attempted to humiliate him into leaving, redirecting the actors even as Berger stood on the sidelines. In all, five directors would work on the film, three that are credited: Powell, Berger, and Tim Whelan, while Zoltan Korda's and William Cameron Menzies's work was unrecognized, although each was given the title of associate producer. Alexander Korda himself would even take a hand at direction. The threat of war began to cast its shadow over the production, and the production designer, Zoltan Korda, was even detained at one point as he attempted to film on location, the authorities having mistaken him for a German agent.

Alexander Korda, however, was undeterred by the events beginning to take place in Europe and the rising cost of the film and even ordered a series of expensive sets torn down, ordering them to be rebuilt larger and with more color. Menzies, who had also worked on the original film, drew nearly three thousand sketches, influencing the final look of the film and, in the process, anticipating Hein Heckroth's later role in the Archers' work. Filming had already lasted two years when the war, so long feared, finally occurred. After briefly occupying himself with *The Lion Has Wings*, Korda moved his production unit to the United States for completion. Not only did this require a change in strategy, for he had intended to film in South Africa, but the passage of time had transformed Sabu from a boy of fourteen to a young man of sixteen, thus requiring further retakes. After filming was completed at the Painted

Desert and the Grand Canyon, the film was finally put together and released in October 1940.

The film was hailed by many as an immediate classic, an opinion many modern reviewers maintain. "The particular glory of this film is its truly magnificent color. No motion picture has been so richly and eloquently hued, nor has any picture yet been so perfectly suited to it."[1] There were some, however, who found the picture to be a shadow of the original. "Beyond six, to all except cases of retarded development and Swahili who are seeing their first magic lantern show, its numerous defects will very quickly become apparent. For one thing it runs almost two hours on almost fifteen minutes of story."[2]

The story opens in the port city of Basra, where a blind beggar and his dog are taken to a nearby palace. Surrounded by maidens, the blind man, Ahmad (John Justin), recounts how he was once the ruler of Bagdad, while the dog had actually been Abu, a young thief. As King, Ahmad is manipulated by his vizier Jaffar (Conrad Veidt), who rules the kingdom through fear and intimidation. When Ahmad walks among the populace in disguise, Jaffar has him arrested as a mad man and thrown into prison. Ahmad manages to escape only through the help of Abu, who has managed to steal a key from a guard, and the two make their way to the city of Basra. Attempting to find food in the crowded market, the pair are surprised by the sounding of horns, which sends everyone in the marketplace into hiding. The princess of the city is to pass by, and, because no man may look on her, all must hide their eyes. Looking down from the roof on which he and Abu have hidden themselves, Ahmad is dazzled by the young woman's beauty and becomes determined to meet her, despite Abu's pleas for him to continue on. Ahmad makes his way to the gardens of the castle, where the princess (June Duprez) initially mistakes him for a djinni. When she learns he is really a man, she too falls in love and the couple declare their devotion to one another. Through his magic, however, Jaffar has also been able to view the princess and journeys to Basra, bringing with him a gift that her father (Miles Malleson) cannot refuse. A toy collector, the king cannot resist a mechanical horse that flies and reluctantly offers his daughter's hand in exchange. The princess, having overheard the exchange, flees the castle grounds, but Ahmad and Abu are discovered in the ensuing search.

When Jaffar catches sight of them, he strikes Ahmad blind and transforms Abu into a dog.

The story returns to the present as Ahmad learns that the princess is in the castle to which he has been taken but that she has fallen into a deep sleep. Ahmad goes to her, and she regains consciousness. On discovering that he is blind, she travels to a ship where a doctor is thought to be able to cure him. The ship is actually Jaffar's, and he takes her prisoner, promising to return Ahmad and Abu to their original form if she embraces him. The princess does; after they have returned to normal, Ahmad and Abu pursue the ship in a small raft, only to be capsized by a great storm Jaffar creates. Abu washes up alone on a beach, and searching for his friend, comes across a bottle containing a djinni (Rex Ingram). The djinni grants the little thief three wishes, the first of which he wastes on a craving for sausage. His second wish is to be reunited with Ahmad, but the djinni informs him he must first steal the all-seeing eye to learn his friend's whereabouts. This accomplished, he is finally reunited with the young king, but, after the pair argue, Abu impulsively wishes for Ahmad to be reunited with the princess. Jaffar is once again attempting to make the princess fall in love with him. With the appearance of Ahmad, however, he has the lovers thrown into chains to await their deaths. His final wish having been used and believing he is unable to save his friend, Abu angrily throws the all-seeing eye. When the eye strikes the desert, a city emerges from the sands. It is the Land of Legend, and the ruler presents Abu with a magic bow and a flying carpet, which takes him to Bagdad just as the executions are to occur. Abu emerges from the sky to kill Jaffar and free his friends. Ahmad once more takes his throne, this time with a queen. Fearing Ahmad will try to domesticate him, Abu takes off on his magic carpet for more adventure.

The Thief of Bagdad helped to further Powell's reputation, in both Britain and the United States, whose market had become crucial to any major British production. Although he was but one of three credited as director, his name seemed to be the most prominent. Forever afterward, the film would be remembered as a work by both Korda and Powell, Berger and Whelan's contributions forgotten along with the countless others who worked on the film. This praise for Powell and the film continued even as his reputation was being resurrected in the sixties. Raymond Durgnat, in a seminal article on Michael Powell, considered *The Thief of Bagdad,* along with *Peeping Tom,* the director's masterpiece. It is a statement that is both overstated and misguided. The film is neither a masterpiece nor a work of Powell's, although his contribution is crucial to what success the film has attained. As Korda's biographer, Karol Kudik, maintains:

> [The] film fails as much in execution as it does in conception. Static camera placements and a plodding editing style, which precludes any imagination in the scene transitions, are bound to undermine the entire atmosphere so dependant on action, movement, and fluid or dynamic cutting techniques. It is not coincidental that all the best scenes, especially the opening harbor sequence with its sweeping and rhythmic camera movements and the scene of Sabu's discovery of the djinni on a deserted beach, are directed by Michael Powell, the one of the five directors whose visual imagination was allowed free reign.[3]

Miles Malleson doubled as actor (King of Basra) and screenwriter, and, although many of his lines have a poetic quality, he has little success fashioning a story. Certainly some of the problems in continuity were the result of the various disruptions the picture encountered, but the central difficulty is due to the decision to divide the central character into two distinct personalities. While Ahmad provides the romantic element of the film, it is Abu who does all of the work and ultimately emerges as the central figure of the film. When Jaffar over-turns their raft, Ahmad is completely forgotten as Abu discovers the djinni, then must recover the magic eye. Adding to this feeling of imbalance is the fact that Sabu is the stronger screen presence. Discounting his good looks, Justin is a vacuous figure, as is the princess as portrayed by June Duprez. The intensity of Veidt's character needs a counterbalance, and only Sabu is able to provide one. The dilemma of having a more interesting protagonist will be repeated in *The Tales of Hoffman.*

The importance of *The Thief of Bagdad* to Powell's career, however, cannot be dismissed, for it anticipated much of his work to follow. It was his first experience with color film, and, if he was not able to determine how it was used, it did prove

educational. Thus, when he was to direct his next color production, he turned once more to the cinematographer of *The
Thief of Bagdad*, Georges Perinal. Powell would later take credit for having had a giant eye painted on Jaffar's ship, ostensibly to distract viewers away from the ship (which was of the
wrong period), but it also established a primary motif of the
film and Powell's career. From a long shot of the ship, the camera moves in on a close-up of Jaffar, his face completely covered except for his piercing eyes. He later attempts to hypnotize
the princess and subsequently strikes Ahmad blind when the
prince declares that "his eyes have been witness" to his treach-
ery. To locate his friend Abu must steal the "all-seeing" eye
from a temple and through it discovers his friend's fate. Then,
it is the all-seeing eye that when thrown to the ground resur-
rects "the land of legend, where everything is possible, when
seen through the eyes of youth." Eyes and the power of gazing
will be repeated in the Archers' *The Tales of Hoffmann*, *Gone to
Earth*, and in Powell's *Peeping Tom*.

As in many of Powell's films, the story is imbued with a
sense of mysticism and prophecy. In the beginning, as Ahmad
walks in disguise among the people of Bagdad, he hears a
prophet speak of a savior who will come from the sky, "the
lowest of the low." These words will be repeated at the conclusion, when Abu emerges from the clouds on his flying carpet.
Yet, the film it most resembles is the Archers' *A Matter of Life
and Death*, for the princess and Ahmad, like Peter Carter and
June, will fall in love at first sight, then suffer through the
threat of being separated. Jaffar's obsession for the princess
anticipates the characters in *Black Narcissus*, *The Red Shoes*,
Gone to Earth, and *Peeping Tom*. Not just his actions predict
Lermontov's; one moment in particular is echoed in the ballet
of *The Red Shoes*. When Jaffar rises up to strike Ahmad blind
and transform Abu into a dog, the shadows of his hands rise
up on the wall. In *The Red Shoes*, the shadows of the shoemaker duplicate exactly this movement as they draw the girl
away from her family.

Created in the midst of the filming of *The Thief of Bagdad*
and released long before it was *The Lion Has Wings*, the first
propaganda film to come out of war-torn England. The war
with Germany had begun, and it looked as if the British cinema "would be the first casualty. A few weeks earlier, cinema

managers had received a Home office circular warning them that during the initial stages of the war all theatres, music halls, cinemas and places of entertainment shall be closed throughout the country."[4] The cinemas were soon reopened, but the status of the film industry remained in limbo. Korda seemed to anticipate this and called together many of his technicians to work on a film whose objective would be to demonstrate the role film could play in the war effort. Ian Dalrymple supervised the production and recalled its inception:

> Whether it was Alex's own idea or he had been unofficially urged to make it, I don't know. What I do know is that he had no financial help from Government: that, as his normal finance was tied up in major product awaiting exhibition, to complete the film he had to pawn his last Life Insurance Policy: that those working on it received token fees, and it was released to Exhibitors on minimal terms: finally, that apart from technical guidance, the content was spontaneous—nothing in it had been imposed by the Central Authorities."[5]

Powell went to Mildenhall to film preparations for the first bomber raid on Kiel canal and to Hornchurch to cover fighter operations. Brian Desmond Hurst filmed the sequences between Ralph Richardson and Merle Oberon and the civilian observer posts, while Adrian Brunel worked on the section dealing with the crisis in Poland. Location work took three weeks, with editing taking place immediately afterward. Finally, footage from Korda's earlier *Fire over England*, concerning the conflict between England and Spain in the 1500s, was incorporated. It received a trade show opening on October 17, after which two hundred copies were distributed, instead of the usual practice of releasing only seventy copies. Most critics of the time panned the film but acknowledged that it served a purpose and had been created in haste. The reviewer for the *Documentary News Letter* was particularly scornful: "This may be 'realism' but it is poor understanding of the psychology of film propaganda."[6]

The Lion Has Wings is divided into three acts, crudely tied together by the recurring appearances of Richardson as a Royal Air Force (RAF) Wing Commander. The first act is almost entirely documentary footage, with a narrator introducing us to Britain, "where we believe in freedom." In the montage that follows, the lifestyles of Germany and Britain are contrasted, as are the personalities of the leaders. While the British involve themselves in recreational activities, the Germans practice marching and military training. Hitler is portrayed as man attempting to "force his outworn ideals on Europe," who requires protection from his people, while the British king is shown to be a man of the people, freely walking among them and even joining in on a popular game of the time. From this the narrator recounts the various acts of German aggression leading up to the war. If the Germans brought on the conflict, the British are well prepared for it, as the narrator promises that British airmen will "only have the finest aircrafts that our factories can produce." He concludes the first section with a forecast of three years for the war.

This segment segues into the fictional material with Mrs. Richardson (Oberon) and June (Duprez) listening to Prime Minister Chamberlain declaring war on Germany. As the anthem is played the two women stand to attention, while their lovers come in, each dressed in military uniform. Wing Commander Richardson (Richardson) reassures his wife that "we've never been better prepared." This is demonstrated as the RAF prepares to bomb the Kiel Canal, where German destroyers are to pass through. The viewer is taken on board an RAF airplane as it journeys to the target, a sequence that the Archers will later re-create more effectively in *One of Our Aircraft Is Missing*. The mission is successful, with the narrator reminding the viewer that the attack was "not upon unfortified towns, but on a heavily protected naval base, a legitimate target." This act concludes with the actual airmen from the mission being introduced as they emerge from their planes.

If the second act demonstrates Britain's ability to attack the enemy, the final act emphasizes its ability to defend itself. Through their espionage network, the British learn that the Germans have planned an air attack on London. The Germans are given their orders in a manner "which is in striking contrast to the friendly atmosphere that is Britain's way," while in London, barrage balloons are released as observers watch the sky for the Luftwaffe. The action abruptly shifts to three hundred years previously, when England was involved in another conflict, this time with Spain. The queen of England (Flora Robson in footage from *Fire Over England*) rallies her soldiers for the conflict, just as the modern day soldiers are similarly preparing. The first wave of German aircraft are met by the English air force and are driven back. The second wave are greeted by antiaircraft guns, then by the RAF, who again emerge victorious. The final wave of Germans are forced to break off their mission when they encounter barrage balloons. Although the Germans turn back, the RAF gives pursuit, eventually destroying most of the German airplanes. Richardson, his busy night finally having ended, returns home exhausted, only to find it is empty. When his wife comes home, she is dressed in her nurse's uniform, demonstrating women's role in the conflict. The film concludes with the Richardsons escaping to the country where they relax beneath a tree and Mrs. Richardson begins to speak on what the war means, making a pledge that will prove ironic in light of Powell's later films. "We must keep our land, darling, we must keep our freedom, we must fight for what we believe in—truth and beauty and fair play—and kindness." In an action that many critics thought served as a perfect comment on the film, Mrs. Richardson's words have fallen on deaf ears, for her husband has fallen asleep.

To attack the film for its naivete and crudity in approach is to ignore the conditions under which it was made. It was produced in a short period of time, when even the government leaders were unsure how to use the medium. Later directors, including Powell, would learn from the mistakes of *The Lion Has Wings*, but that they were even able to produce films may be due to this single film. It is perhaps overstating the facts to claim that the film saved the British industry from being shut down for the duration of the war, but it certainly aided the filmmakers in their cause. Powell's contribution is of interest for its anticipation of the opening of *One of Our Aircraft Is Missing*. On the release of the latter film, many critics thought it was derivative of *Target for Tonight*, not realizing Powell had already created such a sequence in this film. Merle Oberon's final speech is almost Blimplike in her desire for England to win the war, by playing by the rules.

6

Written, Produced, and Directed by Michael Powell and Emeric Pressburger

> The arrows were pure gold
> But somehow missed the target
> But as all Golden Arrow trippers know
> It's better to miss Naples, than hit Margate.
>
> James Agate

For all of its technical faults, *The Lion Has Wings* demonstrated the role film could serve in the war effort and the Ministry of Information (MOI) took notice. Under the direction of Kenneth Clark, a Film Section was created, whose purpose was to sponsor fiction films designed to further the cause of the English struggle. Such a proposal was to prove controversial, with opponents, particularly the Department of Treasury, wondering why money was being transferred from the military effort to fictional entertainment. Clark met with Powell suggesting a story involving minesweeping, but Powell demurred, contending that the last war film had begun with a similar topic. Instead, he asked to go to Canada to develop a film about that country's war effort. He had come across an article by Beverly Baxter that focused on Canada's involvement in the war and in which Baxter had implied that the United States would soon follow its lead. In their film, Powell and Pressburger would also make such a correlation. With five thousand pounds from the MOI to research the project, Powell and his crew boarded a ship bound for Canada. Two days out, Pressburger came up with the story for the film, a German U-boat crew becoming stranded in Canada and forced to make their way to the still-neutral United States to escape.

Powell and Pressburger toured the country, incorporating various communities into their scenario. After coming up with a first draft, Pressburger set to work on a plot line that owed as much to Agatha Christie's *Ten Little Indians* as to Beverly Baxter, and he was assisted with the dialogue by Rodney Ackland. After receiving approval for the project, Powell and Pressburger returned to Canada in April 1940 to begin filming. Eighty percent of the resulting footage was filmed on location as a permanent staff of twenty-five covered fifty-two thousand miles of countryside. Not only did the MOI cooperate with the project, but so too did many of England's most successful actors, as Laurence Olivier, Anton Walbrook, and Leslie Howard all volunteered their services to the picture. An actress, Elisabeth Bergner, would go AWOL from the film, however. From the beginning, her decision to appear in the film was something of a surprise (she had only made five films in the last seven years, all of which had been directed by her husband, Paul Czinner). Bergner made the trek to Canada, but, when the time came to return to England, she balked, instead fleeing to the United States where she was reunited with her husband. Although Powell recast the role with Glynis Johns, he was forced to use some of Bergner's location work. That two actresses could combine for one character prepared Powell for his later experiences with *I Know Where I'm Going* and *The Elusive Pimpernel*, in which lead actors were unable or unwilling to complete location work.

The film was more than just a contribution to the war effort, it was also a declaration by the film industry that it was now prepared to compete directly with Hollywood. One of the premier editors, David Lean, contributed to the film, and Freddie Young served as the cinematographer. Later he would win Academy Awards for two of Lean's productions, *Dr. Zhivago* and *Ryan's Daughter*. For the music, Powell turned to Ralph Vaughan Williams, the influential conductor whose first experience in film this was to be. His music was the first in

Powell's ouevre that influenced the rhythm of the editing. The music he created would later be incorporated into some of his later acclaimed symphonies.

The logistics of the production soon overburdened the Ministry of Information's budget, and the Rank Organization stepped in to purchase the film and complete the financing. It proved to be a smart investment, for 49th Parallel became an enormous financial and critical success, in both Britain and the United States (although its reference to a neutral America was no longer valid). In Britain it became the highest-grossing film of the year and Today's Cinema boasted that "49th Parallel is an event in British production history, a remarkable achievement in many ways, an entertainment feast for all audiences and a natural box office record beater."[1] In the United States, where it was released as The Invaders, the film's success was more than the producers could have imagined. Motion Picture Herald felt that "Michael Powell consolidates his place as one of the minute band of directors in England whose work is equal to the best in Hollywood."[2] Its critical success would carry over into Academy Awards with its nomination in three categories, including Best Picture, but only Pressburger would walk away with an award, for Best Original Story. He did not learn of his victory, however, until well after the ceremony had been conducted, and even then it was through a newspaper report. 49th Parallel was the first in a wave of British films that would make their way to the United States and that for the duration of the war established Britain as the equal of Hollywood in terms of quality.

The film can be neatly divided into four acts, with a prologue establishing the central premise of the film. Each act has a specific ideological agenda, while the entire film delineates the diversity of the Canadian people and landscape. The overriding objective of the film was to demonstrate the resourcefulness and determination of the German military and to introduce the audience to the principles of the Nazi ideology. The film opens as a German U-boat passes through the wreckage of a Canadian freighter it has just torpedoed and picks up some of the survivors, intending to interview the men and photograph them for their records. The Germans' attention to detail and their intelligence of what the ship had been carrying establishes them as an informed adversary (reinforced later by

their producing a detailed map of Canada, which even the locals recognize as exceptional). When one man knocks away a
camera, the Germans retaliate by pushing him and his companions back into the water to fend for themselves. The U-
boat, its location now known to the Canadian authorities,
quickly makes its way north, navigating through the treacherous icebergs. With their supplies becoming scarce, the captain
(Richard George) addresses the men on their assignment, and
at this point Powell begins to incorporate images in the film
that would have been all too familiar to newsreel audiences of
the time. The captain speaks to the men from above, and their
rigid posturing, with their hands outstretched in Nazi salute,
recalls the images of Hitler's speech at Nuremburg as does his
bravado that "today Europe, tomorrow the whole world."

A squad led by Lieutenant Ernst Hirth (Eric Portman) is
sent onshore to serve as the vanguard for the German military
and to retrieve needed supplies, but as the men look on the
U-boat comes under attack from the Canadian Air Force. The
picture greatly exaggerates the capabilities of the Canadian
armed forces at the time, from their tracking capabilities to
their air force, which consisted of only three airplanes, all of
which were used for this sequence. As their ship implodes, the
men can do nothing, realizing their mission has now become
one of survival. Their only chance is to reach the borders of
the United States, the 49th parallel, but to accomplish this they
must first cross thousands of miles of hostile territory. Their
first encounter with Canadians transpires at a Hudson Bay
Trading Post, with Powell cutting from the Germans to the
Canadians inside. French-Canadian Johnnie Barras (Laurence
Olivier) has just returned from eleven months of trapping, not
knowing that his country is at war. As he listens to the factor
of the post, Albert (Finlay Currie), tell him of the conflict in
Poland, he wonders how it relates to him. He is the first character who not only does not understand the meaning of the
struggle but who naively presumes they are safe from the
threat, while discounting the reports of the massacres of Polish refugees. "The Germans are ordinary men same as you and
me. I wouldn't do a thing like that, would you? Well, you can't
tell me they do. That's all newspaper talk." By the end of the
act he will witness firsthand just such carnage.

Albert crosses to the window and comments on the "wind

which is blowing," establishing a running metaphor that runs throughout the film of likening the Germans with the forces of nature. When he turns away, the Germans move unnoticed past the window, and then force their way into the post, introducing the second motif of the film, that the Germans are little more than gangsters, something Johnnie initially mistakes them for. Later the Englishman the Germans encounter in the Rockies makes a similar assumption, and Powell adds to this perception in his presentation of the men, having them loot the trading company and later assault a motorist along the highway. Initially Johnnie fails to take the Germans seriously, boasting that his father had fought "against you the last time. We give you one good licking then and we do it again." The German response is to attempt to assault him, but his Eskimo companion intervenes and is viciously beaten as a result. This does little to dissuade Johnnie's cocksure attitude, and he jeers at their philosophies, winks at one of the soldiers, and pantomimes their marching, which he calls goosestepping.

This sequence establishes Hirth as not only the leader of the party but also the purveyor of the Nazi ideology. His devotion to his cause is contrasted with that of his second in command, Kuhnecke (Raymond Lovell), who, despite an earlier proclamation that he was one of the first to join the party, momentarily forgets himself and becomes involved in a chess match over the shortwave radio. Hirth attempts to indoctrinate Johnnie into the principles of his party, calling his copy of *Mein Kampf* his "bible." For many audience members of the time, this was the first introduction to the Nazi philosophy, and, given the prejudices of the time, Hirth's characterization of the Negro as "silly apes, only one degree above the Jews," may not have caused much consternation. What would have struck closer to home is the German determination to govern Canada, with Hirth asserting that the Germans will set the French-Canadians free. Olivier's performance is offputting with its mannered accent and smart-ass demeanor, yet he will serve as a response to Hirth, arguing that French-Canadians are already free and then sacrificing himself for a cause he at first dismissed. As he lies dying, struggling to speak through his own blood, he is transformed into a poignant character. This abrupt shift in tone, from Johnnie's joking to the violence of the end, is an

example of Powell's and Pressburger's propensity to alter the
cadence of a film.

Most of the violence in the film occurs in the Hudson Bay
sequence, but the viciousness of the assaults remain in the
viewer's mind; an unconscious Eskimo being struck by the butt
of a rifle and left to die in a pool of blood, the sudden erup-
tion of violence when Johnnie attempts to call out on the radio, and, most dramatic, the massacre of civilians at the
outpost. This last action occurs as two men are sent by the
trading company to investigate the disturbance at the post and
are confronted by the Germans. A contingent of Eskimos have
gathered. When the two men attempt to escape, the Germans
fire indiscriminately into the crowd, which includes women and
children. The two young men are killed along with innocent
civilians, including a mother who falls to the ground, her baby
still in her arms.

The next set piece is the most successful of the film but
also the most controversial for its time, for not only its ac-
knowledgement of the large contingent of Germans already living in Canada but also its sympathetic portrayal of a Nazi. The
Nazis come across a German community of Hutterites who left
their country over religious persecution but whom Hirth mistakenly assumes are fifth columnists. Cautiously ingratiating
themselves into the community, the Nazis will not find sympa-
thizers to their cause but another rejoinder to their ideals.
Caught up in the ensuing ideological struggle will be Vogel
(Niall MacGinnis), who is gradually awakened to his conscience.
His dilemma had already been prepared for in the Hudson Bay
sequence, when a dying Johnnie asks Hirth for his rosary, only
to be callously ignored. Vogel, however, returns and silently
hands Johnnie the rosary but then, disturbed by his display of
weakness, viciously carves a swastika in the wall. Later, after
their plane has crashed, Vogel unthinkingly prays over a companion who has died, snapping to attention only after catching
sight of Hirth's reproachful look. In encountering the Hutterites, his morality will be resurrected.

Vogel, like the other Nazis, is disconcerted by the Hutterite
lifestyle in which individuals choose their own role in the community and in which Peter is their leader in name only. This is
in marked contrast to the Nazis' regimented lifestyle, which had
forced Vogel to give up his profession of baker. The conversa-

tion between Vogel and the Hutterite baker anticipates a similar conversation in *A Canterbury Tale* between two men of different countries but of similar professions. For all of their differences, they are united by their passion for baking. Vogel's transformation continues that night as he speaks to Hirth of a young Hutterite girl whose parents had been lost on a ship torpedoed by a U-boat. He wonders about the other innocents killed as a result of their aggression, the most recent example being the massacre at the trading company, although he does not mention this directly. Hirth reminds Vogel that "we are at war. You can't expect to win without the methods of total warfare. Men, women, and children—they are all our enemies and must be treated as such. Do you remember what Bismark said? 'Leave them only their eyes to weep with.'" When Vogel quietly repeats the statement, it is with the realization of just what the war is causing.

The next morning Vogel rises early to bake bread, already rejecting the Nazi sublimation of individuality. When a Hutterite man wonders why he has given up his profession, Vogel reluctantly admits he had no choice. "I didn't want to give it up—I had to." Hirth mistakes Vogel's actions as an attempt to gain the confidence of the community, whom he still assumes to be German agents. Picking up on this tactic, Hirth has the men participate in the harvest, but the analogy of the Nazis being a tempest on the horizon continues as Peter speaks to one of his men who has just returned from the city. The man recounts the troubles of a German family that has been interned, the hostility toward them heightened by accounts of the Nazi attack at the trading company. Looking at the sky, Peter muses that the "air is heavy, I'm afraid we're going to have a storm tonight." Hirth picks up on the analogy in his speech to the community that he gives that night. After addressing the Hutterites as "brothers," he insists that when "one is governed by the deepest of racial instincts, then every other consideration is swept away." He boasts that a "new wind is blowing from the east. A great storm coming across the sea," while, outside the window, an electrical storm is taking place. His rhetoric makes even Vogel uncomfortable; looking into the face of the young girl of whom he had earlier spoken, he can only lower his head in shame. Hirth speaks of the "great sun, which will give us everything we need in life," but, when he invites the others to join him in a salute to their leader, only his own men stand to attention to shout "Heil Hitler," the Hutterites looking on in shocked silence. Vogel continues to distance himself from the others, for although the rest hold their hand out in salute, his remains at his side.

During his speech, Hirth had moved about the room, his voice at a fever pitch, and gestured wildly as he spoke obsessively of his cause. For his response Peter remains seated, his hands folded in front of him and only once raising his voice, yet his speech is as impassioned as Hirth's. He first discounts Hirth's statement that they are "brothers," that he "hates the power of evil which is spreading over the world." By the time the Germans return to their room, all but one have been ostracized by the Hutterites, with only Vogel being offered a place in the community. Yet, individuality cannot be sanctioned in the Nazi crusade, and the next morning Vogel is tried for treason by his companions and summarily executed. The image of Hirth standing at attention, his arm outstretched in salute, as a man is executed, will become all too familiar to audiences of the postwar era.

A second lament of the film on its release was that the Germans become heroic in their struggle as they traverse hundreds of miles of hostile country, with little to get by on but their determination. The audience cannot help but become involved in their quest despite what they represent. The most extreme example is the plane crash, where as the Germans realize they are out of fuel and about to crash, their evident panic imbues them with a display of humanity one does not expect in the portrayal of a Nazi. Powell's intent, however, was not to make the Germans sympathetic but to portray them as both human beings as well as determined adversaries. This approach keeps the film from becoming archaic as many others of the time have become, remaining instead a genuine adventure film. Unfortunately, Powell and Pressburger were not able to maintain this balance between adventure and propaganda, for the suspense generated in the Germans becoming involved in an Indian festival is lost when the remaining two Germans make their way into the Rocky Mountains. There they will encounter an Englishman who is meant to represent an English intellectual who has little use for the war. Philip Armstrong Scott (Leslie Howard) is a caricature of an English dan-

dy, a latter-day Scarlett Pimpernel but stripped of the courage
or daring. Whereas Olivier's character is ultimately redeemed,
Howard's character suspends the film in careful equilibrium.
The failure may be as much Howard's as it is Powell's or Pressburger's, for the actor rewrote many of his own scenes.

The theatricality of Howard's character will be aggravated
by his introduction, sitting in front of an all too obvious backdrop (this in a film noted for its location work). Scott ferries
Hirth and Lohrmann (John Chandos) across in his canoe, decrying the war as a nuisance. "Up here in the Rockies, the war
seems so remote one can't take it so seriously. Of course, one
knows, one half of humanity is trying to wipe out the other
half, but up here among the mountains and the spruce forest
one sees it in perspective, so that it almost seems unimpor-
tant." He takes them to a teepee he has set up in the woods
and proudly unveils his cherished artworks, a Matisse and a
Picasso, and also a German edition of *The Magic Mountain* by
Thomas Mann, three artists who had been banned in Germany—which results in one of the more incongruent sequences in Powell's oeuvre. "Wars may come and go, but art
lives on forever" is Scott's creed. Although it anticipates the
struggle between art and life that will later occupy the Archers,
it lacks any resonance. The encounter with Scott rejuvenates
Hirth, who, as he is taking a shower, dismisses the English as
"soft and degenerate all through," demonstrating his own resolve by rinsing off in cold water. Yet, even this German superman cannot help but shudder from the impact of the water,
providing another instance of humor in the film. That night
Scott is still lecturing, talking of the research he is doing on
the Blackfoot tribes and relating the tactics of that warring
nation with those of the Nazis. Even when Hirth attempts to
escape Scott by going outside, the Englishman follows him, his
presence having become irritating not just to the German but
to the viewer too.

No longer able to restrain himself, Hirth calls Scott weak
and a coward, but neither denigration seems to unnerve the
Englishman, nor is he nonplused when they reveal themselves
to be Germans. Tied up, he is more sensitive to his emotions,
or lack of them, than he is to the physical threat of the Germans. Only when they begin to pitch his artwork and research

into the fire does he finally show any emotion, but even in anger he can only dismiss the men as "spiteful schoolboys." The Germans escape into the woods, but their attempt to steal the horses rouses the rest of the camp and Scott is liberated. Ironically, Howard's character is not redeemed even when he strikes a heroic pose. Having cornered Lohrmann in a cave, he boldly walks toward the entrance even as the man is firing at him, taking a bullet in the shoulder in the process before entering the cave to beat the German up. With each blow he identifies the deed as being "for Thomas Mann, that's for Matisse, that's for Picasso, and that's for me," exacting revenge not for his country but for his lost possessions. Scott emerges from the cave, and his companions are amazed to find the German unconscious. "He had a fair chance. It was one armed superman against one unarmed decadent democrat," Scott claims.

His accomplice having been captured, Hirth continues on alone, eventually making his way on board a train destined for the United States. Hirth has come to personify the Nazi master race, and seemingly the whole world watches in anticipation to see whether he will succeed. At this moment, however, he seems little more than a hunted animal, hiding in the shadows of the railroad car, as another man also stows away on board. When Hirth reveals himself, his companion introduces himself as Andy Brock (Massey), a Canadian soldier overdue on his leave and who grouses about the duties he has been assigned. "I enlisted to knock the hell out of the Germans," the Canadian complains, not realizing that he is face to face with one. When his back is turned, Hirth strikes the Canadian on the head; by the time the man has regained consciousness Hirth is dressed in his uniform. Realizing he has been talking with a German, Brock begins to recant his earlier statements. "We own the right to be fed up with anything we damned please and say so out loud when we feel like it. When things go wrong, we can take it and can dish it out too." What Brock cannot do is to stop the train from entering the United States, and, as the American border agents open the car door, Hirth looks to have been successful in his escape. "We've beaten these dirty democracies, these weaklings. I tell you it's something inside us, something beyond the dim muddied minds of you enemy democracies. What do you know of the glorious mystical ties of blood and race that unite me with every German Aryan?" Yet, for all of his tenacity, the German cannot be allowed to prevail, and Brock manages to convince the patrol to have the train returned to Canada (arguing that he and Hirth are illegal contraband). As they are transported across Niagara Falls, Brock announces his intention of taking back his uniform. The blow he strikes is meant to be a blow against Germany itself, an announcement that the Allies, too, are equally resolute.

49th Parallel, like *The Lion Has Wings*, is a product of its time, but unlike that film, this one remains of interest for its adventure and technique. Powell and Pressburger were directly addressing the issues of the war and its impact on society, as would the films to follow. Powell realized the process involved was often one of prediction: "From then on every film we made during the war sprang organically from the one we'd just made because, first of all, we were guessing a year ahead what the general position of the war would be and what would be the propaganda message. After all, films take a year to make and get out, particularly if you're writing, producing and directing them yourself, and so we had to be good guessers. The only one we guessed wrong on was *A Canterbury Tale*."[3]

The film also establishes a new technical standard for Powell and for the British cinema as a whole. The plane crash equals in suspense and creativity the more famous crash in Alfred Hitchcock's *Foreign Correspondent*, while the opening montage anticipates the importance of music in Powell's films. Vaughan Williams's score varies its style as the images move from the lush wheat fields to the crowded cities of Canada, eventually segueing into the national anthem, then turning menacing as the submarine surfaces. The sequence in which the Germans are given their orders and sent on shore is also a model of economy and the use of ellipsis. The captain gives his speech to the men who are assembled on deck, but, as he concludes and raises his arm in salute, they are already on a boat halfway to shore. The next shot has them answering his "Heil Hitler," but now they are on the shore. In a matter of a few seconds, a half hour of diegesis time has elapsed.

49th Parallel firmly entrenched Powell as one of England's top directors, something for which he had been yearning since the success of *Two Crowded Hours* ten years earlier. Yet, he reached this success with an awareness of Pressburger's importance in all of this. Without him, he was a talented director, with him he was about to create some of Britain's finest films. In his autobiography, Powell takes credit for their unique partnership, recalling a conversation with his agent in which he first brokered the concept of the Archers. Whether this is in fact what happened or not, Powell was making the sacrifice, for the screenwriter in both England and the United States at this time was often unrecognized. Their identities were to merge into one, the Archers, with their name taken from a poem by James Agate. Each film would begin with an arrow striking a target, sometimes hitting the bull's-eye, sometimes just missing, but always striving for the center. If the title signified something new, the men's contribution would be little changed, as Pressburger acknowledged. "I write. He directs. We both produce."[4] Pressburger was also involved in the postproduction, often taking an active role in the editing process. "When things went wrong on the floor, I worked in the cutting room with the editor to put things right."[5] Powell would often relate their partnership to a "marriage without sex," and no analogy seems more apt. While Powell's approach could create tension on the set, Pressburger often served as the calming influence.

An observer on the set of one of their films related how "Pressburger's kindness and generosity transpire instantly when an occasion arises to call them forth. He likes to hear the work of members of the unit praised. When the dynamic personality of Micky [Powell] is removed the unit seems to find it easy to discuss points of interest in the film with him in a way they could not do if they were dealing with the more mercurial temperament of his partner."[6] Like all great directors, Powell had a specific objective in mind when directing, and often this meant he had little patience for those around him. Sometimes this put off an actor, but many, such as Kathleen Byron, came to recognize his ability. "I didn't think Micky was a great director of actors: I thought he used to put people down and upset them. It was only later, looking back at the way he directed, that I realized he was determined to get something from you and didn't mind how you did it. All he wanted was the best for that particular scene."[7]

For their first film, the Archers decided to take the central premise of *49th Parallel*, of servicemen making their way across hostile territory, but change the ensemble to a group of British airmen. The title came from a well-known military phrase of the time, "One of our aircraft has failed to return," but because of the pessimistic sound of this statement, it became *One of Our Aircraft Is Missing*. They first approached Rank Studios about the project, but J. Arthur Rank was skeptical of its commercial potential. With typical bravado, Powell warned Rank that he would come to regret the decision and that after its success he would be the one coming to them. Yet, Rank was not alone in his assessment, and the Archers ultimately turned to British National, which had produced *Contraband*. The MOI, though no longer providing financial assistance to the Archers, did supply them with information on the German occupied country in which the story is set, and the Dutch government in exile also cooperated. Production began on August 11, 1941, with the English landscape substituting for Holland.

For Pressburger, the film allowed him to incorporate one of his passions into the story, soccer (or football as it is known in Britain). One of the British airmen becomes separated from the others and is only reunited with them when he participates in a game of football with some Dutch athletes. For the scene actual soccer stars were part of the action. The excitement that the sport generates for the British is evident even earlier as the servicemen listen intently to a radio broadcast of a game. Powell's central contribution to the film was his casting of Googie Withers in the role of a Dutch resistance leader. Despite his marriage, Powell often had affairs with many of his actresses, but his attraction to them did not affect his judgment about their ability. The passion he felt for Withers, Deborah Kerr, Pamela Brown, or Ludmilla Tcherina carried over into his films, and their sensuality is often apparent.

The debut of the Archers continued their string of successes. "It is in short, a film worth seeing with excellent propaganda value, and is a credit to the British film industry."[8] Ironically, one benefit of Powell associating his name with Pressburger on all of the credits was that he was to receive his only Academy Award nomination, for best original screenplay. (This was the same year in which Pressburger would win for

The Invaders, but for that film the category would be original story, while also receiving a nomination for simply screenplay. What the difference was in the three categories seems indistinguishable).

B for Bertie is overdue from its latest raid. As the men at the airfield wait for its arrival, the film returns to fifteen hours earlier, when its crew was just preparing for the mission, targeting a factory in Stuttgart. After successfully completing the mission, their airplane is struck by antiaircraft fire, and, with its engines on fire, the men bail out over occupied Holland. All but one of the men are accounted for, and, unable to locate their missing comrade, they begin to make their way to the English channel, only to encounter a group of Dutch children. After identifying themselves as English, the men are led by the children to the home of Els Marteens (Pamela Brown), a schoolteacher sympathetic to the Allies' cause. After ascertaining that the men are indeed English, she presents them to the villagers, who supply the grateful airmen with plenty of food. They also agree to help smuggle the men to the English channel via the Dutch underground.

Disguised as Dutch citizens, they are taken to a nearby town, where they lose themselves among the parishioners in a church. The Germans have begun a search for the Englishmen but fail to detect them in the gathering. The local burgomaster (Hay Petrie, a member of Powell's stock company who often portrayed exasperated characters) takes them into his home, where they are nearly given away by a quisling, a Dutchman sympathetic to the Germans. The men attend a soccer match where they are shocked to discover their missing companion among the players on the field. The reunited airmen are placed in a transport truck that carries them to a coastal town and the home of Jo De Vries (Withers), a woman whose husband is thought to have been killed by the British. Because of this, the Germans believe she is sympathetic to their cause, but her husband is actually alive in England and, like her, working against the Germans. Under the cover of an air raid, De Vries escorts the men to her basement, where, after overpowering two German sentries, they make their way into the Channel. As they pass a German sentry, one of them is shot, but he survives and the men make their way onto a rescue buoy, taking the two Germans inside prisoner. A passing ship finally rescues the men, and six months later they take once more to the sky, this time to bomb Germany.

One of Our Aircraft Is Missing does not simply invert the premise of *49th Parallel*, it is almost a reaction to it. The cast of celebrated actors from the first film have been replaced by an ensemble cast made up principally of character actors, and the lush landscapes of Canada have been transposed for an English countryside masquerading as occupied Holland. Whereas the Germans are at the foreground of one story, they are but shadows in the second; whereas Vogel is shot for his religious beliefs and a desire to return to his old life, the English talk openly of their pasts and religious convictions. In fact, the men put to use their past professions in order to survive, the actor providing the group with disguises, the diplomat serving as translator, and the career soldier advising them on how to make their way through a hostile country.

The most dramatic difference with *49th Parallel*, however, is that *One of Our Aircraft Is Missing* has many of the trappings of a documentary. It opens with a Teletype announcing the execution of five Dutch civilians for their complicity in the escape of a group of British airmen, thus grounding the story in reality. The omission of any music (which alone makes this film atypical of the Archer's oeuvre) adds to this quality, as does the extensive sequence that opens the film detailing the raid. It would have called to mind a popular documentary of the time, *Target for Tonight*, but in fact was probably modeled after a similar sequence Powell worked on for *The Lion Has Wings*. Powell bristled at the suggestion that it was a documentary. "It was a detached narrative, told from the inside, of what it is like to be a pawn in the game of total war."[9]

If most of the film has a realistic presentation, the coda the Archers provide to the film breaks this hold. The story ends, and the cast and crew are introduced, then a title stating that "all of them wanted to know what happened afterward to the Crew of *B for Bertie*. So, three months later. . . ." The men are then shown preparing for another mission, this time to bomb Berlin. It would become typical of the Archers' attitude toward film. "Our business was not realism, but surrealism," Powell writes. "We were storytellers, fantasists. This is why we could never get on with the documentary film movement. Documentary films started with poetry and finished as prose. We storytellers started with naturalism and finished with fantasy."[10]

Propaganda was still the intent of the film, and it is no accident that the British survive their ordeal, whereas the Germans were unsuccessful. Certainly they have less terrain to travel, but they also have the support of the Dutch population. The primary objective of the film was both to show the nearly united resistance of the Dutch people and to assert the rationalism of bombing an occupied country. Els Meertens translates for the men her country's motto: "The sea is a common enemy, and against a common enemy we must unite." Her own loyalty is demonstrated by the orange blossoms that she has arranged in a room and a portrait of the queen hidden there. Later the mayor informs them that "we have our own ways of managing things." This dictum will be reinforced throughout the film, as when a group of spectators at a football match are told that fifty of their number must go. Knowing the Nazis' propensity for order, the entire group begins to leave, and a flustered German announcer tells them to ignore the previous command. The sole collaborator of the Germans, a quisling, is showed up, not by the underground but by a young boy. Told by the quisling to take over a batch of records to the German barracks, he instead replaces them with albums of the Dutch anthem. Realizing that they have been made an object of ridicule, the Germans start out searching for the quisling, who now must rely on the underground for safety. The most subtle act of rebellion occurs as a German inspects the church parishioners, looking for the airmen, and all the while the organist quietly plays the anthem.

Jo De Vries also works against the Germans, and it she who puts forth the argument for allied bombing of her country. Only under the cover of an air raid can the airmen escape, for the Germans are forced to take cover. Looking down on the courtyard where the Germans are racing for shelter, Jo says, "You see, that's what you're doing for us. Can you hear them running for shelter, can you understand what that means to all the occupied countries to enslaved people having it drummed into their ears that the Germans are the masters of the earth? Seeing those masters running for shelter, seeing them crouching under tables and hearing that steady hum night after night, that noise which is oil for the burning fires in our hearts." Although Jo can ignore the innocent civilians who are killed in such air raids, the English could not and the bombing of occupied countries was discontinued soon after the film's release.

One of Our Aircraft Is Missing is an entertaining film but a surprisingly forgettable one. The ensemble casting was crucial for the Archers' objective, but it contributed to the lack of focus. It likewise lacks the experimentation one associates with the Archers and resembles many films that went into release at this time, many of which owed their inspiration to *49th Parallel*. Today the primary interest of the film is the character of Sir George Corbett (Godfrey Teale), who accompanies the airmen. He joins the unit at the last moment, and from the beginning his age isolates him from the others. In Holland, he gradually takes control of the situation, even as his companions argue that there is no need for a leader. He is the most qualified of the men to lead, but, he is also the one whose values come under attack. He has little use for women in the war effort, but after encountering first Els Meertens, then Jo De Vries, he is gradually awakened to their ability and value. He is called on to make a toast to Jo De Vries, but he recognizes it as a testimonial to his age, as is her decision to kiss him as they leave. "I suppose that's the one advantage to being old," he says. In the end, his acceptance into the unit is evidenced by their refusal to leave him behind, even if it means their own seizure.

Corbett would serve as the inspiration for Clive Candy, although the men have little in common other than age and a sense that their time has passed. Initially there had been a scene involving Corbett and the pilot, John Glyn Haggard (Hugh Burden), talking of Meertens, to whom the latter had been obviously attracted. Corbett asks whether he will return for her after the war, but John's first concern is simply to survive the engagement. They laugh over the man's pessimism, but then Corbett turns serious. "You know, you'll think me mad, but you are like I was in the past, and you are like I am now in the present." The pilot does indeed think Sir George is mad, but the latter is undeterred. "You've got exactly the same sort of general mentality and character that I had when I was young, and I tell you that in forty years you'll be just like me, a crusty old bugger." The suggestion to expand on this theme into the film *The Life and Death of Colonel Blimp* has been variously credited to Pressburger or to the editor of *One of Our Aircraft Is Missing*, David Lean, but no matter who takes credit for its conception, the final realization of the film would result in the Archers' first masterpiece.

Even with the creation of the Archers, Powell had one more film to direct on his own, a five-minute documentary entitled *An Airman's Letter to His Mother*. A mail carrier walks along a country road and drops a letter into a house. Inside an elderly woman picks it up and goes upstairs to her son's room to read it. The letter is from the woman's son, the narrator (John Gielgud) informs us, who is "missing, presumed dead." The son had left it behind with his station commander to be mailed in the event of his death. Later published in *The Times*, it is now being recounted because the letter "might bring comfort to other mothers and that everyone in our country would feel proud to read of the sentiments which support an average airman in his execution of his present arduous duties."

The letter's objective is to reassure his mother that his death does not mean her "struggles have been in vain. Far from it. It means that your sacrifice is as great as mine." Powell keeps the film from becoming static by having the camera track about the room, also helping to define the dead airman's personality. His photograph is present, as are model airplanes and an airplane prop, that hangs on the wall, attesting to his love of flying, which evidently resulted in his joining the Air Force. The woman is distinguished by her reading glasses and the dog that sits at her side, the disclosure of her features transforming her into an icon for motherhood. The letter concludes by stating that the "universe is so vast, so ageless, that the life of one man can only be justified by the measure of his sacrifice," while the film concludes with the camera tracking through the window toward a cloud that has taken on the shape of the RAF insignia.

7

Stop This Foolish Production

Initially, the script Pressburger began to write in early 1942 was entitled *The Life and Death of Sugar Candy*, but the Archers soon had amended this to *The Life and Death of Colonel Blimp*, incorporating a name familiar to most Englishmen of the time. Colonel Blimp was a featured character in David Low's newspaper cartoons, and he had come to represent all that was wrong with the aged, more entrenched military establishment. The character, which had first appeared in 1934, was on hiatus when the Archers began their film. When they took their script before the Ministry of War, however, the very name *Blimp* was a red flag to them. Ian Christie has painstakingly detailed the government response to the project and how the Films Division characterized the script as "defeatist." The result was that the Archers' initial choice for the title character, Laurence Olivier, was denied release from the Fleet Air Arm, and the use of military equipment was forbidden. Even after the film had gone into production, various factions of the government worked to have it suppressed, with even Winston Churchill taking an active interest in it, as evidenced by the following memo he sent out on September 10, 1942: "Pray propose to me the measures necessary to stop this foolish production before it gets any further. I am not prepared to allow propaganda detrimental to the morale of the Army, and I am sure the Cabinet will take all necessary action. Who are the people behind it?" In the end, all that the government had accomplished was to give the film an air of notoriety.

Because the film's diegesis would encompass forty years, Pressburger carefully researched the period of the film, incorporating not only the major military engagements of the time, but also such details as the public's fascination with Sherlock Holmes, and the type of operas that were then in vogue. What proved to be a godsend for the Archers was Powell's discovery of a small German rule book providing the codes that determined the act of dueling. Pressburger also took note of the advancement of women during this time, so that each of the three female characters with whom Candy would be in love were symptomatic of their particular era. It had been decided that all three women would be portrayed by a single actress, and Wendy Hiller was first approached for the project. Her discovery that she was pregnant caused her to back out at the last minute and forced the Archers to find a quick replacement. Powell suggested Deborah Kerr, a young actress who had made an appearance in *Contraband* but was eventually cut from the film. Despite her youth (she was only twenty), she had already made an impact in films, but it was with this film that she would become a star. The earlier removal of Olivier from the project also resulted in another inspired piece of casting. Powell had first wanted to work with Roger Livesey on *The Phantom Light*, but producer Michael Balcon had dismissed him, believing that his voice was too unconventional. Now as his own producer, Powell took on Livesey for the role of Clive Candy. The only initial choice for a lead role who remained was Walbrook.

Rank Studios, more conscious of the Archers' previous box office success than of the government's resentment toward the film, provided the two men with their largest budget yet. Part of the enormous expenditure was due to the logistics of the project, which occupied most of Denham Studios, but also to the Archers' desire to film in color. They recruited Georges Perinal, whom Powell had worked with on *The Thief of Bagdad*, and also some of the personnel who would become integral to their production unit. Alfred Junge, the great art director who had began his training in the German cinema and who had worked with Powell on *Red Ensign* built the enormous sets required, and Alan Grey produced the music, which influenced the movement of the film.

Filming began on July 8, 1942, but the film was hampered

by not only the government's refusal to supply military equipment but also by the shortage of young men available to fill out the background. Two hundred and fifty Germans were needed for the scene when Candy visits Theo at a POW camp, but less than fifty were available. In an act of ingenuity that would become a trademark for the Archer productions, mannequins were strategically placed throughout the scene. Filming lasted fourteen weeks, resulting in a film that ran nearly three hours. Yet, thanks to the government's reaction the film, advertised as the one the government wanted banned, was a commercial success.

The critics, however, were confused as to how to take the film. "*Blimp's* worst fault—apart from its title and its length, which is two-and-three quarters hours and quite absurd—is an unclarity of purpose. It is a handsome piece. It is frequently a moving piece. But what is it about?"[1] This query by C. A. Lejeune was echoed by many reviewers of the time. Dilys Powell, one of the Archers' strongest supporters, was perhaps most accurate in her assessment, recognizing the ambivalent attitude the directors felt to their central figure. "The moral of his career is left uncertain: with one voice the film censures his beliefs, with another protests that they are the beliefs of all upright men. The portrait presented, in fact, is the portrait of almost any decent, slow-witted, romantic Englishman, with this difference, that not all decent slow-witted Englishmen would show the humanity towards a German refugee shown by this Colonel Blimp."[2]

After Winston Churchill, the greatest opponent of the film may have been M. M. Robson, who published a small book entitled *The Shame and Disgrace of Colonel Blimp*. In it he characterizes the film as "one of the most wicked productions that has ever disgraced the British film industry and inflicted upon the long suffering British people."[3] He then goes on to detail his principal objection to the film:

> Here we are concerned with a specific case, a costly and much patronized film, in order to illustrate how easy it is for the thoughtless to soften a nation's mind in advance to prepare that nation mentally for another dose of illimitable suffering in the future. If the message of *The Life and Death of Colonel Blimp* is absorbed without a vehement protest into the subconscious mind of the nation, it encourages other film makers to do even

worse, and this process need only to be repeated often enough until the manners, the thoughts, the wooly thinking and the antisocial bias of *Blimp* becomes part of the conscious mind of our nation. And what of our future relationships with our Allies and other countries after the war?[4]

Certainly this reaction was among the most extreme, but, similarly, it is hard to believe Robson was alone in his views. It was typical of the way the Archers seemed to strike a nerve with many critics.

The Life and Death of Colonel Blimp began its life as a warning to the British—that the rules of the past no longer pertained to the conflict they now faced—but what emerged more than anything was a lament for the past. Some critics have characterized it as the British *Citizen Kane* (Andrew Sarris among them), but this is perhaps too limiting of a compliment. Hollywood was the world's film capital, employing the finest technicians of the world, in the most advanced studios of the time. The Archers' film was made in the midst of war, when there was always the threat of an air raid and at a time when the British studio was only beginning to assert itself. It is a film light years ahead of its time, particularly in Britain where most films either seemed to be adaptations of literary masterpieces or attempted to mirror reality. *The Life and Death of Colonel Blimp* was neither of these, for it was an original work with no precepts of realism, seeming instead to be more a musical than a war film. It initiated the Archers' most productive period, for they were to produce eight highly original works over the next six years concluding with *The Small Back Room*. While it is not difficult imagining another British director producing *Contraband* or *One of Our Aircraft Is Missing*, it is impossible to imagine anyone but the Archers producing these films. Various factors contributed to this new maturity, not the least of which was the decision to sign with Rank.

J. Arthur Rank's father had made millions in the flour industry, but his son was destined to make his name in films. He had financed a film in 1934 for the Religious Film Society, *Mastership*, but his follow-up would reflect his growing ambitions, for *Turn of the Tide* won a prize at the Venice Film Festival. The lack of support it received from the studio, however,

prompted Rank to purchase all of the Gaumount-British theater circuit. He was often a man more adept at spending money than working toward a goal, but, by the end of the thirties,
he had even accumulated Denham Studios, Alexander Korda's
production unit. With the departure of Korda for the United
States, Rank became the leading figure in British cinema, even
though his biographer would later characterize him as a man
whose "greatest virtue of all was undoubtedly the fact that he
knew nothing whatever about the making of films."[5]

Rank's willingness to spend money, while also remaining
clear of the technical aspects of film, promoted an environment
very conducive to directors. Only the French in the late fifties
enjoyed such freedom, but even they were to be restricted by
financing. Perhaps the most extreme example of Rank's relaxed
spending was his support of Gabriel Pascal's *Caesar and Cleopatra*, whose final production cost was 1.3 million pounds. If
that film was a commercial and critical disaster, his establishment of the Independent Producers was more fortuitous. The
Archers were among the first to sign on, quickly followed by
Carol Reed, David Lean, and Anthony Asquith. Whatever one's
opinion of Rank, there can be no denying his success or his
impact on the Archers. It is hard to imagine another producer,
either British or American, providing them with so much autonomy and financing, as David Lean understood:

> J. Arthur Rank is often spoken of as an all-embracing monop-
> olist who must be watched lest he crush the creative talents of
> the British film industry. Let the facts speak for themselves,
> and I doubt if any other group of film-makers anywhere in the
> world can claim as much freedom. We of Independent Produc-
> ers can make any subject we wish, with as much money as we
> think that subject should have spent upon it. We can cast
> whatever actors we choose, and we have no interference at all
> in the way the film is made. No one sees the films until they
> are finished, and no cuts are made without the consent of the
> director or the producer, and what's more, not one of us is
> bound by any form of contract.[6]

A second factor in the Archers' maturity may have been a
product of the government's reaction to the film. Faced with
the loss of their lead actor and access to military equipment,
the Archers could easily have abandoned the project, but in-

stead the action seemed to galvanize them. Until then, the Archers had often worked in unison with the government's agenda, seeking to create films with specific propaganda precepts while remaining entertaining. *The Life and Death of Colonel Blimp* and the two films to follow were to serve as essays on how the British fought and what values they were protecting. The government action also forced them to rely more heavily on their set decorators, so that these men would become almost equals to Powell and Pressburger themselves. Finally, the government's refusal to release Olivier effectively altered the character of Clive Candy. Olivier certainly had specific ideas concerning the character, and his portrayal would most likely have ignored the more sentimental aspects of Candy. Roger Livesey's rich brogue accent and his ability to create a character who lacks malice results in a figure that is more sympathetic and less a target of derision.

This impression of a talent being liberated is evident in the opening, which immediately creates a sense of release. A Teletype types out an order for the Home Guard exercise that is to occur at midnight, and a fleet of motorcycles carry the message out into the country. The camera hurtles along with the riders, the music adding to the sense of rhythm, and the vehicles begin to fan out until only one is left speeding along a deserted road. The music comes to a stop when the rider is knocked off his cycle by a rope strung across the road by two sentries. From the spacious outdoors, the Archers cut to the interior of a barn, where Lieutenant Spuds Wilson (James Mc-Kechnie) is in the midst of shaving when the message is brought in. If Powell had often experimented with the movement of the camera, the Archers were soon to display a willingness to place the camera in unwieldy positions, to the point where the viewer is made aware of its presence. Here, the camera is in the loft looking down on Wilson as he complains to his men of the civility of the exercise, with its exacting rules, but also its demand to "make it like the real thing." After reluctantly taking on the assignment, Wilson decides to take a page from the Japanese and carry out a surprise assault. His men start out in transports for London, with their first stop being a roadhouse where Wilson's girlfriend Angela is relaxing. Later we discover that she is the driver for the leader of the exercise, General Clive Candy, and that from her Wilson learns the general's location. Now, however, the camera remains outside with the men, who stand around waiting for Wilson and casually greeting Angela as she emerges from the building, only realizing as she reaches her vehicle that she is attempting to escape. Wilson is located inside nearly unconscious and, after mustering his men, takes off in pursuit of Angela, who has gone to warn the "wizard," the reference calling to mind one of Powell's favorite films, *The Wizard of Oz.*

The race to the club where Candy is unwinding is like a dance, with the vehicles moving in and out of traffic in order to secure an advantage, and Angela arrives first, but Wilson and his men are close behind. Her attempt to forewarn her commander in chief proves ineffectual, and Wilson's men fan out throughout the club searching for their quarry, finding him asleep among the rising steam, only clad in a towel. The setting and his appearance would have been familiar to audiences of the time, for this was often the manner in which David Low's character was depicted. Candy takes no notice of the activity around him and is annoyed at being awakened. Only gradually does he realize what has happened but his continuous entreaty that "war starts at midnight" has no effect on the younger man. Wilson's response is to reinforce the leitmotif of the film, that the enemy is not bound by a code of honor or rules. "We agree to keep the rules of the game, and they keep kicking us in the seat of the pants! When I joined the Army, the only agreement I entered into was to defend my country by any means at my disposal, not only by National Sporting Club Rules but by every means that has existed since Cain slugged Abel." Wilson's manner becomes even more impudent as he makes references to the general's size and moustache. No longer able to contain his anger and frustration, the elder man begins to strike out, and, as a stunned Wilson attempts to block Candy's punches, the pair fall back into the pool. "You laugh at my big belly, but you don't know how I got it. You laugh at my moustache, but you don't know why I grew it. How do you know what sort of man I was, when I was as young as you are, forty years ago, forty years ago . . . ?" The last words gradually become lost in the water in which the men have fallen, and the camera pulls back to disclose a motionless pool. Suddenly a young man emerges from the water and breaks into an aria as he makes his way up the stairs. The young man is Clive Candy and we have indeed gone back forty years.

Music is important as a way to enhance not just the choreography of movement, but also a motif, as it is introduced. The aria Candy is whistling, for example, will be referred to constantly in this section. Another soldier joins in with him and it proves to be Hoppy (David Hutcheson), a companion who had served with Candy in the Boer War. Their impromptu duet disturbs an older general who berates the men first in the steam room then in the lobby, only to recognize Candy as a hero from the Boer War. Thus, when Candy is introduced, his moment of distinction has already passed, although it will be constantly alluded to, most often through the aria. This section is also the most visually stunning of the film, as the year 1902 is re-created, with hansom cabs the primary means of transportation, but automobiles just being introduced and hot potato vendors not only selling food but providing warmth to Candy and Hoppy. The latter begins to relate to his friend a letter he has received and the ensuing dialogue seems more from a musical than from a war film.

> "Remember that interview you gave *The Times*?" Hoppy asks.
> "Don't tell me you read it?"
> "Me? No. I have a niece, who has a governess, who has a sister."
> "Pretty?"
> "Never laid eyes on her, but she read it."
> "Who?"
> "My niece's governess's sister."

The content of the letter concerns a German agent who is spreading rumors of British atrocities in South Africa, with specific references to the town where Candy had been stationed. Candy approaches the War Office about traveling to Germany to put a halt to the rumors, but the official he meets with is more interested in Sherlock Holmes's latest escapades, the author of which Candy admits to knowing. The politician lovingly recites a line from the latest installment: "'A lovely evening my dear Watson. I really think you will be more comfortable outside than in.' Sarcastic devil, that Holmes. I once had a CO [commanding officer] just like him." Candy's petition is nearly lost in the discussion, but he emerges from the meeting with orders not to travel to Germany. Undeterred, he leaves for Germany, his act of insubordination echoing that of Wilson in the prologue, with both men rebelling against an order they believe is wrong. The raison d'etre for the film had been the supposition that Wilson is Candy's doppleganger, a version of himself at that age.

The Life and Death of Colonel Blimp is a film of striking images, and the introduction of Edith Hunter is one of these. Standing at a window, she moves across the lobby to the soft elegiac music that will be not only her signature music but also the theme for Candy's lost love. She is clothed in a long, flowing, dark blue gown and wearing the first of many distinctive hats, in this case a large-brimmed one that extends out nearly a foot. After greeting Candy and expressing surprise that he traveled to Germany simply on account of her letter, she begins to assume almost the role of an educator. She tells him of the difficulties the British currently face in Germany, evidence of which is her recent dismissal from her position as nanny, then tells him of Kaunitz (David Ward), the man spreading the propaganda. The irony, of course, is that British atrocities were documented during the Boer War, a fact that only the most well-read moviegoers of the time could have known. For the first time, dueling is mentioned, as Edith announces that it is a "proud father that has a scarred son, and vice versa." Edith also subliminally establishes her intellectual superiority to Candy as she corrects him in his allusion to Stanley and Livingston. He is taken back by the manner in which she seems to rebuke him, a state of affairs that continues into their next sequence.

The serenity of their first encounter gives way to the chaotic pace of the cafe where they hope to meet Kaunitz. The camera opens on the orchestra, the conductor flailing about with his baton in time to the music, but, as the camera pans about the exorbitant cafe, the movements of the patrons and waiters are also in sync to the music. Two Germans meet across the table and bow to one another before slamming down their mugs on the table, each gesture seemingly choreographed. There is a constant sense of rhythm throughout the locale, and here we encounter for the first time the Archers' obsession with creating a composed film. Powell would often refer to the cli-

max of *Black Narcissus* as the beginning of the experiment
while decrying *The Life and Death of Colonel Blimp* as little
more than a black-and-white film that had been shot in color.
Neither of these statements rings true, for intuitively the Archers were already beginning to combine the soundtrack and
image into one experience. Powell's statements also discredit
the work of Alfred Junge and Georges Perinal, who as art director and cinematographer combined to create one of the most
beautiful color films of its time, not to be surpassed until the
Archers' own *Black Narcissus*. Powell's definition of the composed film and its antecedents in film history will be examined
later, but it is sufficient to realize that even now, with the war
not yet half over, the Archers were already beginning to look
toward the future.

As Candy and Edith take their seats, the orchestra is performing the "Mill Which Went 'Round and 'Round," but the
music fades to the background as he remarks that the embassy has proscribed him from taking any action. An inadvertent
repercussion of his refusal to take action is that she too will
be forced to withdraw to Britain, to a family who will take her
back but which to her represents a loss of independence. She
admits her options are limited to either marriage or life as a
nanny, but her principal allure is her ability to speak German
and teach manners. He believes the latter is important, but
she turns it on to his profession. "While you men have been
fighting, we women have been thinking," she informs a startled
Candy. She then makes a statement concerning South Africa
that will be echoed throughout the film: "Good manners cost
us six thousand men killed and twenty thousand wounded and
two years of war, when with a little common sense and bad
manners there would have been no war at all." Just then
Kaunitz makes his entrance, accompanied by members of the
German military. The sight of Kaunitz causes Candy to hesi-
tate and instead of "retreating" he calls over a waiter to request a song, the aria that he had earlier hummed and that
had been the only music available to them when he had been
holed up with Kaunitz for weeks. This initiates the next musical set piece of the film, in which the music develops into both
a literal and a symbolic anticipation of the duel.

The first note of the music is in time with Candy's nodding
of his head to the orchestra, and, as the aria begins, Kaunitz's

head turns in recognition, his movement also to the beat. He immediately orders a waiter to have the music stopped, but Candy prepares a counterattack, sending his waiter down to purchase beer with which to bribe the orchestra members. The two men pass one another on the steps, their quick steps like those of a dancer. The men at Kaunitz's table are gesturing for the orchestra to stop, further evidence of the choreography involved. The orchestra discontinues playing, but with the arrival of the beer and with Candy making like a conductor, lifting his hands up and bringing them down, the music commences once more. Kaunitz angrily slams his mug to the table and hurries up the stairs, the dance about to reach its completion. Glancing in Candy's direction, he turns his concentration to the orchestra, then a sense of recognition passes across his face as he perceives Candy's presence and turns back to him. The music has brought the two foes together and set into motion the events leading up to the duel. The action that follows is almost anticlimactic, with Candy confronting not only Kaunitz but also the German soldiers who accompany him, the result of which is a challenge to a duel.

The preparation for the duel lasts ten minutes, with the underlying theme of the film brought out to its fullest: Candy's fidelity to the rules. From the confrontation with the Germans at the cafe, the Archers cut to two pairs of military boots walking along a sidewalk, each step in rhythm with the music, and the camera remains with them as they enter an embassy. Only then are full figures of the military men revealed, as they march purposely to the office of the British ambassador. The music fades as the Germans question the embassy man over Candy, and they are relieved to discover he is a British officer. The announcement of the duel sets into motion a scene more reminiscent of an Ernst Lubitsch operetta than of a military drama, with the shocked official racing off to relay the news. The camera looks down a corridor as the man enters a number of rooms, a growing number of officials trailing after him as in a promenade.

Candy accepts the challenge, and his government reluctantly goes along with the duel, believing his refusal would result in a public relations disaster. Representatives of the German military and the British government meet to discuss the rules of the engagement and announce Candy's opponent, Theo

Kretschmar-Schuldorff (Anton Walbrook), a man chosen at random to represent the Germans. The duel is to occur in an immense gymnasium that nearly overwhelms the participants (in fact a matte was utilized to increase the sense of depth). Candy arrives first, and his calm manner belies the risk involved, his interest on who his opponent is to be. A group of German soldiers parade in, but his competitor remains obscured until each man has taken his place opposite the other. The German is momentarily disconcerted by Candy's smile in greeting.

The duel itself loses its importance once it begins, serving as a mechanism for bringing together Candy and Theo, and ultimately Edith. For the Archers it is the preparation of the duel that is significant, and now as it begins the camera retreats, rising to the ceiling and passing through a skylight. Snow is falling, and the camera tracks down to a waiting carriage, where a hand is wiping away the frost from a window. Inside Edith nervously waits for the outcome of the duel, but her companion, Babyface Fitzroy (Frith Banbury), does little to assuage her fears, remarking that he hopes no one is killed. As he attempts to reassure her of Candy's fencing abilities (he has won awards for his prowess), the gates open and the first of two Red Cross wagons pass through. The duel has ended with no indication of who won or the health of the participants. In fact, both men have been injured, with Candy receiving a cut to his upper lip, prompting him to grow his distinctive moustache. In his confinement in the German hospital, Candy comes to befriend his German opponent, and the two spend the time playing cards, with Edith acting as translator. After months of recuperation, Candy is finally discharged, but now he must face a second challenge as the underlying theme of the film is introduced, one of lost love.

Candy is in the midst of packing when Theo enters the room, his uneasiness apparent to us but not to his English companion. In imperfect English he makes known his love for Edith, whom he wrongly assumes is Candy's fiancee (the government having established this as the motive for the duel). Theo expects the announcement to incite a second duel, but not for the last time Candy surprises him with his reaction, as the Englishman congratulates him, genuinely happy with the news. What Candy does not realize is that he too loves Edith, but this is only apparent to him when he congratulates her on the engagement. Pulling back from kissing her, his face registers a change in emotion and he stumbles over his words as he attempts to make a toast. He returns to England alone but with an ideal of his love having been established, and he even takes out Edith's sister in a misguided attempt to re-create the passion. He takes a room in his aunt's mansion and begins to hunt wild game, the passage of time delineated by the heads that appear on a wall, accompanied by the sound of gunshots. The plaque below each of the trophies indicates the passing of time, the camera finally descending on a German helmet, signifying the commencement of the First World War.

In this sequence, the primary themes of the film emerge again and we witness for the first time Candy's detachment from the realities of war. Confronting a group of German prisoners, he attempts to question them on Theo's whereabouts, while rebuking the Germans' willingness to use torture to obtain information. The men say nothing. After Candy has departed, the South African sergeant who takes over the questioning establishes that he will not take the tempered approach of Candy. When Candy later receives word that the war has ended, he tells Murdoch that British have demonstrated that "right is might after all," adding that "clean fighting and honest soldiering have won."

While in Flanders Candy catches sight of Barbara Wynne (Kerr), a young woman who bears a striking resemblance to Edith. He has entered a church that has been converted into a hospital and as he sits among the hundreds of nurses, seated at the tables, he catches sight of her. Before he can speak, she has moved on and is lost in the crowd. When he speaks of the experience, he compares it to seeing an Indian rope trick. "You hear about the thing. You hope to see it—and you see." Having ascertained from what district the nurses are, Candy reunites them after the war on the pretense of a benefit, through which he meets Barbara. Of the three characters that Kerr will portray, Barbara has the shortest screen time, but this is to be expected for she is the realization of an ideal. When he asks her why she has agreed to marry him despite their differences in age, her response is whispered to him as they sit on the grass, her family's estate behind them. "I'm marrying you because I want to join the Army and see the world. I'm marrying

you because I love watching you play polo. I'm marrying you
for fifty reasons that all means that's how I imagined my future husband." Certainly she is how Candy conceives of his
wife, but their happiness will be transient for she will die before Britain enters World War II.

Through various mechanizations, Theo and Barbara will be
destined never to meet, although he and Candy are reunited
soon after the war's cessation. Candy has learned that Theo is
interned at a POW camp, but when he and Barbara travel to
meet him, an embittered Theo rebuffs him. Only as he is about
to be repatriated to Germany does Theo finally contact Candy,
who is in the midst of entertaining some colleagues. Theo is
invited to join them but is visibly uncomfortable as the discussion turns to the conditions of the POW camps and the ad-
justments his country will be forced to face in peace-
time. Candy's attempts to reassure him only substantiate his
naivete. "You got the wrong end of the stick, old man. The war's
over. There's nothing to bear malice about. You're a decent fellow and so are we." Theo wonders about the Germany to which
he will return, one that is as much a prison as the one from
which he has just been released, and he emerges from the
encounter convinced that Germany will once more assert itself
as a military power, while Britain will be weakened by a paci-
fist movement. This scornful digression is out of keeping with
Theo's character and when he is introduced again, there is no
sense of gratification in his predictions having proven correct.
Sitting before a British tribunal, hoping to gain entrance into
England, he is not just older but also more subdued. During
the questioning, he provides insight into what he has endured
in the years between the wars, as he was forced to watch his
wife die and witness his son's conversion to Nazism.

For Pressburger, *The Life and Death of Colonel Blimp* was
his most cherished film. In Walbrook, he found his perfect
mouthpiece, just as he had in *49th Parallel* and would later in
Oh Rosalinda!! As in all of these films, Walbrook is called on
to deliver a monologue that relates to the experience of the
emigre. "The truth about me," he says, "is that I am a tired
old man who came to this country because he is homesick.
Don't stare at me, sir, I am all right in the head. You know
that, after the war, we had very bad years in Germany." He

goes on to relate how he had been driving through the German countryside when he came across the nursing home where he had first met Candy and Edith. He admits he wrote to Candy for help but received no reply, only to have the Englishman surprise him once more by appearing at the hearing to take him home. If the central thread of the film is of a lost love, it is also of a friendship that endures, mirroring Powell and Pressburger's own relationship.

Candy has now been transformed into the figure we had met in the opening, although at this moment he is a member of the military, having been reactivated. After becoming reacquainted with Theo, he finally confesses to him his love for Edith and presents a painting of Barbara, commenting on the resemblance between the two women. Having grown old with Edith, Theo cannot see the similarity between the two, but he does recognize his wife's likeness in Candy's driver Angela. Angela admits she was surprised at being chosen as his driver, that it was a "seven hundred to one. Makes me bit of an outsider." Both the audience and Theo, however, realize that Candy has once more experienced the "Indian rope trick." The Archers were often careful to shroud their individual contributions to a film, but in the conversation that follows it is Powell's addendum to the dialogue that gives Angela's character an identity. Theo has told her that she has a lovely name, but she wants no part of it. "I think it stinks. My friends call me Johnny."

Candy's loyalty to the precepts of acceptable behavior in wartime eventually catches up to him, for as he is about to give a radio address on the battles at Dunkirk, he finds himself replaced, his speech having been found to be too defeatist. In it Candy had denigrated the Germans for their atrocities and stated that he would "sooner accept defeat than victory if it could only be won by those methods." Even Theo recognizes the absurdity of Candy's convictions, that Candy has "been educated to be a gentleman and a sportsman. But this is not a gentlemen's war." He characterizes Candy as a soldier out of step with the time. "It's a different knowledge they need now, Clive. The enemy's different, so you have to be different too." Candy is unwilling to accept this, but he does not give up on life, instead taking on a role in the Home Guard. His accomplishment is denoted by the magazine covers on which he appears, but he also suffers more hardship, losing a close companion and his home.

The film now comes full circle as the events leading to the assault on the steam room are repeated, with additional material included. This elliptical format is representative of much of the Archers' work, which either used a flashback or returned to the setting of the opening. Wilson's subjugation of Candy comes through intelligence (learning of the general's whereabouts from his girlfriend) and aggressiveness (attacking before the war is to begin), but he engenders little of our esteem. Although we know his motives are justifiable, it is Candy's defeat that remains in our mind, as well as his determination not to give in to cynicism. Standing at the remnants of his destroyed home, he looks out at Wilson's soldiers passing by in a parade as he tells Angela that the exercise will be repeated and that Wilson's actions will come under review. He admits little will come of it, instead relating Wilson to his own experience. "When I was a young chap," he says, "I was all gas and gaiters with no experience worth a damn. Now, tons of experience and nobody thinks I'm any use. I remember when I got back from Berlin in '02. Old Betteridge gave me the worst wigging I ever had. And when he invited me to dinner, I didn't accept—often wish I had. Yes, I think I will invite him to dinner. And he'd better accept, d'you know." The film ends not with a condemnation of Candy's convictions but more a wish that such values could still exist.

If *The Life and Death of Colonel Blimp* represented a break with the conventional British cinema, so too did *The Volunteer* appear to be a reaction against Britain's documentary movement. Powell had little enthusiasm for the project, which was begun at the request of Ralph Richardson, a close friend of Pressburger's and a member of the Fleet Air Arm. Just as he had with *A Canterbury Tale*, Powell found Pressburger's script to be too convoluted, involving a "story within a story and the episodes he wanted were difficult to obtain—we were a bit early for that sort of thing."[7]

The interiors for *The Volunteer* were filmed at Denham, and scenes aboard a navy ship were filmed on a training ship. The scenes of Richardson as Othello were set in the New Theatre in St. Martin's Lane. These two settings hint at the peculiar dichotomy of the film, where the boundary between the military and the theatrical are constantly blurred. Richardson thinks back to before the war, when he had been essaying the role of Othello and was continually irritated by the actions of his dresser, Alfred (Pat McGrath). Alfred constantly makes a mess of things, and Richardson has little hope for him, particularly after he declares his intention to join the service. When war is declared, Richardson begins making propaganda films and is visited by Alfred, who declares his enlistment in the Fleet Air Arm. Richardson will also join this branch of the service and one day is contacted by Alfred, who is to perform in a play with his unit and wishes to borrow an artificial beard. Alfred still seems the clumsy buffoon who constantly exasperated the actor during his theater work. When Richardson encounters him next, he has been assigned to a carrier as a mechanic. The ship has recently been in a confrontation, but Alfred admits he spent most of it in the sick bay, something that does not surprise Richardson. When Richardson views footage of the encounter, however, he observes Alfred boldly working to repair a plane while under fire and becoming wounded in the process. Richardson emerges from the screening with a new regard for his former dresser but when he goes to congratulate him, he finds the man asleep in a hanger, exhausted from his work. Later, while walking with his daughter, Richardson comes across a parade and discovers Alfred being honored for his bravery. The film concludes with the actor asking Alfred for his autograph, just as the dresser had earlier asked Richardson for his.

The film opens with a close-up of Richardson's legs propped up on a fireplace, the perspective his, as he begins to narrate the tale. From the mantle he takes down a photograph of the cast and crew who had worked on his production of *Othello*; holding a magnifying glass to the image he introduces Alfred. Richardson's narration continues even as he is introduced coming into his dressing room, still in the guise of Othello, and is met by Alfred. Richardson recalls the conversation that had taken place, and it is his voice that originates from Alfred's mouth. The initial tone of the film is one of slapstick, with Alfred a figure of ridicule, but, as is typical of the Archers' work, the tone shifts abruptly. The theatrical world is constantly

aligned with that of the theater of war, with Richardson remarking that it "was the end of one world and the beginning
of another." He emerges from the theater, to be greeted not by
autograph seekers as earlier, but by the sight of men placing
sandbags in preparation of war.

Richardson's next move is into a studio, where he is
dressed as a beefeater. "We were making a propaganda film.
With the outbreak of the war actors donned historical costumes
and gave powerful speeches about the wooden walls of England," a comment that relates to Powell's earlier work on *The
Lion Has Wings*. When Richardson does enter the services, he
still appears to be assuming a role, as when he has a rendezvous with a ship and is surprised by the attention his appearance engenders, only to realize the fuss is over the reels of
film that have also arrived. The presentation of the battle sequence in which Alfred is transformed into a hero is one of
detachment, with the viewer constantly aware of the audience
watching the footage of the battle. The film Richardson views
is actually the Archers' approximation of a documentary, as we
witness the training the men endure and the application of the
knowledge in battle. The captain narrates the footage, even invoking the cinema itself when he mentions Algiers and recalls
the Charles Boyer movie of the same name. Our attention is
alternately drawn between the battle on the screen and Richardson's reaction to it. When the film is over, the others depart, leaving Richardson alone with his thoughts. In many
respects the film is of his own transformation from actor to
spectator, which will culminate in his later asking Alfred for an
autograph, providing an ellipsis to an unusual film.

8

Our Journey's Just Begun

With *The Life and Death of Colonel Blimp*, the Archers examined how the British fought; now they decided to explore the values they were fighting for with *A Canterbury Tale*. For Powell the film was to be "an examination of materialism (in the form of the organist/soldier played by Dennis Price) against idealism (as exemplified by the young American soldier). That was really the reason for making the film, because we thought the moral issues of the war were almost as exciting as the war that was being fought. The whole idea was to examine the values for which we were fighting and to do it partly though the eyes of a young American who was training in England."[1]

Powell decided to set the film in Chillingbourne and Canterbury, the area in which he had grown up, but it was Pressburger who decided to incorporate Chaucer's tale into the diegesis, creating a story of three modern-day pilgrims. The film reunited Deborah Kerr and Roger Livesey from *The Life and Death of Colonel Blimp*, but the former was forced to back out due to a binding contract with M-G-M and the latter departed on his own after finding the script incomprehensible. In Kerr's place, the Archers cast Sheila Sim, a young actress just beginning in film, and Eric Portman took on the role of the magistrate. For the American soldier, Powell turned to an actual member of the U.S. military, Bob Sweet, who was currently in an Army performance of *Eve of St. Mark*. Sweet had been a schoolteacher before the war, and *A Canterbury Tale* was to be his only film, for after the war he returned to the classroom.

Wartime restrictions prohibited Pressburger from traveling to Kent, where the production company would spend six weeks, but he was in constant touch with Powell and faithfully viewed the dailies. The Archers are noted for their color films, but their black-and-white productions were often just as sumptuous. They benefited from the involvement of Erwin Hillier, a cinematographer and sometime artist who had been discovered by F. W. Murnau. Although Hillier was not to work with Murnau, he did collaborate with Fritz Lang, and his work here reveals his expressionist background. His use of shadows and landscape would be one of the features singled out by critics of the time. What did not meet their approval would be the scenario. "*A Canterbury Tale* is a remarkable film, in which Michael Powell, the writer, has given Michael Powell, the director, a pretty shabby story and the second Powell has almost managed to get away with it."[2] Not only does this comment ignore Pressburger's role completely, but it fails to appreciate the complexity of the story, which many mistook as a mystery. Powell himself, perhaps mindful of the criticism, found that the script was one of Pressburger's more "complicated ideas and I really let him down by insisting that it was simplified."[3]

Powell's assessment is one of the few instances of his underestimating his own abilities. The very locale presented him with a chance to produce a personal film, as even he recognized:

> I expected that it would be a far more personal film than it turned out to be. I was working, creating a story in the country I was born in, the "garden of England," a chalky country of bare downs and shallow valleys, of chestnut woods and little chuckling streams, of slowly turning water and windmills, and white-capped osthouses with the bittersweet smell of hops drying in the kiln. All this I knew from my childhood, yet somehow I failed to get it on the screen. No doubt it was because the principal characters were all strangers to my countryside. They were intruders—well meaning, but still intruders.[4]

Yet, if Powell did not recognize the characters, he was still able to imbue the film with his own personal style; and if Pressburger's characters were not necessarily true to reality, he managed to create his own milieu. *A Canterbury Tale* is one of the most dramatic instances of Powell trusting Pressburger completely even if he maintained doubts and in the process inadvertently created a masterpiece.

The film would not be released in the United States until 1949 and then in a severely truncated format that included a prologue set in New York where Sweet is recounting the story to Kim Hunter. This version found little favor with critics or audiences and has since been forgotten. The Archers' original work also begins with a prologue, opening with a passage from Chaucer's *The Canterbury Tales*, thus invoking the spirit of the earlier work on the present film. From an ink drawing of the pilgrims, the Archers cut to the same pilgrims moving along the road to Canterbury. A falconer releases his bird and watches it soar across the sky, then, in a brilliant match cut, the bird is transformed into a British fighter plane. As in Stanley Kubrick's *2001: A Space Odyssey*, the passing of an extended period of time has been encompassed in a single shot, for the narrator informs us that six hundred years have transpired since Chaucer's tales. The soldier looking up at the plane is the earlier man's descendant, and we are told that "although so little has changed since Chaucer's day, another kind of pilgrim walks the way," and a tank hurtles across the landscape. "Our journey's just begun," he relates, while in the distance a train is passing through the countryside.

The film proper opens in darkness as a train is pulling into a station, the stationmaster calling out the stop as well as the next destination. Believing the stop to be Canterbury, American serviceman Sergeant Bob Johnson (Sweet) leaps from the train just as it is pulling out, only to realize too late that he has arrived at Chillingbourne, the last stop before his destination. From this moment on, he will be in a state of confusion, unsure of English customs or even how to conduct himself in a blackout. In fact, a primary thesis of the film will be the various misconceptions the characters maintain about one another. Not only will Sweet's preconceived impressions be examined, but so too the British perception of Americans and how the rural people view those from the city and vice versa. The British fail to identify Sweet as a sergeant as his stripes are the opposite of those of an English sergeant, while he finds it difficult to believe Chillingbourne is a town.

In the darkness of the blackout, Sweet is introduced to two other new arrivals, Sergeant Peter Gibbs and Alison Smith, who has come to Chillingbourne to serve as a field hand. The stationmaster is reluctant to allow her to walk the streets alone, claiming that the magistrate would not approve. Even before he has been introduced, Thomas Colpeper's authority is demonstrated as the stationmaster invariably alludes to his laws. There is a second justification for Alison's having an escort, which is made apparent as they make their way in the darkness. She is assaulted by someone who pours "sticky" stuff into her hair. The trio give chase, seemingly cornering him in a building revealed to be the town hall. This opening is a typically daring move by the Archers, with most of the action obscured in darkness for nearly six minutes. Only after they have entered the town hall are the features of Alison and Bob introduced and it will be even longer for Peter, as he has hurried off to catch his bus. The blackness will be a striking metaphor for the emotional darkness in which each of the characters will find themselves.

In the town, the local constable is busy playing cards and shows little inclination to pursue Alison's assailant, dismissing their claim that the "glueman," as he refers to the assailant, has entered the building. Alison learns that she is the eleventh "incident," and their attempts to hurry along the search of the building only anger the constable. "We may be slow in Chillingbourne, compared with London ways," he says, "and we ain't no G-men either, but we know our duty and we have our methods." A cursory search of the building reveals that someone is indeed in the building. The introduction of Colpeper reinforces his position as a figure of higher authority, the camera passing through the door and ascending the stairs, at the top of which is a beam separating Colpeper from the others. On it is written "Honour the Truth," but his objective will also be to honor the past. He casually orders the constable out for coffee while asking to see the young American. In his conversation with Bob, Colpeper alludes to one of his obsessions, that one must actively participate in life. Bob admits that he has spent most of his time in England in movie theaters, preferring to watch films. "It's a great thing to sit back in an arm chair and watch the world go by in front of you," he says. This statement is the antithesis of Colpeper's philosophy, and he mimics what Bob's response would be were he asked what he had seen in England. "Oh, I saw a movie in Salisbury and made a pilgrimage to Canterbury and saw another one.'"

Because the police constable had not known Colpeper was in the building the audience immediately suspects him and the Archers do not leave the audience in suspense long. During his conversation with Bob, the air raid warden calls out to Colpeper to close his curtain, which is permitting light to escape. After the American has gone, the constable returns to the curtain and, touching it, whispers his own name twice as if chastising himself. The Archers, as Hitchcock would later do in *Vertigo*, have gone against the central precept of a mystery by revealing to the audience the object of the search, then compounding it by having Alison immediately come to suspect him. She is introduced to him, her hair still wet from an unsuccessful attempt to wash the glue out, and identifies herself as the laborer sent to work for him. Colpeper wants no part of her, however, having believed the agency would be sending a man. His belief that a woman can contribute little to the war effort calls to mind Corbett in *One of Our Aircraft Is Missing*. He is also concerned about the army unit stationed outside town; although she argues that she has no interest in the men, he wonders whether the opposite will be true. Their conversation is interrupted by the sound of something in the next room, and, after a reluctant Colpeper finally opens the door, they find that his warden's uniform has fallen from its hanger. This will be enough to cause her to suspect Colpeper, and that night she recruits Bob into helping her discover the glueman's identity. Yet, as we already know the outcome of the search, our interest will be on Colpeper's motives and interrelations of the characters.

After agreeing to stay on in Chillingbourne, Bob must still adapt to his milieu—to a quarter that is called a shilling, to traveling on the opposite side of the road, and to receiving tea in the morning instead of coffee. Conversely, he will also learn that he has much in common with the English, which is brought out in a conversation he has with a wheelwright. Jim Horton (Edward Rigby) runs a wood mill, as does Bob's father back in the States. The two men discover that the techniques to treat wood handed down through the years by the English are the same ones passed on to Bob by his father. Alison is surprised by the rapport between the men, and Bob admits

that they both speak "the same language." Confused, she responds that she is "English, and we don't speak the same language," not realizing that although she is of the same country,
she is not of the same background, for her status as a city
dweller makes her more a foreigner than Bob. Ironically, this
theme, as Anthony Aldgate and Jeffrey Richards identify it, of
"the city dweller, the product of the urban culture, [having] lost
touch with his rural roots and the values they embody,"[5] will
be embodied more in Peter than in his two companions, for
although he occupies the smallest amount of screen time, he
will emerge as the primary antagonist to Colpeper.

In addition to their inquest, each of the characters will also
be coming to terms with a loss. Peter's lost passion will be
more ethereal, a loss of desire for his vocation, whereas Bob
and Alison are dealing with missing loved ones. Their wagon
having made its way out into the country, Bob tells Alison that
he has not heard from his girlfriend in six weeks, causing him
to believe she has left him. Alison recounts her own lost love,
a geologist who had first introduced her to the area but is now
a serviceman missing in action. This explains her motivation
for having moved to Chillingbourne, for "if there is such a thing
as a soul he must be here somewhere." She will also prove to
have an affinity for those in the country, as in her conversation with her employer's sister. Alison and Prudence Honeywood (Freda Jackson) are loading hay onto a wagon, when the
older woman asks her to describe the life she left behind in
the city. Alison begins, but Prudence anticipates her description of her home, asking if the street Alison had lived on had
been a long block where every house had a different sort of
sadness. The woman's entire life is crystallized in the next line:
"The only man who ever asked me to marry him wanted us to
live in a house like that. I'm still a maid." She tells Alison to
call her Pru. "I don't like Prudence, the name or the quality."
Although it was Powell who was raised in the English countryside, it often seemed to be Pressburger who advocated such a
way of life. Even in such an impersonal work as *The Elusive
Pimpernel*, Pressburger managed to get across his philosophy
by having the central villain, Chauvelin, admit "that these country people I do not trust. They are always thinking of their
families, their fat families, their fishing, their farms. When do
they think of our revolution?"

Peter finally returns to the story when his unit overtakes Alison's wagon, having picked it as their target for their military exercise. His off-hand remark that she was only an "objective" obliquely refers to her actual role in the drama unfolding. Peter tells her of a lecture that Colpeper is to present that night and convinces her to attend, where Bob is also in attendance. Many in the audience have little interest in listening to the lecture, with one there only so that he may read his book by the projector's light. Yet, Colpeper will gradually draw them in as he relates their experiences to that of the original pilgrims who were composed of a similarly diverse group. When one asks why he has solicited them, the magistrate admits it is "human nature when you hear something interesting to pass it on," a statement that also unites him with Powell. "The ancient pilgrims came to Canterbury to ask for blessing or to do penance. You, I hope, are on your way to secure blessings for the future."

Having begun as Colpepper's victim, Alison has developed into a kindred spirit. When she and Bob pass by an exquisite home, she wonders what it would be like to grow old in such a place, only to discover Colpeper is the man wielding the scythe in the backyard, the activity also uniting him to the past. They share an obvious affinity for the Pilgrim's Way, and, as he speaks in the shadows during his lecture, his words often seemed addressed directly toward her, although even he is not yet aware of this. This is developed through the mise-en-scene, with each of their faces framed in close-up, only their eyes highlighted in the darkness. He advises his listeners to "follow the old road and as you walk think of them and the old England," something she will in fact do later. The address concluded, he is about to begin the slide show when the projector fails, fulfilling Bob's earlier prophecy that "free shows" always have catches. At this moment Colpeper's own awakening begins as Alison demonstrates her own knowledge of the countryside and further disconcerts him by presenting to him precious coins excavated in the Pilgrim's Way. She has shamed him into realizing that by ignoring women, he effectively halved his audience; when he admits as much, her one-word response is cutting: "Pity."

The lecture and slide show complete, the group emerge from the building into the darkness where once again Bob is reproached for using his flashlight in the blackout, inadvertently providing him with their first piece of evidence. "Topography plays an important part in my expose," he tells them in words that could also characterize the Archers' work. Bob realizes that the light which had come from Colpeper's window on the night Alison had been attacked had not been there when they first arrived at the town hall. Alison still cannot believe that he is the glueman. "What motive could he possibly . . .," but her sentence is left incomplete as the soldiers run off in pursuit of their bus. Yet, the film has already begun to delineate his motives. Some critics have labeled Colpeper a misogynist ("a bachelor, living alone with his mother, entirely self-absorbed and didactic"[6]), but only one statement by Colpeper really identifies him as such. When asked by Bob about a bucket on a rafter, Colpeper responds that it is a "ducking stool, very sensibly used for silencing a talkative woman." His living with his mother and even his attacks on women have their motives in the war, for many families in wartime moved in with one another, while many residents were concerned about soldiers taking an interest in local women. Even one of the glueman's victims recognizes the central axiom of her attacker, admitting that it has kept her true to her boyfriend, who is stationed far away.

The role of Esmond Knight in *A Canterbury Tale* cannot be overlooked, for he was an integral member of his stock company, particularly to this film. His relationship with Powell dated back to the quota quickies, and here he was called on to portray three characters, the narrator who opens the film, a British soldier who becomes friends with Bob at the lecture, and, most unsettling, the village idiot whom the soldiers encounter in the darkness after the lecture. Not only do the Archers portray the character as a stammering simpleton, they permit the soldiers to ridicule him openly. Yet, after the man has walked off into the mist, the camera momentarily holds on him as he stands on the hillside, transforming him momentarily into a mystical figure. This shot looks forward to Colpeper's own mutation into a mystical character suggestive of Prospero in Shakespeare's *The Tempest*, a work that Powell had long dreamed of filming.

Peter grows impatient with the pace of the investigation, deciding to call on Colpeper at home, hoping to find material tying him to the nights of the attacks. Almost from the moment that they sit down in Colpeper's den, Peter cannot mask his antagonism toward the magistrate, even speaking derisively of his hobby, mountain climbing. The dialogue will disclose Peter's own lack of passion for his vocation. "Why climb to the top at all? What's wrong with the valley?" "The answer is in yourself" is Colpeper's rejoinder. Peter does not lack ambition; he has also given up on his dream, for he had once been determined to be a church organist but had settled for being a cinema organist. Colpeper muses that "there are two kinds of men: one who begins by studying Bach and Handel and ends up by playing 'I Kiss Your Hand Madame' and the other, who climbs Mount Everest one step at a time." These words are echoed later when Peter begins to play the "Toccata" by Bach at Canterbury Cathedral. Peter emerges from the confrontation with Colpepper's guilt confirmed (his fire warden schedule cor - responds to the nights of the attacks) but also with his old dream resurrected.

Colpeper's influence on the trio has already begun as Alison begins to walk along the path of Pilgrim's Way, literally hearing the voices from the days of yore, as Colpeper had suggested. When he calls out to her from his resting place in the grass, she is startled and he anticipates her dilemma. "It's a real voice you heard, you're not dreaming." He invites her to sit beside him on the grass, and she tells him that this is near where her fiance's caravan, or trailer, had been camped. She tells him of her fiance and of his father who had disapproved of her because she had been a shop girl. "'Good family,' 'shop girls.' Rather dilapidated phrases for wartime," Colpeper muses.

"Not for Geoffrey's father. It would have taken an earthquake," Alison says.

"We're having one," he concludes.

Colpeper admits he still believes in miracles, but Alison lacks such conviction. Their conversation is interrupted by Bob and Peter's arrival, but, not wanting to be discovered, Colpeper and Alison lie back in the tall grass. The men speak of their life before the war, then Bob concedes that he has enjoyed his experience in Chillingbourne, that since he has arrived in Europe "something's been wrong with me." In pursuing the glue-man, his mind had been kept occupied, thus releasing him

from his burden, but Peter too has undergone a transformation, as evidenced by his climbing the hill. When they joke
about "Gluepepper" their silent audience realizes his identity
has been exposed, and, after they leave, Colpepper quietly
walks off.

The next morning the trio board a train for Canterbury,
their journey nearly complete, but Colpeper is also to make
the trip, to assume his post as a magistrate. He enters their
compartment, aware of what they intend to do on arriving in
Canterbury, but, although Bob and Alison are sympathetic to
him, Peter is determined to denounce him. Attempting to clarify his motive, Colpepper tells of having endeavored to lecture
before the war but was unable to find a receptive audience.
The arrival of the army camp looked to him to be a miracle,
providing him with a prospective audience, only to discover
their attention was on the local women. He began the attacks
not only to obtain an audience, but to protect the virtue of the
women in town, many of whom had boyfriends stationed many
miles away. Peter wonders how he would have ruled in such a
case, but Colpeper argues that there is a "higher court than
the local bench of magistrate." He looks contemplatively out
the window at Canterbury Cathedral, which has come into view,
the structure becoming an integral part of the mise-en-scene
for the final third of the film. Peter attempts to distance himself from the pilgrims, claiming to be neither seeking penance
or offering blessings.

"Perhaps you're an instrument." Colpeper muses.

"I'll believe that when I wear a halo around my neck," Peter replies, not realizing that just such an effect has been produced, for as the train enters the station a light shines behind
his head. Arriving at Canterbury, the four move off into divergent paths, with Peter proceeding to the police department,
where he deliberates for a moment. The outcome, however, is
already out of his power for the superintendent has already
left for Canterbury Cathedral to participate in the service honoring Peter's unit. On the off chance of catching up with him,
Peter moves to the cathedral, where even he, on entering the
hallowed halls, is awestruck. The organist passes by him, and
Peter asks him whether he knows where the superintendent is.
The man has little patience for the inquiry and continues up
the staircase not realizing he has dropped a sheet of music. It

drifts down the stairwell landing gently at Peter's feet, like a divine message. He picks it up and reverently moves up the stairs, coming to an enormous church organ, the type he had long dreamed of playing. The fantasy reawakened, it is finally consummated as the organist allows Peter to perform, his choice being Bach's "Toccata."

As Peter's music begins to fill the church, Bob is walking below, equally inspired by the surroundings. Marveling at the architecture, he whispers that "my dad's pa built the first Baptist church in Johnson County. Well, that was a good job too." Alison has continued on to locate her caravan, passing by the ruins of homes whose owners have left behind markers announcing their new addresses. Finding the warehouse, she pulls off the covering of the caravan, causing debris to fall down, and is further dismayed to find the tires have been removed for scrap and that the interior is filled with dust and moths, who are eating at the curtains. In tears, she runs from the caravan, slamming the door, and is startled to find Colpeper standing in the doorway of the warehouse. She complains to him of the moths, but he acknowledges that there is "something impermanent about a caravan. Everything on wheels must be on the move." The warehouse owner arrives and asks Alison why she did not leave her address, for her fiance's father has been waiting for her. The young man has been found alive and is recovering in a hospital in Gibraltar. Ecstatic at the news, she reenters the caravan, throwing open the windows to let in the light and chase off the moths. In the distance is the Canterbury Cathedral. Leaving the caravan, she looks around for Colpeper, but he has moved on, his influence in Alison's life concluded. Many critics relate the magistrate to the character of Puck, becoming less an aggressor than a magical agent.

Bob finally encounters the army buddy he had first set out to meet, and he immediately surprises Ernie Brooks (Charles Paton) with his knowledge of the Pilgrim's Way. Like Joan Webster in the film to follow, however, Bob is skeptical of the blessings involved. Ernie's face lights up as he sarcastically asks whether he looks like a "heavenly messenger," for he has brought with him the highly coveted letters from Bob's fiancee. The delay was the result of her having joined the Women's Army Corps and having been stationed in Australia.

With the three pilgrims having received their blessings, all that is left is the ceremony at the cathedral. As Peter's unit marches in, Alison stands with her fiance's father. Colpeper is poised in the entrance, motionless, with his eyes closed as if imagining himself once more in Chaucer's time, while the choir sings "Onward Christian Soldier." The film closes as it had opened—with a long shot of Canterbury Cathedral from the hill along Pilgrim's Way.

Many critics, particularly British ones, have criticized the Archers for often seeming unfocused, complaining that their stories needed to be tightened. This complaint had been made against *The Life and Death of Colonel Blimp* and was to be heard on subsequent film. Yet, *A Canterbury Tale*, as with the others, has a specific rhythm, more frantic in the opening but gradually becoming more leisurely as the story progresses. For example, at one point, Bob finds himself in the midst of a game of war between the local children; instead of interrupting, he tags along, only addressing the boys after one side has lost. The effect is that we, like Bob, learn to relish the ambience of the township. Like *Brigadoon*, it is a community held in time, with little evidence of modern technology (no automobiles are visible except for the military transports).

9

Let's Have Another Go at It

I Know Where I'm Going began as an afterthought. Powell and Pressburger had been commissioned by the Ministry of Information to prepare a film that would help to improve relations between Great Britain and the United States, which had become strained from the pressures of war. The unavailability of Technicolor film stock, however, put this project on temporary hiatus; in the interim, the Archers began work on a more personal project. Despite the failure of their previous film, the Archers were still interested in its themes. "A Canterbury Tale was made as a crusade against materialism and Emeric said, 'Well let's have another go at it.'"[1] The result is another film in which the characters are confronted by an environment and society that are the antithesis of their own. The failure of the previous film had not been lost on the Archers, however, and the result is a film that addresses its themes on a more passionate level. It is among their most fondly remembered works, with only *The Red Shoes* surpassing it in popularity.

For Pressburger, writing *I Know Where I'm Going* was remarkably fast. "It burst out—you couldn't hold it back."[2] He wrote the script in four days, then presented it to Powell in a routine they had developed in preparing their films. Pressburger would work alone on the first draft to develop the structure of the film, "but if I don't succeed and yet know I'm on the right track, I start writing and suddenly, it's as if the characters take over and they bring me so far that I can't stop again and set up the whole structure. But if I can help it, I never sit down to write the real script until I know where I'm going and I've worked out the rhythm and so on beforehand. I'm very musical and that might have something to do with it."[3]

Powell would then go over the script, making modifications as he went. He would incorporate not only his own material but also any information he had acquired while scouting locations, in this case "bringing in all I had learnt of the authentic dialogue, atmosphere and names of the Western Isles. I ransacked Monty McKenzie's potboiling novels for Gaelic phrases and idioms. As soon as I completed the first few sequences, and numbered them with regular script numbers, I turned them over to Emeric for him to agree or disagree, or to point out to me that I had entirely missed the point of the scene."[4]

One point of contention involved Torquil MacNeil's (Roger Livesey) relationship with Catriona Potts (Paddy Brown). Sequences were included that told of their past love affair, but Pressburger, perhaps receptive to any digressions from the main story line and also having little fondness for Brown, eventually excised most of this subplot. For Powell, however, allusions to their relationship remain. In one sequence Torquil was to have entered the castle, unaware that Catriona has followed him, "drawn there by the same inspiration as him, the same legend. I think there is much more goes on in life—below the surface— than people realize. I like these unexpressed things, they can be enormously effective in a film. I think I probably learned that from seeing the early German films which were full of unexpressed and beautiful ideas—films like *Destiny*. In other words I'm a great 'eye' but I also believe there's more than meets the eye."[5] This sequence was filmed, but all that remain of it are a few stills.

For Powell it was the preproduction that was often the most laborious.

You are then dealing with something which does not yet exist. All your preliminary work for months is performed as if it were blindfold. You can't compare making a film to work in any other medium. Even making a play is different. There is no film until your first day when your first shot is shown to you on the screen. Until then even you yourself do not know what you have done. You may know what you wanted to do, but you do not know that you have done it. It is this that to my mind makes the stage of preparation the hardest, this working for something whose existence is still completely hypothetical.[6]

James Mason and Deborah Kerr were the first selections for the leads, but Mason was put off by the extensive location work the film seemed to warrant, and Kerr was bound by a contract with M-G-M. Wendy Hiller, whom Kerr had replaced on *The Life and Death of Colonel Blimp*, now returned the cour-tesy and took on the role of Joan Webster. In the interim, Rog-er Livesey had read the script and actively campaigned for the role of the Scottish laird, not caring that the part called for someone much younger. He lost weight and dyed his hair, only to find another obstacle had presented itself, as he was bound by a contract to appear in a play in London, making travel to Mull impossible. The lessons of *49th Parallel* had not been lost on the Archers, however; although it seems as if Livesey hikes all across the island, a double was in fact used for his location work. Filming on the island would take six weeks, with Press-burger only visiting the island twice during this phase of production. Instead, he occupied himself with the sets being built and carefully overseeing the rushes. The interiors were to be filmed at Denham, but the climax of the film, set in a whirlpool, was to take place in a water tank using tech-niques similar to those used in *The Ten Commandments*. The three occupants of the small boat that is nearly drawn into the giant whirlpool were buffeted about, while water was constantly poured over them. The final cost of the film would be two hundred thousand pounds; much of it used for the whirlpool sequence.

Complications arose in the production, with Powell having an affair with one actress (Pamela Brown) while alienating an-other (Hiller), plus the usual problems associated with working on location. Yet, despite these and all of the technical chal-lenges the film presented, the result was a commercial suc-cess, helping Rank overcome the financial difficulties it had sustained as a result of the failure of Gabriel Pascal's costly production of *Caesar and Cleopatra*. The critics, however, though admitting it was a better film than *A Canterbury Tale*, were still not convinced it was a masterpiece. "Michael Powell's new film *I Know Where I'm Going* is a disap-pointment, because it has all the makings of a good picture, but has mixed them with some of the tricks of a very bad one."[7]

From the moment she could crawl, Joan Webster seemed to know instinctively in which direction her life was heading—

up. When she was only five, she was already asking for silk
stockings; at twelve, she was riding with the milkman, not willing to wait for the bus as the other children did. By the time
she is 26 she seems on the verge of reaching her objective, as
she announces to her father her engagement to Sir Robert Bellinger, the owner of the chemical factory in which she works.
The wedding is to take place on the island of Kiloran, in the
Western Hebrides, necessitating Joan's traveling a great distance on a variety of vehicles. On arriving at Port Ellaig, the
last stop before Kiloran, her journey abruptly ends, for a dense
fog makes further travel impossible. Also stranded is Torquil
MacNeil (Livesey), a resident of Kiloran home on leave from the
navy. The marooned travelers are taken in by Catriona, a young
woman whose demeanor confounds Joan. As they prepare for
bed, Torquil counsels Joan to count the beams above her bed
to have her prayers answered. Despite her cynicism, she prays
for the wind to blow off the fog and awakes the next morning
to find her invocation has been more than answered, for a gale
has now blown up. Still unable to reach Kiloran, Joan and
Torquil start out for a hotel, passing Moray Castle along the
way. Having learned of the curse the castle contains for the
laird of Kiloran, Joan begins to venture in, but her enthusiasm
is dampened by Torquil's confession that he is the actual laird
and her fiance only leases the island.

Using a wireless, Joan contacts her fiance, who advises her
to call on the Robinsons, the "only people worth knowing in
the area." Originally satisfied to stay at the hotel, Joan becomes
disturbed over her conflicting emotions toward Torquil and
eventually seeks refuge with the Robinsons (Catherine Lacey
and Valentine Dyall). Circumstances bring the two together,
however, for the Robinsons take Joan to a neighboring castle,
on whose owner Torquil is already calling. He is to attend a
ceildh that night, a sixtieth anniversary celebration for a couple who work in the castle, and Joan accompanies him. Although content to watch from the outside, the couple is
eventually drawn in and spend the night dancing together. The
next morning Joan is even more desperate to leave, and, although the storm has not abated, she bribes a young man,
Kenny (Murdo Morrison), to take her across the treacherous
seas. Only after Catriona tells Torquil of Joan's true reasons
for leaving does he resolve to accompany her. The rough seas

disable the engine; as Torquil and Kenny rush to repair it, the small boat is drawn toward the Corryvrekan, the second largest whirlpool in Europe. They succeed in restarting the engine, just as the boat is being pulled into the whirlpool. Wet and exhausted they return once more to Port Ellaig. The next morning finds the gale has dissipated, and, finally free to leave, Torquil walks Joan part of the way to her ship. Their paths diverge at Moray Castle, and she asks of him one favor, a kiss. After he enthusiastically obliges, she continues on, and he decides to venture into the castle, no longer concerned for the curse. He comes to the plaque relating the curse, but, as he recalls the words of his nanny, he is surprised to hear the sound of bagpipes. Looking down from the ramparts, he witnesses Joan returning up the path, leading the bagpipe players who were to have played at her wedding. He races down the steps and emerges from the castle to embrace Joan, who finally admits her love for him.

If *A Canterbury Tale* had been imbued with the spirit of Chaucer and of English history, *I Know Where I'm Going* is infused with the Scottish legends and air of mysticism Powell had encountered on *The Edge of the World*. Joan first encounters the legends that will impact her life on her arrival in Port Ellaig, as her driver relates the curse on the laird of Kiloran. A past landlord of the castle had found his wife in the arms of another man and, after storming the castle in which the lovers had sought refuge, returns with them in chains to Moray. The two are thrown into a well to drown, but, before the woman dies, she places a curse on her husband and all of his descendants who dare enter the castle. Torquil will abide by the curse, not so much because he believes in it, but because his ancestors have always honored it. "My father never entered Moray Castle, nor did my grandfather or his father, nor will I." That Joan has little regard for the curse or for the other legends she encounters is apparent, but contained within them are portents of her future; she will succumb to their bidding by the end. Told that a prayer will be answered by counting the beams above her bed, she finds herself instinctively doing just this, but, in asking for the wind to blow off the fog, she unwittingly brings on the gale. The contents of the curse of Moray Castle will not be revealed until the end, but it will impact not only Torquil's life but also her own, for the MacNeil who steps across the threshold will be forever chained to a woman.

If the legends that Joan encounters challenge her beliefs, the residents of the island will challenge her ideals. According to Powell, it was "necessary to bring on to the screen a whole new world, full of people with their own standards and judgments, dependent upon one another, feudal, democratic and totally devoid of materialism."[8] Highland economics are constantly alluded to, a philosophy of life where one is content with what one has. The embodiment of these convictions, however, is less Torquil than Catriona, who is presented by the Archers as an almost mystical character, similar to the type into which Colpepper is transformed in *A Canterbury Tale*. She is introduced emerging from the fog, led by three great hounds and carrying a gun in one hand and two dead rabbits in another, a modern day Diana the Huntress. As Powell relates, he filmed Catriona's sequences so that she was linked "half-consciously and half-unconsciously with what was going on—not exactly spying on things but being drawn."[9] Her presence is felt even when she is silent, as when Joan packs her belongings having just bribed Kenny to take her across the sea. In the entire scene she speaks but one line, and this is to introduce Bridie (Margot Fitzsimmons), but her eyes speak volumes. If she enlightens Joan about Highland economics, she also is cognizant of Torquil and Joan's true emotions. This role of bystander and penetrating observer anticipates Brown's later role in *The Tales of Hoffmann*.

Like Alison in the previous film, Joan is from the city, this time Manchester, and she is introduced in this milieu making her way through a crowded smoke-filled nightclub, where it is evident that she is a regular. The ambiance is suggestive of the screwball comedies of the thirties, which Powell had first imitated in his quota quickies but here are better incorporated into the style of the film. She is meeting with her father, but their relationship is not immediately discernible in their easy manner with one another. She constantly calls him "darling" and later asks him to dance with her, as they had when she was younger. When their table is called, he follows after, carrying her coat and purse like a faithful lover, and it will emerge that in fact he is the same age as her fiance. Her love for Sir Robert Bellinger is based not on passion but on ambition, and, when she tells her father of her engagement she presents to him not a photograph but a work pass. He muses that she cannot marry the company, but she replies smiling, "Oh, can't I?"

As Joan makes her journey, she goes over her itinerary but is constantly distracted by the wedding gown that hangs above her, encased in a plastic sheath. She looks at herself in the mirror, and this scene serves as the bridge to the dream that follows. According to Ian Christie, the sequence has the "confusion and logic of a real dream,"[10] opening with the dress abruptly disappearing from the sheath, but the wedding she dreams of is not to Bellinger but to his company, symbolized by machinery shot in negative. The pallor of her appearance makes her seem more like a mannequin than a woman of flesh and blood and foretells her role in Bellinger's life, as not a companion but a possession. Significantly her father assumes the role of the priest who performs the ceremony and as he asks whether the factory takes Joan as its wife, the train whistle blows, signaling her arrival at her first station.

Bellinger will never be shown in the film, but his ideals will be constantly in evidence, and, as we do of the island of Kiloran (which is never reached), we develop a strong impression of him. Over the wireless he advises her to call on the Robinsons, but their home is in marked contrast with Catriona's. Where her dogs roamed free, the Robinsons' pair of dogs sit motionless in their basket. Instead of engaging Joan in a conversation, Mr. and Mrs. Robinson speak at her. The locals have little use for either the Robinsons or Bellinger, whose building of a pool on an island and having fish imported are ridiculed by them.

Joan's attraction to Torquil is developed gradually, only brought to the surface when they attend the Campbells' ceildh. Content at first to watch from outside, she stands on a ladder while he stands below her, his arms protectively about her. He explains to her what is taking place, the ritual recalling similar gatherings in John Ford's westerns. As the song "Nut Brown Maiden" is performed, he relates to her its lyrics; when he comes to the line "you're the maid for me," he turns purposely toward her. His forthright manner disconcerts her, but she finds herself unable to escape, for the elder Campbell has emerged from the home to invite them to participate in the celebration. Ironically, the bagpipe players that entertain the gathering were hired by Joan's fiance and are likewise stranded by the storm. That night, she returns to her room, the image of her dancing with Torquil literally swirling about her head, as she prays desperately for the gale to end. Her need to leave is intensified by her increasing passion for the young Scotsman, and her determination not to be dissuaded from her objective causes her to bribe Kenny and thus risk all of their lives.

Kenny is at the center of the second romance depicted in the film, one contrasted with that of Joan and Torquil. Kenny is in love with Bridie, but he cannot marry her until he has saved enough to purchase a half interest in his father's ferry business, which is approximately twenty pounds. She is content to wait, but he is more anxious, particularly after witnessing a soldier making a pass at her. Thus, his own desperation motivates him to take the risk and accept Joan's offer of twenty pounds to ferry her across the sea. Bridie is more willing to wait, content with what they have and concerned over what she could lose. She goes to Catriona's home to confront Joan over the matter, the shadows in the house creating the type of mise-en-scene obviously indebted to the Germans. Joan is in the midst of packing as Catriona looks on, her eyes speaking volumes. Throughout the sequence, Catriona will have but one line, to introduce Bridie, but her significance is evident, particularly as she comforts Bridie, her eyes registering her disapproval of Joan's actions. When Torquil, having failed to dissuade Joan from leaving, disparages of her behavior, it is Catriona who informs him of her real motivation for departing.

The staircase, so prominent in many of Powell's and the Archers' films, is most effectively used in the confrontation between Joan and Torquil over her decision to leave. Bridie is descending the staircase as Torquil arrives, and she pleads with him to stop Joan from going. Torquil enters Joan's bedroom and accuses her of being conceited, still misconstruing her rationale for leaving. She attempts to escape, but he pursues her, catching up to her on the staircase, where the railings and the shadows produced by them form an enclosure that seems to entrap her. She is forced back against the wall in an effort to evade his wrath, but his harangue is only beginning, and he pulls her back onto the stairs to stand over her. Her anxiety is apparent, but it is not due so much to his attempts to coerce her as to her emotions, which are spilling over. She persists in leaving, and in frustration he pushes her away, and, clutching her suitcase, she finally makes her escape down the staircase and strides through the hallway. She may have succeeded in evading Torquil, but nature's power is evidenced by the billowing curtains and the leaves blowing on the floor. This sequence will be in marked contrast to the one in which they return to the home, having successfully escaped the whirlpool. The camera is positioned at the top of the staircase as they make their way up, emerging from the shadows that now lack menace.

The whirlpool sequence is a starting achievement, but it is more than just a display of technical skills. The legend of Corryvrekan is first introduced when the pair attempt to contact the island over the wireless. A painting depicting the legend is displayed prominently, and Torquil begins to recount the legend of how a prince was challenged to anchor his ship off the whirlpool, using lines made of three different materials, the last of which is the hair of maidens thought to be true to their lovers. Torquil's story is interrupted and is not to be completed until they venture out in the boat, which Ian Christie identifies as the moment in which they leave the "here and now of 1945 and enter the realm of legend."[11] Joan finally asks him to finish the story, so he tells of how all but one of the lines had broken, the last being the one made of the hair of maidens true to their lovers. Unfortunately, one of the maidens had been untrue, causing the line to eventually give and thus sending the boat to its demise. That Joan, Torquil, and Kenny manage to extricate the boat from the drag of the whirlpool serves as testimony to her own devotion to Torquil.

If I Know Where I'm Going is ostensibly a love story, it is also another illustration of the Archers' self-reflexivity. In the film's opening montage, Joan is introduced at the age of one, crawling across the floor, but the credits are incorporated directly into the sequence, appearing on the side of her baby bed. As she grows older, we are given further evidence of her ambition, with subsequent credits appearing on the sides of the wagon and on a factory gate. Later, as Joan is being met at a railway station by two men, one of the men's hat begins inexplicably to emit smoke, followed by a jump cut to the stack of the train similarly discharging smoke. The Archers often broke down the barriers between the audience and the screen, as if they reveled in reminding them that it is only a movie they are viewing, not reality. Proof of this has already been anticipated in *One of Our Aircraft Is Missing*, with its coda, and in *The Volunteer*, where Ralph Richardson speaks to the audience of his dresser, the camera initially serving as his eyes. It would culminate in Powell's *Peeping Tom* but is also is in evidence in *Oh Rosalinda!!* where Anton Walbrook enters through a door to greet the audience and take them into his confidence. Such an approach was also the cornerstone of their next film, which not only combined black-and-white footage with color but also manipulated time and space. Conductor 71, arriving on Earth from the monochrome heaven, watches as the flower on his lapel turns red and comically bemoans that "one is so starved for Technicolor up there." It is a line that invariably draws laughter but that for British critics of the time, was an unforgivable transgression. It is also what Powell was referring to when he later spoke of *A Matter of Life and Death*: "I was able to step out of conventions."[12] Certainly much of what Powell and the Archers attempted was based on this same premise.

Like *The Red Shoes*, *I Know Where I'm Going* is a fable, and, because of this, it too retains a strong emotional appeal. It evokes a world no longer in existence and portrays a passion no longer evident in films. It is a world for which many continue to search. Many still make a pilgrimage to the small island, looking for the hotel where Joan and Torquil stayed and the phone booth sitting on the edge of a waterfall and to exploring the castles that added to the film's texture.

10

Invention, but Logical Invention

A Matter of Life and Death began production on the day the Japanese officially surrendered to Douglas MacArthur. The war that had so impacted the lives of so many and had so infused the work of the Archers was now over. Powell and Pressburger would soon turn their focus to other themes, but first they had to complete a film that, like *49th Parallel*, was begun at the government's request. The basis for the story was an account in the German newspapers of a British airman who had fallen from his airplane and survived, despite his not having a parachute. Pressburger fashioned a script centered on an airman who survives such a fall, but only because the messenger sent from Heaven to retrieve him has lost him in the fog. When Heaven attempts to correct its mistake, the man is understandably reluctant to leave Earth, and a trial begins to determine his fate. Powell initially had reservations about the project, having little interest in producing a fantasy. Only after it was decided that the man would be suffering from a head injury and that the sequences in Heaven were his hallucinations did he become interested. In the end it would become his favorite film.

David Niven was brought in to play the British airman, in what was to be his return to film after four years in the service. In that time he had only made one film, the critically acclaimed *The Way Ahead*. For his costar, who was to be an

American, the Archers decided to take a page from Hollywood and conduct an exhaustive talent search. Their search would ultimately end in the entertainment capital, where it was Alfred Hitchcock who came to the Archers' assistance. He had worked with a young woman just the day before who had served as Ingrid Bergman's stand-in for *Notorious*. Kim Hunter had appeared in a half dozen films but had yet to make an impact. She was languishing under a contract to David O. Selznick, but the Archers were able to obtain her services. The rest of the cast would be filled out with actors who had already worked with the Archers. Roger Livesey for once was the first choice for a role, as the character of Dr. Frank Reeves was written specifically for him. Marius Goring had briefly appeared in *The Spy in Black* and was soon to gain fame for his role in *The Red Shoes*, while Kathleen Byron, making her first appearance with the Archers, also was to gain eventual notoriety with them for her portrayal of Sister Ruth, the nun who goes mad in *Black Narcissus*.

The production of *A Matter of Life and Death* was the largest attempted in British cinema since *The Thief of Bagdad*, and, as always with an Archers film, the look was carefully worked out before production. Forty-six detailed sketches were prepared and twenty-four series of architectural drawings drawn up, while detailed scale models were created, primarily for the sequences set in Heaven. The largest set piece for the film was the enormous escalator in heaven that weighed eighty-five tons and had 266 twenty-foot steps. The decision was made to film the heaven sequences in black and white, creating further difficulties. The footage was filmed in black-and-white, then reproduced in dye monochrome. For Powell, the film would be his "most perfect film: the technical perfection and the fact that it is a most wonderful conjuring trick to get handed."[1] Yet, the magic was to have a basis in reality, for the fantasy was to take place in the pilot's head, hallucinations resulting from the injury.

As was to be expected, many British critics were dissatisfied with the film. Dilys Powell wrote that "*A Matter of Life and Death* remains an audacious, sometimes beautiful, but basically sensational film about nothing."[2] Ironically, in her obituary of Powell some forty years later, she stated that "for some of us it is the best thing Powell ever did."[3] Without question the film's fantasy element had little chance of finding favor with many critics in Britain. "The film has technical originality and a firmer narrative shape than anything we have seen from Michael Powell and Emeric Pressburger who wrote, produced and directed it. But it is even farther away from the essential realism and the true business of the British movie than their two recent films, *I Know Where I'm Going*, and *Canterbury Tale*."[4] For John Ellis, this was the point at which the British critics turned against the Archers, "when quality critics, engaged in defining a 'native British realism' became disenchanted with the very different work of Powell and Pressburger."[5] The film had greater success in the United States, although its title was changed to *Stairway to Heaven*, which seemed to hint more at a fantasy than a conflict between life and death.

With his airplane shot up by antiaircraft fire and accompanied only by his dead radioman, squadron leader Peter Carter (Niven) speaks to whom he thinks will be the last person ever to hear his voice, an American WAC named June (Hunter). After quoting poetry to her and passing on a message to his mother, he finally admits to her that he has no parachute and that he has chosen to jump from the airplane instead of crashing with it. A distraught June cannot dissuade him. As Peter leaps from the airplane, his radioman waits in Heaven for his arrival. Peter, however, does not arrive at his appointed time, and, as warning bells ring in Heaven, the pilot awakens on a sandy beach, which he assumes to be the hereafter. This view is reinforced by his discovery of a young boy playing the flute, but as Peter speaks to him, he discovers that he is in fact near an air base, and a plane hurtling overhead confirms the fact that the Englishman has somehow survived. In the distance a young woman can be seen riding her bike, and Peter instinctively realizes it is June, to whom he has already developed an attraction. She too is shocked to find him alive and, like him, has already fallen in love with someone she has only just met. Peter begins to romance her, but, as they sit under the moonlight sky, she falls asleep. He attempts to wake her but is startled by the appearance of a Frenchman, claiming to be an emissary from Heaven. Conductor 71 (Marius Goring), who has stopped time, admits it was because of the thick English fog that he had missed Peter and that he has now come to retrieve him. Peter is understandably reluctant to give up his life, arguing that it is only because of Heaven's mistake that he has fallen in love with June. Unable to take Peter by force, the conductor makes a retreat, promising to return.

When Peter tells June of his encounter, she contacts Dr. Reeves, a noted neurologist who agrees to examine him, not only because the case intrigues him but also because he admires Peter's poetry. His diagnosis of Peter's disorder, which includes hallucinations and headaches, is that it is the result of a head trauma he had received some time earlier. He takes Peter into his home as he prepares for the necessary operation, while the American continues to receive visits from Conductor 71, who announces that a trial is to be convened in Heaven to determine his fate. The prosecuting attorney is to be Abraham Farlan (Raymond Massey), the first American killed in the American Revolutionary War and who holds all Englishmen in contempt. Peter is given the opportunity to choose his defense attorney from anyone in Heaven. Believing his patient's fate is tied to that of the trial, Dr. Reeves encourages the operating physician to schedule the surgery on the same night as the trial. When the night arrives, Peter is still struggling over who to have represent him, but Dr. Reeves is more concerned by the delay of the ambulance. Riding off on his motorcycle to search for the ambulance, he nearly runs into it and, in his effort to avoid an accident, he crashes his motorcycle and is killed, thus providing Peter with his counsel.

Conductor 71 and Dr. Reeves appear in the operating room to retrieve Peter and take with them a tear from June's cheek, which they believe is proof of her love. The trial occurs in a giant auditorium where an infinite number of people, seeming from every nationality (except presumably those of the Axis powers), gather in expectation. Dr. Reeves and Farlan debate not only whether the couple is in love but whether love is even possible between an Englishman and an American. Farlan is initially concerned with portraying the English as aggressors, pointing out the number of countries with whom they have been at war. Dr. Reeves, however, returns the case to its central argument, whether Peter and June are in love. The courtroom adjourns to the operating room, as June and Peter are called to testify. Believing love is the strongest force of all, Dr. Reeves asks June to take her lover's place on the stairway to Heaven, and, as Peter is restrained, she is transported toward

Heaven. The escalator, however, abruptly stops, and June races down to Peter, their love having been proven to be stronger than the laws governing the hereafter. Having won his case, Peter is supplied with a new date on which to appear in Heaven. In his hospital room, Peter regains consciousness, having survived his operation and his trial.

The first image of the film is not of an airman or the war but the universe, as a Heavenly voice begins to give a tour. As the camera pans about the planets and stars, the narrator points out a nova, declaring that someone must have been "fooling around with a uranium atom." This opening recalls the American film, *It's a Wonderful Life*, which went into release at the same time, but if that film examines what would happen if a man had never been born, this one wonders what would happen if a man failed to die at his appointed time. From the universe, the camera moves in on Earth, then in on a city on fire, only to become lost in the thick English fog. It is May 2, 1945, two days before the war is to end. Voices can be alternately heard, first that of Winston Churchill giving a speech, then that of an English pilot calling out. A woman's voice responds and June is introduced, speaking over a radio, the only person in a control tower. She asks for the pilot's location, but he responds by quoting a verse from Walter Raleigh. When his plane is revealed, it is a dark silhouette against the nighttime sky, one of its engines in flames. As the camera begins to pan the cockpit, further damage is revealed, for the controls are shot up and its undercarriage is missing, making a landing impossible. Peter's face is covered with soot and blood as he once more quotes poetry to her, then tells her of his dead radioman, Bob Trumpshaw (Robert Coote), who lies beside him staring blankly into space. From this point on, the sequence is composed entirely of close-ups as if they are the only two people left in the world. He gives her a message to pass on to his mother, and, with her voice quivering she asks whether he has been injured, only to have him respond by asking once more what her name is. She finally tells him and he admits that his problem is that he intends to bail out but has no parachute. After asking for her description, he questions her on her background, admitting he likes being "alone" with her. Their conversation, seemingly having no relation to the futility of his situation, causes her to cry out that it is "such nonsense."

There is a poignancy to their words, not just for our realization of Peter's probable fate but also for a love that is destined
never to occur. Granted, our realization that this is a commercial film foretells their eventually meeting, but this in no way
detracts from our emotional involvement.

The film now shifts to the central premise of the film as
Peter asks June what she thinks the "next world's like. I've got
my own ideas." Then he leaps from the plane wondering whether he will have "a crop or wings." As he is lost in the fog, his
last words are repeated, and the next image is of him floating
unconscious in the water. When he does come to he is on an
empty beach. As he walks around, he comes to a sign warning him to keep out, but he does not know whether it is Heav-
en or Hell from which he is being prohibited. He obeys the
sign and goes off in the opposite direction, coming across
the young boy, who reveals to him that in fact he is still on
Earth. Yet, his ideas concerning Heaven still influence what
is to happen, and, as an opening title announces, this is a
"story of two Worlds, the one we know and another which exists only in the mind of a young airman, whose life and imagination have been violently shaped by the war." Peter's point of
view infuses the film, at times even subjectively, and references are made to this throughout the film, as when Dr. Reeves
praises his prose, admitting he likes his "point of view." The
representation of Heaven is one filtered through the mind of
not just a poet but also a serviceman, where airmen arrive to
find a Coke machine waiting for them and where matters of
love and country are debated in front of an audience of servicemen and women.

The Heaven portrayed has been variously described as a
representation of Nazism (this description courtesy of M. Robson, who had come out so strongly against *The Life and Death
of Colonel Blimp*) to that of a "futurist Utopia. It's a planned
society. It's machinelike (one mounts to it on an inexorable
escalator, hence the film's U.S. title, *Stairway to Heaven*). This
stairway is flanked by the imposing but dead-white statues of
such great idealists as Plato (whose Utopia is, of course, thor-
oughly totalitarian). As Tories claim planning drains colour from
life, so here, Technicolor of earth pales to celestial monochrome.
Heaven's values are those of the collectivity (as opposed to the
selfless individualism of romantic love). Planned, bureaucratic,

idealistic, totalitarian, colourless, theoretic."[6] Raymond Durg-nat's description is, however, no more successful than Robson's, for, in fact, individuality is allowed in Heaven (witness the con-ductor's behavior) and matters of the heart can be debated.

The expressionists had provided the Archers with the first experiences of portraying the state of mind of a character and here they would take it to its logical extreme. Previous attempts had been made, as in Joan Webster's dreams in the previous film and even after there would be more examples; the dance in *The Red Shoes*, the nightmare in *The Small Back Room*, and the stories Hoffmann relates to the patrons in the bar. Dr. Reeves characterizes the hallucinations as a "combination of vision, hearing, and of idea," then later tells the operating phy-sician that Peter's troubles are compounded by his imagina-tion, that he has "too good of a mind." If all that occurs in Heaven is of Peter's creation, the Archers also present his per-spective as he is wheeled in for surgery, the camera shooting up at the ceiling as he is wheeled through the hospital. The hospital attendants look down on him, attempting to reas-sure him, while a concerned June looks on from the side. The subjective camera reaches its apex as Peter is given anaesthe-sia and we witness his eyelid closing from the inside. As the screen is enveloped in darkness, the camera pans down and we are transported to the entrance of Heaven, where the re-cently deceased pass through and where Conductor 71 is greet-ing Reeves.

The two central figures of the film, Peter and Dr. Reeves, delineate the divergent personalities of the Archers themselves. Peter, the poet, is like Pressburger, willing to believe in fan-tasy. He works with words, while Reeves is concerned with the visual experience. Reeves does not discount Peter's stories, be-lieving this could be damaging to his psyche, but he is also determined to find a legitimate cause for them. Similarly, Pow-ell is willing to work in fantastic settings, but only if they too are grounded in reality. "I like to have fantasy based on some-thing real because life is far more fantastic than fantasy, and although most people won't understand it I just can't go with pure fantasy. Although I'm good at fantasy, as pure fantasy I would be no good at all."[7] Dr. Reeves is introduced looking through a camera obscura, a device that uses mirrors to

allow him to look out over the entire town. June muses
that he is "surveying his kingdom," and he admits the device
alters reality, so that "you see it clearly and at once, as in a
poet's eye."

The film ultimately fails for the very reason it had been
created: to demonstrate the historical bond between the United
States and England. The Archers did a disservice to themselves
by having the matter settled in a courtroom, because this
allowed for only a static milieu as Powell had learned in
The Night of the Party. For all of this film's technical advancement, the Archers have only slightly more success here. Powell always disparaged of lengthy dialogue sequences, and in
Pressburger, a writer whose rhythmic style of writing emphasizes the image as much as the spoken word, he found
his perfect companion. Once the two attorneys take up their
positions, the film is overwhelmed by dialogue and ideology.
Even Powell conceded that he was not "happy about the ending, but that's the relic of the propaganda period—the request
of the M of I."[8]

The trial sequence lasts over twenty-five minutes and opens
in a large auditorium where an infinite number of spectators
are taking their seats, with the front rows occupied by members of the military from nearly every nation and era. Farlan's
polemic focuses on the nationalities of Peter and June, and his
tirades against the English soon become jingoistic. He identifies three issues that must be addressed: whether Peter should
have died, whether June is in love with him, and, whether he
is in love with her. In fact, however, his arguments are based
on the divergent nationalities of the participants, something the
Archers had already examined; Farlan's argument that the love
affair came about because Peter was thousands of miles from
home and lonely, "the love of the moment," had been among
the issues against which Colpepper had been working in *A Canterbury Tale*. As the lawyers argue over the relations between
the United States and England, the fate of Peter and June is
momentarily forgotten, brought back only when June's tear is
introduced. "Here in this tear are love, truth and friendship;
these qualities can build a new world today and must build a
better one tomorrow," Reeves informs the jury.

Now the operating room and the courtroom come together
as Peter and June are finally given the chance to testify before

the final verdict is to be decided. Farlan questions Peter on how he fell in love with June and whether he would die for her. "I would, but I'd rather live," he replies, an answer that startles even Farlan. "Young devil," he blurts out, then quickly apologizes to the court. June is called as a witness and Farlan asks whether she would take Peter's place to prove her love, a remark that upsets Peter, but Reeves builds on this, telling her to take her lover's place on the stairway. The escalator begins to carry her toward Heaven but abruptly stops. June races down the stairs to embrace Peter, while Reeves provides his summation. Repeating Farlan's earlier boast that "in the whole universe nothing is stronger than the law," he now amends it to be that "on Earth, nothing is stronger than love." Even the judge will declare that "love is Heaven, Heaven is love." The film ends with one more cinematic trick, as the conductor tosses from Heaven a book he had borrowed from Peter. It travels to the other world, eventually appearing in the coat that June is removing from a chair in Peter's hospital room. When he awakens, the trial is complete and the visions have passed. Yet, for Peter and the Archers, another world was about to begin.

11

Something in the Atmosphere Makes Everything Seem Exaggerated

For nearly eight years, Powell and Pressburger had worked with one purpose: to create films related to the war and its effect on the people of England. There were still many wounds to heal, both physically and emotionally, for the English and Pressburger, who was haunted by the fact that his mother had not survived the war. He felt guilty for his not having done more to obtain her freedom and could only guess as to her fate, for the last report of her was that she had been interned at Auschwitz. According to his grandson, Kevin MacDonald, the effect on the Archers was that Pressburger "stopped writing original stories. Perhaps he found it too painful to confront his inner life."[1] There was also a sense of displacement for the Archers, for with their identity so long tied to the war, they now lacked motivation. In fact, for a time it seemed as if the Archers' time had passed and rumors emerged that they would pursue separate careers. Pressburger for the first time entertained the notion of directing, his subject being his earlier *The Miracle in St. Anthony's Lane*, while Powell would direct Nigel Balchin's *The Small Back Room*. Eventually, however, both men recognized their need for one another and looked for another project on which to collaborate. This is perhaps why, for the first time since their debut on *The Spy In Black*, they turned to a novel for inspiration and in the process unconsciously found their next objective: to create a composed film.

Pressburger's wife Wendy had introduced him to the novel *Black Narcissus*, written by Rumer Godden. The story is of an order of nuns who attempt to establish a convent in the Himalayas but ultimately fail, with one of their number dying. In contrast to the liberties taken with *The Spy In Black*, the Archers remained remarkably faithful to the original work, as many of its themes corresponded to their own, in particular the influence of the environment on the participants. This is apparent in a passage from the book, which ironically also calls to mind Powell's first critical triumph. Commenting on the landscape surrounding the proposed convent, a priest remarks that "it feels . . . like the edge of the world; far more remote than it actually is, perhaps because it looks at such immensity. And the wind! It's very pure and healthy, of course, but—if you don't like it sisters, you must say so. Don't be tempted by it if you think it's too lonely and strange."[2] The modifications made, though minimal, add to the sense of isolation the nuns will experience, even called upon by a priest at one point. The characters also undergo a transformation: Dean is no longer the devout character who builds an altar for the nuns, and Sister Ruth does not don a red dress as she will do in the film. The Sister Ruth of the novel is concerned about the loss of her beauty, while the Archers' character will be one more representation of obsession.

The Indian setting seemed to call for extensive location work, much like the Archers had already done with *A Canterbury Tale* and *I Know Where I'm Going*, but almost immediately Powell dismissed this approach, having experienced with Ingram the dilemma of uniting location work with studio sequences. Powell had become fascinated with a new process that used back and front projection techniques to create a landscape inside the studio. The independent frame was a misguided attempt by the Rank Studios to actually package a film, to create all of the elements of a motion picture so that it could be filmed in a number of languages but for a minimum of cost. It seemed to be the antithesis of Powell's desire to manipulate the mise-en-scene, for in fact it took power away from the director. The complexity of the process as well as the possible constraints it created made it impractical, although Powell was the last to admit this. It awakened in him, however, a determination to control every aspect of the mise-en-scene as only the animators such as Disney could do. The set decorators, particularly Alfred Junge, who had been so crucial to *A Matter of Life and Death*, were to gain in prestige with the Archers, becoming key figures in the films to follow.

The Archers had attempted to obtain Deborah Kerr for both *A Canterbury Tale* and *I Know Where I'm Going*, but her contract with M-G-M had prevented this work. This time the Archers were able to prevail upon the studio to loan her out, further evidence of their increasing influence. For the lead actor, the Archers first considered Robert Donat before settling on David Farrar, an actor whose intensity was in contrast to Roger Livesey's easy-going manner. The characters he would create for the Archers would reflect a return to the types of the German cinema, tortured characters on the edge of an abyss. The costume designer for the film was Hein Heckroth, a man who would influence the look of many of the Archers' greatest films, here creating forty sketches. Production began on May 23, 1946, and, although it would finish on schedule, had gone substantially over the budget. Yet, the money spent manifests itself on the screen, and the film became a commercial success on both continents.

The film was almost universally praised for its mise-en-scene, with Jack Cardiff receiving an Academy Award for his work. In what would become a recurring theme for the critics, however, the Archers were criticized for creating a beautiful film but one lacking a persuasive story. "Michael Powell and Emeric Pressburger have come so close in executing a perfect fusion of all the elements of cinematic art—story, direction, performances and photography—that one wishes they had hit upon a theme at once less controversial and more appealing than that of *Black Narcissus*"[3] Even the author of the novel Godden was dissatisfied with the final film, believing it was "counterfeit," because of its studio setting. "I suppose I was so unhappy because I knew what the film could have been."[4] This view was echoed by, of all people, Michael Balcon, the influential producer with whom Powell had worked early in his career. "The documentary movement was in my view the greatest single influence in British film production and more than anything helped establish a national style. With *Black Narcissus*

The Archers were stepping yet further away from this supposed 'national style.'"[5] To the Archers, this remark could have only seemed like praise. Still, just as many critics conceived of what the Archers were undertaking. "The natural color is beautiful; but, more, the rhythm of camera movement is recurrently used in combination with a vertinting of the whole scene, at significant dramatic moments, to produce a poetic emphasis we have not seen before."[6]

In Calcutta, an order of nuns arranges to establish a new convent in Mopu, the site being the former harem of an Indian king. The Mother Superior informs Sister Clodagh (Kerr) that she is to be made Sister Superior of the convent, which is also to serve as a hospital for the locals and a school for the young women. She is to be accompanied by four other nuns, most of whom have been selected because of a specific contribution they will be able to make, such as gardening or nursing. The exception is Sister Ruth (Kathleen Byron), who is chosen because of her physical and emotional difficulties, the convent at Mopu being her last chance. Arriving at the convent, they are greeted by Mr. Dean (Farrar), an Englishman who is to help them establish the retreat but whose unrefined manner conflicts with the nun's sensibilities, particularly Clodagh's. They are also unsettled by the fact that their patients and students have been compensated for attending. On the first night, the nuns begin to feel the inexplicable effects of the environment, becoming easily fatigued, breaking out into spots, and becoming distracted by the constant gale. Although the natives come to accept the nuns, Dean warns them not to take on any serious medical cases, for if the patient were to die, the nuns would be held accountable.

The women's trials are exacerbated by the arrival of a young Indian woman, Kanchi (Jean Simmons), who Dean intimates was once his mistress, and General Lei (Sabu), the young son of their benefactor, who wishes to obtain an education. The atmosphere continues to impair the nuns, particularly Clodagh and Sister Philippa (Flora Robson), who are confronted by reminders of their past. For Clodagh the order had been less a vocation than a chance to escape the embarrassment of having been abandoned by her fiance, and now she finds herself reliving these emotions. The discord with Dean escalates, and, when he arrives at the Christmas Mass drunk, she forbids him from returning, which enrages Ruth. She accuses Clodagh of being in love with Dean, her own infatuation for him similarly transparent. When a baby in their care dies of natural causes, the natives hold the nuns responsible. As they seek refuge on the grounds, Clodagh discovers Ruth in her room no longer wearing her habit but a scarlet dress, rejecting entirely her vocation. She manages to escape from Clodagh and make her way to Dean's home, but his rebuff of her advances only accelerates her descent into madness. Ruth returns in secret to the palace. As Clodagh begins to ring the bell, Ruth attempts to push her off the cliff. In the struggle, Clodagh manages to hold onto the rope, but Ruth loses her footing and falls to her death. The nuns' mission having been a failure, they pack up to leave, just as the rains begin to fall, fulfilling Dean's earlier prophecy that they would not make it to the rainy season.

For all of the success of *Black Narcissus*, it was never a film to which either member of the Archers seemed particularly endeared. For Powell, it was a technical exercise, a preparation for his ultimate objective of a composed film: for Pressburger, it was simply an adaptation of another person's work. Yet, it remains one of their finest achievements, both visually and thematically. The Archers return to the fanaticism of *49th Parallel*, for although the methods and objectives of the nuns' order and the Nazi Party are obviously at odds, both groups require their members to subjugate their individuality. Clodagh's failure is her inability to give herself over to her vocation; she instead struggles with ghosts from her past. Like Vogel in the earlier film, Clodagh cannot ignore her experiences, nor the emotions that are rekindled by the environment.

The extraordinary hold of the mountain is proclaimed in a letter Dean has written to the order, in which he relates the history of the palace and its grounds. The influence of the gale is already present as he tells them that he lives in the valley, "out of the wind," as if even he is not immune to its effects. The power of nature and its ability to determine events is a common theme of Powell's and the Archers,' dating back to *The Edge of the World* and featured most prominently in *I Know Where I'm Going*. The magnificence of the land serves as a distraction from the nun's prayers, while the wind that affects them physically also makes them susceptible to their memories. Almost immediately the women's health deteriorates as they break out in a rash and grow weak from the change in atmosphere. Yet, the beautiful landscape is the greatest distraction for the nuns, as evidenced in Philippa's struggle. When she is supposed to pray, she instead finds herself looking out at the horizon, and, when advised by Clodagh to throw herself into her work, she displays her hands, the callouses on which serve as testament to having already attempted this. It is this confrontation that initiates Clodagh's own internal struggle. Yet, Clodagh's difficulties are evident even before her journey to Mopu, just as Ruth's neurosis is.

When the Mother Superior announces that Clodagh is to be the youngest woman ever appointed in her position, a hint of a smile passes across Clodagh's face. The almost subliminal display of pride is not lost on the older woman, who advises, "spare her some of your own importance," with Ruth. When Clodagh asks whether she regrets her decision to make her a Sister Superior, the elder admits she does not think that she is "ready for it and . . . [will] be lonely," reminding her that "the superior of all is the servant of all." Dean will similarly display a lack of faith in Clodagh's preparedness, although for different reasons, even echoing the Mother Superior's earlier statement when he introduces the holy man by identifying him as a "superior being like yourself."

Ruth emerges as Clodagh's alter ego, giving life to the emotions Clodagh is struggling to contain, particularly her attraction to Dean. She is not introduced until the nuns arrive at Mopu, when she rings the church bell located on a giant precipice. She looks down the cliff, both repelled and attracted by the height. She is constantly at odds with the others, hysterically ridiculing the natives, whom she dismisses as "smelly," with little need of education. Dean is the first one to treat her with kindness, as she later confesses to him, but she misinterprets it. Her neurosis is channeled into her obsession with Dean, for whom she is constantly watching. When he arrives, she is the first to greet him, like a young woman waiting on a suitor. Clodagh's struggle with Ruth is intensified by the latter's perception that they are rivals for Dean's affections. Clodagh accuses her of "thinking too much of Mr. Dean." Ruth retorts, "All the same, I notice you're very pleased to see him yourself." When he ultimately rejects her, it sends her over the edge, both emotionally and literally.

If Ruth is a portrait in obsession, Clodagh is another in a line of characters who are torn between their vocation and their desires. As with the others, her difficulties are accentuated by the environment but also by her past and the history of the palace. She begins to recall the love affair that drove her into the convent, remembering not only the passion of being in love but also of a dog hunt. She is also disturbed by the knowledge that the palace had once been occupied by the general's mistresses, and images of the concubines appear throughout the palace. Their presence is also brought out in Dean's letter as he makes reference to Angu Ayah (May Hallatt), the former caretaker of the palace, who lives "with the ghosts of bygone days." Ayah is introduced standing before a painting of the bejeweled women who had once occupied the rooms, and she imagines them calling out her name, as if she lives between the past and the present. Clodagh will have most of the paintings removed, but the murals remain as does their spirit, which is embodied in Kanchi, the young woman brought to the convent by Dean. Thinking she is alone, she engages in an erotic dance, and this scene looks forward to her role as lover of the young general, in effect his concubine. When Ruth flees from the convent, she will also be incorporating these spirits. "Ruth's resurgent sexuality [is] related to the irrepressible history of the place (the burning candle being, of course, a Christian symbol). This relatively simple equation is then brilliantly compounded. As Ruth flees down the corridor, she catches a lace curtain, thereby uncovering a statue of the dancing Shiva (Nataraja) which the curtain was intended to conceal. Since, in traditional Hinduism, Shiva is 'the destroyer,' this is doubly significant."[7]

From the beginning a tension develops between Clodagh and Dean, as he ridicules her position and her faith. When he brings Kanchi before her, he purposely asks Clodagh whether she has any questions concerning her, making it clear that she had been his mistress. She masks her feelings for Dean with hostility, but, when the baby dies, she has no alternative but to turn to him for help and in the process let down her guard. He arrives at night, and they walk out onto a patio, not realizing that Ruth watches from inside, her face criss-crossed by the honeycombed shadows of the window. The posture of Clodagh and Dean is almost like that of suitors, reinforcing Ruth's perception of their relationship. In one of the few instances of his showing Clodagh respect, Dean carries his hat in his hand as he tells her of the change he has noticed in her, that she is more "human," but what to him seems a compliment is to her a sign of weakness. She confesses to him the particulars of her joining the convent, the abandonment by her fiance and the resulting need to escape Ireland, then turns to her most recent failings. "I had to take in the young general. I couldn't turn out the old man, I couldn't hide the mountain." Attempting to comfort her, Dean makes a remark that many critics would have found ironic, that there is "something in the air which makes everything exaggerated."

This overstatement of emotions is most evident in the extended sequence, which, for Powell, would become the *raison d'etre* for the film. The composed film was not a new concept but simply a new name for an old idea, whose antecedents were not just the silent movies, but the animated films of Disney. The most accomplished of the silent directors, particularly among the Germans, were able to control not just the image but the speed of the film, while the background music provided by the piano player served to heighten the emotion. Sound meant that the image often was eclipsed by dialogue and that the film speed was predetermined. Disney managed to overcome this, having his animators create characters whose movements were often determined by the music. The Archers had already attempted a composed film in *The Life and Death of Colonel Blimp*, but then it had been an unconscious attempt. This may have initially been the case with *Black Narcissus* also, but it was very much a conscious objective for them by the time production ended. "In *Black Narcissus*, I started out almost as a documentary director and ended up as a producer of opera, even though the excerpt from the opera was only about twelve minutes long."[8] While Pressburger was schooled in music, Powell had an intuitive sense of music, and their films reflected the influence of music on the action of the screen.

The sequence begins with a close-up of Ruth, who has just observed the conversation between Dean and Clodagh, and her image is superimposed over a tracking shot through the jungle, where the natives are beating their drums. The drums have already been associated with death, and the Archers cut from the motion of one of the men bringing his hand down to the darkened interior of the palace, where a billowing curtain echoes the previous movement. A light appears in the left corner, followed by Clodagh, carrying a lantern. She descends the staircase and walks along the hallway, reassuring herself that each of the nuns is asleep. Outside one room, however, a light is visible beneath the door, but when she knocks it is extinguished. Clodagh attempts to force open the door, but, as a cut to the interior reveals, it is blocked by a chair. It is Ruth's room. When Clodagh advises her to open the door or awaken the others, the chair is removed, but only as the door opens and the lantern lights the room is Ruth revealed, dressed in a red dress. Clodagh's look of shock is heightened by the sound of a chorus rising up on the soundtrack.

Clodagh closes the door, still clinging to the hope that she can save Ruth, but instead she only demonstrates once more her own weaknesses. The chorus continues to provide an undertone to the emotions being played out, but it is the women's eyes which garner our attention, Ruth's red-rimmed eyes serving as testament to her madness, while Clodagh's register her anxiety. Clodagh attempts to convince Ruth to wait until morning before leaving and sits down at a small table to pray with her, but the latter is unswayed. Ruth takes her place opposite her and begins methodically to apply lipstick, her red lips in brilliant close-up before the camera pans up to her eyes, which are taking in Clodagh's reaction. The passage of time is delineated by the melting of the candle, interspersed with images of the concubines on the wall. Clodagh has fallen asleep, her Bible falling from her hands as the candle is extinguished. She stirs just as Ruth escapes from the room, her maniacal laughter mingling with the chorus as she closes the door behind her. Clodagh's cries awaken the others, and the women huddle in the darkness, their white garments crisscrossed with shadows. The ambience resembles a Gothic melodrama, with the women racing around the courtyard, resembling spirits in their white garments.

A search of the palace grounds fails to turn up Ruth, who is nervously making her way through the forest in an effort to find Dean's home. The viewer cannot help but be reminded of Disney's *Snow White and the Seven Dwarfs* where the forest seems to come alive as a frightened Snow White attempts to escape her stepmother. Dean watches from the protection of the trees as Ruth arrives expectantly at his home, although he does not recognize the intruder. The soundtrack now carries a soft elegiac violin concerto as Ruth moves longingly about the room, picking up his personal belongings. Still unaware of who the intruder is, Dean comes up behind her and is startled to discover that it is Ruth. She blissfully tells him of her decision to leave the order, but he as yet does not understand her motivation. He offers to find her passage to a nearby town, and she responds by declaring her love for him. This too surprises him, but he maintains his composure until she accuses him of being in love with Clodagh. He shouts that he cannot "love anyone," a telling insight into his own internal struggle. At the mention of Clodagh's name, Ruth's hysteria reaches its zenith as she repeats her name, the screen becoming infused in red as she faints. In an action that anticipates Ingmar Bergman's *Persona*, the screen literally tears apart.

When Ruth comes to, she is more composed, but the sweat that covers her forehead is a reminder of her disorder. Her eyes are more focused, and she tells Dean that she will return to the convent alone. As he places a coat around her, she kisses his hand. She races off into the darkness as he watches after her, his concerned expression fading into that of Clodagh, waiting nervously at Mopu. She stands at the edge of the cliff, her figure in silhouette against the backdrop of the Himalayas. Her young servant comes up to her, and his pulling at her garment causes her to turn around in fright. The young boy moves off as Clodagh is photographed in long shot, the tracking camera revealing the viewpoint to be that of Ruth's cover. Her eyes are revealed in a tight shot, the sweat even more pronounced, as she watches Clodagh enter the chapel. Inside Clodagh kneels down to pray, but a sound from behind her causes her to turn around again in terror, the choir rising up in exclamation once more, but she is unable to discern from where the sound came. Ruth has already made her way upstairs, watching Clodagh from the loft as she takes a drink of water. The camera tracks with her as she moves outside to ring the bell, her apprehension increased by the cliff before her. She is in the process of ringing the bell when the door opens to reveal Ruth, her face now a ghastly white as if already dead. She slowly moves in on the unsuspecting Clodagh then rushes at her in an attempt to push her over the side. Only Clodagh's grip on the rope saves her as she falls over the edge. Ruth attempts to pry her fingers loose as Clodagh attempts to pull herself back onto the surface. In the struggle Ruth loses her footing and plunges over the edge, as a shocked Clodagh holds her hand to her mouth. This last sequence most certainly influenced Hitchcock, most obviously in *Vertigo*. The sequence concludes with birds rising up from the valley where Ruth has fallen to her death. The emotional struggle has ended in death, but it anticipates the next stage of the Archers' career, with its coalition of music and visuals to further involve us in the character's mind.

12

Nothing Matters but Music

The tremendous commercial and critical success of *Black Narcissus* allowed the Archers nearly total freedom in the choice of their next project. Pressburger suggested a script he had written in 1937, *The Red Shoes*. Loosely based on a fable by Hans Christian Anderson, it was intended to be a vehicle for Alexander Korda's wife, Merle Oberon. Its setting was a ballet company, and, if backstage musicals were nothing new, ballet at least suggested something more unique. The script, however, was designed to exploit Oberon's limited dancing skills, and the dance sequences were secondary to the story. Still, Pressburger felt the script was one of his best. Without Korda realizing who was purchasing it, the Archers surreptitiously bought back the script. When Powell read it, he had two preconditions: that a ballet be created specifically for the film and that the leading performer be a ballerina. Powell felt that the script "had all Emeric's usual charm and ingenuity and rather stronger character drawing than usual. The viewpoint of the storyteller was from the outside, looking in. But the script was ten years old, and the prewar conventions of this kind of star vehicle showed up very plainly."[1]

Hans Christian Anderson's "The Red Shoes" is a violent fairy tale with only a superficial relation to Pressburger's story. On the eve of her mother's funeral, a poor girl is given a pair of shoes, handmade of red cloth by her grandmother. Religious

153

ceremonies run throughout the story, from the girl's confirmation to her final encounter with an angel. While wearing the shoes, the girl begins to dance uncontrollably, the shoes now in possession of her body. Near exhaustion, the girl finally persuades a woodcutter to cut off the shoes, and both the shoes and her feet dance off. Fitted with crutches, the girl continues to attend church, until she is taken up to Heaven to be reunited with the shoes. The theme of Anderson's story is one of vanity; the film's theme will be one of art versus love, as Pressburger understood it. "The germ of the whole thing, in one sense, does lie in Anderson's story, for the ballet grew out of that story, and the main plot out of the ballet. One stage followed another. Above all, I wanted to have a film in which a work of art would not merely be discussed, but in which it would appear. That was my aim."[2]

The Archers had already surrounded themselves with some of the finest technicians available, and they applied the same standard with the dancers they engaged. Robert Helpmann had already worked for the Archers, portraying the quisling in *One of Our Aircraft Is Missing*, but his reputation had always been in ballet. One of the men under whom he had studied was Leonide Massine, then recognized as one of the finest choreographers in the world. Helpmann was to serve as choreographer for the film, with Massine creating his own interpretation in the role of the Shoemaker. For the lead actress the Archers were to choose a relative unknown. If Helpmann and Massine were in the later stages of distinguished careers, Moira Shearer's was just beginning. Only twenty-one, Shearer was a dancer in a distinguished dance company when Powell approached her about the film. Not only was she an exceptional dancer, but her beautiful looks and fiery red hair made her seem a natural screen presence. She was reluctant to take the part, however, believing it did not offer the opportunities the theater did and that in fact it could set her career back. In the years following the success of the film, a dispute arose between Powell and Shearer over what caused her finally to change her mind. He believed that it was for the money, whereas she maintained that she simply gave in to the pressure.

I told Mr. Powell, as politely as I could, that I didn't want to do this and returned the script. I just thought the story was silly and banal. But he kept insisting. Finally, he went away saying, "I shall go around the world and find the perfect dancer for this part." I was delighted. Well, in 1947, Powell was back bombarding me with letters. By this time, Leonid Massine and Robert Helpmann were going to be involved in the movie, and I felt that with those names Powell would at least get the balletic things right. Still, I held out, because I simply did not like the story. But there was no stopping Powell. He badgered and badgered. Finally, Ninette de Valois, our ballet company director, sent for me and said, "Will you please make this movie, and get this man Powell off our backs.[3]

Production for the film began even as *Black Narcissus* was still being filmed, but two of the key figures in that film were about to be replaced. Alfred Junge was to create the sets for *The Red Shoes*, but unbeknownst to him Hein Heckroth was to design the ballet. When Junge learned of this he resigned, and Heckroth then assumed full responsibility for the production design. Powell would later try to characterize Junge's departure as being of his volition, that he believed the Archers were going too far with *The Red Shoes*. Although this statement is hardly accurate, it must be conceded that Heckroth was about to take the Archers to a new level, his influence on the films to follow as great as Powell and Pressburger's. For this film alone he created over two thousand sketches, which determined not only the look of the film but also camera placement. The second member to be replaced was Alan Grey, although like Junge he was initially to work on the film. The music he created, in particular the ballet sequence, satisfied no one. He was replaced by Brian Easdale, who was to work on five more pictures for the Archers as well as Powell's *Peeping Tom*.

Scheduled for fifteen weeks, the filming subsequently took twenty-four and the final budget of 551,927 pounds was considerably more than the amount originally approved. Rank worried it would never recoup its cost, leaving the company with another expensive failure like *Caesar and Cleopatra*. The British film industry was in another state of flux, the strides made in the Second World War having been wiped out by a single act of Parliament. Believing it was helping the native producers, the British government applied a large tax to all imported films, not realizing that while the Americans could get by without the English market, the opposite was not true for British films. The American reprisals that followed cut sharply into the English producers' profits, resulting in another depression. This, combined with the fact that Rank's spending had finally caught up with him, caused the banks to force him to turn over control of his company to John Davis, his chief accountant. Davis was to severely curtail the freedom that directors had enjoyed at Rank, and soon many of their greatest directors were to leave in a mass exodus. Only an offer from Alexander Korda to buy *The Red Shoes* outright convinced them they might have something on their hands, but even then they released the film with little fanfare.

The fears of the producers concerning *The Red Shoes* could not have been eased by the initial reviews, which were mixed, at best. Some felt that Powell and Pressburger had indeed created a "perfect film,"[4] but others decried it as "pretentious, but empty."[5] Even the most optimistic of critics, however, could not have predicted the success that the film would ultimately engender. In both England and the United States, audiences started lining up soon after the film debuted; eventually it made anywhere from five million to twenty million dollars, depending on the source. It also created tremendous interest in ballet itself, particularly among women. "There has never been a picture in which the ballet and its special, magic world have been so beautifully and dreamily presented as the new British film, *The Red Shoes*."[6]

Through the years commentators have agreed on two aspects of *The Red Shoes*: that no one could have anticipated or accounted for its tremendous appeal and that the story line is its weakest element. Shearer's appraisal of the story being "silly and banal" was echoed by many critics, and even its admirers often dismissed the story as "kitsch." This last characterization is especially perplexing, for ballet films were taboo at the box office, particularly one that had at its centerpiece a fifteen-minute ballet sequence. The film succeeds because it appeals to an emotional level, but its story is a complex examination of an artist unable to reconcile himself with his own desires. It is a film with many of the themes of *Black Narcissus*, but in which the order of the nuns gives way to the insulated world of the theater, and Sister Ruth's neurosis is echoed by Boris Lermontov's. It is a complex examination of a maestro as he creates first a work of art, then a great ballerina, but who finally reveals himself to be human, albeit a particularly venomous one.

Lermontov is a compendium of three real-life impresarios: Serge Diaghilev, Alexander Korda, and Michael Powell. Diaghilev obviously provided the model for Lermontov, for he was one of the greatest ballet impresarios ever to live, who was commercially successful but constantly experimenting with the medium. His tribute to Pavlova, following her death, of using a spotlight to take her place on stage would be re-created in *The Red Shoes*, as would be his dismissal of a dancer for having married. Korda's influence on the character is less obvious, but as he was the one who first commissioned the screenplay, Pressburger looked to him for inspiration. Lermontov's cosmopolitan manner reflected that of the great film producer. It was during the revisions of the screenplay that Powell's character traits were incorporated into the story, consciously on Pressburger's part, perhaps less cognizant on Powell's. Lermontov is called an "attractive brute," which corresponds to many of the characterizations of Powell as does Vickie's assessment that he is a "gifted, cruel monster." Certainly these last words could have summed up actress Moira Shearer's opinion of Powell. He remained aloof from many in his film company, but he pushed them to heights they never realized were possible. He also often took chances on relative unknowns, not just actors but also technicians, as evidenced by his promotions of Heckroth and Easdale on this film. Lermontov is the first of a series of artists who will serve as the protagonist for the Archers and for Powell. Hoffmann, Mark Lewis, and Brad Morahan in *Age of Consent* are the most obvious, but less obvious is Powell himself in *Return to the Edge of the World*.

The opening of the film evokes the excitement and aura surrounding the ballet as a group of students are literally held back at the door of the theater company. When the doors are finally opened, they nearly trample one another in their race to obtain seats. The students are divided into two groups, those attending for the dancing and those only wishing to hear the music. This conflict will be brought out later in the discord between the dancer and the young composer, who will eventually become lovers. Among those attending for the music is Julian Craster, a music professor who has created the score for the ballet, *Heart of Fire*, and has little use for ballet. When he recognizes the music as his own, he leaves the theater in disgust and writes an angry letter to Lermontov, which he later tries unsuccessfully to retrieve. Yet, his desires are not dissimilar to those of Lermontov, who often proclaims that "nothing matters but the music." Hired to coach the orchestra, Julian takes the task to heart, even making corrections in the music that only he and Lermontov know to be his own. Later, when he is presented with the original score to *The Red Shoes* for which he is only to make revisions, he instead creates an entirely new score.

The opening sequence is a brilliant interplay of three separate dramas, Julian recognizing the music as his own (his perspective presented through a montage of the orchestra), Lady Neston (Irene Brown) anxiously waiting to see whether Lermontov will accept her invitation, and her niece, Vickie Page (Shearer) appearing transfixed by the dancers. Lermontov's prestige is discernible in the excitement he generates on entering the auditorium, as deified as the dancers with whom he works. After reluctantly accepting the invitation to the party, he is annoyed to discover that he is to watch a dance recital. He wants no part of the proceedings, telling Lady Neston that he thinks of his art as a religion. "One doesn't really care to see one's religion practiced in an atmosphere such as this." When Vickie finally presents herself to Lermontov, she is undaunted by his refusal to see her impromptu recital and instead registers her obvious desire. When he asks her why she must dance, she instead asks him why he must live.

"I don't know exactly, but I must," he replies.

"That's my answer too," she says.

Like Julian, Vickie is offered an opportunity with Lermontov's dance company, and both report to work on the same day. In entering Lermontov's company they effectively enter into a new world, and this portrait of the insulated community of ballet has contributed much to the film's success. There is a sense of how isolated each dancer can be, greeting each visitor as competition, as well as the discipline and work required, all of which is offset by the potential rewards. Vickie finds herself simply another in a handful of women to whom Lermontov has offered a position in the company. She must even receive Lermontov's approval to return to her previous dance company for a single performance, but here she once more gains the impresario's attention. The fortunes of the Mercury Theatre are in marked contrast to those of the Ballet Lermontov: a record player takes the place of an orchestra, painted backdrops serve as the set, and the auditorium is small and cramped. As she is completing a pirouette, Vickie catches sight of Lermontov in the seats, his gaze focused on her. Her eyes in close-up register first an expression of surprise, then anticipation, and finally confusion as he seemingly evaporates, like an apparition. She is to remain with the company as it travels to Monte Carlo, although she is still a member of the chorus.

Yet, even as Vickie's star is rising, an awareness of her future confrontation with Lermontov develops. The prima ballerina of the company, Irina Boronskaja (Ludmilla Tcherina), announces her engagement, and, as the company gathers about to offer congratulations, Lermontov is noticeably missing. Like a character in film noir, he stands alone in his office, in darkness, enveloped by cigarette smoke. Lermontov is presented as a nocturnal figure, often losing himself in the shadows as he observes those around him and wearing dark sunglasses when outside. He immediately loses interest in his prima ballerina, declaring within earshot of Vickie that "you cannot have it both ways. The dancer who relies upon the doubtful comforts of human love will never be a great dancer." Grischa argues that human nature cannot be altered, but Lermontov is convinced that it can at least be ignored. Certainly for all of her talent, Boronskaja had been unprofessional, invariably arriving late for rehearsal and quarreling with the choreographer. Yet, it is only marriage and the commitment it signifies that prove intolerable to Lermontov. Even as Boronskaja is making her good-byes, Lermontov is making preparations for his next ballet and his next discovery.

Soon after arriving at Monte Carlo, Vickie receives a note asking her to call on Lermontov, and, believing it to be a social request, she arrives dressed in an elegant gown, a tiara on her head as if she were a princess. The fairy tale quality is reinforced as she passes through a large wrought iron gate, with music filtering down from the mansion above. Before her stands a giant staircase, where weeds protrude through the cement. Lifting her gown, she moves up it, like Cinderella preparing to set foot into the ball. Even before she has entered the mansion, however, she realizes that she has misinterpreted the note, for it is in fact a production meeting. The subject of the meeting is Lermontov's latest production, *The Red Shoes*, for which Vickie is offered the lead despite her lack of experience. Lermontov confesses to her that his colleagues do not share his enthusiasm for her, but his confidence in her will be more than justified, as will his decision to let Julian rewrite the score.

Even before offering the part to Vickie, Lermontov had assigned Julian to rework passages of the preexisting score. As he mentions the ballet's name, Julian drops into a trance, already imagining the score that he will create. Lermontov's passion for the ballet is evident, not just in the enthusiasm he demonstrates in recounting the story but also in his unconscious action of stroking a statue of a pair of ballet shoes. For Ian Christie this fetishist action indicates that Lermontov has a "perverse, passionate identification with *The Red Shoes* as an allegory of dance itself."[7] On arriving at the conference in which Vickie is offered the lead role, Julian finds Lermontov demonstrating his frustration with the entire score. Julian momentarily takes him back by presenting to him an entirely new score, which all recognize as a masterpiece. Lermontov does not let Julian enjoy his moment for long, quickly sending him off to work on the orchestration. Passages of the score have been anticipated throughout the first half, with even a blowing newspaper that catches on Julian's feet serving as inspiration.

The ballet is the centerpiece of the film, and in it the Archers encapsulate the film's themes and conflicts. The sequence begins in a conventional manner, with the curtain opening up on the dance, the perspective that of the audience in the balcony. There is a cut to a closer view, now registering the viewpoint of those in the front row and finally to that of a dancer on the stage, as the Girl enters on the arm of the Lover. That the dance will be presented through Vickie's eyes is announced almost immediately as she walks up to the Shoemaker's window, admiring the pair of red shoes that he offers. She imagines herself wearing the shoes; when he places them before her, she jumps into them, their laces magically wrapping around her ankles. It is an action that could not occur on a stage as performed and prepares us for a sequence that takes place as

much in the Girl's mind as in an actual location. On its release, some critics were disturbed by such effects, feeling that
the ballet was "marred in spots by the most abandoned use of
the sort of trick photography usually associated with something
like *The Goldwyn Follies*."[8] At the time of its production, some
debate arose over whether the Archers in fact intended to film
the ballet in a traditional manner. *The Times* reported that
Powell "plans to direct this without any cuts to show that it is
being performed in a theatre. It will be arranged and photographed, he says, as a cinematic composition, something like
a Disney subject. There may even be a few seconds break in
the picture, we understand, when the camera draws back at
the end of the ballet, giving the movie audience a chance to
applaud if they are so minded."[9]

Hindsight indicates that these statements did not reflect the
Archers' true intentions. The ballet had initially attracted Powell to the project, and it would be the ballet which would garner the most attention. "For me the ballet of *The Red Shoes* is
a gathering together of my whole accumulated knowledge of
the film medium—disciplined by music, enhanced by colour,
with the very maximum of physical action—which films should
transfer better than anything—and at the same time a distilla-
tion of story-telling. It is a gathering together of all we've learnt.
My memory goes back to the very first films. My ambition goes
far ahead of today."[10] The past that Powell brings to the film is
the expressionist films he had long admired, and here again
he was allowed to incorporate their influence into his film. If
the first half, where the Girl is transported by the red shoes
away from her lover, occurs in a theatrical setting, the second
becomes the manifestation of Vickie's psyche, incorporating her
fears not just in performing her first major work but also in
her conflicting feelings toward Lermontov and Craster. The
movement into the second half will occur as Vickie's dancing
is suddenly slowed down. "I always tried to shoot scenes at
different speeds, even dialogue scenes: anything from ten to
twenty-nine, although, of course, you know it'll be projected at
twenty-four frames per second. But every shot has its own
viewpoint, its own pace, its own mood. We didn't shoot Moira
at normal speed in her dancing scenes onstage; it was eigh-
teen or nineteen."[11]

Returning home, fatigued by the shoes, the Girl is held

back from entering her home by a shadow. It is the Shoemaker, and his movement reproduces exactly that of Jaffar in *The Thief of Bagdad*, and the Shoemaker's powers will be similar to the magician's. Yet, Lermontov had also been called a magician, and Vickie imagines for an instant that it is him before her, not the Shoemaker. This gives way to that of an image of Julian, and she races at the figure passing through it to enter another world, a surrealistic landscape from which she suddenly falls through space. A newspaper swirls about her, eventually becoming transformed into an actual figure who briefly dances with her, before once more taking the shape of a newspaper. The Shoemaker returns, and the image is dominated by red flashes as she effectively enters the world of Dante's Inferno, with figures grabbing out at her as her anxiety increases. Lermontov's Svengali-like control over Vickie has already been established, but the dance also serves notice as to Julian's influence on her. The "ballroom sequence" had been cut by Lermontov, but Julian had boasted that audiences would imagine it anyway; in fact, this is where the Girl will appear. He also had suggested Vickie imagine herself to be a flower or a bird, and this advice is given a literal translation as the action gives way to that of paintings depicting just such representations. If the ballet contains reminders of the past, it is more important for its portents of the future, most obviously her growing attraction to Julian as she imagines him rising from the orchestra pit to take the stage, only to be replaced by the Lover.

If Julian and the Lover are identified as one, then so too are the Girl and Vickie. In the final act of the ballet, the Girl arrives at a church, having danced all night, where the shoes preclude her from entering. The Lover emerges, having in the interim become a priest, but the Shoemaker arrives once more to assert his authority. The congregation and the priest having filed into the church, the Shoemaker offers her a knife with which to cut the bindings of the shoes. As she slashes at her feet, the blade becomes a tree branch, and she throws it away in frustration, only to witness it becoming a blade once more as it becomes embedded into the ground. The Lover/Priest emerges from the church, and, as the Girl falls into his arms, she gestures for him to remove the shoes. Once done, the Girl dies and the Shoemaker returns the shoes to his window. The ending anticipates the ensuing tragedy, but it differs in one significant point. The Shoemaker is unaffected by the Girl's death, but Lermontov will not be so immune.

Vickie's success is sudden and overwhelming, as she goes on to perform to perfection the leads in some of the world's greatest ballets. After Vickie's debut, Lermontov had boasted that he would create out of her a great dancer: "I want to create, to make something big out of something little." If he attempts to characterize his interest in her as a project, there are also hints as to his growing passion for her as a woman. His struggle echoes those of many expressionist figures, and Walter H. Sokel's characterization of the protagonists in German literature applies equally as well to him: "The poet stands on the margin of life, longing to be in the center. But something in himself bars him from ever reaching it, from ever partaking of the world's warmth and love."[12] On the night of *The Red Shoes'* premiere, he hesitates before Vickie as if to confide in her, then walks off, noticeably agitated, as if forced once more to deny his emotions. Once Vickie's reputation has been established, he makes plans to take her out to dinner, only to learn she has purportedly joined the others at a birthday party. A man who has purposely distanced himself from his company, Lermontov surprises everyone by making an appearance at the gathering. At this moment, when his guard is down, he learns of Vickie's romance with Julian. He makes no intimation to his companions of his feelings, but his features have suddenly hardened. In a film in which close-ups serve as exclamation points, this single act is particularly chilling.

Despite his own precept that "music is all that matters, nothing but the music," Lermontov loses all sense of objectivity. He watches Vickie's performance with an obvious disdain and tears into Julian's work, particularly when the latter innocently acknowledges that he and Vickie are in love. Despite the fact that nearly all agree that Julian's latest score is a masterpiece, Lermontov discards the work and fires the composer. Vickie and Julian both leave the company. When she meets with Lermontov to discuss the situation, he admits that "Mr. Craster has been unwise enough to interfere with certain plans of mine, and that is something I won't permit." With their departure, Lermontov's frustration only intensifies, as he learns of Vickie's marriage to Julian. The Archers pan from the an-

nouncement of the marriage to an ashtray, the numerous cigarette butts serving notice to how long he has been locked up
in his room. Clutching the letter, he begins to slam his hand
into it as he strides angrily around the room. Coming to a large
mirror, he looks purposely at his reflection then suddenly slams
his fist into the glass. The blood seeping from his hand breaks
the spell, and he turns on the light before unlocking the door
for his attorney. If the landscape of Monte Carlo is at odds
with the dark rainy streets one associates with film noir, the
film's dark central character rivals Humphrey Bogart's character in *In a Lonely Place*. Perhaps the greatest indication that
his dissolution with Vickie is of a different nature than his
break with Boronskaja is that he invites the latter back into
his company, her earlier transgression forgiven.

For a brief instant, Lermontov nearly gives in to his passion, setting down to write a letter to Vickie, but once more
fate intervenes, as his servant announces Lady Neston's presence in the evening's audience. Learning that Vickie is expected to visit her aunt, Lermontov waits for her at the railway
station as her train arrives. Trains appear throughout the film,
and even Lermontov admits they are "destined to meet in railway stations." On the night Vickie and Julian had learned of
their new assignments (to write and perform *The Red Shoes*),
a train had passed underneath the balcony, enveloping the two
in dark smoke. It had been on a train that Vickie attempted to
talk Lermontov out of firing Julian, and now he reciprocates
the action by arriving to urge her to put the red shoes on once
more. Lermontov, as would many reviewers, attempts to characterize the conflict as one between career and marriage, but
Vickie has continued to dance, albeit with less respected companies. The only evidence of her longing to return to the Ballet
Lermontov is a sequence at night of her secretly taking the
shoes from a dresser drawer and caressing them. Yet, this sequence had opened with a fade-in from Lermontov at his desk
and concludes on a similar image, so that the sequence is actually a creation of his own desires. The struggle, in fact, is
between two men over Vickie's soul, just as the Lover and the
Shoemaker had fought for the Girl's.

That Vickie has no control over her destiny is evidenced by
the climax of the film. As she prepares for her return, she listens to the broadcast of the premiere, and is shocked to hear

that Julian has taken ill. Glancing up, she catches sight of him in her mirror. This introduction makes him first appear to be a specter, but the look of anger and disappointment on his face is all too real. He confesses to her that he would gladly give up his career for her and wonders why she will not do the same for him. It is not her career, however, that he wants her to forgo but the influence of Lermontov, who now appears in the room. Lermontov obviously relishes the struggle, as he tells Vickie that if she leaves, she will never be allowed to dance in *The Red Shoes*. She clutches her face in agony as tears stream through her makeup, but once more she has no involvement in the final decision. When Vickie proves unwilling or unable to leave with him, a shocked Julian kisses her, while Lermontov exuberantly clasps his hands together in anticipation of victory. Vickie is already wearing the red shoes as she walks to the stage, something crucial to the film's ending but that Pressburger felt was illogical. Powell's romantic sensibilities eventually overruled Pressburger's more pragmatic literary senses, reasoning that Vickie was only breaking the shoes in, and her attendant walks beside her with the other pair of shoes.

The Girl and Vickie have now coalesced into one. As she walks, her movements are stilted as if she is a zombie. As the overture for the ballet begins, the shoes seem to take possession of Vickie, and she races down the steps and out onto the balcony. Hearing his name called, Julian looks up as Vickie either leaps or falls from the balcony, just as a train is passing underneath. Her motivation left purposely vague, the Archers manipulate time, for although she has yet to die, a stunned Lermontov takes the stage. He is photographed from a distance, but as he speaks, in words that seem dredged up from his soul, the camera moves in to a medium shot. "Ladies and gentlemen, I'm sorry to tell you that Miss Page is unable to dance tonight, nor indeed any other night. Nevertheless, we've decided to present *The Red Shoes*. It is the ballet that made her name, whose name she made. We present it because we think she would have wanted us to."

Just as had been done when Pavlova died, a spotlight takes the place of Vickie, moving about where she would have danced, while at the railway station Julian cradles Vickie's bloodied figure. She motions for him to remove the shoes. When

Julian performs the act, she dies, while on the stage the Shoe-maker is replacing the shoes. Critics were critical of such a grisly ending, perhaps unaware of how violent the original fable had been. The film, however, was to anticipate a new phase in the Archers' career. In *Black Narcissus*, the directors had for the first time experimented with uniting music, edit-ing, and cinematography into one experience. *The Red Shoes* took the process one step farther, but it was *The Tales of Hoff-mann* that took the experiment to its natural conclusion. Yet, *The Tales of Hoffmann* will prove to be a visceral experience, whereas *The Red Shoes* remains an emotional one. "I think the real reason why *The Red Shoes* was such a success was that we had all been told for ten years to go out and fight for de-mocracy, for this and for that, and now that the war was over, *The Red Shoes* told us to go out and die for art."[13]

13

My Best Film

It is no accident that Michael Powell ends the first half of his autobiography with the release of *The Red Shoes*, for, although they did not realize it at the time, the freedom and success that the Archers enjoyed throughout the war and the years immediately following were about to end. At the time, in returning to Alexander Korda, the man who had brought them together, they believed they were solidifying their independence, not realizing that his ambitions were to conflict with their own. Korda was still attempting to compete on an international level and for this he needed access to the American markets. Initially it looked as if the Archers would determine their projects, for their first work was an adaptation of a book that Powell had long dreamed of filming, Nigel Balchin's *The Small Back Room*. It was a story that seemed to be the antithesis of *The Red Shoes*, for the bright colors of Monte Carlo were replaced by a London under siege and filmed in black and white. British moviegoers had lost their appetite for wartime films, so that from the beginning its commercial potential looked limited. Ironically, *The Small Back Room*, like *The Red Shoes*, had originally been owned by Korda but had been sold to Independent Producers, so that now he was forced to buy back the material at a cost of ten thousand pounds. It proved to be a smart investment, for afterward the Archers signed a long-term contract with Korda for five films. In effect, however, they were signing their own death warrant.

The Small Back Room, published in 1943, concerns the political maneuvering that transpires in an office whose assignment is to test and report on military equipment. The book's narrator, Sammy Rice, is a man crippled by an artificial leg and with little appetite for the "back-room politics" that is rampant in his unit. Despite the inducements of his girlfriend, Susan, Rice is content with his consultative position. The climax of the book takes place on a beach, where Rice works to defuse an explosive charge that the Germans have been dropping over London. The book concludes with Sammy returning to Susan, his standing unchanged.

In adapting the work, the Archers retain most of the characters and incidents of the book but omit many of the episodes dealing with the political intrigue. Their focus is on Rice, a man tortured by his handicap who as a result loses himself in alcohol. The defusing of the mine becomes in effect a cathartic event out of which Rice becomes determined to establish his own unit. For Powell it is the "story of a hunted man who discovers a reason for living. I think that it is my best film."[1] Just as with *A Matter of Life and Death,* another film he often cited as his favorite, Powell's attraction to the project was more for the technical challenge it presented than necessarily for the themes it examined.

In signing with Korda, it was Pressburger who would the most affected by the new arrangement. If he had served as an adapter on *Black Narcissus,* it was still a film that paralleled his own interests. With *The Small Back Room* and the films to follow, Pressburger was forced to forgo many of the intimate touches that so infused his finest work. Powell would also be constrained by the arrangement, although he was still able to occupy himself with the technical challenges that the films presented, and he remained determined to create a composed film. If *The Small Back Room* provided little chance for this, he remained intrigued by the climax of the book, the defusing of a bomb. It was on this sequence that the Archers began filming in April 1948. In the book, the action occurs on a sandy beach, but the Archers transplant it to Chesil Bank, whose pebbled surface adds to Sammy's difficulties and contributes much to the tension. Isleworth Studios was the setting for most of the interiors, which were filmed in an atmospheric, noirish style, reminiscent of Powell's final quota quickies. For the cast, Kathleen Byron and David Farrar were reunited from *Black Narcissus*, although this time she was allowed to give a more restrained performance.

The film was not a commercial success, the public having become anesthetized to the problems of the veteran, and the critical opinion seemed tepid. Using the Archers' own logo as a guide, *Variety* wrote that the directors "come close to missing the target altogether."[2] A British reviewer's praise was only slightly more complimentary, finding it "ably produced, and the direction, with one or two lapses, is extremely efficient."[3]

In 1943 London, Sammy Rice (Farrar) is a member of Professor Mair's (Milton Rosmer) research department, reporting to the government on military equipment. Involved with a secretary from the department, Susan (Byron), Rice is in constant pain due to an artificial leg and he often attempts to relieve it through alcohol. He is approached by Captain Dick Stuart (Michael Gough), who is investigating a series of mines that the Germans have been dropping over London and whose victims have been unsuspecting civilians, most often children. Rice agrees to help Stuart but his attention is currently on the Reeves gun, a weapon that many in the government want approved despite the military's wariness. Although the unit is still working on the gun, Mair's personal chief, R. B. Waring (Jack Hawkins), has already given the office's support of it. At a meeting in which the various factions involved with the gun meet with the minister, a reluctant Rice is forced to admit that the gun still has problems. This statement further undermines Mair's position, which has already been damaged by the resignation of the minister who had supported his independent unit.

Rice's difficulties carry over into his relationship with Susan, and the two often fight over his self-pity and lack of enterprise. After one argument, Susan leaves him, and a bitter Rice becomes violently drunk, only to be contacted by Stuart, who has found two of the mines on a beach in Chesil Bank. Rice manages to gather himself together, only to find on arriving at the site that Stuart has been killed attempting to defuse one of the booby traps. After going over Stuart's notes, Rice makes his way across the rocky beach to where the mine lies. He makes it to the juncture at which Stuart had been killed but, recognizing the latter's mistake, manages to complete the operation successfully. When Rice returns to London, he receives an offer to form his own unit, one responsible to the military. After accepting the offer, he returns to Susan, his life seemingly in order.

With the film's opening, the Archers return to the setting of *Contraband*, while Powell re-creates the noirish world of *Crown v. Stevens* and *Her Last Affaire*. A car makes its way through the blacked-out streets of London, its passenger an army captain looking for answers. Stuart arrives at a government building looking for Professor Mair's division, but the transitoriness of the organization is apparent from its being listed on a paper sign taped below the fixed plates of the other units. Walking up the stairs, bathed in darkness, he finds Mair in his office looking through a microscope. After listening to Stuart's problem, Mair counsels him to meet with Rice, one of his assistants. Although Rice is not in, the secretary offers to locate him. Stuart's interest in Susan is apparent, but her knowledge of Rice's routine hints at their relationship. She first calls his flat but, not finding him, calls the Lord Nelson Pub, where the bartender recognizes her voice and assures her that Rice is there. Moving to the other side of the bar, he pauses in front of Rice, telling him simply that "she says you're to wait." Noticing Rice kicking at his leg, the bartender asks about the artificial leg and whether he is taking dope for the pain. "You won't give me the dope I need," he replies, but the bartender reminds him of what happened the last time he had whiskey, intimating his potentiality for violence.

Stuart and Susan arrive at the pub and immediately wonder about Rice's sobriety, but he anticipates their question. "Don't worry, I'm sober," he says, then he takes them to his flat. If Rice's state of mind is constantly called into question, his expertise is never in doubt. Stuart relates to him of a series of booby traps that the Germans are dropping on London but of which they have no description because all the civilians who have come across them have died. All that has been found is a cylinder, which Stuart carefully hands to Rice, who examines it, then flips it carelessly across the room to the captain, much to Susan's horror. It is, in fact, a Thermos, presumably dropped from a German plane as the explosives were dropped over the countryside. After agreeing to assist Stuart, Rice asks him to return to the pub for a drink, conceding that he does not keep any in his room. Stuart purposely looks at the bottle of whiskey setting on a table, and Rice uncomfortably responds that they are "keeping this one for V-Day." Beside it is a photograph of Susan, and Stuart realizes their relationship, and, although she is careful to point out that she lives across the hall, her presence is felt throughout the room.

The world that the characters inhabit is a dark one, both emotionally and aesthetically. They are often lost in the shadows, whether in their laboratory or a nightclub, and they are constantly intruded on by those around them. According to one critic, "The film brings a noir oppressiveness to social reality, without using crime, neurosis or the notion of an underworld as distraction or scapegoat, and belongs to the small and select group of film noir whose flagship is *Citizen Kane*."[4] In a nightclub, the couple are confronted by an overbearing young woman who entreats Rice to dance while her soldier-boyfriend is doing the same with Susan. At Mair's laboratory, his colleagues serve as a microcosm of the various stages of matrimony, from the young lovers unable to spend a minute without speaking to one another to the nervous explosive specialist who worries about his wife's perceived indiscretions.

Rice's personal struggle will be symbolized by not only his prosthesis but also the whiskey bottle he keeps on his living room table. His refusal to remove his prosthesis in front of Susan even when it is causing him pain becomes to her a representation of his refusal to give himself completely to her. Instead, she must engage him in mind games, in which she offers alcohol to him and through which he finds the strength to reject the temptation. His dependence on her is evident when he believes she has stood him up for their weekly date, and he nearly gives in to his desire to drink from the bottle. When she does leave him, he becomes violently drunk. Yet, their relationship is more than just one of dependence, for it is also grounded in masochism, something that even they recognize. He constantly seeks to drive her away, but the actions seem more a test of her love than an actual desire to end the relationship. "I take things from you with both hands," he says. "I always have, I always will. I keep kicking this foot of mine. When I have a bad patch on I like someone to flutter around, so that I can be a perfect swine to them. And you still seem to like it." Her response is just as telling: "Wouldn't it be silly to break up something we both like, only because you don't think I like it?" At the heart of their dilemma is not only his self-pity, but also his refusal to advance himself in his vocation. When the minister is replaced, Susan realizes that Mair's office will be closed or taken over by someone else and that Rice will do nothing to prevent it. "You'll hang around hating it and expecting everybody else to be sorry for you."

If Colonel Holland (Leslie Banks) physically resembles the elder Clive Candy, he is not a Blimpish figure, for he is well aware of not only the requirements needed for the gun but also the political maneuvering that influences its approval. He questions Rice on the unit he works for and correctly reasons that it is accountable to no one, in either the military or the government. "Lots of responsibility and no power. It's not right, you know. It's not right." This characterization also applies to Rice himself. He is the most qualified of Mair's men, but he is content to remain working with his figures, becoming uncomfortable when called on to give an opinion. That the numbers mean little in the scheme of things is apparent in the Archers' approach to the meeting, with the viewer distracted from the debate by the sounds of construction outside, then by a soldier who closes the windows in compliance with the blackout. In the end, Rice's figures have proven nothing, and this fact causes the minister to withhold authorization of the gun.

Throughout the film, the politicians and office workers are made to appear removed from reality, concerned more about their personal agendas than whether the gun can save lives. The minister of finance (Robert Morley) visits Mair's unit, and the scientists attempt to enthrall him with experiments unrelated to their work, while he takes an interest in a calculator, whispering to his guide that the men enjoy it when he feigns interest. Yet, it will be Waring, who personifies all that Rice detests in the politicking, concerned more with appearances than facts. The personnel chief has a petition put up to provide him with an office to announce his prominence and that of the unit. "The sale side has to impress people," he says. Rice and Waring come to personify the two factions of Mair's unit, one searching for knowledge, the other attempting to use that knowledge for political gain.

Yet, despite the prominence of the back-room politics, the film's focus is on humanity. Only two deaths occur in the film, one onscreen, the other off, but both are presented in very harrowing, very human terms. The first is a young soldier who has come across one of the mines. Not knowing what it was and fearful that his friends would think him a coward, he picked it up. When Rice arrives to question him, he has only scarcely survived the night, and the doctor believes it is a miracle that he has lasted as long as he has. The young man regains consciousness for a brief moment, and Stuart, believing it the last opportunity to secure any information, screams at him to answer his question. The boy does, then immediately dies. Stuart, having sat with the soldier through the night, leaves the tent, ashamed of what he was forced to do and also sad at the loss of a nineteen-year-old boy. The second death is of Stuart himself. He is already dead by the time Rice arrives, but a young servicewoman begins to read back to him the notes Stuart had dictated to her as he attempted to defuse the mine. She sits in the back of an army truck, nervously clutching the papers that only she can decipher, while Rice stands beside her smoking. Renee Asherson's rendering of the role creates a scene of quiet pain. As she nears the moment when the bomb had exploded, her voice begins to crack. Her sense of loss adds to ours, and Rice's is that of someone genuinely decent. The Archers were often accused of dealing in abstract ideas, but this scene demonstrates their films often had an emotional center.

For all of the critical accolades, one sequence, which lasts over three minutes, was often singled out for criticism. "The lapse which it is most hard to forgive is that into surrealistic camerawork illustrating Sammy's internal struggle with himself when, with his morale at its lowest ebb, he thirsts to open a bottle of whiskey."[5] Rice has returned to his flat and, believing it is Wednesday, the night he and Susan have set aside for one another, prepares to go out. As he continues to glance at his watch he gradually becomes agitated. He dials the phone to check the time, which is 7:53, long past the time at which they meet. Foreboding music commences, while the bottle of whiskey on the table is placed in the foreground. The ticking of the clock intensifies as it becomes 9:10, and the camera moves inside of the clock to show the timing mechanisms at work. Shots of the clock are interspersed with shots of his face, as it gradually overwhelms him. The whiskey bottle also becomes similarly exaggerated, and Rice's attempts to scream are silenced as the bottle moves in on him, now twice his size. He runs at it, and the bottle returns to normal as he falls against the table. Such a sequence could have been overlooked by the critics had it been presented as a dream or in a genre film that allows for such breaks with reality, but such a transgression here was tantamount to suicide. Yet, one can understand the Archers' motivation, for it was one more attempt to present a sequence introspectively. For Tom Milne, the difficulty of the scene is not its presentation but its failure to address Rice's real dilemma. "It isn't vulgar, it is beautifully executed and certainly as resonant as the much lauded delirium tremens sequence in *The Lost Weekend*; but it is unnecessary, because what matters here is not the presence of the whisky bottle so much as the absence of Susan."[6]

The aspect of the book that most attracted Powell was the extended bomb sequence, which is not simply an exercise in suspense; it is a matter of whether Rice can defuse the bomb, and also whether he can overcome his personal demons. It comes at his darkest moment, when he believes that he has lost Susan and is in danger of losing his position, and he finally succumbs to alcohol. Having become violently drunk at the pub, he returns to his flat to drink from the bottle that has represented his struggle. As he picks it up, he notices that the portrait of Susan is gone, as is her pet cat, and their absence further incenses him. He turns even more violent, smashing the empty frame and knocking the phone off the receiver when it rings, thinking it is Susan. As the phone dangles from the table, he hears not Susan's voice but Stuart's, announcing that two mines have been discovered. Splashing cold water on his face, he attempts to compose himself enough to comprehend what Stuart is telling him. The mines have been found on a beach in Dorset; Stuart claims one for himself and asks Rice to examine the other. In darkness and shadows for most of the film, Rice arrives at the open beach in daylight, the change in atmosphere providing a setting for his redemption.

The beach where the mines have been discovered is made up of pebbles, making the footing unsteady, but Rice is also hampered by the effects of his hangover. As the army unit looks on, he begins with the same experiments that Stuart had performed, testing the mine for metal and heat effects while still maintaining a safe distance. These steps completed, he moves in on the mine, carrying a telephone over which he will dictate the steps he is taking. During the sequence, the Archers will constantly cut away to the men observing Rice and the young woman dictating his notes, so that they take on the role of spectators. A combination of strain, the heat, and his hangover soon has his forehead bathed in sweat, and more than once he slips, nearly setting off the mine. As he reaches the point where Stuart had accidently detonated the mine, the soldiers grow concerned about his stamina. "He's all in—he'll never make it." Rice, however, is able to find the second trembler of the bomb, and, with the job successfully completed, he falls back onto the beach physically and emotionally drained. Later he will call it a "personal matter," and even Major Strang (Anthony Bushell), who had once seemed skeptical of his ability, finds praise for him. "Anybody ever has any doubts about what you can do with your hands, your arms, or any other part of you, you send them around to see me," he says. It is this prejudice, more than anything, that the mine has come to represent for Rice, for in conquering it, he has also conquered his suffering. He returns to London accepting an offer to create his own unit in the army (which surprises even General Holland) and returning to Susan, no longer burdened by his disabilities.

14

They Seek Him There, They Seek Him Everywhere

The Small Back Room was not a financial success, but it was a return to favor with the British critics, who could forgive the momentary lapse of taste in the dream sequence. Without realizing it, however, the independence that the Archers had so carefully built up effectively ended when they signed a five-picture contract with Korda. As if sensing that their moment had passed, Powell and Pressburger no longer used the title of the Archers to identify themselves, although their partnership would forever be known by that designation. Almost immediately they came to regret it, as Korda first assigned them to a remake of his own earlier triumph *The Scarlet Pimpernel*. Korda had directed the film in 1935, and Leslie Howard was so identified with the role that he had even starred in an updated war film in 1941 entitled *Pimpernel Smith*. David Niven was to have the unenviable task of taking over the role of English aristocrat Sir Percy Blakeney, who moonlights as the rescuer of French citizens due to face the guillotine. Powell must have thought he had left behind such assignments when he had directed *The Night of the Party* in 1935, but now he found himself and his partner doing little more than adding color to another man's film. The suggestion that they turn the story into a musical was rejected out of hand, and Pressburger struggled with the script, continuously going over Baroness Orcy's books but unable to maintain interest in them. Only when he decided the

approach needed to be more tongue-in-cheek did he finally
come through with a script. Surprisingly, this sense of fun even
extended to the production, which Powell characterized as
among the most enjoyable of the Archers' career. What makes
this surprising is that the Archers were confronted with two
actors who presented different difficulties for the production.

The Archers are often remembered for the performances of
their actresses, but Margaret Leighton was an actress with
whom Powell could do little, dismissing her as a "wooden" performer. Niven had already successfully worked with the Archers
but wanted no part of this production, believing he would be
lost in the shadow of Leslie Howard's portrayal. Yet, he was
under contract to Samuel Goldwyn, the producer who received
the rights to the American release of the film in exchange for
Niven's services. In a fit of pique, Niven failed to turn up for
the location work, requiring the Archers once again to double
an actor on location.

Despite all this, the Archers roamed across Europe, filming
at a chateau in the Loire Valley and sequences in Bath and
Marlborough, as well as the climax at the spectacular Mont St.
Michel. It was not simply the French countryside that fascinated the Archers but also the production design created by Hein
Heckroth. His influence with the Archers continued to develop,
and the sets he created were based on what Kevin MacDonald
characterized as "essential detail."[1] Not only did he forgo the
usual practice of creating an entire set, but he often used
painted backdrops and gauze wall hangings with objects painted on them. Powell felt the sets were "worked out splendidly. I
mean, we had agreed there would be no mouldings and fussy
details, and in some cases even the mirrors and the furniture
were a painted replica of the real thing. Because of the rich
colors we had kept the colours subdued."[2] This style was to
serve as a precursor for the Archers' *The Tales of Hoffmann*
and *Oh! Rosalinda!!* and Powell's later *Bluebeard's Castle*.

Despite working with an unhappy lead actor and an actress who seemed to display little emotion, the Archers were
satisfied with the rough cut of the film. The climax, set on
Mont St. Michel, where the tide moves in on the mountain and
suddenly turns it into an island, needed some additional
footage, but they had prepared for this by setting aside some
of their budget to cover such a contingency. The Archers, how-

ever, were once more to receive a shock, a further reminder of their new restrictions. Goldwyn had viewed the rough cut and was offput by the Archers' tongue-in-cheek approach. He called for new footage to be shot that would bring the film closer in spirit to not only the original book but also Korda's earlier film. The Archers wanted no part of this and filed a lawsuit, to which Goldwyn responded with a countersuit, and eventually the Archers were forced to acquiesce to the demands. This was not to occur until after they had completed *Gone to Earth*, which would have its premiere two months before *The Elusive Pimpernel*.

The final result pleased no one, particularly the critics, who, not knowing the circumstances that had influenced the film, blamed the Archers for the failure. The critic for *The Times* wrote that the Archers "throw themselves on the Technicolor paintbox like a couple of intoxicated infants, digging deep into the crimson and overlaying the story with a wealth of ornament and decoration. Occasionally they achieve a striking effect, but generally the screen has much the same effect on the senses as a prolonged blare of trumpets."[3] Some critics were astute enough to realize that the true difficulty with the film was the incompatibility of the story with the Archers' previous work. "It is difficult to see why such skilled and experienced craftsmen as Powell and Pressburger should have chosen a subject so unsuited to their somewhat exotic tastes."[4]

In 1792, the Scarlet Pimpernel has gained notoriety in Europe for his daring rescues of Frenchman sentenced to die by the guillotine. The true identity of the Pimpernel is known only to his men, for Sir Percy Blakeney's (Niven) reputation is of a dandy, known more for advising the Prince Regent on his clothing and for engaging him in games of chance. Blakeney's wife, Lady Marguerite (Leighton), knows nothing of her husband's extracurricular activities, only that relations with him are strained over her involvement in the denouncement of the first French family executed by the tribunal. Marguerite's brother, Armand St. Just (Edmond Audran), is one of the Pimpernel's men. While on a mission to France, he is detained by the Citizen Chauvelin (Cyril Cusack), the French ambassador who is determined to capture the Pimpernel. At a party honoring the Prince Regent (Jack Hawkins), Chauvelin approaches Marguerite and offers her a letter incriminating her brother in ex-

change for her helping him learn the Pimpernel's identity. Fearful for her brother's safety, Marguerite spies on a man known
to be in the Pimpernel's company and from him discovers that
the Pimpernel is returning to France. She relays the information to Chauvelin, only to discover too late that the man she
has betrayed is her husband. Determined to save him, Marguerite journeys to France accompanied by one of his men,
unaware that Percy has already escaped from Chauvelin. He
and his men take the French citizens they have rescued to Mont
St. Michel, only to find Chauvelin waiting for him and already
holding his wife captive. Percy offers himself in exchange for
his wife's freedom, then once more manages to elude Chauvelin's trap, having replaced the Frenchman's firing squad with
his own men. Chauvelin is further shocked to see the soldiers
he has placed around Mont St. Michel nearly drowned by the
incoming tide. As the waters rise, Percy and his large contingent of volunteers and freed Frenchmen prepare to board a ship
to take them to England. As the ship sails, Percy is reconciled
with his wife, having finally realized that she was innocent of
any indiscretion.

It is difficult to evaluate *The Elusive Pimpernel* as an Archers' film, for there is no way of knowing what their intended
film would have been or how much the final product has been
shaped by the hands of its producers. What had been envisioned as a musical, then something of a satire, in the end
became little more than a costumed adventure film with few of
the touches one associates with a work by the Archers. The
music often overwhelms the images, while the editing has a
disjointed quality with a propensity for close-ups, which are
most obviously not the style of the Archers. The miscasting of
Leighton furthers adds to the difficulties, for the central theme
of the film is of a love betrayed, but there is none of the passion required for such a drama, with Leighton often registering
desire with a look of bored incomprehension. Blakeney has lost
himself in his cause, trying to forget his wife's apparent denouncement of a French family. When one of his men comments on the tragedy of his having lost his love for his wife,
Blakeney returns that he is "desperately in love with her—that's
the tragedy." When Blakeney learns the truth of what occurred
and holds his wife for the first time, remarking that "Chauvelin said you'd be free the moment I die and not a moment

sooner," the declaration lacks the resonance of the MacNeil curse in *I Know Where I'm Going*.

One can appreciate *The Elusive Pimpernel* on a technical level as Powell began to return to his roots in the silent cinema, with sequences alternately reminding one of Rex Ingram and the costumed epics of D. W. Griffith. The Archers' mise-en-scene is often sumptuous: a group of women doing their laundry in the river as the Pimpernel's men make their escape in the distance, a bed of flowers out of which a group of rioters emerge to attack the castle in the background, and the sequences at Mont St. Michel, where the tide hauntingly moves in on the French troops and turns the mountain into an island. It is Abel Gance, however, who is paid homage in the sequence involving the prince's costumed ball, when he participates in a game of blind man's bluff. Just as Gance incorporated the camera into the action in *Napoleon*, here we look through the small slit in the prince's blindfold, which allows him to view the ample bosoms of the young women who encircle him. In another instance the Archers seem to anticipate the future of film, in a sequence Powell was particularly proud of. Chauvelin believes he has finally captured the Pimpernel but fails to notice the Englishman switching his snuff for pepper. When the unwitting man inhales a pinch of the pepper, he begins to sneeze uncontrollably, with each fit highlighted by a great flash of sparks, which in turn serve as jump cuts that allow for breaks in continuity. One sneeze finds him transported from one end of the room; another brings him to where he is about to be lowered into a cellar. This bit of self-consciousness is also evident in the staging of Percy's reading of his poem about the Scarlet Pimpernel. Set in a steam bath, not only does the setting recall the opening of *The Life and Death of Colonel Blimp*, but so too do the bloated military leaders who lie about on the stone surfaces. The general's obvious disdain for Percy's effeminate manner does not prevent him from relating to them the poem, and, as he speaks the lines "They seek him there, they seek him everywhere," he is able to move about the room seemingly at the speed of light. These sort of jump cuts would later be reinvented by Jean Luc Goddard and others members of the French New Wave.

The travails with Samuel Goldwyn served as a precursor for the Archers' next film, for once again they found themselves

with another American producer, this one even more notorious
for his interference. On May 14, 1948, Korda and David O.
Selznick entered into an agreement that was to result in four
films. Carol Reed was to direct both a version of *Tess of the
D'Urbervilles* and a script by Graham Greene entitled *The Third
Man*; Sidney Gilliat and Frank Lauder were to film *The Doctor's Story*; and the Archers were to adapt Charles Dickens's,
A Tale of Two Cities, which Selznick had already produced
in the United States. In the end only two films would be
produced by Selznick and Korda, Reed's *The Third Man* and
Gone to Earth, the latter taken from Mary Webb's novel. The
first would be an international critical and financial success,
while the latter would end in lawsuits and the dissolution of
the agreement.

Powell first suggested *Gone to Earth*, having long been an
admirer of Mary Webb, perhaps because her stories were often
set in the countryside in which he had grown up. Korda was
again agreeable to the project, because he already owned the
rights to the novel, whereas Selznick looked on the story as an
ideal vehicle for his wife, Jennifer Jones. Pressburger began
writing the script in January 1949, and all through the process he was inundated with memos from Selznick, which he
politely ignored, but in the end all were to prove satisfied with
the final draft. (Later, however, in another statement that
seemed to reflect his change in attitude toward his films based
on their eventual response, Powell decried, "We never licked the
script. I doubt if Mary Webb could ever be licked.")[5]

Selznick's reputation was one of constant interference, particularly in the films he produced starring Jones, so that as
the July production date neared, the Archers braced themselves
for his interference, only to receive a reprieve. Selznick became
ill with the flu and was forced to leave for the United States to
regain his health, not to return until filming had been nearly
completed. Powell was pleasantly surprised by not just Jones's
ability but also her easy manner with the cast and crew, and,
as in the calm before the storm on their last film, the production proved to be a happy experience. Location work was completed in Shropshire, once again returning Powell to another
setting from his childhood, but this film was to prove more
personal for him than *A Canterbury Tale* had been. "All around
us, from our crowd of locals, from our artists, and from the

Michael Powell.

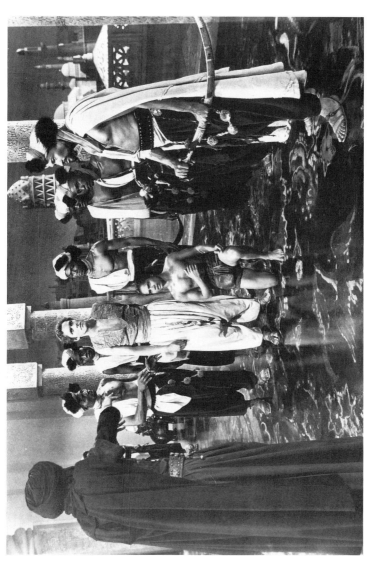

Jaffar (Conrad Veidt) strikes Ahmad (John Justin) blind and will soon transform Abu (Sabu) into a dog in *The Thief of Bagdad*.

Coshenille (Frederick Ashton), Coppelius (Loenid Massine), and Spalanzani (Robert Helpmann) in *The Tales of Hoffman.*

Johnnie Barras (Laurence Olivier) in *The 49th Parrallel.*

The Crew of *B for Bertie* wait anxiously to learn their fate. Sir George Corbett (Godfrey Teale), Frank Shelley (Hugh Williams), John Glyn Haggard (Hugh Burden), Geoff Hickman (Bernard Miles), and Tom Earnshaw (Eric Portman) in *One of Our Aircraft Is Missing.*

The German Theo Kretschmar-Schuldorff (Anton Walbrook) and the English-man Clive Candy (Roger Livesey) toast one another in *The Life and Death of Colonel Blimp*.

Theo and Angela (Deborah Kerr) can do little to console Candy.

Thomas Colpepper (Eric Portman) draws the suspicions of Alison Smith (Sheila Sim) in *A Canterbury Tale*.

Torquil MacNeil (Roger Livesey) and Joan Webster (Wendy Hiller) fight the elements and one another in *I Know Where I'm Going.*

An angel (Kathleen Byron) and Bob (Robert Coote) look down on heaven in
A Matter of Life and Death.

Sister Clodagh (Deborah Kerr) and Kanchi (Jean Simmons) in *Black Narcissus*.

The dance of the Red Shoes with the Girl (Moira Shearer) torn between her lover
(Robert Helpmann) and the shoemaker (Leonid Massine).

Vickie (Shearer) finds herself similarly torn between her husband Julian Craster
(Marius Goring) and Boris Lermontov (Anton Walbrook) in *The Red Shoes*.

Hazel Woodus (Jennifer Jones) comforts her pet fox in *Gone to Earth*.

Dr. Dapertutto (Robert Helpmann) and Giulietta (Ludmilla Tcherina) in *The Tales of Hoffmann*.

The Graf Spree meets its fiery end in *The Battle of River Plate*.

The German General Karl Kreipe (Marius Goring) is helped up a Cretan hill by Major Patrick Leigh-Fermor (Dirk Bogarde) in *Ill Met by Moonlight*.

A poster for *Peeping Tom*.

Cora (Helen Mirren) and Bradley Morahan (James Mason) in *Age of Consent.*

onlookers, I was being reminded of my mother's tales and of my childhood visits to Worcestershire. Even the landscape, with its abrupt changes from civilization to savagery, contributed to the story and helped the actors. I think it was, perhaps, because the story and my own feeling for the countryside were both so intensely regional that the French public liked the film so much."[6] A crude sound stage was built at an aerodrome in Shrewsbury for the interior sequences, particularly the fair.

In August, however, Selznick returned, and with him so did a sense of foreboding. He was unimpressed with what had been filmed and immediately began offering suggestions that he felt were more in keeping with Webb's original work. By the time the picture was completed, the suggestions had turned into threats as Selznick, borrowing a tactic from Goldwyn, argued that the picture was not what he had initially agreed to. Eventually the Archers found themselves once more in court over one of their films, but the ruling this time left the Archers with some measure of control. The Archers could keep the film as it was, but, due to the wording of the contract, Selznick was free to release his own version in the United States. This was nothing new for the Archers—their films were often altered for their American release and just as often given new names. *The Spy in Black* became *U-Boat 29*, *Contraband* was renamed *Blackout* (a title even Powell seemed to prefer to the original), and *49th Parallel* was severely edited before becoming *The Invaders*. More dramatically, *The Life and Death of Colonel Blimp* was released simply as *Colonel Blimp*, with nearly a half hour of the film excised, including its flashback format, while a new flashback was created for *A Canterbury Tale*. Later, the final act of *The Tales of Hoffmann* was shorn of most of its footage for its American release. Nothing, however, compared to the alterations the Archers' current film would be subjected to, for *The Wild Heart*, as Selznick renamed the film not only was cut from 110 minutes to 82 but received entirely new footage by Rouben Mamoulian. Selznick initially wanted the Archers to film the new sequences that he had devised, but they obviously passed on such an ordeal, as did many of the directors to whom Selznick offered the work. The cast and crew were brought in nearly a year later to film the sequences, and Selznick was not to release his version for another two years after *Gone to Earth* premiered. Selznick, however, was to have the last laugh, because his film is the only one available in the United States and it also turns up many times on television in England.

Both versions of the film initially were to find disfavor with the critics. The critic for *Monthly Film Bulletin*, reviewing *Gone to Earth*, found that "Powell and Pressburger appear to have inflated it to an allegorical statement of spiritual and carnal love fighting it out over an innocent being, and their slow, stilted, portentous method made the slight story seem even more ridiculous than perhaps it is."[7] *Variety* would review both films and dismiss the first version as "primarily a simple yarn about simple people, it is without finesse, polish or sophistication. Dialog just about emerges from a monosyllabical state."[8] The critical drubbing of *The Wild Heart* can perhaps better be understood, considering the revisions that took place, although once again it was the Archers who were called to task, not Selznick. "The characters—a wild and beautiful gypsy girl, a headstrong foxhunting squire, a tender and understanding clergyman—all beg for definition and development, but they have [been] ruthlessly subordinated to a shapeless story [that] builds to an exciting, yet meaningless finale."[9] Reviewing the original film much later, the critics again found another masterpiece that had been overlooked. "*Gone to Earth* is unmistakably a Powell-Pressburger picture with its sensuous, dramatic, often lurid use of Technicolor, the flamboyant sets and designs, the heady mixture of the sacred and the profane, and a mystical love for the English countryside, placing it squarely outside the dominant British realist tradition."[10]

In the early years of the nineteenth century, Hazel Woodus (Jones) is the beautiful, untamed daughter of Abel Woodus (Esmond Knight), a coffin maker, beekeeper, and musician. The pair live on God's Little Mountain, where she cares for a pet fox, protecting it from the many hunters in the area. Her mother had been a gypsy, who left to her daughter a book of spells, which guide Hazel's life. After traveling to a nearby town to purchase a new dress, Hazel is forced to make her way back in darkness and is nearly run over by Jack Reddin (David Farrar), a local squire with a reputation for womanizing. He offers to put her up for the night, but, after he makes advances toward her, she escapes and instead spends the night with his servant, Andrew Vessons (Hugh Griffith). The next morning Vessons takes her home, promising not to tell Reddin where she lives. A gifted singer, Hazel and her father are to perform at a gathering honoring the new minister, Edward Marsten (Cyril Cusack), but along the way the pair argue, and Hazel impulsively promises to marry the next man to set foot on God's Little Mountain. Marsten is immediately entranced by Hazel and invites her to supper the next Sunday. Reddin, meanwhile, has been searching the countryside for Hazel, but she has come to associate him with the Black Huntsman and thus hides from him in fear. Marsten has learned of Hazel's promise and proposes to her, later making a vow to God that he will not treat her as his wife until she first comes to him. They agree to marry in August, the week after the county fair.

While attending the fair, Hazel is discovered by Reddin, who forces her to meet with him later. He is unable to dissuade her from marrying Marsten, and the wedding takes place after Hazel is first baptized. Marsten adheres to his promise to God, but Hazel is confused by his lack of passion. Having performed one of her mother's incantations to learn what to do, Hazel believes she is compelled to meet with Reddin and, after making love to him, returns to his manor. Their relationship causes a scandal in the county, although Marsten is the last to know of his wife's indiscretion. Hazel comes to regret her decision to live with Reddin, troubled by his rough manner and hunting, while also longing for the company of her pet fox. Marsten finally comes for her and, although shocked to discover she came of her own free will, takes her back to his home, where his mother immediately threatens to leave unless he rejects Hazel. The community also ostracizes the couple, forcing him to give up his ministry. As Reddin and his men are in the area hunting, Hazel grows concerned for her fox and goes off in search of it. She finds it, but the hunting dogs, having caught the scent of the fox, give chase. In escaping, Hazel falls into an abandoned mine shaft and is killed.

This plot synopsis is, for the most part, the story encapsulated in both *Gone to Earth* and Selznick's version of *Wild at Heart*. Because of the differences in approach taken to each film, and because Selznick's is the film more readily viewed today, both films must be taken into account. The only signif-

icant plot detail added by Selznick is to have Hazel, as in the
novel, become pregnant with Reddin's child. Yet, the material
that he excised from the original and the new material directed
by Mamoulian create an almost entirely different story, one
more melodramatic than the Archers'. According to one reviewer, "The re-editing destroyed *Gone to Earth's* lyrical construction, its almost musical momentum."[11] As always with an
Archers' film, their film had a specific movement, with each
sequence segueing into the next. This is not the case with
Selznick's version, which, in addition to changes made to keep
it more in line with the original work, has heightened the sense
of fate controlling Hazel's life. Hazel, confused over her husband's behavior, consults her mother's book of spells to determine what she should do. The book advises her to place her
shawl on a rock formation; if, after she has walked around it,
the wind causes it to flutter, then she must leave with Reddin.
Of course it does, but in the Archers' version, the sequence is
more complex. After the placement of the shawl, she is to listen for the music of the fairies, and, as she stands in the night,
she does indeed hear the music. What she does not realize is
that it is her father's music, the viewer discovering this as the
camera pans across the valley. In the Archers' films, more often than not characters precipitate events, and the actions of
the central figures result in the tragedy.

The film that the Archers produced is further proof of Disney's influence. Pam Cook describes how the "low-angled shots
of black trees swaying ominously are accompanied by a
soundtrack of hunting music, thudding hooves and chanting
voices whose reverberations have almost physical impact, both
evoking the Black Meet in Hazel's mind and creating a more
general sense of dark, hostile forces threatening humankind."[12]
This description could easily apply to Disney's *Snow White and
the Seven Dwarfs* or the later *The Legend of Sleepy Hollow*. As
in many of Powell's and the Archers' films, the landscape takes
on a personality of its own.

The struggle, as in *The Red Shoes*, is over a woman's soul,
and the triangular relationship is also found in *I Know Where
I'm Going*, where the woman must choose between a romantic
figure and a more sedate lover. As with Joan, Hazel lacks a
mother and openly rebels against her father. Her perception of
marriage, however, is influenced by her mother's proclamation

that it is "tears and torment. She said keep yourself to your-self. Eat in company and sleep alone." This view is reinforced by her marriage to Marsten, which is lacking in emotion. This lack of passion does not signify a lack of desire but is instead tied to an ill-advised prayer he had made on the night of their proposal: "What I want is not for myself. I want to protect her, to change her, in my house, like a flower. And this I promise. I shall ask nothing of her, nothing until she wants to be a wife to me." This promise, no matter that it is of pure intentions, ultimately results in tragedy. Having been introduced to sen-suality by Reddin, Hazel is distressed by her husband's unwill-ingness to take her in his arms, eventually thinking of him as more of a parental figure than a lover. ("You're my father and mother both"). Marsten eventually gives in to his desire. Hav-ing left Hazel's room, he pauses in the hallway and returns to her door, only to find it locked. Ironically, it is his confusion that has caused her to lock her door, as she pulls out her mother's books of spells in the hopes of finding an answer to her conflict. In fact, their fate may have been determined at the moment of his proposal to her, for in the distance can be heard the hunter's horn.

Hazel is an objective, just as Alison Smith had been in *A Canterbury Tale*, and an object of desire, as Vickie had been in *The Red Shoes*. She is introduced racing with her pet fox, at-tempting to escape the hunters. After making her way safely into her home, she boasts to her father that she "could hear the Black Huntsman's horn," a mythical figure associated with death. If this alludes to her own fears, she will find herself pursued throughout the film by men desiring her for her looks. On traveling to town, she meets her young cousin, whose at-traction to her is immediately apparent, particularly to his mother. She wants no part of Hazel staying overnight, recog-nizing the threat she is to men. "It's a disgrace the way you look. You quite draw men's eyes." Her reaction anticipates that of Marsten's mother, whose reticence toward Hazel is also based on social prejudice. "She is not of your class, Edward," she advises him. Certainly both men's eyes will be drawn to Hazel, as when Reddin takes her to his home the first night. He has offered her a new dress to wear, and leaves the room only to hold back at the window as she begins to undress. He is a voyeur just as Mark will be in *Peeping Tom*, but so too will

Marsten, for he finds himself attracted to a young woman with whom he has nothing in common. She arrives at the fair accompanied by her father, and Marsten's eyes follow her movements as she walks past carrying her parasol, already tempted by the woman who will draw him away from his calling.

Prophetically, Hazel's first encounter with Reddin is in a moment of fear. Walking down a country road at dusk, Hazel hears the sound of an approaching horseman. Thinking it is the Black Huntsman, she starts to run, only to be nearly struck by Reddin's carriage. At first he simply offers her a ride, then invites her to spend the night at his manor, arguing that it is too late for her to make her way home. As always with the Archers, the use of color has psychological implications. The dress Hazel has purchased is green, but after it is ruined by the accident, Reddin offers her a red one. She holds it up to her body, admiring it, but discards it for her own, torn dress when she catches him watching her. That it is red is significant, for Reddin will soon represent to Hazel not just passion, but also fear. It is evident in the red roses she brings to him when they finally agree to meet and are trodden under his feet after they have made love. Red is also seen in the fires often found in the background of Reddin's sequences—for example, in the fireplace in his home and the torch visible between Reddin and Hazel's father when the latter attempts to purchase her.

When Hazel rejects Reddin's advances, he calls out to her in the darkness into which she has escaped that he has "never run after a woman in my life," but, in fact, this is what he will do most of the film. If Reddin is often portrayed as the aggressor, who continuously pursues Hazel even after marriage, his personality is shaded so that there is a hint of his own vulnerability. In Reddin, the Archers again examine the psychology of obsession, as he rides about the countryside looking for the woman who rebuffed his advances. When he does find her, he first attempts sexual blackmail, then offers her father money to let him take her away on the eve of her wedding. On the night of her wedding, when the guests having finally departed, she looks out the window of her new home, and Reddin stands silently at the fence, like the minister who haunts the children in *The Night of the Hunter*. Later, when the pair have argued, Hazel attempts to escape into the bedroom, but he breaks the door down. His threat of violence gives way to anguish, how-

ever, as he breaks down and clutches at her waist as she
strokes his hair. She remembers that on the first night that
they had made love, he had also broken down in tears.

Although fearful of Reddin, Hazel also enjoys his attentions.
As Vessons gives her a ride home, she makes him promise not
to tell his master where she lives, but, as she continues to
repeat the request, while looking longingly back at the manor,
it is obvious she hopes that he will break his promise. This
attraction will not be lost on Reddin, who later, on meeting
with the newly married Hazel, confidently tells her she will meet
with him, "because you'll want to come." Yet, their relationship
is overshadowed by her natural fears. On hearing his voice
outside a tavern in which she and her father have stopped,
she leans forward in expectation, only to pull back in fear on
hearing a woman compare him to the Black Huntsman. Even
she realizes that her fate is tied to that of her pet fox, warning
her pet that the "world's a big spring trap and we're in it."
This is given a physical representation when she marries
Marsten, with her animals in cages all about her and her own
freedom restricted by the bonds of marriage. Yet, it will be
Reddin whom she will accuse of having "the blood of foxes on
him," and it will be his dogs, in pursuit of the fox, that cause
her to fall to her death.

The film also returns to a favorite theme of Powell and the
Archers: the need to reject the influence of a parental figure.
The mother's admission that she knows where Hazel is finally
brings about the rejection of matriarchy that restrained
Marsten. He goes to Hazel, demonstrating a passion that had
been lacking in their previous encounters. "I've come to take
you home," he angrily tells her while decrying that she has
told a "great many lies. Well, I'm not particular." Yet, when
Reddin arrives, Hazel offers her own representation of her husband, calling him "my soul." Looking purposely at Reddin,
Marsten wonders whether she would ever call him that. When
they return to his home, his mother remains, but the bond
will now be completely severed as she asks whether he intends
to put Hazel before her. When she cries out that she will not
stay under the same roof as Hazel, his response is in his expression, and, looking into his cold eyes, she is distressed.
"What are you staring at?" she wonders. "The world, Mother,"
he replies, as if for the first time aware of her hypocrisy. Yet,

her reaction is no different from that of the other members of the community, who also embrace religion but cannot forgive others' sins. The members of the town council call on him, ordering that the "adulteress must go," but their proclamation has the same impact as the mother's earlier declaration. He shocks them by announcing that he is forgoing his post as pastor, intending to move on to another community, taking Hazel with him, whom he believes is innocent of wrongdoing. "How do you know it was Hazel's fault? It was mine. I could try and explain, but not to you. You think everyone has a price," his last remark calling to mind Reddin's earlier attempt to purchase Hazel from her father. Hazel is an unwitting pawn in a drama over which she has no control. In effect, so were the Archers.

15

A Composed Film

The Archers' return to the Korda fold had not proven fortuitous for either side. The Archers, who had gained their reputation for original works, found themselves adapting projects already owned by Korda, while the Hungarian producer was disappointed that the commercial success of *The Red Shoes* had not been repeated. This film initiated their next, a project that originally appealed to both sides. Sir Thomas Beecham, the musical conductor on *The Red Shoes*, suggested to the Archers that they attempt an opera, but his first two suggestions, *Carmen* and *La Boheme* were immediately rejected by Powell. He argued that these works would result in filmed opera, offering limited cinematic potential. Beecham's third suggestion was more to his liking, Offenbach's *The Tales of Hoffmann*. Hoffmann's works had a profound influence on the German filmmakers of the twenties, and the three tales contained in Offenbach's opera, linked by the figure of Hoffmann himself, seemed to be just what Powell was looking for. To ensure that Korda would approve the project, the Archers first recruited many of the participants from *The Red Shoes*, including Moira Shearer, an actress whom Korda had long been desirous of for his studio. In addition to reuniting some of the greatest dancers available, they resolved to recruit some of the world's finest singers. Although most were only called on to sing, dubbing the voices of the dancers, the central character, who was not required to dance, required a more traditional opera singer. Robert Rounseville had already essayed the role of Hoffmann on stage before being cast. The only other actor with opera experience was Ann Ayars, who had also gained experience in MGM musicals.

Only a seventeen-page script, providing little more than stage directions, was prepared, while Dennis Arundell wrote a new translation of the libretto. The Archers first considered filming on location in Germany and Venice, but, after returning to the England, they decided to do as they had with *Black Narcissus*, creating a film entirely in a studio. This was to give them more control over the mise-en-scene, as would the decision to record the music first to be played back during filming, allowing not only the dancers more freedom but also the camera. Unfettered by the unwieldy equipment required for sound films, the camera operators could easily move around, providing movement that surprised even the Archers. In effect, they were creating a silent film, even able to control the speed of the film and reversing the image to control the movement of a character. It also allowed them to film in Shepperton Studio, where Korda had filmed the epic *Things to Come*, but that had been seldom used since. Filming began on July 10 and would last eleven and a half weeks, with the budget being a surprising small three hundred thousand pounds. This amount was due to the cost measures Hein Heckroth used to create a film that looks much more expensive but for which a predetermined camera placement was required, as Christropher Challis recalled. "In the early planning stages of the picture, we decided first on the effect we wanted, then designed and built the set accordingly—and then only just what was required. The economy thus effected was enormous."[1]

This project was one of Powell's most propitious experiences, for he was not only finally achieving his objective of the composed film, but also returning to his roots in the silent cinema. "My life and work had come full circle. I was never more happy."[2] This was the Archers' first experience with a true musical, but Powell found that his profession and that of a composer had many similarities. "Composers and film makers think very much alike. Their tempos are very closely related to our cutting tempos, their longuers and their statements are very similar to ours. Whereas, even with a writer as clever and subtle as Emeric I always had this continual battle with words."[3] *The Tales of Hoffmann* would free Powell from any reliance on dialogue, for the composed film was a "method which allows for complete pre-planning of every aspect of the production to achieve a single, intense, expressive end under the guidance of the music. It is the music that carries the emotional meaning of the movie—watching a 'composed film' one is struck by how similar the experience is to listening to a full-scale orchestral work."[4] Pressburger's role as writer was thus once more diminished, so that even in this triumph the seeds for their later dissolution were evident.

The response of many British critics was to be expected. "Probably the material itself is quite intractable, but the trouble is that behind all the effects, the strivings, the opulence and the apparatus, there seems no clear sense of direction, no single purpose at all. In this way it is the most spectacular failure yet achieved by Powell and Pressburger, who seem increasingly to dissipate their gifts in a welter of aimless ingenuity."[5] A critic for *Sight and Sound*, however, more accurately described the picture as a "gigantic Panorama of dreamland and nightmare, sometimes rising to enchanted heights, then falling to dismal banality. The new Powell-Pressburger picture, like much of their work, is a baffling, tantalizing, but eminently noteworthy piece of perverse brilliance."[6] Reviewing the film years later, Thomas Elsaesser found the film to be "no doubt seriously flawed, over-ambitious and uneven. It creates a confusing complexity, in which images of startling force are side by side with a rather too obtrusive, mechanical symbolism. But it is a film which is genuinely disturbing, not least by its uncompromising pessimism."[7]

The writer Hoffmann is attending the ballet, *The Enchanted Dragonfly*, in which his latest love, Stella (Shearer), is the prima ballerina. During the intermission he escapes to Luther's Tavern for an ale, but he is surrounded by college students who entreat him to tell one of his stories of the "folly of love." After first recounting a story of a hunchback who had fallen for Stella and had been rejected, Hoffmann relates three tales of his own failure with women. In the first, a young Hoffmann falls in love with an inventor's daughter, Olympia (Shearer), not realizing she is the mechanical creation of Spalanzani (Leonid Massine). Providing the eyes for the doll is Coppelius (Robert Helpmann), a rival of Spalanzani's. When the latter's check bounces, an enraged Coppelius returns literally to tear apart Olympia before a stunned Hoffmann. In the second tale, Hoffmann confronts Dr. Dapertutto (Helpmann), who entreats a beautiful woman to steal the author's soul. Giulietta (Ludmilla Tcherina) succeeds, but Hoffmann manages to win it back after battling a rival suitor. The final story is the most tragic, as Hoffmann visits a Greek island where his former lover, Antonia (Ayars), is held in seclusion by her father (Mogens Wieth). A beautiful singer, Antonia is forbidden to perform as her poor health makes such an action fatal. The father's anxiety increases with the arrival of Dr. Miracle (Helpmann), who had played a part in his wife's death and who brings on tragedy once more by entreating Antonia to sing, thus precipitating her death. By the conclusion of the final story, Hoffmann has lost himself in alcohol and suffering and can only look on as Stella leaves with Councilor Lindorff (Helpmann), who is revealed to have been the antagonist in each of the three tales.

Offenbach's opera is based primarily on three Hoffmann tales, *The Sandman*, *A New Year's Eve Adventure*, and *Councillor Krespel*, the first of which supplied not only the story for *The Tale of Olympia* but also the framework for the opera. In *The Sandman*, the antagonist of the opera is drawn, for the young man who falls in love with Olympia lives in constant fear of a man he only refers to as the Enemy. Offenbach will create such a character in Councilor Lindorff, who emerges as the antagonist in each of the stories. Hoffmann held a profound influence over the German expressionists with his tortured souls struggling to survive in an oppressive atmosphere. In contrast, Offenbach's reputation was for lighthearted operettas, including those on which Pressburger had worked in the thirties; but *The Tales of Hoffmann* had been his final work, and he would die with it uncompleted, thus leaving no definitive version. The Archers, with the complicity of Beecham, made some alterations in the work, most obviously the transformation of the opera that had opened the film to a ballet. By creating the Dragonfly Ballet, the Archers provide more screen time for Moira Shearer, while also paying further homage to Walt Disney. In many respects, the film that it most resembles is *Fantasia*, but, as Howard Roller notes, "the demands of Hoffmann are more complex, since it must convey the fantastic delusions of Hoffmann's mind while being faithful to the opera text. *Fantasia* could simply free-associate to the musical piece

without any restriction."⁸ The backdrop for the ballet is obviously modeled after Disney's animation, with the young girl
ending the piece by racing onto the leaf of a plant. The film
thus becomes a compendium of a variety of disparaging influences, from the dark atmosphere of the German cinema to the
bright colors of Disney's cartoons.

The film opens with Stella, the ballerina, performing, but
our interest is not as much in what is taking place on the
stage as off. She has moved to the edge of the stage to pass a
note to her servant, Andreas (Philip Leaver), but he is inter-
cepted by Councilor Lindorff. Lindorff's introduction is among
the most striking images of the film, with double doors opening to reveal him, standing in front of a red backdrop, his tails
in one hand and his cane in the other. Two men sit asleep just
in the doorway, and, after awaking them with a blow from his
cane, he strides past them, the camera now observing him
from above as he moves in and out of three chairs, his coat
trailing after him like a reptile's tail. His offer of money to
Andreas for the note is rejected, but, as the servant moves off,
Lindorff maneuvers himself to impede the servant's progress,
increas-ing the amount. Their movements, as with many of the
sequences in *The Life and Death of Colonel Blimp*, are methodically choreographed, the dancing backgrounds of the two actors apparent.

At the intermission of the ballet, the audience departs except for Hoffmann, who holds back still transfixed by Stella's
performance. The music begins to build as Hoffmann is photographed in medium shot, and there is a cut to an announcement from Luthor's tavern offering ale to those in attendance
and then to the marquee outside the tavern as the student's
voices can be heard beginning to exalt the properties of beer
and wine. It is as if everything is being held back, only to be
released by a cut to a stairway, the camera tracking down it
as a student races down the steps to join his companions, who
begin circling around, their arms intertwined. Lindorff also
comes down the stairs, pausing momentarily on the landing,
allowing the camera to pan down to the stairwell below, where
Nicklaus stands. Each action, from the lifting of a cape to the
movement of a character's eyes or the simple drinking of ale,
is conducted to the timing of the music.

"The Tale of Olympia" is the most lighthearted of the tales, with the Archers constantly experimenting with lighting and visual effects that have their roots in the silent era, most obviously Georges Melies. Images are reversed, puppets are transformed into lifelike characters who serve as a chorus for the action, and the sound effects enhance the mechanical nature of the figures. Hoffmann is a student who declares his intention to devote himself to study, forgoing love. Yet, as had been put forth in *The Red Shoes*, it is impossible to sublimate emotions. On catching sight of Olympia, he immediately becomes entranced by her beauty, not caring that she lies motionless on her bed. It will be Spalanzani's rival, Coppelius, who completes the subterfuge of Hoffmann, presenting to him a pair of glasses that give life to inanimate objects ("Look and see all you want to see"). From this point forward, he is unable to discern fantasy from reality. In all of his stories, Hoffmann is accompanied by Nicklaus, a character of ambiguity for not simply sexual identity (a male figure portrayed by an actress) but also for motivation. As played by Pamela Browne, the film initially was to contain a scene that revealed the character to be a muse, her skin bathed in gold. Nicklaus is often aware of the duplicity being exercised against Hoffmann; although he often attempts to warn the author, he also participates in the mechanizations working against him. It will be Nicklaus who purchases the glasses for Hoffmann and later, knowing that Olympia is a "never-was thing," helps to wind her up. Throughout Nicklaus often seems to take pleasure in Hoffmann's predicament.

Hein Heckroth's importance to the Archers is no more evident than in this film. He envisioned each of the tales being dominated by a particular color, in this case, yellow. A visitor to the set related Heckroth's set design. "An ornate swinging bed in the middle of a completely circular room. Walls were of yellow dyed muslin; the entrances a clever arrangement of drapes. Two yards away hung a further circular sweep of muslin. At the back again a yellow-painted backcloth. The impression of depth through the gauzes, and of reality to the cellophane chandeliers hung between the two layers, was achieved by the lighting."[9] Heckroth would create a similar set for *Bluebeard's Castle*, but there the dominant colors would be black and red. Despite the beauty of the mise-en-scene and the frivolity of the story, it will end in tragedy, as Coppelius, having learned he has been cheated, returns to dismember Olympia. With one of her legs still dancing, Hoffmann sits down beside the head of his beloved, and, as springs pop from her head, they are transformed into the ripples in the waters of Venice, the setting for the next story.

"The Tale of Giulietta" is the most sensual of the stories, as Hoffmann, older but apparently not much wiser, is confronted by the beautiful courtesan, Giulietta. She is introduced riding in a gondola, accompanied by Dapertutto, a magician who wishes to possess Hoffmann's soul. She stares into the water, her face reflected on its surface, in a shot similar to one used by Powell in *The Edge of the World* and later in *Bluebeard's Castle*. The reflection begins to sing, foretelling the use of a person's reflection as a mirror to the soul. She passes by Hoffmann, who watches on from a bridge. On the shore waits her present lover, Schlemiel (Massine), whose loss of his soul is evident by his deathlike complexion, and he fingers a key that will become another signifier for the soul, anticipating Powell's later use of the key as a metaphor in *Peeping Tom*.

Hoffmann opens this tale once more making a resolution, this time declaring himself able to withstand the women's charms, passing through an orgy to which he pays little notice. It is one of many startling images in the sequence, most of which are related to sensuality: Giulietta dressed in white stepping over the bodies of past lovers, being beguiled by Dapertutto with a jeweled necklace he has transformed from candle wax, and, finally, the duel between Hoffmann and Schlemiel that transpires in silence on a gondola, giving it a detached dreamlike quality. Hoffmann wins the duel not through skill but because Schlemiel accidentally glances his sword against Dapertutto, who then allows the author to slay his opponent. The central theme, the struggle for the possession of a man's soul, dates back to *Faust*, and the Archers will use F. W. Murnau's silent version of the story as their model. The devil in that film anticipates the character of Dapertutto, even to the clothes he wears.

The passion of the second story is in contrast to the final act of the film, "The Tale of Antonia," which is more classical in its approach. This act is marked by an air of austerity and death, akin to that with which Powell had opened *The Edge of the World*. This sequence would come under the most criticism, particularly from Korda, who failed to recognize that the themes of this act had the most in common with those of *The Red Shoes*. Hoffmann and Nicklaus have traveled to a Greek island, where his lover Antonia is forbidden by her father to sing because of the frailty of her constitution. Her own dilemma is whether to practice her art or to live, but, as in *The Red Shoes*, her fate ultimately resides in another. The father wants no part of Hoffmann, believing he will entreat his daughter to sing; even the author, while yearning to hear her sing, recognizes the hazard it presents. Dr. Miracle (Helpmann) arrives on the island soon after Hoffmann and eventually gains control over Antonia. The father, having been witness to Miracle's role in his wife's death ("he never cures, he destroys"), becomes even more fearful for his daughter, hiding her away in her room. Miracle possesses abilities similar to those of Dapertutto, and, as he sits down on the couch Antonia had only recently occupied, he makes as if he is treating her, while in her room Antonia is compelled to sing, thus giving herself away.

Antonia imagines Miracle entering her room, but each attempt to escape the room finds her once more back in it, until in despondency she throws herself off a cliff that has opened in her room. She awakens in her room from the nightmare, but not from the suffering. Miracle convinces her that Hoffmann is in league with her father, then has the statue of her mother, which stands in her room, begin to entreat her to sing. Just as the ballet in *The Red Shoes* represented the mind of Vickie, so too does this imagery reflect Antonia's sense of foreboding. She imagines herself taking the stage, where the statue of her mother already stands, while Miracle serves as both conductor and musician. She pursues her mother's likeness through a forest but finds herself enclosed by fire, which becomes the torches that encircle the stage on which she begins to sing. Even her father is compelled to participate, as Antonia's aria gains in intensity. A helpless Hoffmann can only watch as she falls dead back into the arms of Miracle, who now removes his mask revealing himself to be Lindorff. The central antagonist of each act is also revealed to be Lindorff, his role in Hoffmann's tragedy now divulged.

The Tales of Hoffmann is a dazzling accomplishment, from a technical standpoint one of the greatest films that was ever created. It remains, however, more a cerebral experience than an emotional one. Robert Rounseville gives a staid performance as Hoffmann, creating a character that is more acted on than one that takes action. This is the fault not of the actor but of the character and the Archers' fascination with the composed film. It is unusual in a musical that it is not the music one remembers but the visuals. This film was Powell's chance to pay tribute to the silent films in which he had received his training, and it would have served as a fitting end to the Archers' career, even if Pressburger's contribution did not equal that in their greatest works, for it once more reinforced their reputation as romanticists.

Despite the film's success, relations with Korda had not improved. When they could not agree on another picture, the Archers were allowed out of their contract. Five years separated the release of *The Tales of Hoffmann* and the Archers' next feature, *Oh Rosalinda!!*, the longest hiatus of their career. This respite was partly due to a lack of interest for directing on Powell's part and to their inability to obtain backing for the projects that did interest him.

The years with Korda had precipitated a strain in the relationship between Powell and Pressburger, and by 1952 each man seemed to have his own agenda. Powell turned to the theater, first directing Siobham McKenna in *Heloise* and then bringing to the stage Raymond Massey's adaptation of Bruce Hamilton's *The Hanging Judge*. Although neither play was a commercial success, Powell considered *The Hanging Judge* to be "one of the happiest memories of my life."[10] Pressburger, meanwhile, had become infatuated with a German film entitled *Das Doppelte Lottchen* and convinced Korda that an English adaptation would be a commercial success. Powell wanted no part of the project, so, for the first and only time in his career, Pressburger served as both writer and director. The film was a complete failure, further proof that one of Powell's attributes was to constrain Pressburger's propensity for fantasy and sentimentality. Also at this time, Powell attempted his most ambitious project, a television series entitled *Powell's Tales*. Each episode was to have involved some of the finest talent available, both in front and behind the camera, some of which he details in his autobiography. An example was his intention of having Dylan Thomas adapt Homer's *The Odyssey*, which would have starred Orson Welles. Powell could interest no one in the

series, nor did he have any success gaining interest in a cinematic equivalent of the idea. The only project which came to
fruition of this series was a thirty-minute short film, *The Sorcerer's Apprentice*, that received only a limited release.

Powell's work bears little resemblance to the Disney interpretation, which appears in *Fantasia*, as if he were consciously
reacting against the earlier work, eschewing the bright colors
for a dark, nightmarish milieu that he would later repeat in
Bluebeard's Castle. The camera opens on a curtain through
which the silhouette of a castle can be discerned, and the interior resembles more a cavern than a castle. Inside the apprentice (Sonia Arova) is approached by the sorcerer, who is
accompanied by two ballerinas dressed as cats (only Arova is
identified in any account of the cast). Once the sorcerer departs, the apprentice uses a conjuration to help him complete
the task he has been assigned, to transport buckets of water.
He transforms a broom into his assistant, commanding it to
carry the water, but just as Joan's prayer in *I Know Where I'm
Going* is too potent, so too is the apprentice's incantation. As
the castle fills with water, the apprentice struggles to remember the magic words with which to stop the broom, and in
frustration he takes an ax to it. This action results in even
more brooms being conjured up, and only the return of the
sorcerer puts a halt to the misadventure, the film ending with
the broom once more taking its original form.

The film is Powell's closest approximation of the world of
Calgari and German expressionism in which he grew up, the
sorcerer resembling not only Jaffar in *The Thief of Bagdad* but
also an earlier role of Conrad Veidt's, Ivan the Terrible in *Wax-
works*. The setting has a heightened artificiality, and the
grounds surrounding the castle are of a dead forest. The film
is a trifle, a throwaway, but an interesting portent of where
Powell's ambitions were being diverted.

As other projects fell to the wayside, Powell found himself
being pressured by other members of the Archers' company to
film *Oh Rosalinda!!*, Pressburger's modern-day adaptation of
Johann Strauss's operetta *Die Fledermaus*. The inspiration for
the film had come about when Korda had flown Powell and
Pressburger to Vienna to attend a performance of *The Tales of
Hoffmann*. Although they missed all but the final minutes of
the play, Pressburger was fascinated by the circumstances of

Vienna. The city was still governed by the Council of Four Powers, with military representatives from France, the United States, Russia, and Britain alternating military rule. In adapting *Die Fledermaus*, Pressburger created a character representative of each governing body but with a Viennese, Dr. Falke, as the central figure. Falke seeks his revenge on a Frenchman, who in turn is married to the title character, while her prospective lover is an American. The British and Russians would be represented by a prison commandant and a general, respectively. Powell's lack of enthusiasm for the project was augmented by his disdain of operetta in general, and he hoped to salvage the undertaking by enlisting an international cast made up of Bing Crosby, Maurice Chevalier, Orson Welles, and Anton Walbrook. Almost immediately compromises were required, with only Walbrook eventually cast in the film. Michael Redgrave became resolved to undertake a musical and insisted that his own voice be used, and Mel Ferrer managed to attach himself to the project, primarily because the Archers were attempting to work with Ferrer's wife, Audrey Hepburn, on another film. Ludmilla Tcherina would give life to Rosalinda, the woman sought by all.

The five years the Archers were away from film were among the English cinema's most traumatic, as it faced the same difficulties that American producers were encountering. The competition from television had resulted in a loss of attendance, and various measures were taken to contend with this problem, one of which was to increase the size of the screen. Having overcome the restrictions of the Technicolor camera on their last film, the Archers now found themselves bound by the cumbersome process involved in CinemaScope. For a director whose signature was his moving camera, Powell suddenly found his hands tied. With Hein Heckroth again serving as production designer, the film was guaranteed a unique mise-en-scene. "Hein designed sets for this medium that were wide, shallow, and splayed, with large areas of colour between the decoration. I was able to plan the action in the foreground. I wanted the actors to have the freedom of movement, to be larger than life and I wanted the sets to frame the action and set it off."[11] In the end, the film found little favor with the British public or critics. "The plot loses itself in hopeless convolutions; the presentation of songs and comedy alike is wearily heavy; the design is a scrapbook of a sort of Teutonic House-and-Garden contemporary."[12] The reviewer for *Variety* was more accepting, calling it a "lavish production, highly diverting and spectacular. This should make for offbeat, light entertainment anywhere."[13] Despite this pronouncement, the film was never released in the United States, further proof of the Archers' perceived decline in marketability.

In occupied Vienna, in the spring of 1955, Dr. Falke is about to exact his revenge on the French Colonel Eisenstein (Redgrave), who the night before had placed the inebriated Viennese in the lap of a Russian statue. Brought before the Council of Four Powers, Falke implicates Eisenstein, who is dismayed to learn that he has received an eight-day prison sentence for his practical joke. Eisenstein's wife, the beautiful Rosalinda, is being pursued by an American serviceman, Captain Alfred (Ferrer), with whom she had once had an affair and who extends his leave on hearing of her husband's sentence. Falke convinces Eisenstein to postpone his assignation at prison in order to attend a party he is hosting for the Russian General Orlovsky (Anthony Quayle), to which he has also invited Rosalinda's maid, Adele (Anneliese Rothenberger). Having created a phony story to obtain the night off, Adele makes off with one of her mistress's gowns, and Falke sets his plan into action by telling Rosalinda of her transgression and, more important, of her husband's extracurricular activities. Alfred has been taken off to prison, having been mistaken for her husband, and Rosalinda puts on an evening gown and mask to attend the party.

Rosalinda arrives at Orlovsky's party, and, as Falke had anticipated, Eisenstein not only fails to recognize her but becomes infatuated with her. Having gained his attention, Rosalinda departs from the party, taking with her Eisenstein's prized watch. Desperate to know the identity of the woman and retrieve his watch, Eisenstein diffidently departs for prison, not realizing his drunken companion is the prison commandant. His confusion intensifies when he finds someone in his place in the cell, but Alfred's boasting of his affair sets Eisenstein off in search of his wife. With Alfred and the commandant in pursuit, Eisenstein makes it to the hotel, where the celebrants have gathered in the courtyard. They listen in as Eisenstein threatens his wife, but the timely chiming of his watch causes him to recognize the woman at the party as Rosalinda. It is her turn to feign anger, but soon they embrace, as Dr. Falke basks in the success of his practical joke and Alfred is returned to prison, having once more been mistaken for Eisenstein.

Oh Rosalinda!! is aligned with *The Tales of Hoffmann*, because of its musical format and its use of dubbing and incorporation of images from the silent era. The result, however, is a poor imitation of the previous work. In *The Tales of Hoffmann*, the Archers had used dubbing because it allowed them to recruit the finest dancers and unite them with professional singers. Here it is done only because of the limited skills of the actors they had chosen. Certainly many singers could have essayed these roles, in particular, the role played by Ferrer, who compounds the situation by also demonstrating his limited acting ability. The two actors who are most successful in their roles are, not surprisingly, alumni of the Archers, whose casting provides insight into the psyche of both Powell and Pressburger.

Powell later expressed dissatisfaction with Anton Walbrook's performance, but he is in fact the heart of the film, making it seem less a British product than a European one. In the prologue, Walbrook enters through a door to address the audience, the most obvious example of the Archers' breaking down the screen's plane. He establishes the premise of the film (his seeking revenge on Eisenstein) as well as his occupation (a black marketeer), before asking whether he can get the audience anything before the story begins. This calls to mind his earlier performance in Max Ophul's *La Ronde*, but whereas in that film he assumed a variety of roles in the compendium of romantic conflicts, here his objective is announced from the beginning. After being detained by the Four Powers, he introduces the flashback that recounts how he had become the victim of a practical joke. Yet, for most of the film, he is a director, carefully orchestrating the activities, even in the practical joke played on him. Having passed out after a night of celebrating, Eisenstein is placed in the lap of a Russian statue, where he is discovered the next day. The joke receives a lot of press, but only because Falke reenacts the event for the media.

If Falke's activities relate him to Powell, he also embodies the beliefs of Pressburger, just as he had in *49th Parallel* and

The Life and Death of Colonel Blimp. As is to be expected, he is
supplied with a monologue that reflects Pressburger's sentiments, but here it seems unsuitable among the champagne
glasses and singing maids:

> Ladies, sweet charming ladies. And gentlemen. It's four o'clock
> in the morning, and the air of Vienna is like champagne. When
> I am soaked in champagne, I love everybody. I love the whole
> world, in particular, of course, our dear friends, the British,
> the French, the Russians, and the Americans, who have been
> spoiling us Viennese for so many years, now. And when I say
> spoiling, I am not thinking only of your champagne, and whis-
> key, vodka, and Coca-Cola. We are proud that you love us, so
> much, and we can assure you that we love you too. But even
> the dearest friend loses a bit of his attraction if he overstays
> his time. Don't you agree? So, if you don't mind go home. Come
> back. As our guests. But, please go home.

Another part of Falke's disposition reflects Powell's libido,
for his obsession with Rosalinda mirrors Powell's own with
Ludmilla Tcherina. The film is as much a statement on sensuality as *Black Narcissus* had been. When Falke speaks Rosalinda's name he often does so as an exclamation of passion, and
he constantly speaks of her beauty. In *The Red Shoes*, Ludmilla had played a dancer who was less physically striking than
elegantly continental, but, in *The Tales of Hoffmann*, she had
embodied a sexual predator, whose slimmer figure was accentuated by her costumes. Powell openly professed his attraction
to Tcherina, and in this film he revels in the opportunity to
display her magnificence, photographing her in a bathtub or in
gowns that fall from her shoulders, while also allowing her to
display her comedic skills. When Alfred is about to be led away
to prison, he does so only because it allows him the opportunity to impersonate her husband and thus receive a good-bye
kiss. One wishes that Powell could have moved his camera
around her, as he would have in most films, but here he seems
restricted by the CinemaScope process. Instead, the Archers'
mise-en-scene often uses natural triptychs, as in one scene in
which Rosalinda is bathing in one room, Arthur is shaving in
another, and Adele is speaking on the phone in a third.

If expressionism as a style was considered to be a reaction
against the status quo, then *Oh Rosalinda!!* is by its very na-

ture an expressionist film. It is a reaction against not just realism but most specifically *The Third Man*, considered by many to be England's greatest cinematic triumph. Not only do both films use the same settings, but Falke's profession is similar to Harry Lime's, dealing on the black market. Yet, the bombed-out ruins of Carol Reed's films are here replaced by the stylized settings created by Hein Heckroth. It is a film based not on actuality but on the history of cinema. It is the world of Ernst Lubitsch and Rene Clair, as in the following exchange between Orlovsky and Falke: "What is reason in our language?" "I'm afraid you haven't got a word for that."

Throughout are images that also remind one of various genres related to the silent era. The opening newsreel, which details the discovery of Falke in a statue's lap, reminds one of the opening of Chaplin's *City Lights,* and the arrival of the Russian firemen calls to mind the Keystone Kops. The most overt example is when a drunken Major Frank (Dennis Price) returns to his prison feeling the effects of alcohol. The office that he enters begins literally to twist and turn, much like the inebriated sequence in *The Last Laugh* had, and the design of the room is Caligariesque with its use of diagonal shapes. When the sergeant enters the room, the colonel sees two of him, but, instead of simply doubling the image, the Archers use two actors who only remotely resemble one another.

Only the Archers could have attempted to unite so many divergent styles in one film. If the film does not measure up to their lofty standards, it was once again an announcement of their individuality. This could not be said of their final films.

16

Like a Ministry of Information Documentary Film

By 1956, Powell and Pressburger had collaborated on sixteen films, but Powell had directed only one in the past five years, and it was one in which he had little interest. The eventual dissolution of the Archers would not be the result of a clash of egos, for they had long since adapted to one another's idiosyncrasies, but more of a realization that each man's goals had changed. There were still projects to be produced, but the incentives of the past were gone; as a result, their creativity had declined. Ironically, their partnership was to end with two films set in World War II, the very event that had originally given their partnership meaning and a purpose. However, the lack of these two qualities is sadly apparent in both films. Like *I Know Where I'm Going*, *The Battle of the River Plate* began its inception through happenstance, with the Archers having received an invitation to attend the Mar Del Plata in Argentina. Believing they needed some reason for attending the gala celebration, they hit on the idea of researching a film on the English pursuit of the German pocket battleship, the *Graf Spree*. After their initial inquiry into the project, they managed to obtain the backing of Twentieth Century-Fox.

The pursuit of the *Graf Spree* was one of the most famous naval battles in World War II, garnering headlines even in the United States, then still two years away from entering the war. The *Graf Spree* had been wreaking havoc on British shipping, while continually frustrating the British navy with its ability to lose itself in the Atlantic Ocean. Eventually the ship was engaged in battle by three British cruisers, and, although the *Graf Spree* managed to escape, it was forced to seek refuge in the neutral port of Montevideo, ostensibly to receive repairs. The Uruguayan government, feeling pressure from the respective governments of the participants, limited how long the ship could remain safely in port. With the British navy rumored to be amassing a great fleet just off the coast of Montevideo, everyone anticipated an epic battle, but the captain of the *Graf Spree* stunned everyone by scuttling his ship. The British were thus denied a victory, while the Germans lost one of their most effective weapons. The story had already been filmed earlier, as *For Freedom*, and had even included some of the actual participants in the production. In preparing for the film, Powell and Pressburger interviewed as many of those involved as possible, including Captain Patrick Dove, an British captain taken prisoner on the *Graf Spree*, who also served as an adviser.

The primary dilemma facing the Archers was that the facts did not present them with a linear story line. The action begins on the German ship, then shifts to the English pursuers, and concludes in Montevideo, where the attention is divided between the behind the scenes politicking and the action on the sea. For the first act, the Archers benefited from their discovery of a small book by Dove, whose ship was among the last sunk by the *Graf Spree* and who had been taken on board as a prisoner. The relationship that developed between Dove and the German Captain Hans Langsdorff was reminiscent of that between Theo and Clive in *The Life and Death of Colonel Blimp*. In the second half of the film, however, this story line is necessarily forgotten as the focus shifts to the political maneuvering of the various governments and the anticipation of a great sea battle. Here, Pressburger was saved by his discovery that an American journalist had broadcast radio reports back to the United States of what was occurring. This character will serve as the narrator for the final events leading up to the destruction of the *Graf Spree*.

With the backing of the American studio, the Archers then obtained the assistance of three countries' navies. When Powell had directed *The Fire Raisers* just two decades earlier, he had been forced to make do with a small model, which, when exploded, was nearly overwhelmed by an air bubble. For this film, not only was Powell free to roam the great cruisers provided for the film, but the spectacular climax featured a twenty-three foot model, exact in every detail. The *U.S. Salem* doubled as the *Graf Spree* while the *Sheffield* and the *Jamaica*, two British cruisers, masqueraded as the *Ajax* and *Exeter*, respectively. The third British ship, the *Achilles*, had been rechristened the *Delhi* by the Australian navy but temporarily reclaimed its old name. Although the producers were hoping for Jack Hawkins to portray the British Commodore Henry Harwood, who leads the British fleet, the part eventually fell to Anthony Quayle. Ian Hunter, who had worked with Powell twenty years earlier, returned to portray the captain of the *Ajax*. Lionel Murton would portray the American radio announcer Mike Fowler, who becomes the commentator for the second half of the film. Although Powell enjoyed his experience on the film, it is due more to his fascination with the ships put at his disposal, than with the script.

For all of the innovation the Archers had put into their film, it is ironic that *The Battle of the River Plate*, one of their most pedestrian projects, would be among their most financially successful. The reviewers too, though restrained in their praise, singled out the film for being devoid of the eccentricities they had come to despise in the Archers' films. "At times it seems that Messrs. Powell and Pressburger are chafing at the limitations of the semidocumentary technique they rightly employ and longing to venture into waters even more romantic than those of Montevideo, but, if they feel the temptation, they honorably resist it."[1] A more accurate assessment came from The *Saturday Review* which found the film to be a "beautifully photographed, absolutely shapeless report on the British naval tactics that led to the scuttling of the famed German raider."[2]

The development of the relationship between Dove (Bernard Lee) and Langsdorff (Peter Finch) occupies the first half of the film, as the British captain is taken prisoner, still protesting that his ship was within neutral waters. Brought before Langsdorff, he continues his protestations and is immediately taken aback by the response. Although he concedes that neither man will agree on whether the ship was safely in neutral waters, Langsdorff instead offers a compromise, providing the British captain with a receipt for the loss of his ship. Langsdorff will prove to be a reluctant soldier, not enjoying sending ships to the bottom of the sea and accepting Dove as his equal, taking him into his confidence about the *Graf Spree's* mission and providing him access to the ship. The film is most successful in presenting the spectacle subjectively as we become caught up in the events that are overwhelming Dove. He stands on a small lifeboat that carries him toward the German ship, passing through the black smoke emitted from the wreckage of his own ship. The small boat is lifted from the sea and lowered into the bowels of the *Graf Spree*, the giant doors closing behind it, engulfing him in darkness. Dove obviously relishes the opportunity to explore the ship, looking in obvious admiration when the *Graf Spree* receives the transfer of fuel from another ship, as the waves violently buffet the two crafts and supplies are passed over on a rope. When other British prisoners are transferred aboard the *Graf Spree*, there is a sense that Dove yearns for the independent status provided to him by Langsdorff. The first act ends with the British prisoners wondering whether the British can ever overtake the faster, more power-ful German ship.

The friendship between Dove and Langsdorff is the only relationship that occurs in the film; once this thread is lost, the film becomes simply a spectacle, albeit a stunning one. If the film is atypical of the Archers' work, it is that its focus is on not an individual but an event. The sea battle is breathtak-ing, but the film fails when the action gives way to conversa-tion, Pressburger's ear for dialogue no longer in evidence. Most embarrassing are the scenes below deck involving the British prisoners, which remind one of the television show *Hogan's Heroes*, even with the constantly ridiculed German sergeant. The Archers attempt to maintain the central thread of Dove and Langsdorff, but, once the *Graf Spree* enters the Port of Montevideo, the British captain becomes merely a spectator from shore. Only the destruction of the *Graf Spree*, its hull bursting into flames against the setting sun, can provide one more startling, hypnotic image. Dove meets with Langsdorff one more time, as the German captain seeks refuge on another ship, his own still exploding in the distance. Langsdorff is vis-ibly strained, haunted by the loss of his ship and his own feel-ing of guilt over having put his ship in jeopardy. Although his ship could have outrun the British pursuers, he had chosen to engage them and in the end missed his opportunity to escape. What could have been a poignant ending is now anticlimatic.

Powell was so intrigued by the story that he wrote his second book, an account of the events surrounding the *Graf Spree* entitled *Death in the South Atlantic*. It is more successful than the film because it is denser, with Powell able to juxtapose the facts with the personal stories of the participants. In the preface, Powell expressed his reason for undertaking the project: "I began to wish this varied and unique experience could be preserved in some more permanent shape than a film. I have two sons. I wanted them to read this story and possess it. I wanted unborn boys and girls to pick it up one day and read it and absorb it into their experience. A film can entertain millions, but it can seldom be possessed by them. A book can; and that is why I have written this book."[3] Nearly forty years later, *The Battle of the River Plate* is available on videotape for all to view and possess.

Just as the Archers began their partnership with a film set in an occupied country, so too would they end it. They had first begun researching the project in 1951, with Pressburger having read William C. Moss's book *Ill Met by Moonlight*, his account of the kidnapping of a German general on Crete. Powell began location work on Crete and immediately fell in love with the island and its people. He hoped that Pressburger would make the Cretans central to the script.

> I proposed to open with the German paradrop on the island: hundreds of armed paratroopers turning the sky black like a crowd of locusts, while the islanders fight and die in defence of their homes and families. He had heard my stories about Xan Fielding and Paddy Leigh-Fermor, and had listened to my pleas for at least three or four subplots, love stories or murders, to criss-cross in and out of the main plot of the kidnapping of the German General. An action film like this needed to have big names and daring stunt men, and the best part would be the German General; the more formidable he was, the greater glory for his kidnappers—and then he would have to make several attempts to escape and nearly succeed.[4]

Film producers were cautious about films set in a war still so fresh in everyone's mind, and the project, like many in which the Archers were involved at the time, seemed destined to become little more than a treatment. After the commercial success of *The Battle of the River Plate*, however, the Archers were able to interest Rank in the project, although the contract they received reflected their lack of influence in the British cinema. Their salary was their lowest since the mid-forties, when they were just establishing their prominence. Powell's initial enthusiasm for the project was dampened by the script that Pressburger presented, which he recognized as a poor imitation of their previous films. He singled out the ending, as the kidnappers return to the German general the belongings that he left along the way in hopes of giving away their location. This act causes him finally to accept them as professional soldiers, but it reminded Powell too much of *Contraband*, in which the British return to the Danish captain the watch he had lost. The final script is even more of a patchwork of their previous films, in particular *One of Our Aircraft Is Missing*. Powell wanted a romantic interest added to the story, despite the fact that no such relationship existed in the real story, but then much of the story was of Pressburger's own creation.

Powell was also disappointed in the casting of the film. He envisioned Orson Welles, James Mason, and Stewart Granger in the lead roles but in the end would have to settle for Dirk Bogarde and the little known David Oxley as the two leaders of the unit. The part of the general, which Powell thought needed someone of the stature of the late Conrad Veidt, fell to Marius Goring. He lacked the intensity required of the role, adding to the difficulties, which Powell only aggravated in his decision related to the location work. Despite his infatuation with Crete, Powell was unable to film on the island, the instability of the government at the time making such a proposition risky. Instead, the location work would be completed in the Alps Maritimes, near a hotel that Powell owned. Powell's lack of interest in the film continued even as filming began, and he was often absent from the set or, when he was available, kept to himself. Pressburger was also in attendance, but he and Powell communicated little; the partnership which had once seemed based on intuition, now was grounded in silence. The Archers had reached their peak with *The Tales of Hoffmann*, and the epilogue that followed did little to enhance their reputation. "To put it squarely, this dawdling directed entry lacks genuine suspense, wartime urgency and genuine humor, while straining frightfully hard for chuckles all way."[5] Another reviewer agrees: "One waits in vain for some of the physical excitement which was communicated in W. Stanley Moss's book; but the Powell and Pressburger team shows little confidence in the potentialities of the battle of wits between kidnappers and their distinguished quarry."[6]

American Captain W. Stanley Moss (Oxley) travels to Crete, where he is to meet up with Major Paddy Leigh Fermor (Bogarde), a prominent figure in the Cretan underground. Their mission is to kidnap General Karl Kreipe (Goring), the German in charge of the occupying army. As the general makes his way from the headquarters, his staff car is stopped by Moss and Paddy, who are disguised as German MPs. Confiscating the car and with the general safely held down by two members of the Cretan underground, Moss and Paddy successfully pass through the various checkpoints along the way. The German army discovers Kreipe's disappearance and begins an intensive search as the kidnappers take to the hills of Crete. The Cretans receive word that the cave to which they have taken the general is no longer safe, but, after making their way down the treacherous terrain in the darkness, they discover the message has been misinterpreted. They also learn that their rendezvous ship is to arrive in a few days' time, forcing them to travel even in daylight.

The men eventually make their way to the rendezvous site, only to find a German patrol encamped on the beach. Having little respect for the Cretan population, Kreipe attempts to trick a young boy into giving away the group's location, providing him with German coinage with which to buy highly coveted German boots. As the boy makes his way to the camp below, Kreipe confidently tells the group of his subterfuge, but, as the men look down, the boy instead leads the Germans away from the beach. Paddy had discovered the general's plan and used it to his advantage, having the boy escort the Germans into an ambush. Having finally reached the beach, the men are faced with one more hurdle: to signal the ship in Morse Code when, in fact, no one knows how. Only the timely arrival of the leader of the Cretan underground, who does know the code, manages to get Paddy and Moss onto the ship along with their captive. As the ship makes its way to Egypt, they return to the general the personal effects he had left behind as clues for his pursuers. Impressed by their resourcefulness, he characterizes them as professionals, having once dismissed them as amateur soldiers.

Viewing the film some thirty years after its completion, Powell was "surprised by how bad the film was. It wasn't entertainment, it was like a Ministry of Information documentary film."[7] There is little to identify this as the work of the Archers, and it is conceivable any of a number of directors could have directed this project with little change in style. In fact, the Archers had become something neither man had ever been interested in: documentarists, albeit ones willing to play fast and loose with the facts. More important, the production qualities that had highlighted the Archers' work are also noticeably absent. Hein Heckroth's noninvolvement on the last film was not as noticeable, for there was little need for a production designer of his stature; a more innovative cinematographer was required. Despite their affection for color, the Archers had created many stunning achievements in black and white (witness *A Canterbury Tale* and *I Know Where I'm Going*), but this is not the case with this film. Here the darkness is designed to amplify the confusion of the protagonists, leaving them and the audience unaware as to where the Germans are, but, because the pursuers are not even in the vicinity of the kidnappers, this approach comes across as subterfuge.

The film opens with a quote from Homer's *The Odyssey*, as a narrator informs us that in "1944, three thousand years after Homer's time, Crete was fighting another Homeric battle, this time against occupying Germans." These words, along with the quotation, echo the prologue of *A Canterbury Tale*, but whereas the earlier film is imbued with the spirit of Chaucer, this film does not call to mind Homer's epic struggle. Neither the story nor the characters are epic; in fact, the story is almost too slight for the telling. Moss's account is of a long journey where the chief obstacles were the landscape, the insects and a German general who seemed almost conciliatory in defeat. Although the abduction of the German was certainly daring, the kidnappers ran into few difficulties, and the Archers were forced to construct their own version of the raid. The ending, in particular, bears little relation to the facts, with the Archers having their party arriving at the beach where they are to rendezvous with their ship, only to find a German patrol already encamped there. When not content with creating their own version of events, the Archers deceive the audience by building up suspense only to reveal at the last moment that nothing in fact is happening. Making their way in the darkness, the Cretans realize that they are being followed and wait for a German patrol, only to be overtaken by a herd of sheep that is following their donkey.

With the dissolution of the partnership, Powell and Pressburger were finally allowed to establish their own identities, only to discover that life on their own was not so easy. Pressburger had little desire to direct again, the failure of *Twice upon a Time* still fresh in his mind. The reasons for the failure, however, seemed lost on him, for *A Miracle in Soho*, which he wrote and produced, was equally saccharine. Powell was having similar difficulty with his next film. He had gone to Spain to shoot another ballet film, but it was to have little relation to the success of *The Red Shoes*. "*Honeymoon* was not a lucky picture. In everything I did or proposed to do I was frustrated, or nearly so."[8]

The film received only a limited release, and viewing it today is difficult. The reviewer for *Monthly Film Bulletin* gives the most extensive synopsis of the film:

> Kit Kelly, a wealthy Australian farmer, arrives in Spain with his beautiful bride, Anna, for a motoring honeymoon. Stopping at a wayside cafe, they watch a dancing display and meet Antonio, who is on the look-out for talent for his ballet company. Anotonio's interest in Anna increases when he discovers that she was a famous ballerina before her marriage, and his efforts to interest her in his new production make Kit jealous and morose. Antonio takes Anna to some of the favorite tourist spots and tells her the story of "The Lovers of Tereuel," which has provided the subject for his ballet. Tired of his rival's attentions to her, Kit accuses Anna of making a fool of herself: shortly afterwards Anna is taken ill. In her delirium she dreams of Antonio's ballet, at the tragic climax of which she is luckily awakened by Kit. They are reconciled. While recuperating in hospital Anna is visited by Antonio, who hints cheerfully that he will be looking out for her during his coming world tour.[9]

The reviewer for *Monthly Film Bulletin* thought that *Honeymoon* "confirms the recent decline of its director. Basically, the film is an enormous travel poster of the most blatant kind, full of fast cars, sumptuous hotels, elegant dresses, flowing money and lovely scenery with never a spot of dirt or a hint of discontent to cloud its beautiful vision,"[10] The film does have its defenders, however. "*Honeymoon* provides greater pleasure. In its plot premise—a ballerina torn between her husband and a male ballet mentor—the piece is an agreeable if minor echo of *The Red Shoes*. But the resemblance extends to Powell's characteristic use of colour harmonies, as well as to the atmospheric ballet world evocation."[11]

17

The Morbid Urge to Gaze

For too long the misconception has persisted that *Peeping Tom* and the critical reception it received effectively ended Michael Powell's film career. Powell had often been depicted as an outsider in the English cinema (an image that he worked to sustain), and the reaction he received on this film seemed to be the logical consequence, that in breaking so much with the mainstream cinema, Powell had in effect committed cinematic suicide. This attempt to turn Powell into a martyr is not born out by the reality of the situation. He was to continue directing after the film's release. One of the benefits of the second volume of his autobiography is his detailing of a number of projects, which for various reasons never came to fruition and none of which are related to *Peeping Tom*. Powell's difficulties mirrored those of many of the great directors of his generation, all of whom struggled to find financing in England. Sir Carol Reed directed but three films in this same period, none of them in Britain, while Anthony Asquith was only slightly more productive with six films, but his films received mostly international financing. The most successful director of this time was David Lean, but the three films he made in the sixties were international productions, with none of them set in his native country.

The British cinema was again facing a crossroads, for television had cut drastically into its audience. In 1954, 24.5 million people went to movies; in 1960, it was only 10 million. Large British and American coproductions such as *The Bridge*

over the River Kwai were commercially and critically successful, but they hardly reflected British society. Many young film
critics, several writing for the magazine *Sequence*, had already
become disillusioned with the mainstream cinema and channeled their frustration into a documentary movement dubbed
the Free Cinema. Karel Reisz and Lindsay Anderson were the
main proponents of the movement, and the success of their
documentaries occurred at the same time that a new social
realism was taking place in English novels and theaters. By
1961, this conviction resulted in a British New Wave, often
dubbed Kitchen Sink realism for the working class milieu that
served as the backdrop for their stories, that was created by
the same directors who had worked in the Free Cinema.
Reisz's *Saturday Night and Sunday Morning* was the most
commercially successful of these films and is, in fact, one of
the British cinema's most successful films since the thirties.
The movement would not last long, and today many of the
films seem archaic; but once more an emphasis was put on
realism, and the nearly universal condemnation by the mainstream press of *Peeping Tom* reflected this. The truth is, Powell could have released *The Red Shoes* at this time in British
cinema history and fared little better.

It was in this environment that Powell began to look for
his next project, his first British film in twenty years for which
he would receive sole directorial credit. He first labored on a
film biography of Sigmund Freud, collaborating with Leo Marks,
a young writer who had once been a code specialist in the
army. Powell and Marks had completed their research and were
in the midst of writing their script when John Huston's film of
the same subject was announced. Their project no longer seeming viable, Marks suggested an original idea, but one related to
psychology, of a murderer who films his victims as they die.
Powell was intrigued by the story and began working with
Marks "in the same way that I have always worked with Pressburger; that is to say, we discussed a sequence together and
at times, I would say to him that as a director, I didn't see
things in the same way: as a matter of fact, sometimes we had
a very precise idea of what we wanted to capture, but sometimes only an image which we hoped to develop, like in a sym-
phony. There was much more dialogue in the first screenplay
than in the final version."[1]

Despite the limited budget required for the film (it would come in at just under 125,000 pounds), Powell had difficulty finding a backer, with Rank being among the first to pass on the project. Eventually the National Film Finance Corporation provided the funding, although it was to be filmed at Rank's studio. Powell approached Laurence Harvey about the lead role, but Harvey had just gained attention for his work on *Room at the Top* and was preparing to leave for Hollywood. Instead, Powell found his actor while attending a party. Mark Boehm was the son of the famous conductor, Karl, and had already worked in a pair of films when Powell chose him for the role of Mark Lewis. The lead actress would also have a famous father, for Anna Massey was the daughter of Powell's longtime friend Raymond. The cast would be filled out with similar unfamiliar names, with two obvious exceptions. Moira Shearer was in the midst of pursuing an acting career and was signed for a small, critical role. For Lewis's father, Powell himself essayed the role, having already appeared in a number of his earlier films. These were to be slightly more substantial than Hitchcock's famous cameos, for he was the radio operator in *One of Our Aircraft Is Missing* who announced the *B For Bertie* delay, and in *The Edge of the World*, he was the yachtsman who had brought Andrew back to the island. This was his most significant portrayal, made even more personal by his use of his own son Columba to portray the young Mark.

The responses to the film have already been well documented in Ian Christie's work and Powell's autobiography where he reprints them as if they were a badge of honor. Yet, one must remember that Britain at this time had few antecedents in the horror genre, the obvious exception being the movies produced by Hammer Films. Although these films were commercially successful, they were all but ignored by critics. More meaningfully, *Peeping Tom* was a film that openly challenged viewers, and the response of the critics reflected this. Sometimes the reviewers themselves had conflicting feelings about the film. In *Films and Filming*, the reviewer called it a "brilliantly made film" but later commented on the "creative dishonesty of *Peeping Tom* that reflects the sickness of much Western cinema."[2] For others it was merely an extension of the eccentricities that had run throughout the Archers' films. "Setting such immediate comparisons to one side, it must be admitted that Michael Powell's new film appears to be part of a logical progression from the straightforward brutalities of *49th Parallel* through the more sophisticated activities of the Eric Portman character in *A Canterbury Tale* who was given to putting glue into the hair of the Kentish maidens, and through the disagreeable final scenes of *The Red Shoes*."[3]

Yet, not all of the critics came out against the film, although even many of these found the subject distasteful. "It is an uncomfortable theme, yet one which is fraught with suspense. That expert movie-maker has invested it with a maximum of cinema excellence and all the quality of which he is capable."[4] The French were among the first to recognize the film for what it was: "a delicately nuanced psychological study of an authentic film auteur, who pushes a particular conception of the direction of actors to its limits. For voyeurism alone is not enough to explain the character of Lewis: he is also, and at one and the same time, a sadistic film-maker and murderer, with these different facets forming a coherent whole."[5]

Peeping Tom, however, remains a film over which critics are still divided. "'*Peeping Tom's* rediscovery, I fear, tells us more about fads in film criticism than it does about art. Only someone madly obsessed with being the first to hail a new auteur, which is always a nice way of calling attention to oneself, could spend the time needed to find genius in the erratic works of Mr. Powell."[6] Today the film is among the most analyzed films in recent memory, by not only feminist critics but also those interested in its psychological implications and its reflection on cinema itself.

At times Powell attempted to distance himself from the primary figure of the film, crediting the film's success to Marks, but there can be little doubt that it is among his most personal projects. Voyeurism had been a central motif to his career, dating back to *The Thief of Bagdad*, and the central character bears an obvious relation to Lermontov and Hoffmann. In addition to essaying a major role in the film and using his son, Powell also incorporated many references to his previous works, at one point filming on the very location where his directorial career began. The alleyway that leads to the tobacco shop had been among the locations used in *Two Crowded Hours*. Mark provides Helen with a dragonfly pin, bringing to mind the ballet that opens *The Tales of Hoffmann*, while the use of Moira

Shearer and Miles Malleson recalls earlier triumphs. The producer featured in *Peeping Tom* is obviously modeled after John
Davis, with whom he had come into so much conflict at Rank.
It was also a technical challenge, allowing him to experiment
with not only the images but also the soundtrack, incorporating the sound of a clock's ticking in many sequences and even
accentuating the sound of the protagonist's heart to demonstrate his anxiety.

Most important, the film allowed Powell to comment on the
very medium in which he was working. Christian Metz fashioned the term *mise en abyme* to refer to films that looked back
on themselves, the most obvious examples being the early films
created in the French New Wave. More than one reviewer credited Powell's film as being the only English heir to this movement, because the studio settings allow him to examine his
vocation, and the central premise is of a character who fancies
himself a film director ("I hope to be a director very soon").
"*Peeping Tom* is a very tender film, a very nice one," according
to Powell. "Almost a romantic film. I was immediately fascinated by the idea: I felt very close to the hero, who is an 'abso-
lute' director, someone who approaches life like a director, who
is conscious of and suffers from it. He is a technician of emotion. And I am someone who is thrilled by technique, always
mentally editing the scene in front of me in the street, so I
was able to share his anguish."[7] Powell's assessment not withstanding, the film remains an uncomfortable experience, as it
implicates the viewer in the proceedings and concludes with
no one emerging unscathed. Certainly many of the Archers'
films had pessimistic endings, as in the case of *The Red Shoes*
and *The Tales of Hoffmann*, but this film leaves us with no
antagonist with which to lay blame. In fact, the antagonist here
has died long before the story is even begun.

A single eye in extreme close-up, opening and looking into
the camera, is the first image of the film but also a leitmotif of
Powell's career, from the *Thief of Bagdad* on through his association with Pressburger. When one recalls close-ups from these
films, it is often of a character looking off at someone; Jaffar's
piercing eyes as he begins to hypnotize the princess; Vickie
pausing momentarily during her performance and catching sight
of Lermontov in the audience; Sister Ruth, bathed in sweat, as
she contrives to murder Sister Clodagh; Lindorff lifting an eye-

brow in anticipation as Hoffmann begins to recount one of his
stories. These are but a few examples, chosen at random, from
an oeuvre dominated by the power of gazing. *Peeping Tom*, by
its very title, has already alerted us that voyeurism will be the
focus of our attention.

From the eye, Powell cuts to the object of the stare, a street
scene at night where a young woman stands on the sidewalk,
looking into a shop window. Her manner and appearance identify her as a prostitute, but the scene looks more like a studio
setting than an actual English street. It will later be duplicated
in a backdrop with which Mark will photograph a model. A
man enters the frame, his back to us, and his whistling recalls
the child murderer in Fritz Lang's *M*. He too will prove to be a
murderer, but he is also a director, as a cut to a camera hidden in his overcoat indicates. Once again Powell cuts from the
mechanism of vision to the subject being viewed, but the image is divided into quadrants by the camera. Already the camera seems united with the protagonist, and Powell's
remembrance of the first time he picked up a camera could
also be Mark's: "My eye became a lens, my brain a machine
for measuring movement at different speeds. I discovered the
beauty of image. Suddenly I discovered that all these new elements would combine to obey me. I was amazed."[8]

The camera and the man move in on the woman, who takes
no notice of him until he is almost upon her. As she turns to
face the camera in close-up, she speaks the first words of the
film: "It'll be two quid." Behind her is the window through
which she had been looking, and in it is a prediction of her
fate, for the shop window includes the disembodied parts of
mannequins. Although no response is given, the woman turns
and walks off, passing under an archway as the camera tracks
after her. As the woman begins to put her key into a door, the
camera pans down as the man examines a film box before discarding it into the trash. That the man is wearing no gloves
and leaves a clue so close to the scene of the crime announces
his desire to be caught. The two proceed up a staircase as an
old woman comes down, giving a look of contempt as she
brushes past the camera. On entering the prostitute's flat, the
camera impassively observes the woman as she begins to undress. She seems oblivious to the man's presence, only looking
up after his hand passes across the camera, inducing a click-

ing sound. Her look of puzzlement turns to one of apprehension as the camera begins to advance on the woman, who pulls back, her eyes widening. The camera moves in tightly as her mouth opens to let out a scream, and there is an abrupt cut to a projector as the credits are finally played. What it is that has caused her so much alarm will be the film's MacGuffin.

From production we now move to postproduction as the previous sequence is screened. The man sits in front of the screen, his back still to us, and like the sequence aboard the aircraft carrier in *The Volunteer*, the audience finds itself in an unusual position, our attention divided between what is on screen and what the spectator is doing. In inspecting the footage being screened, we notice that details have been omitted, such as the discarding of the film container. That the film being screened lacks a soundtrack and is in black and white relates it to a silent film; this point is reinforced by Brian Easdale's score, which is only piano music. At the moment of her murder, as the woman's face is in extreme close-up, the man falls back into his chair, an action that some have related to a sexual climax. "Mark's first orgasm in the film occurs as he is projecting his movie of a whore's murder; his ejaculation coincides with the arrival of Michael Powell's directorial credit on the film which encloses Mark's film."[9]

This relating of the murders to a sexual act would be echoed by many feminist critics, but this view is based on the supposition that Mark is performing a cinematic rape, when in fact he has yet to develop a sexual identity. Emotionally, he is still a preadolescent, dominated by the spirit of his father. In fact, his identity remains sublimated by his camera, his features not being revealed until the next sequence when he is filming the police investigation of the murder. A policeman asks him what newspaper he represents, and, in the first of many heavily coded statements, he replies, "The Observer." In filming the investigation, Mark completes the final action of the murder, for, as William Johnson has discerned, each murder is divided into three acts: the actual murder, the screening of the murder, and finally follow-up filming of the investigation. Only in the last murder, when the police are moving in, is Mark unable to complete all of the phases.

Incorporated into the film's diegesis will be two documentaries, the one being created by Mark and a second one already completed by his late father. This allows Powell to satirize the documentary movement with which he had so often been at odds, for both men initiate the events that they film while controlling their subjects, thus negating their role of the passive observer. For his own documentary, however, Mark is both a spectator and a participant, and Powell's presentation of the opening implicates the viewer also into both roles. Ironically, the objective of Mark's film is not only to record the women's murder but also to force them to serve as witness to their own deaths by the use of a mirror. "I made them watch their own deaths and if death has a face they saw that too," he says.

The first murder is seemingly executed indiscriminately (although his choice of his victim fulfills a particular scheme), but the two that follow will be drawn directly from Mark's sphere. In addition to his work on his documentary, Mark also works as the photographer of nude models and as a focus puller for a movie studio. The photographing of the nude models conjures up an image of a voyeur, but his manner belies this impression, for he goes about his work impassionately. As he arranges the shoot, he seems oblivious to the model, Milly (Pamela Green), and even she realizes that he is more comfortable with his camera. "What do you have under there, a girlfriend?" she wonders as he puts his head beneath the camera's covering. Later Mark's second victim will comment on his ease with his camera. "You're so at home with that camera. You make me feel at home too. You have it in you, boy." Even the woman he comes to fall in love with will worry that the camera has become an "extra limb."

The camera serves to define Mark's personality as evidenced when he meets Milly's companion, Lorraine (Susan Travers), a model who until the point of their introduction had stood at the window in profile. She turns to reveal a face grossly disfigured by a harelip, her features nearly duplicating the distorted image of the woman in the mirror of his camera. As she tells him that it is her "first time," referring to her modeling, he has become disconcerted, reaching for the film camera with which he is filming his documentary. He moves in on her, transfixed by her appearance; unconscious of his surroundings, Mark whispers that it is his "first time, too," his words relating it more to a sexual act than one of filming. "Don't be shy. With me it's my first time too. In front of eyes like, eyes so full of . . . " If the sentence is left incomplete, the absent word will prove to be *fear*, the subject of both his father's and his own documentary.

The film's diegesis is of Powell's own profession, for Mark's final vocation, a focus puller in a film studio, allows the director his greatest opportunity at self-reflexivity. The head of the studio, Don Jarvis (Michael Goodliffe), is patterned after John Davis, who is introduced dictating a memo on cost control, advising his directors that if "you can see it and hear it, the first take's OK." Not only will Mark ignore this precept, continuing to kill as he searches for the perfect shot, but so too will the director on the production Mark is working. The shot is of the actress fainting, but the marker announces this as the forty-ninth take. In another irony of the film, the director, Arthur Baden, is portrayed by Esmond Knight, who by this time was legally blind. Sitting off to the side is the stand-in for the actress, Vivian (Moira Shearer), patiently waiting, for her work on not only this film, but also Mark's.

Although many critics identify the thesis of Mark's film as the murder of young woman, it is, in fact, an examination of a murderer, the conclusion to the film begun by his father. What Mark intends to be the climax of the film will be the solving of the crime by the police, and toward this end he gradually draws his divergent worlds together, by committing murders at the film studio and later at the newsdealer shop where he photographs the models. The murder of Vivian is the longest sequence of the film and in many respects the most shocking. Just as Hitchcock's killing of Janet Leigh in *Psycho* was an unheard of act, so too would be the murder of an actress of nearly equal stature, Moira Shearer. Whereas Leigh's murder is shocking for its unexpectedness, the viewer is all too aware of what Shearer's fate is to be, so that our discomfort develops even as she serves as his accomplice. For the first time in the film, Powell cuts away from Mark to focus on another character, as Vivian hides from the studio guards after hours. She makes her way into a set calling out Mark's name, but he announces his presence first with a spotlight that shines on her. When Mark finally emerges, he is confident that they will not be disturbed as he has turned on the red light, which signifies that filming is in progress. The red light also calls to mind not only the prostitute but also Mark's secret chamber. That this act could result in his being found out does not matter to him at this point, only that he is undisturbed. "The difference is a perfect image. I've waited a long time for this. What does it matter? I stand to lose nothing." The title of the film on which they are working, *The Walls Are Closing In*, is shown, foretelling Mark's own destiny.

As the title suggests, Mark is more than just a cinephile, for he is compelled to watch others, most often through the lens of his camera. As he returns home, he instinctively looks through the window of the downstairs tenant, who is in the midst of celebrating her birthday. The frame of the window duplicates the crosshairs of his cameras, as he is also the subject of another's gaze. The celebrants have noticed the encroachment, but Mark is unconscious of the fact that he is now the subject of their attention. When he does notice, he hurries off, but Helen Stephens (Massey), instead of being perturbed by the intrusion, invites Mark to join the party. He demurs, escaping to the safety of his screening room. As he takes his place at his projector, Helen knocks at the door, bringing with her a piece of her cake. His unfamiliarity with societal customs is evident as he awkwardly invites her in, then attempts to offer her something to drink, realizing too late that all he has is milk.

Helen will appear to offer Mark a reprieve from his deadly vocation, but in fact she will be drawn into it, as he takes her through the curtains that separate his living quarters from his laboratory. She muses that it is "so completely unexpected," the room resembling a dark cave, even to the sound of water dripping. On the shelves is an assortment of cameras; in the cabinets are reels of films, one of which Mark takes out. Having first considered showing Helen the footage involving the murder, he instead pulls out one of his childhood, but it will be equally as disturbing. The footage of the young Mark introduces the second documentary contained in the film and provides the foundation for Mark's psychosis. A. N. Lewis (Powell), a noted psychologist, had conducted experiments on his young son of which he kept a record on film and that Mark now screens for her. The first image of the young Mark is as he sits on a fence, and his father pans to what he is watching, a young couple kissing on a park bench, thus relating his gaze to voyeurism. The father holds the image until even Helen is disturbed by the invasion of privacy. "What a strange thing for your father to photograph," she wonders, but she continues watching, already drawn into Mark's world.

Helen's discomfort will only increase as she views the young Mark being awakened by a bright light, then pulling back in terror as a lizard crawls up his bed. This action duplicates exactly that of the prostitute in the first sequence, and Mark takes out his camera to film Helen's reaction to the screening. She makes him shut off the camera, but he holds tightly to it, caressing it as he hears his father's voice, not on the screen but in his mind. She asks him to explain what it all means—"I like to understand what I'm being shown"—ignoring his request for her to leave. Even more disconcerting is the father's footage of Mark visiting his dying mother. According to Kaja Silverman, "not only does Dr. Lewis orchestrate the crises, but these crises are all key moments within the Oedipal narrative: the castration threat, the primal scene, the loss of the mother, and access to the paternal legacy, here represented by the gift of a camera."[10] Mark speeds up the film, racing through his mother's funeral and burial, only returning to normal speed when his stepmother is introduced, emerging from the sea clad in a bikini.

The image of the stepmother provides if not the motivation for Mark's killing, at least the reasoning behind the victims whom he chooses, for in some manner all relate to her. The stepmother, Successa (Margaret Neal), holds the camera as the father presents Mark with his first camera on the eve of his honeymoon. The timing is significant; having only recently lost his mother, he must now face the loss of his father, for even when the elder Lewis returns, his attention will be divided between his experiments and his nubile young wife. Mark's first action on receiving the camera, after looking through the viewfinder, is to turn the camera on his stepmother, thus presenting himself with the first image of his own documentary. The prostitute who is his first victim bears a physical resemblance to the woman, as will Milly. In fact, it is Milly whom the woman most resembles and Mark's earlier remark when he photographs her to "look at the sea," relates to the first images of Successa, emerging from the sea. Vivian does not physically resemble Mark's stepmother, but at one point she takes a place behind a camera, duplicating Successa's act of photographing Mark as he had photographed her. She is in reality only living out the role of a stand-in once more, while her death also serves as the mechanism that draws the police ever closer to Mark.

Despite the disturbing undertone to their first meeting, Helen will return and begin the process of socializing Mark. She will begin to fill the void left by his mother, as he had unconsciously anticipated when he put his hand on her shoulder while the footage of the mother is introduced. Mark has assumed his father's legacy, even to living in his study, his many publications reverently aligned on the bookshelf. Even his position as a focus puller could serve as a description of his father's work as a psychiatrist, and one of Dr. Lewis's colleagues, on meeting Mark, muses that he "has his father's eyes." Helen at first attempts to draw him away from his vocation, convincing him to leave behind his camera on their first date, its absence apparent when he comes across a couple kissing and unconsciously reaches for it. Again he loses himself in his gaze, making the couple aware of his presence, and it is only the intervention of Helen that draws him away. Their date would seem to provide an interlude for Mark, but Powell superimposes the montage of their date with images of his laboratory, while the soundtrack is dominated by the sound of his developing timer. Mark's fate is predetermined; whereas Susan could ultimately save Sammy Rice in *A Small Back Room*, Helen's intervention in Mark's life is too late, something even he realizes.

Even Helen inadvertently involves herself in Mark's struggle as she tells him of her own pet project, the writing of a children's book. Its title, *The Magic Camera*, relates it to Mark's own career, and its story of a camera whose photographs reveal the child in the adult also comments on his documentary. Although she is only asking him what technique would be best, he quickly offers to take the photographs for her. "There are some things I do for nothing," and Boehm's reading of this line gives it a haunting quality. It also refers to his primary vocation, the documentary for which he is working independently.

As Mark anticipated, the murder of Vivian brings the police directly to him, and even they are drawn into the world of the cinema. Not only are they unwitting participants in Mark's documentary, but they also emerge as amateur cinephiles. One detective wants to stop at his home on his way to investigate Vivian's murder to pick up his autograph book, while another invokes a line well known to audiences, "I tawt I taw a putty tat." when Mark nearly gives himself away while filming their investigation. In their inquiry, the police stand around the production unit, as engrossed in what is happening with the actress and her exasperated director as they are in searching for a murderer. They take little notice of Mark's activities as he films them, only asking that the footage does not appear in the local cinema, while another muses that he is being given a "screen test." They also serve as the antagonists for Mark's documentary, as evidenced by a conversation he has with a fellow technician, who has asked him why he is filming the investigation.

"It will complete a documentary."
"Documentary? What's it about?"
"Hmm."
"What's it about?"
"I'd rather not tell you until it's finished. And it will be soon."
"Suppose they catch you" [referring to his filming of them].
"Oh, they will. They look very efficient."
"Don't you mind."
"No."
"Mark, are you crazy?"
"Yes [Mark laughs]. Do you think they'll notice?"

The police will be the mechanism by which Mark is found out, but Helen's mother serves as his conscience. The editing constantly relates them, as when her pouring of a glass of whiskey segues into that of him pouring his developing fluid. Even before they have been introduced, Mrs. Stephens (Maxine Audley) is uneasy about Mark, and, when they meet, he senses her distrust. Whereas he is related to the sense of sight, her world is made up only of sound, yet the two prove to have much in common. She tells him that her life has been destroyed by a doctor whom she had trusted, thus making her blind, while Mark had been betrayed by his father, a psychiatrist. She is able to move easily around his room, admitting that she visits this "room every night. The blind always live in the room they live under." Mark has arrived home from his date with Helen and takes his place at his projector, only to be startled by a sound from the darkness. Turning his light in that direction, he finds Mrs. Stephens standing against the wall, her cane in her hand, which she holds out in front of her, the pointed tip recalling the blade of Mark's camera. She asks him to take her to his "cinema," and he obliges as the images of Vivian's death are being played (providing a startling effect when the image of Vivian is superimposed on his suit, distorting her appearance into that of a skull). He forgets Mrs. Stephens's presence and he lunges at the screen in anguish, as he cries that "the light fades too soon."

One of the most haunting elements of the film is the matter-of-factness with which Mark approaches his murder, but here his disappointment over the inferior quality of the footage results in a desperate attempt to make Mrs. Stephens his next victim. He turns the camera on her, and, although she cannot see the blade, the heat from the lamp causes her to pull back, dropping her cane in the process. She is framed by the white screen on which he has just viewed his footage, but he regains his composure and, after turning off the camera, hands her back her "eyes," her cane. Once more having the advantage, she advances on him, making her way easily about the room, while he stumbles backward. Entering into the next room, she walks to the door, commenting ironically that "all this filming isn't healthy." She urges him to seek help and, until he does, forbids him from seeing Helen, not realizing that her daughter is his only hope to find salvation. He reluctantly agrees. After walking her down the stairs, she begins to feel his face. He recognizes the action as her attempt to "photograph" him, and, as Laura Mulvey points out, in a film noticeably lacking in eroticism, there is a sensual quality to this encounter.[11]

The introduction of Helen and her mother into Mark's life arrives too late to save him, as he learns when he seeks the advice of a psychiatrist whom the police have stationed on the production unit. The man recognizes Mark's father and during the conversation is more interested in obtaining access to his colleague's papers than in helping Mark overcome his disorder, which he diagnosis as "scopophilia. The morbid urge to gaze." His diagnosis that a cure could take years of therapy discourages Mark, and he endeavors to complete the work at hand, calling the newsdealer shop to set up an appointment with Milly. When he arrives, his employer is closing up and hands Mark the key with which to lock up, not realizing the implications of this act. Keys are a recurring motif of the film, serving as a signifier for sexual maturity. On her twenty-first birthday, Helen is presented with a large facsimile of one, the reference to her sexuality not lost on her as she playfully chases the benefactor. Mark also speaks of keys, telling Helen that he has no locks in his apartments because his father never trusted him with keys. When Helen is about to visit Mark, her mother advises her to take along her key, also phrasing it in sexual terms. "Mine needs oiling, yours needs exercise." Thus, as Mark is presented with a key he cannot help but smile at the implications, even as he leaves from the murder scene, he pauses to contemplate it before dropping it in the mail slot.

The murder of Milly is the climax of Mark's film, but, like the duel in *The Life and Death of Colonel Blimp*, it occurs off-camera. Likewise, as the duel is significant for bringing together Theo and Clive, this murder serves to bring together the police and Mark. From the beginning, Mark had encouraged the police's involvement, even handing to them the murder weapon at one point (the movie camera), but he had not counted on his involvement with Helen. He returns to his apartment to wait for their anticipated arrival, only to find Helen already there. She had come to his apartment to present him with a copy of her book, with the inscription "from one Magic camera which needs the help of another." After setting it beside his projector, she finds herself unable to resist its temptation and turns it on, thus uncovering Mark's hidden vocation, for the footage is of Vivian's murder. She is in the midst of absorbing the horror when he comes in, and even then she attempts to reject what her eyes have witnessed. In contrast, he is more concerned with avoiding her gaze, fearful of his own reaction to her emotions. "You'll be safe as long as I can't see you frightened." He admits to her that this had been his father's laboratory also and turns on the tape recorder with which he can monitor all of the rooms, adding one more layer to the film. She continues to urge him to divulge how he murdered the young women. "Show me or I'll remain frightened the rest of my life," she tells him, not realizing her request will lead to an even greater terror. Taking out his camera, he finally reveals

what to now has been kept from the audience, that a mirror
has been mounted on it. Powell had incorporated mirrors into
his mise-en-scene even in his quota quickies, and his later
work with Pressburger, but here, although revealed at the end,
a mirror provides the impetus for the film.

Mark's role as victim and aggressor converge as the police
move in on him. He smashes the window to film them con-
verging onto his apartment building, and they pull back, mis-
taking the apparatus for a gun. One man remarks that it is
only a camera, but his companion is not comforted by this:
"Only?" It is this moment for which Mark has prepared, and,
as a shocked Helen looks on, he shows her the ending to his
film, revealing a series of cameras that have been carefully positioned. He runs through a gauntlet of flashing cameras arriving at his "magic" camera, which he has mounted to the wall,
holding back for a moment as he admits to Helen that he feels
fear. She attempts to stop him, but he pushes her to the
ground and impales himself on the blade.

As Peter Wollen has discerned, the bright lights of the flashing bulbs remind us of the light with which Mark's father
had often awakened him with as a child. "He has turned his
father's murderous gaze upon himself in order to liberate
himself from it."[12] Yet, even at the end the father will have
the last word. The police break down the door to find Helen
unconscious and Mark dead. The camera begins to draw back
as an audiotape from Mark's past is heard, with Dr. Lewis's
voice telling his son, "silly boy, there's nothing to be afraid
of." If in death is Mark finally free of his father, it is the elder
Lewis who has the final word. The audiotape runs out of the
recorder, the tape spiraling around.

While still reeling from the reception of *Peeping Tom*, Powell began work on his next project, *The Queen's Guards*, which
would be his final English film. It too would receive a critical
pounding, but this time Powell agreed with the reviewers. He
was intrigued by producer Simon Harcourt Smith's idea of setting a film against the backdrop of the queen's annual review
of her troops, admitting he was a "sucker for stories about the
services."[13] Unfortunately, there was little agreement on the
story ultimately created for the film, and the collaboration with
writer Robert Milner was not an easy one. If the resulting story held little interest for Powell, he did find much to occupy

himself with the production. The Massey family were again to make an appearance; this time not only would Raymond Massey appear but also his son Daniel. Once more the government assisted Powell, perhaps recognizing the film more as propaganda than a criticism of the service, allowing Powell to accompany a unit to Libya. This footage, along with that of the ceremony of the queen's inspection of the guard, provides the film with many breathtaking images. Powell was to work in VistaVision, his second experience in a wide-screen process, the first being the less successful *Oh Rosalinda!!* (from an aesthetic standpoint).

The response of the critics could perhaps be better understood this time as they found much to fault with Powell's film. "Michael Powell's flag-waving piece would be distressing if it weren't so inept."[14] Surprisingly, some critics enjoyed the film. "Powell has directed with meticulous attention to detail and, without getting bogged down too much in any one facet, has been able to present a well-drawn picture of the life and thoughts of the average Guard officer."[15] Raymond Durgnat was perhaps allowing for both point of views when he assessed the film as a "mixture of the sublime and the ridiculous, often occurring simultaneously."[16]

As the queen's annual inspection of the Queen's Guards is taking place, John Fellowes (Daniel Massey) thinks back to the events that led him to his position of being the captain of the guard. As a cadet first entering the training academy, he had shown little promise, and he still is prone to making mistakes even after two years of training, as when he leads his group into an ambush. It is a mistake similar to the one that had cost his brother's life at Horseshoe Oasis in the Second World War. John is haunted by his brother's death, and, when another cadet, Henry Wynne Walton (Robert Stephens), taunts him over it, the two fight. Called before the commander, the two cadets make peace, with Henry offering John a ride home. John's father, Captain Fellowes (Massey), is an army historian whose own career was cut short by a bullet that has left him with a severe limp. He anxiously invites Henry into the home, recognizing him as a potential audience for his lectures, thus making him a latter-day Thomas Colpepper. As John stands uncomfortably off to the side, Captain Fellowes recounts the exploits of his deceased son. From that night, John and Hen-

ry's friendship gradually develops, although it constantly undergoes strain.

John introduces Henry to his girlfriend, Susan (Elizabeth
Shepherd), only to see them develop their own relationship.
John, however, manages to console himself with Susan's room-
mate, Ruth (Judith Stott), only to discover that her father has
little regard for his profession. George Dobbie (Ian Hunter) still
feels the effects of having been injured at the Horseshoe Oasis
and believes that the Guard's inefficiency precipitated the crisis. This is the same assault in which John's brother had died,
and he discovers soon after, in a letter that his father had withheld from the family, that his brother had died under dubious
circumstances. Having been entrapped by the enemy, the young
man had executed a prisoner he had been responsible for, and
this action brought on violent reprisals. Wanting to protect his
son's reputation and also unwilling to admit his deficiency,
Fellowes had kept the information a secret. John's own unit is
sent to the Middle East, where their assignment is to rescue
an Arab general. Although the mission is a failure, the general
having been executed by the rebels, it is a personal victory for
John, as he finds himself in a similar situation to that of his
brother. A prisoner escapes, but John is unwilling to shoot an
unarmed man and allows him to flee. The action returns to
the diegetic present, the elder Fellowes looking with pride as
John participates in the ceremony honoring the queen.

For all of the diversity of Michael Powell's work, he had
seldom worked in films that could be categorized as genre films,
at least not from *The Life and Death of Colonel Blimp* on. Perhaps the closest he had come was with *The Red Shoes*, with
its tale of a dancer becoming an overnight star, then forced to
choose between her career and her love, but even that film has
more of the trappings of a film noir, than of a musical. *The
Queen's Guards*, however, takes its plot from dozens of war
films, dating back to the silent era. Its plot involving a successful soldier looking back on his career develops along specific genre requirements. The bumbling cadet becomes the
experienced, seasoned soldier; the two cadets who begin as
antagonists become best friends; a young man finds himself
continuing his family's custom of a military life and, most significant, must emerge from the shadow of a deceased brother
who died in warfare.

Certainly there is much wrong with *The Queen's Guards*, but its underlying subtext involving the Fellowes family is a portrait of an atmosphere as stifling as the one in which Mark presumably grew up. Henry is invited into the Fellowes household and is immediately questioned on his family's military background, causing him later to characterize the elder Fellowes as being "like some aristocratic custodian of a military museum." In fact, the home resembles more a museum than a living quarters, with the rooms cluttered with not only military artifacts but also reminders of the deceased son. As he lectures to his captive audience, Fellowes gradually loses himself in alcohol, and Henry and John finally escape to the bedroom. The mother comes in, questioning Henry on a companion he had mentioned, but becomes upset when he refers to her son as deceased; she believes he is simply missing.

After she is gone, Henry questions John on his nickname, Dawson, and the latter admits it is from when as a boy he had pretended to serve as his brother's batman, or orderly. His father, however, had said that guard's officers don't have "batmen, only servants. Well, I was his servant. My father still thinks of me in that way." Henry says, "So do you, don't you?" "No. I try to live up to David's memory that's all." Henry then asks him whether he intends to spend the rest of his life walking in his brother's footsteps, but John admits he has no alternative: "I can't help it." Like many of Powell's characters, John is tortured by something over which he has no control. His brother's room has been kept the same, and even John sometimes wonders whether he is not alive: "He's dead all right, but not in this house." Even in his relationship with Ruth, John cannot escape the memory of his brother, for her father blames the guard for his men being killed at the Horseshoe Oasis, the very battle in which his brother had died under questionable circumstances.

It becomes apparent that John must both overcome his brother's memory and gain his father's acceptance. He accomplishes the latter on the eve of his departure for the Middle East, when he learns the truth of his brother's death. After confronting his father about withholding the truth, he prepares to leave, only to be handed his brother's cap badge, as his father for the first time addresses him as John. He will in effect exorcise all of his spirits when he finds himself in a situ-

ation that duplicates the circumstances under which his brother
had died. His unit finally having taken possession of the enemy's fort, John is responsible for a prisoner who attempts to
flee. Whereas his brother had shot such a man, John allows
the man to escape uninjured. Confident that it was the right
choice, he visits his brother's grave in an encounter that recalls the films of John Ford.

The film returns to the present as the ceremony reaches
its climax. His health having prevented him from attending, the
elder Fellowes begins to make his way to an upstairs room,
using the trolley system designed by David. As Nigel Andrews
and Harlan Kennedy observe, staircases were to take a prominent role in a Powell film one last time. "The stairs are aglow
with such an eerie light (is this a satiric version of Powell's
earlier *Stairway to Heaven?*), the perspiring effect on Massey's
face seems so disproportionate to the event, the camera angles—extreme high, extreme low—are so vertiginous that the
scene seems like the dying gasp of the British Empire itself."[17]
It was also to be the dying gasp of Powell's British career.

18

Something More Personal

Michael Powell did not realize it at the time, but his career in the British cinema had ended. He was to produce one more film in England and would find work in television, but the final feature films on which he was to work would be produced in foreign countries. It was not that he had given up on the English cinema, for he was continuing to work on projects, but the one that most interested him was set in Australia. In 1962, Powell came across a book entitled *They're a Weird Mob*, written by Nino Culatto, which he later discovered was the pseudonym of John O'Grady. He immediately became infatuated with the first person account of an Italian reporter who finds himself stranded Down Under and gradually ingratiates himself with a group of laborers, while also falling in love with a rich Australian. Powell was not the only one to find promise in the novel, however, for Gregory Peck had already optioned the book, but, when the actor was unable to procure financing for the project, he relinquished the rights to Powell. The final budget for the film was six hundred thousand dollars, with one third coming from the Rank Organization, another portion from Britain's National Film Finance Corporation, and the final third from a group of Australian investors. It proved to be a long, complicated process, and it would not be until 1965 that it finally went before the camera. In the interim, Powell busied himself with a film brought to him by his old colleague Hein Heckroth.

Heckroth was in the midst of designing *Bluebeard's Castle*, the German opera by Bela Bartok, with a libretto by Bela Balazs. Norman Foster was both to produce and star in the opera, which lasts only sixty minutes and in which much of the action is restricted to a single set. It hardly offered the cinematic opportunities of *The Tales of Hoffmann*, but Powell and Heckroth were to turn this austerity to their advantage, creating an expressionistic psychodrama, where lighting and decor convey the nightmare which is Bluebeard's life. As with many of the Archer' films, Heckroth was instrumental in determining the final look of the film, as Powell admitted. "At the same time quite a few of the images in Hein's story board are, what one might call, of the common currency of surrealism. Hein was above, everything else, a surrealist painter and was a member of one of the original surrealist groups. Surrealism is very sympathetic to the cinema and very sympathetic to me. The script that I wrote first—this doesn't differ from it much I think—was written after listening to a recording several times and looking at the score quite a bit. Then I wrote the script, visualizing it in terms of a picture."[1]

Bluebeard's Castle is sung in German, and the copy held by the British Film Institute contains only a few titles, the first of which introduces the opera as the story of a "curious woman. She was curious about a man." Judith is the seventh wife of Bluebeard, and he takes her to his castle, where he tells her of the seven rooms that he keeps locked. After she entreats him to keep no secrets from her, he reluctantly offers her the key to the first room; as the opera progresses, he relinquishes each of the final six keys. Each room reveals some aspect of his kingdom, from the armaments to his treasures and vast properties. If the rooms progressively divulge facets of his personality, they also contain portents of death, with even the clouds becoming red with blood. Bluebeard becomes agitated with her endeavors to determine what is behind each door, but she continues on, finally pressuring him to open the last door. Behind it are the images of his past wives, either carved in stone or encased in shrouds, and she realizes too late that the foreshadowing of death in the rooms is related to her. She now joins his other wives, surrounded by the swords she had discovered in the armament room and a crown she had found in another. A disheartened Bluebeard is thus left alone once more, as the final line "henceforth all shall be darkness" relates his own torment.

Bluebeard's Castle continues the theatrical style that char-acterized *The Tales of Hoffmann*, *The Sorcerer's Apprentice*, and *Oh Rosalinda!!*, which is almost minimalist in its approach. Papier-mache swords are suspended from the ceiling, and the expansive room where most of the action transpires is un-adorned except for the bed and gauze and muslin, which stand out against the black background. The use of red is thus all the more shocking when juxtaposed with the dark shadows. Throughout the piece, there is a sense of entrapment, of not just Judith but also Bluebeard, who cannot escape his lonely fate. When respites to the conflict emerge, they are transient; when they enter his garden, for example, she runs away in fear. In the sixth room of the castle is a lake, and, looking at her image in the water, Judith is shocked to find blood falling from the sky like droplets, gradually transforming her image into red. This is perhaps Powell's darkest tale, both literally and figuratively, and it contains once more a character who is destined to sacrifice any chance for love. The films to follow will be just the opposite, for despite the struggles he would face in his career, Powell's optimism was being liberated.

The production of *Bluebeard's Castle* took only six days. With *They're a Weird Mob* still unfolding, Powell turned to tele-vision to occupy himself. His inaugural work was for a series entitled *Espionage*, and he also directed episodes for *The De-fenders* and *The Nurses*. This work not only provided him with needed income, it also enabled him to reunite with some of his colleagues from the past. Anthony Quayle, Roger Livesey, and Pamela Brown are found among the credits, while one, "A Free Agent" for the series *Espionage,* was written by Leo Marks. Marks also wrote the only English film that Powell produced in this time, *Sebastian*, a comedy involving an Oxford professor who becomes involved in the Secret Service. It was not a pleas-ant experience for Powell, and the resulting film by director David Green was quickly forgotten after its release in 1968.

Powell returned to *They're a Weird Mob* and wrote the ini-tial screenplay, but he was unsatisfied with the ensuing work, nor was he pleased with the script produced by the novel's author, John O'Grady. He turned in desperation to the one man

who could always fashion a strong script for him, Emeric Pressburger. In the years since dissolving their partnership, Pressburger had gradually moved away from film to begin a
successful career as a novelist. It was not that he abandoned
film but that film had seemingly abandoned him. In 1958, he
had toured India with David Lean, researching a proposed film
on Ghandi, but the screenplay that he produced so displeased
Lean that he ultimately fired Pressburger. He also worked unsuccessfully on a project for Ronald Neame, who had once
served as a cinematographer on *One of Our Aircraft Is Missing*.
Forgotten by an industry to which he had contributed so much,
Pressburger turned to writing, a medium that allowed him complete control over his work.

Killing a Mouse on Sunday was published in the fall of
1961, and it was an immediate success, both critically and in
sales. The book was set in the years following the Spanish Civ-
il War along the French and Spanish border and concerned an
old man, who had once been a hero in the war but now is
ridiculed by those around him. He sets off on an expedition to
cross the border, conscious of the ambush that has been set
up for him. What is unique about the story is that it is told
through the point of view of four characters, with each accounting for two chapters. If the goal of the expressionists had been
to take the viewer into the characters' minds, Pressburger
was doing just that with his novel. The complexity of the
work seemed to offer few cinematic possibilities, but its commercial success could not be ignored, and Fred Zinnemann
eventually obtained the rights to the book. Even on a project
based on his own material, Pressburger could not find work,
as his draft was rejected in favor of another writer's. The resulting film, *Behold a Pale Horse*, featured Gregory Peck and
Anthony Quinn in the cast, but even with these names it was
a commercial failure.

The book's success only emboldened Pressburger, and he
went to work on his second novel. He began to write a novel
that was

> less reliant on adventure story conventions, something more
> personal. This was a mistake because the deeper he looked in-
> side himself the darker, the more painful, and the less read-
> able the results. The preoccupations which he had shied away

from in the post-war films took hold: Nazism, the Jewish experience and his own failure to belong. The darker aspects of his imagination which had only surfaced sporadically in the Archers' films—in Lermontov in *The Red Shoes*, in Colpepper in *A Canterbury Tale*—began to override everything else.[2]

The Glass Pearls was all of this, the story of a Nazi scientist who conducted heinous experiments on Jewish prisoners during the war but afterward attempts to live in anonymity in London. His own paranoia ultimately causes him to take his own life. It is a story with little of the humanity that enlightens Pressburger's finest work. The book would be savaged by the critics, and a disillusioned Pressburger would attempt to write only one more book in his lifetime, although he was to later cowrite a novelization of *The Red Shoes* with Powell. Now he turned to film once more, providing much needed assistance to the screenplay of *Operation Crossbow*, a star-studded adventure film set in World War II. As if attempting to start over and escape the burden of his own past, he used the pseudonym of Richard Imrie. It was under this name that Pressburger wrote the screenplay for *They're a Weird Mob*.

Powell first approached Peter Finch about the lead role, but the latter declined, suggesting instead an Italian actor, Walter Chiarri, who had gained a measure of fame in comedies. It must have been a strange experience for Powell, for none of the technicians with whom he had worked on his previous films were around, nor did any carryovers appear in the cast. Yet, Powell enjoyed the experience, and the resulting film would prove to be a huge commercial success in Australia, grossing over three million dollars and initiating a new surge in Australian film production. Its success was not duplicated in England, however, where once again critics took the opportunity to dismiss Powell's previous achievements. "The strong point of Michael Powell's films has always been their splendid disregard for what lesser men might reverence as good taste, discretion and all that."[3] Yet, many critics, though faulting the opening, thought that the film as a whole was enjoyable. "Michael Powell seems ill-at-ease during the chummily extrovert opening, with its repeated assurances that Australia is a big, big country and its endless jokes about a foreigner's difficulties in understanding the slang; but after the film stops trying so hard to be jolly, the quieter sequences in which the Italian learns to live his new life are moderately successful."[4]

Italian Nino Culatto (Chiari) arrives in Sydney, Australia, expecting to take on the position of sports editor for the magazine that his cousin has started. On arrival, however, he is dismayed to discover that the magazine has gone out of business and his cousin has fled to Canada, leaving behind only a trail of debts. Kay Kelly (Clare Dunne), the daughter of the building's owner, has little sympathy for Nino's plight, immediately setting her creditors on him. With little money and unable to find work as a journalist because of his difficulties with Australian colloquialisms, Nino takes on a job as a laborer, while covertly living in the magazine's abandoned offices. He is ill prepared for physical labor, arriving the first day dressed in a suit and nearly exhausting himself in his efforts to keep up with his Australian companion. Despite his inexperience with the language and the position, the workers take to Nino, with his supervisor, Joe Kennedy (Ed Devereaux), even taking him in. With his first check, Nino attempts to reimburse Kay for some of his cousin's debts and for the time he spent living in the office, but she wants no part of it, instead preferring to have her lawyer settle the matter.

Even as she pursues legal action against Nino, Kay's attitude toward him perceptibly changes, becoming annoyed when he fails to turn up at the beach, as he often had in attempts to pay her back, then becoming jealous on seeing him with another woman. The other woman, however, turns out to be a member of an Italian family who has asked him to participate in her wedding. Kay's change in demeanor toward Nino is evidenced by her transformation in appearance, as she relinquishes her prim appearance for a more feminine one, surprising her employees by going to a beauty salon. In the meantime, Nino has begun to set down roots in Australia, even purchasing a piece of property overlooking the sea on which he intends to build a home. Having reconciled with one another, Kay and Nino must now gain the approval of their respective families, Nino's coworkers serving as his surrogate family. Kay's father wants no part of an Italian laborer, until Nino reminds him of his own working-class background, and, to Kay's surprise, the two men take to one another. The introduction to Nino's associates is equally as inauspicious, with the workers nervously attempting to demonstrate their social graces for her while sitting uncomfortably in their suits drinking tea. Kay breaks the ice, however, by asking for a beer. As the suits are discarded and a barbecue is begun, the film ends.

It is no accident that Pressburger would be called on to help with the script of *They're a Weird Mob*, for its central conflict of an immigrant adjusting to a new country, not only mirrors his own past but also invokes memories of *The Life and Death of Colonel Blimp* and *A Canterbury Tale*. Much of the initial humor of the film concentrates on Nino's attempts to understand the local colloquialisms and customs. He has answered a classified in the newspaper; in talking to his prospective employer, he is constantly flustered by the man's directions. Only through the intervention of two operators listening in on the conversation is Nino able to ascertain where he is to report, but his difficulties continue, for his adjustment is to not only a new culture but also manual labor. He is dressed improperly for his first day, but he throws himself into the work, while his Australian companion takes a more leisurely approach. Within an hour Nino is exhausted, but in time he acclimates himself to the job, impressing his once-skeptical companions. Acceptance into their world means visiting the pub, where he is introduced to Australian beer and the hangover that it brings on. Evidence of their friendship is their quick response to another man's taunting of Nino.

This was Powell's first comedy since the thirties, and he initially seems out of sorts with the material, particularly in the opening, which relies too much on crude sight gags to introduce Australia (the inverted image of people walking is meant to indicate the country's Down Under philosophy). In the introduction, a narrator attempts to explain the customs of the Australians while also poking fun at them. He characterizes Australia as a "nation of sportsmen," while onscreen two hunters back into one another, then subsequently one is shot at by the other, who has mistaken him for game. Yet, once the story starts, Powell settles down and the film obliges with many humorous sequences, many resembling something from a Jacques Tati film. Forced to spend the night in the abandoned office of his magazine, Nino sets about making a home, fashioning a couch out of stacks of magazines and using pages as towels.

The themes and conflicts of *They're a Weird Mob* return Powell to those of *I Know Where I'm Going* with a heroine forced to conquer her own business aspirations and prejudices to accept her lover on his terms. Kay is openly antagonistic toward Nino as much for his nationality as for his cousin's debts, for which she holds him accountable. When he strives to pay back the money a little at a time, she fails to recognize his virtuous intention but mistakes it as his effort to impede her court action. He characterizes her as someone who throws herself into her work, and to her employees she is a cold, unemotional individual. Clare Dunne was the last of Powell's red-headed actress, and, like those before, she undergoes a transformation. The alteration of a passionless nature into a more feminine, sensual disposition was first brokered by Powell as early as *The Love Test* in 1935.

The success of *They're a Weird Mob* allowed Powell to direct a second film in Australia, which was to be his final film. *Age of Consent* was written in 1938 by Norman Lindsay, a well-known Australian author, who also worked as a painter and political cartoonist. The novel perhaps mirrors a conflict in Lindsay's own life; it concerns an artist who is struggling to find his desire to paint.

> He had not been aware of putting the doubtful rewards of his forty years' work under inspection. Now those were presented to him in a muddled perspective of appalling monotony; year in, year out, a certain number of pictures painted and peddled for small sums so that he could go on painting and peddling more pictures. Was that an objective sought and attained? an objective that in being sought became the thing sought? A disgusted mumble rejected a concept of art as a carrot eternally dangled out of reach. Damne, there ought to be more in the business than that.[5]

This statement could also have applied to Powell's own struggles, particularly in the fifties and sixties.

Bradly has escaped to an island off Australia in an attempt to isolate himself but instead encounters a young woman who rekindles his enthusiasm for his art. Dressed in rags, Cora seldom speaks to those around her and spends her time selling crawfish and fowls to obtain money to procure the booze that her grandmother craves. Bradly takes to painting her, but

their work is disrupted first by the appearance of an acquain-
tance of his who is hiding out from the law, then by the accu-
sations of the grandmother who claims that he is prostituting
Cora. All is eventually resolved when the grandmother is accidently killed and the house guest flees the island, believing the
police are on to him for outstanding debts.

In adapting the tale, Powell and screenwriter Peter Yeld-
man updated the time period and transposed the location from
the New South Wales Coast to the Barrier Reef. The character
of Bradly, as envisioned by Lindsay, was an overweight mid-
dle-aged man with a scraggly beard, hardly the image that one
had of James Mason. He would take the role and also serve as
the film's producer. It was perhaps his casting that necessitat-
ed a second change in the character, transforming him from a
man whose only contact with women had been with prostitutes
to one who opens the film making love to a woman. Ironically,
the actress who plays the small part, Clarissa Kaye, would
eventually marry Mason. For the part of the young woman who
serves as the inspiration for Bradly, Powell cast Helen Mirren,
who had already made a name for herself by signing with the
Stratford-on-Avon Shakespeare company. The budget was 1.2
million dollars, most of which came from Columbia Pictures in
England. Shooting began in March 1968 in Brisbane and on
Dunk Island off the Queensland Coast. A few interior sequences were filmed at Ajax Studios in Sydney, Australia.

By the time of *Age of Consent*, few critics were even paying
attention to Powell. "Given the convincing and humorous development of this island duo, it is only a pity that the film's
side-line sketches are meager distractions rather than embel-
lishments,"[6] wrote one British reviewer, while once again foreign critics were not as trenchant in their reviews. "The film
has plenty of corn, is sometimes too slow, repetitious and badly edited, almost as if scenes had been deleted. Yet, the picture has immense charm and the actual photography
(particularly underwater scenes) and superb scenery make it a
good traveling ad for the Great Barrier Reef area, where most
of it was filmed."[7]

An established artist living in New York, Brad Morahan
(Mason) has become disillusioned with his profession and the
commercialism surrounding it. He escapes to Brisbane, Australia, to forget about his art, eventually making his way to a

small island off the coast renouncing his profession thorough-ly. He is content with exploring the island and painting his hut until he comes across Cora (Mirren), a young woman who sells food to pay for her grandmother's gin. The girl is hiding away supplementary money in order to leave the island to become a hairdresser, but toward this objective she has begun stealing. Brad gets her to promise not to continue, offering instead to pay her to be a model; although he takes the brush up begrudgingly, he is pleased with works that he produces. Their collaboration comes to an end with the appearance of Ned Kelly (Jack MacGowran), a companion of Brad's from Australia who is hiding out from the authorities over some outstanding alimony bills.

Ned settles in with Brad, not realizing that the beautiful young woman he occasionally catches a glimpse of is working for Brad. No longer able to pursue his craft, Brad can only look on in frustration as Ned begins to woo one of the women on the island. Only when the woman's advances become too aggressive for him does Ned finally leave, taking Brad's money and some of his sketches in the process. Despite the losses, Brad is relieved to continue his work with Cora, although he realizes she will soon have enough money to escape her grandmother. The old woman, however, finds Cora's money, and then comes across her posing nude for Brad, whom she accuses of statutory rape. A flustered Brad attempts to mollify her, but when Cora discovers that her money is missing, she confronts the grandmother. In the ensuing struggle, the older woman falls to her death. Ironically, a constable has arrived at the same time, intending to inform Brad of Ned's capture. While Brad distracts the policeman, Cora moves the body, making it appear that she fell off a cliff while in a drunken stupor. With all of the diversions seemingly eliminated, Brad prepares to continue his painting of Cora, only to find that his model is reluctant to continue. She believes that he is only interested in her as a subject, but in fact, he has fallen in love with her, just as she has with him.

For Powell, the artist could finally reconcile himself to his art and his obsession. Lermontov could not possess Vickie Page, nor could Hoffmann any of his many loves. Mark Lewis meets Helen too late, already nearing the completion of the documentary contrived by his father. Brad boasts that he is immune to sexual desires, recalling Hoffmann's declaration, and that a week of lovemaking can be succeeded by a protracted period of chastity. When he first gazes on Cora and begins to paint her, there is little to suggest that he has any feelings toward her other than as a subject for his canvas. She awakens in him, however, a new passion for his art and in the end is shocked to find that she wants to leave him. "You only want me for the pictures," she cries, going out into the water, the sea having often been her sanctuary. He chases after her, shouting that she has "given me back my eyes. You taught me to love again. I'm alive," he tells her as she swims around him. "It's all because of you." The result is one of the most optimistic conclusions in Powell's oeuvre, one not found in the book.

The character of Brad, as introduced in the film, is one who is attempting to escape the demands of both his art and civilization in general. The film opens beneath the sea, but, as the credits roll, the film segues into the artificial environment of an aquarium as the real-life sounds of the city are heard on the soundtrack. Brad looks in at the aquarium through a shop window, imagining life away from civilization, but the watch that floats in the tank (the timepiece had been found still working on a barrier reef) brings him back to reality, and he hurries off to his meeting with his publisher. His dissatisfaction with his art perhaps echoes Powell's concerns from the time: "If someone had told me, when I first wanted to be a painter, that I'd end up living the way I do, I'd never had started." His incentives for beginning his career are Powell's own. "It was my way of responding to the things I love, light, color, people, sensuality, but I'm out of touch with them now." He escapes from New York to Brisbane, but, in the midst of making love to an old girlfriend, he is reminded of his prominence, for the television is broadcasting an earlier interview with him.

On arriving at the island, Brad is content to explore and clean up the cabin, his only apprehension coming from the reminders of other people that he encounters. Finding paint cans in a storage shed, he starts giving the hut an identity, the walls calling to him more than his canvas does. Powell's focus was often on an artist's obsession with his work, but here the artist has lost his way. He will rediscover it through his encounter with Cora. For Powell, the artist could finally reconcile himself to his art and his obsession with another. In a demonstration of his art, Brad creates one of the most stunning images of the film. As Cora lies on the sand, eventually falling asleep, he creates a nude image of her out of sand. When she wonders how he knew what she looked like nude, he muses that he has "eyes."

It will be through Brad's "eyes" that Cora will also become aware of her own sensuality. Certainly it is evident to others, in particular, a young man who attempts to rape her, but she demonstrates no modesty about taking off her clothes for Brad. Only when she looks at Brad's painting does she become conscious of her body; when she returns to the squalor of her bedroom, she begins to examine it in a cracked mirror. Her grandmother finds her and begins to beat her, accusing her of being sinful, but Cora is not the subservient girl she had once been. She breaks the woman's cane and shoves her back over a table, shouting that she is not to "treat her like a child, I'm not anymore." The encounter serves as a portent to the later fatal struggle, in which the grandmother falls to her death.

Like *They're a Weird Mob*, *Age of Consent* is not a perfect film, certainly not up to the technical standards of Powell's earlier films and again burdened with ill-advised humor, much of it from the character of Ned Kelly. Yet, it serves as a fitting finale to Powell's cinematic career, providing him a chance to lay to rest many of the demons that had haunted his earlier characters. The portrait of an artist rediscovering his passion ultimately foretells Powell's own career, for although his film career was over, he was soon to find other creative outlets and also happiness with a younger woman, just as Brad apparently does with Cora.

19

This Is My Life

Michael Powell's work in film had come to an unceremonious end at the age of sixty-four. Many men would have been content to retire at that age, but Powell was possessed of a keen mind and a strong heart, and he could have comfortably continued working for another fifteen years. That he was not allowed such an opportunity might be labeled a tragedy, another great film director discarded by a commercially minded film industry. Orson Welles is perhaps the most notable example, but Powell had witnessed firsthand such an ending to a great career with his mentor, Rex Ingram. He would also observe the other end of the spectrum with his old colleague, Alfred Hitchcock, who was working on a film up to the moment of his death, even though most around him knew that it was destined never to get past the scripting stage. Powell's fate was neither of these, for he was to find a new way to channel his energy, ultimately creating masterpieces for two other mediums.

Powell continued to work on film projects, the most interesting of which was a long-cherished dream of filming William Shakespeare's, *The Tempest*, which included James Mason among its proposed cast members. None of these projects were to come to fruition, and by 1972 the only opportunity presented to him was a sixty-minute children's film, albeit one with his old colleague Emeric Pressburger. Pressburger had lived during most of the sixties in Austria, but in 1970 he had moved to a small cottage in Ipswich, where he would live out his final years. Soon after Pressburger returned to England, Powell persuaded him to write a story for the Children's Film Foundation, of which he was a board member. Pressburger submitted a story entitled *The Wife of Father Christmas*, which Powell would rename *The Boy Who Turned Yellow*. Christopher Challis signed on as cinematographer, and filming began in March 1972. By the fall of that year, it had gone into release. The public for which it was intended loved it and it received the distinction of being voted the most popular children's film for not only that year, but also the next. The critics were as usual divided, with Richard Combs bemoaning that a "lot more detail goes into building up to the appearance of the extra-terrestrial stranger than is in fact spent on his subsequent adventures; and for all the sumptuousness of the color effects, it seems unlikely that children will be satisfied with so little in the way of explanation."[1]

Viewing the film today is difficult, and one must rely on reviews of the time for its plot. The story concerns a young boy, John Saunders (Mark Digham), who visits the Tower of London, taking with him his pet mouse, Alice, who becomes lost in the monument. Unable to locate his pet, he returns home distraught and is sent home early from school the next day because of his fatigue. On the way home, he inexplicably turns yellow; although the doctors can find no cause, they do not believe him to be at risk. That night he hears a voice emanating from his television set, and he encounters Nick (Robert Eddison), whose name is short for *electronic*. He tells John that as a result of his transformation, he can now travel on waves of electricity at the speed of light. Nick accompanies John to the Tower of London, where they attempt to rescue Alice, but the young boy is discovered by the Beefeaters and sentenced to die. He manages to escape through a television set, only to wake up in his classroom, his past adventure having been a dream. Yet, he exhibits an unexpected knowledge of electricity and on returning home finds Alice has been recovered and that she has given birth to a brood of mice.

The commercial success of *The Boy Who Turned Yellow* did not translate into any other projects, and Powell found himself turning to writing once more. He had already authored two books, but both had been nonfiction works related to his films. He now took a hand at fiction, although the inspiration for the story was an actual murder case and had once been the basis of a property that the Archers had envisioned filming. The murder of an English family while on vacation in France in 1953 had made headlines throughout the world. It was thought that the murder had been an act of revenge, as many of the local men had been members of the French resistance and one of the victims had been a member of a military unit. What had interested Pressburger in the story was that the police, unable to find the murderer, sent a young policeman into the region to live undercover, hoping he would discover the murderer's identity. The project never came to fruition, but Powell retained the rights to it after their separation. *The Waiting Game* is a slight book, only 175 pages in length, but surprisingly effective in delineating characters and the Irish landscape where it was set. It ends in a typical Powell fashion, with the central figure, having been shot by the murderer, lying in his girlfriend's arms, with a car advancing on them. The readers are left to decide on their own whether the car contains help or the murderer.

At this time the renewed interest in Powell and the Archers really began to take hold. There had always been defenders of their work, most notably Raymond Durgnat, but in 1971 the first extensive retrospective of their films occurred. Kevin Gough-Yates supervised the retrospective and conducted the first of two extensive interviews with Powell on his work. The second would be in conjunction with the Brussels Film Festival in 1973, where among the films being screened was *The Edge of the World*, a film that had always held a special place in Powell's heart. It had been forty years since Powell and his crew had traveled to Foula. To mark the event, the British Broadcasting Corporation decided to reunite the surviving members and send them back to the island to learn what effect the film had on the island and what changes it had undergone. The new footage would serve as a prologue and an epilogue to the original film to be aired on the BBC. The result was *Return to the Edge of the World*, and it was to be Powell's final cinematic masterpiece.

The BBC provided Powell with fifteen thousand pounds to produce the film, and he immediately set about locating members of the cast and crew who were still alive. John Laurie was among the first to sign on, despite his doctor's pronouncement that he had only two years left to live. Powell was not as for-

tunate with Niall MacGinnis, who declined to participate, and
Eric Berry, who was on tour in the United States in a musical. He was able to persuade Hamish Sutherland, who played
the catechist in the film, and the former Frances Reidy, now
Mrs. Michael Powell, but although she appears in the film
for an instant, she would not make the trek to the island.
From the technical side of the production, Sydney Streeter not
only appeared in the film but also served as associate producer. For their second trip to Foula, Powell and his crew
had "facilities we wouldn't dream of in 1936. We flew over sea-
cliffs that were inaccessible to us in those days, and we mar-
velled at the colour of the island. But the film's colours were
not the colours of the island; they were the colours of Fujicol-
or. The island, stern and wild and in black and white, had a
character of its own. It was beautiful in an entirely different
way."[2]

The film is as much a statement of nostalgia as *The Life
and Death of Colonel Blimp* had been. It opens as did *The Edge
of the World*, with a man returning to a place he has long since
left behind, in this case Pinewood Studios, but that had once
been the site of the Rank Organization. Riding in a jeep, Powell travels to the setting for many of his greatest films, but the
studio, like Powell, shows the passage of time. As his vehicle
comes to a stop, he looks directly into the camera. "My name
is Michael Powell, I'm a film director. This is my life." He speaks
of his introduction to film, the discovery of the film magazine
that first captivated him, then goes on to recount his first film,
a "thriller." He remembers coming across a newspaper article
on the evacuation of the island of St. Kilda, and a map locating it off the Scottish coast. Admitting that he could not gain
access to St. Kilda, the camera pans across the map to Foula,
and the actual island is introduced from a distance, as the
credits begin. Powell is visible walking along the cliffs, a small
figure against the immensity of the island's natural landscape.
The sea violently buffets the rocky coastline, as the camera
pans across the cliffs and John Laurie takes over the narration. "This was where a young film director called Michael Powell brought us in 1936 to make a film about the death of an
island. It started out just a film, but it became an experience
that changed all our lives."

Laurie speaks to us of the island's history and of the birds that inhabit it. Laurie and Powell will spend the rest of the film alternating as narrator. The plane containing the returning members of *The Edge of the World* arrives on the island. Laurie greets the residents of the island as if he were reuniting himself with members of his family, while Powell strolls about the island in a cap that makes him look like an elderly Sherlock Holmes. The assemblage moves on, and Laurie turns to the camera to introduce himself. "You may have seen me around. After all, I've been acting for fifty-seven of my eighty-one years." He recalls some of his greatest roles, ending with the character of Peter Manson. Walking with the son of a resident of the island who had worked on the film, he recounts the film's plot and the two families who came into conflict, the Mansons and the Greys. In the meantime, Powell has walked off alone, coming to rest upon a grassy hill. He begins to take off his sweater as he looks directly at the camera. "Don't tell anyone I'm a poet. A poet is not without honor, save in his own country, and I suppose that's why most of my biggest chances were given me by Hungarians or Americans," noting in particular American Joe Rock who produced the original film. "When it was shown in London, it didn't exactly set the Thames on fire," and he adds that it was the American critics who discovered the film. When Laurie joins up with him and they begin to reminisce, the actor remembers it as "the golden days, Michael." Sitting on the grass with members of the cast, he muses on it being spring and how much time has passed since then, some forty-two years. It was at this point that the original film aired.

At the conclusion of the original film, Laurie is in close-up, his face reacting as if he has just experienced the film once more. Passing through a gate, he surveys the island as he remembers the cast members who have died. This theme is picked up by Sutherland, the catechist of the film, who remembers other members who could not make the trip. Admitting that the "mind's gone a bit," he reads from a list of the natives who have died, the camera panning across the graveyard. "God bless them all," he says. Powell returns as he introduces Streeter, "who speaks for the technicians." Even he has become an icon, for most of the production crew have long since died. Sutherland asks the islanders what impact the film had had on Foula, and one admits that the island received much publicity because of the film. Yet, the film also inadvertently hurt the island, for many who read of the filming assumed that Foula was also about to be abandoned; as a result, many technical advances were not installed. Laurie now proclaims the island's present success, as off-shore drilling is taking place. Looking at the oil tanks that line the island, Laurie muses it "was Thomas Carlyle who said it, the age of miracles has passed? No, the age of miracles is forever here," and a montage of the islanders follows, while one resident plays the violin, recalling a similar interlude in the original work. The closing credits appear as the camera pans once more across the island, with only its natural sounds heard on the soundtrack.

The Return to the Edge of the World is a lament to a cinema that no longer exists and to the men who worked in the British film industry but are now dead or dying. It opens in a film studio that appears to be little more than a ghost town and concludes with the words of a man who was even then dying. Yet, it is not a eulogy but an attempt to recapture an experience. Thanks Laurie's personality, the experience is renewed, so that even if we recognize the actor's fate as predetermined, he remains optimistic, embracing life. It is a world that has somehow remained untouched in all the years since *The Edge of the World*, even with the oil rigs lying offshore.

In looking back at his career, Powell had inadvertently discovered his future. He had become the grand old man of the British cinema, and, if his compatriots did not recognize it, the Americans would. *The Red Shoes* remained the Archers' most fondly remembered film, and there was always talk of taking it to Broadway. Perhaps because its dance sequence was so much a product of the cinema, the project never came to fruition. Still, it was to find life in another medium, as Powell and Pressburger collaborated on an adaptation of the film for Avon Books. Released in 1978, the book does little to add to the mystique of the film, but it is interesting in continuing the Archers' tradition of attempting to delineate a character's thoughts, for the dance of *The Red Shoes* will be presented subjectively, with the dancer relating her feelings as she performs. It had been obvious that Lermontov had been based on Diaghilev, and references to him are made throughout:

They were legendary characters, these Russian impresarios: yet to call them impresarios was like calling Rembrandt a portrait painter, Mozart a musician, Einstein a mathematician. First came Daighilev. He started it all; the others followed. It takes years to train and create a ballet dancer, but impresarios drop from the cloud like angels, rise from the gutters like gods. They come in all shapes: cultured and barbarous, proud and meek, ruthless and gentle, continuously in need of funds and rolling in luxury. In their breast burns a sacred flame of passion for their chosen art: and whereas artists are prepared to sacrifice themselves for their art, those impresarios are ready to sacrifice everybody else.[3]

It would be interesting to know whether this were Powell's own recollection of his career or Pressburger's assessment of his old partner.

Powell was to have one more experience in film, but it was not to be a happy one. He is credited as western version supervisor in *Pavlova: A Woman for All Time*, but just as his title has little meaning, so too did his involvement. He was originally recruited as the codirector of the film, which was to recount the life of Anna Pavlova, one of the premier ballet dancers of her time. "It will not be a repeat of *The Red Shoes*. What we are aiming at is much more a realistic, gritty film, almost a comedy. Even the ballet scenes will be shot from backstage rather than front-of-house: to emphasize that it's a hard working, sweaty world. The beauty and the work must co-exist— just as in Pavlova herself we must find both the tempestuous and the graceful."[4] Powell's participation in the film was a result of his relationship with Erwin Hillier, who had served as the cinematographer on *A Canterbury Tale* and who was to direct this film. In the end, neither man was to contribute very much to the film, with Powell's chief duty seemingly to be the translator for the Russian director who was eventually credited with the film. The British-Russian coproduction was not to be released until 1983 and would quickly die an ignominious death.

It is perhaps fortunate that Powell's work on *Pavlova: A Woman for All Time* had not been more extensive, for he was to find a new outlet for his talent. He had come across a book by David Thomson, *A Biographical Dictionary of the Cinema*, and by chance opened it to the passage devoted to his own career. He had been aware of the critical reassessment taking place involving his work, but for the first time he found in print someone who recognized the quality of his films. "There is not a British director, working in Britain, with as many worthwhile films to his credit as Michael Powell."[5] So pleased was he with Thomson's assessment that he took the unusual step of writing the critic, and the two began to correspond with one another. In addition to his writing, Thomson was a professor at Dartmouth College in New Hampshire and managed to obtain for Powell the post of artist in residence. While Hollywood had not been able to beckon Powell in the thirties, he now finally moved to the United States and would reside there for most of the last years of his life. In addition to his salary, Powell received lodging and was called on to give lectures, make appearances at important functions, and in the process produce a five-minute film with the film class. The subject was *A Wizard of Earthseas* by Ursula K. Le Guin, and it was evident to those around him that his passion for film had not diminished.

In addition to discovery by film historians, Powell also came to the attention of many of Hollywood's biggest names, young men who were revolutionizing the industry. Martin Scorsese had grown up watching many of the Archers' movies on Saturday nights, on a program entitled *Million Dollar Movies*. Despite being severely edited to allow time for commercials and being aired on a black-and-white television, Scorsese recognized in them something unique. Having become a renowned director in his own right, Scorsese managed to obtain a meeting with Powell, and out of it emerged a strong friendship that had a profound impact on the last years of Powell's life. Scorsese would even be able to receive a credit on a Powell film, as he helped reconstruct the much-neglected *Peeping Tom*, finally providing it with an American premiere. It would also be through Scorsese that Powell would come into contact with Francis Ford Coppola, who recruited him to work in a post similar to that with Dartmouth in his ill-fated studio project, Zoetrope. In many respects, Coppola's undertaking resembled Ingram's earlier attempt to reject the predominance of Hollywood and establish his own film community. Unfortunately, Powell found himself with little do and was unimpressed with the films that the company produced, in particular *Hammett*.

A second introduction was to prove more fortuitous. Scorsese was completing *Raging Bull,* the editor of which was Thelma Schoonmaker. She was forty years Powell's junior, but there was a similar passion for film that helped transcend the age difference.

For all of the triumphs of this period, there were disappointments and tragedies. In 1983 Powell's wife Frankie died, and five years later his other partner in "marriage" would also die. Pressburger had witnessed the resurrection of the Archers but was always cognitive that Powell was garnering most of the attention. At times this caused him some consternation, but for the most part he was content with his anonymity. Pressburger's health began to deteriorate, and in 1983 he was injured in a fall, which only added to his difficulties. It became hard for him to express himself or even take care of his daily needs, so that in the spring of 1987 he was moved into a nursing home. He lived there for nearly a year and died in his sleep on February 5, 1988. He was eulogized as a great screenwriter, but this praise seems too limiting, considering his divergent responsibilities in the Archers. Powell remembered him as "immensely courageous. I admired his courage, his honesty and his lovely sense of humor—a real deep humor about human beings."[6]

Although Powell grieved for their losses, their places would be taken by others. His friendship with Scorsese only deepened, while his relationship with Schoonmaker underwent a change, for she became his wife one year after Frankie's death. Both Scorsese and Schoonmaker were to figure prominently in Powell's last project, the recounting of his life story. While many directors have taken pen to hand to write their autobiography, most were content to encompass their life in one book. Powell began to work on his memoir at Dartmouth and his goal was not just to recount events of his life but to summarize the British cinema of the time in which he worked. Even he often admitted that his story was not a linear one.

> Do I digress? Well, I digress. This book is not a history of the movie business, but the story of one man's love-hate relationship with it. Art has its historian in every century. From Benvenuto Cellini to Kenneth Clark, we learn most from their personal memories, experiences, opinions. Do I claim to sit with

the Masters? Yes I do. I served my apprenticeship and I became a master in my chosen profession in the twentieth century. I am writing this lengthy book because I conceive of it as my duty to do so, but I should be making a film of it. There are not many men in my profession who have had my experience and are still alive and who can get it all down.[7]

Six years in the making, the result is a stunning portrait of a country and its films. Without question Powell was proud of his accomplishments, but he was also willing to acknowledge his shortcomings, as in his recollection of his first marriage, which had lasted all of three weeks. Ironically, the most compelling passages are not of his filmmaking career but of his growing up in Canterbury. Throughout, he relates his various fixations with certain actresses, so that his obsessions call to mind characters in his own films. There are factual errors in the book, which is almost beside the point because, as in his films, he is presenting his own interpretation of reality. Some boasts are hard to believe, but even many of these prove to be accurate. He takes credit for suggesting to Scorsese that he film *The Raging Bull* in black and white; in fact, Scorsese has admitted as much. He would also be quick to point out the contributions of those with whom he worked, in particular Emeric Pressburger. The first book ends with the release of *The Red Shoes*, but, even by cutting off his memoir at this point, he was left with a manuscript over seven hundred pages long.

The critics would find much to praise in the book. "I don't think anyone has attempted to do what this book does," wrote one, "and I really think of it as more of a social history of the way film has developed over this century from the silent era, through quota quickies and then the war when its value as a form of propaganda was realized. After all, what is a nation without its cinema, without a means of expressing its national identity to the world: it's like a person without water or food."[8] Another reviewer said: "The leisurely pace and many digressions are not everybody's cup of tea; however, readers willing to give themselves up to the work at hand . . . will be rewarded with an intimate view of British film-making filtered through the eyes of a charming vibrant man whose love of life and of people colors everything he attempts."[9]

As Powell's heath failed, first from a stroke, then from cancer, the completion of the second volume of his autobiography became a race against time. No longer able to write, he dictated to Schoonmaker, who recorded his account of the breakup of the Archers and the difficulties he faced with *Peeping Tom*. The result is not the literary masterpiece of the first book but a more poignant account, as Powell constantly makes references to his own mortality, hoping only to live long enough to reach the book's logical conclusion, the death of Emeric Pressburger. He would survive until the manuscript was complete, but he would die before it was to be published.

Michael Powell died on February 19, 1990, and was eulogized as "one of the true creators of British cinema."[10] William K. Everson, who became a friend of Powell's thought that "few men in any field of art have left behind such an outstanding legacy. By rights, Michael Powell should be buried in Westminster Abbey along with England's other great writers and poets, but he'd have found that stuffy and wouldn't have wanted it."[11] In fact, Powell was buried at a cemetery at the Holy Cross Church in Avening, England, the church where he had been married and which was within sight of his home.

Notes

Introduction

1. *Movie*, Autumn 1965, p. 18.
2. *Midi-Minuit Fantastique*, October 1968, p. 14.

Chapter 1

1. Michael Powell, *A Life in Movies* (London: William Heinemann, 1986), p. 71.
2. Kevin Gough-Yates, *Michael Powell in Collaboration with Emeric Pressburger* (London: British Film Institute, 1971), p. 1.
3. Powell, *A Life in Movies*, pp. 158–59.
4. Ibid., p. 168.
5. Ibid., p. 219.
6. *Times* (London), August 12, 1931.
7. *Variety*, July 21, 1931.
8. Gough-Yates, *Michael Powell*, p. 2.
9. Allen Eyles and David Meeker, *Missing Believed Lost* (London: British Film Institute, 1994), p. 37.
10. Powell, *A Life in Movies*, p. 223.
11. Gough-Yates, *Michael Powell*, p. 2.
12. *Everyman*, February 11, 1932.
13. *Biograph*, March 23, 1932.
14. *Picturegoer*, December 3, 1932.
15. Eyles and Meeker, p. 43.

16. *Picturegoer*, April 1, 1933.
17. Gough-Yates, *Michael Powell*, p. 3.
18. Ibid.
19. *Monthly Film Bulletin*, July 1935, p. 90.
20. *Monthly Film Bulletin*, March 20, 1936, p. 126.
21. Gough-Yates, *Michael Powell*, p. 3.
22. *Monthly Film Bulletin*, April 30, 1936, p. 62.
23. Gough-Yates, *Michael Powell*, p. 3.
24. Eyles and Meeker, p. 65.

Chapter 2

1. Powell, *A Life in Movies*, p. 215.
2. Ibid., p. 225.
3. George Perry, *The Great British Picture Show* (London: MacGibbon, 1974), p. 15.
4. Kevin Gough-Yates, *Michael Powell* (Brussels: Film Museum, 1973), p. 2.
5. *Everyman*, December 10, 1931.
6. Gough-Yates, *Michael Powell* (1971), p. 14.
7. *Variety*, February 20, 1934.
8. *Monthly Film Bulletin*, January 1935, p. 116.
9. Ian Christie, *Arrows of Desire*, p. 15.
10. *Monthly Film Bulletin*, January 1935, p. 116.
11. *Monthly Film Bulletin*, July 1935, p. 89.
12. Jack Ellis, *A History of Film* (Englewood Cliffs, NJ: Prentice Hall, 1979), p. 96.
13. *Monthly Film Bulletin*, October 1935, p. 145.
14. Powell, *Million Dollar Movie*, p. 16.
15. *AIP*, December 1985, p. 9.

Chapter 3

1. *New York Times*, September 4, 1938.
2. Michael Powell, *200,000 Feet on Foula* (London: Faber and Faber, 1938), p. 48.
3. Ibid., p. 187.
4. Ibid., p. 223.
5. *Monthly Film Bulletin*, July 21, 1937, p. 13.
6. *Nation*, September 17, 1938, p. 278.
7. Gough-Yates, *Michael Powell* (1971), p. 3.
8. Gough-Yates, *Michael Powell* (1973), p. 12.

9. *Sight and Sound*, Autumn 1978, p. 228.
10. Powell, *200,000 Feet on Foula*, p. 302.

Chapter 4

1. Powell, *A Life in Movies*, p. 81.
2. Christie, *Arrows of Desire*, p. 22.
3. *Monthly Film Bulletin*, October 1984, p. 318.
4. *Box Office*, September 28, 1934, p. 41.
5. MacDonald, Kevin, *Emeric Pressburger: The Life of a Screenwriter* (London: Faber and Faber, 1994), p. 155.
6. *Rob Wagner's Script*, January 25, 1941, p. 16.

Chapter 5

1. *New York Times*, December 6, 1940, p. 28.
2. *New Republic*, October 21, 1940, p. 870.
3. Karol Kulick, *Alexander Korda: The Man Who Could Work Miracles* (London: Allen, 1975), p. 131.
4. Robert Murphy, *Realism and Tinsel* (London: Routledge, 1992), p. 4.
5. Ian Christie, *Powell, Pressburger, and Others* (London: British Film Institute, 1978), p. 26.
6. *Documentary News Letter*, January 1, 1940.

Chapter 6

1. *Today's Cinema*, October 10, 1941, p. 7.
2. *Motion Picture Herald*, November 8, 1941, p. 349.
3. *Sight and Sound*, Winter 1978, p. 10.
4. Monk Gibbon, *The Red Shoes Ballet: A Critical Study* (London: Saturn, 1948), p. 53.
5. Powell, *A Life in Movies*, p. 389.
6. Gibbon, *The Red Shoes Ballet: A Critical Study*, p. 53.
7. Brian McFarlane, *Sixty Voices* (London: British Film Institute, 1992).
8. *Monthly Film Bulletin*, April 30, 1942, p. 42.
9. Powell, *A Life in Movies*, p. 389.
10. Ibid., p. 532.

Chapter 7

1. *The Observer*, June 13, 1943.
2. *Times* (London), September 17, 1943.

3. M. M. Robson, *The Shame of Colonel Blimp* (London: Sidneyan Society, 1944), p. 4.

4. Ibid., p. 22.

5. Alan Wood, *Mr. Rank* (London: Hodder & Stoughton, 1952), p. 121.

6. Ibid., p. 125.

7. Gough-Yates, *Michael Powell* (1971), p. 3.

Chapter 8

1. *Sight and Sound*, Winter 1978, p. 11.

2. C. A. Lejeune, *Chestnuts in Her Lap*, p. 121.

3. Gough-Yates, *Michael Powell* (1971), p. 7.

4. Powell, *Million Dollar Movie*, p. 67.

5. Anthony Aldgate and Jeffrey Richards, *Britain Can Take It* (Cambridge: Blackwell, 1986), p. 48.

6. *Monthly Film Bulletin*, November 1984, p. 356.

Chapter 9

1. *Monthly Film Bulletin*, October 1984, p. 317.

2. Gough-Yates, *Michael Powell* (1971), p. 14.

3. Gough-Yates, *Michael Powell* (1973), p. 12.

4. Powell, *A Life in Movies*, p. 468.

5. *Sight and Sound*, Winter 1978, p. 12.

6. Gibbon, *The Red Shoes Ballet: A Critical Study*, p. 50.

7. Lejeune, *Chestnuts in Her Lap*, p. 159.

8. *Sight and Sound*, Summer 1990, p. 182.

9. *Monthly Film Bulletin*, October 1984, p. 318.

10. Ian Christie, *I Know Where I'm Going* (Criterion laser disc).

11. Ibid.

12. Gough-Yates, *Michael Powell* (1971), p. 18.

Chapter 10

1. Gough-Yates, *Michael Powell* (1971), p. 8.

2. *Times* (London), November 3, 1946.

3. *Times* (London), February 25, 1990, p. E4.

4. Richard Winnington, *Drawn and Quartered* (Saturn Press), p. 69.

5. Christie, *Powell, Pressburger, and Others*, p. 79.
6. Durgnat, Raymond, *A Mirror for England: British Movies from Austerity to Affluence* (London: Faber and Faber, 1970), p. 30.
7. Gough-Yates, *Michael Powell* (1971), p. 8.
8. Ibid., p. 8.

Chapter 11

1. MacDonald, *Emeric Pressburger: The Life of a Screenwriter*, p. 261.
2. Rumer Godden, *Black Narcissus* (London: World Film Publications, 1947), p. 35.
3. *New York Times*, August 14, 1947, p. 29.
4. Rumer Godden, *A House with Four Rooms* (London: 1989), p. 53.
5. Michael Balcon, *Michael Balcon Presents . . . A Lifetime of Films* (London: Hutchison, 1969), p. 136.
6. *Monthly Film Bulletin*, May 31, 1946, p. 60.
7. *Framework*, Winter 1978–1979, p. 13.
8. Powell, *A Life in Movies*, p. 583.

Chapter 12

1. Powell, *A Life in Movies*, p. 614.
2. Gibbon, *The Red Shoes Ballet: A Critical Study*, p. 54.
3. Ibid., p. 60.
4. *New York Times*, January 10, 1988, p. 22.
5. *Nation*, November 6, 1948, p. 529.
6. *New York Times*, July 27, 1947.
7. Ian Christie, *The Red Shoes* (Criterion laser disc).
8. *Nation*, November 6, 1948, p. 529.
9. *New York Times*, July 27, 1947.
10. Gibbon, *The Red Shoes Ballet: A Critical Study*, p. 78.
11. *American Film*, July 1990, p. 36.
12. Walter H. Sokel, *The Writer in Extremis: Expressionism in 20th Century German Literature* (Palo Alto, Calif.: Stanford, 1959).
13. Powell, *A Life in Movies*, p. 653.

Chapter 13

1. *Midi Minuit Fantastique*, October 1968.
2. *Variety*, August 11, 1948.
3. *Monthly Film Bulletin*, March 31, 1948, p. 40.
4. Ibid.
5. *Monthly Film Bulletin*, November 1984, p. 40.
6. Ibid., p. 359.

Chapter 14

1. MacDonald, *Emeric Pressburger: The Life of a Screen-writer*, p. 305.
2. Powell, *Million Dollar Movie*, p. 49.
3. *Times* (London), November 6, 1950.
4. *Monthly Film Bulletin*, December 1950, p. 184.
5. Gough-Yates, *Michael Powell* (1971), p. 8.
6. Powell, *Million Dollar Movie*, p. 67.
7. *Monthly Film Bulletin*, October 1950, p. 149.
8. *Variety*, September 27, 1950, p. 8.
9. *Saturday Review*, June 28, 1952, p. 27.
10. *Films and Filming*, November 1986, p. 35.
11. *Monthly Film Bulletin*, December 1986, p. 353.
12. Ibid.

Chapter 15

1. *American Cinematographer*, May 1951, p. 194.
2. Powell, *Million Dollar Movie*, p. 94.
3. Roy Armes, *A Critical History of British Cinema* (London: Secker and Warburg, 1978), p. 223.
4. MacDonald, *Emeric Pressburger: The Life of a Screen-writer*, p. 270.
5. *Monthly Film Bulletin*, May 1951, p. 278.
6. *Sight and Sound*, May 1951, p. 278.
7. *Brighton Film Review*, no. 1, 1968.
8. *Perfect Vision*, Summer 1993, p. 116.
9. *American Cinematographer*, May 1951, p. 176.
10. Powell, *Million Dollar Movie*, p. 208.
11. *Sight and Sound*, November 1955, p. 5.
12. *Monthly Film Bulletin*, December 1955, p. 4.
13. *Variety*, November 1955.

Chapter 16

1. *Times* (London), October 30, 1956.
2. *Saturday Review*, September 14, 1957, p. 30.
3. Michael Powell, *Death in the Atlantic* (London: Hodder & Stoughton, 1956), p. 1.
4. Powell, *Million Dollar Movie*, p. 218.
5. *New York Times*, April 25, 1958, p. 32.
6. *Monthly Film Bulletin*, December 1956, p. 63.
7. Powell, *Million Dollar Movie*, p. 364.
8. Ibid., p. 388.
9. *Monthly Film Bulletin*, February 1962, p. 32.
10. Ibid.
11. *Films and Filming*, December 1981, p. 18.

Chapter 17

1. *Midi Minuit Fantastique*, October 1968, p. 14.
2. *Films and Filming*, May 1960, p. 26.
3. *Monthly Film Bulletin*, April 1960, p. 66.
4. *Daily Cinema*, April 1, 1960.
5. Christie, *Powell, Pressburger, and Others* (reprint of review by Jean-Paul Toruk that originally appeared in *Positif*, 1960), p. 60.
6. *New York Times*, October 14, 1979, p. 65.
7. *Midi Minuit Fantastique*, October 1968, p. 14.
8. *AIP*, December 1985, p. 9.
9. *Film Comment*, September 1979, p. 59.
10. Kaja Silverman, *The Acoustic Mirror: The Female Voice in Psychoanalysis and Cinema* (Bloomington: Indiana University Press, 1988), p. 33.
11. Laura Mulvey, *Peeping Tom* (Criterion laser disc).
12. *Sight and Sound*, December 1984, p. 21.
13. Powell, *Million Dollar Movie*, p. 410.
14. *Monthly Film Bulletin*, November 1961, p. 172.
15. *Variety*, October 25, 1961.
16. Durgnat, *A Mirror for England*, p. 54.
17. *Film Comment*, June 1979, pp. 54–55.

Chapter 18

1. Gough-Yates, *Michael Powell* (1973), p. 16.

2. MacDonald, *Emeric Pressburger: The Life of a Screenwriter*, p. 378.

3. *Times* (London), October 20, 1966, p. B17.

4. *Monthly Film Bulletin*, November 1966, p. 56.

5. Norman Lindsay, *The Age of Consent* (New York: 1938), p. 33.

6. *Monthly Film Bulletin*, December 1969, p. 256.

7. *Variety*, May 14, 1969.

Chapter 19

1. *Monthly Film Bulletin*, October 1972, p. 208.

2. Powell, *Million Dollar Movie*, p. 556.

3. Michael Powell and Emeric Pressburger, *The Red Shoes* (New York: Avon, 1978), p. 6.

4. *Film Comment*, June 1979, p. 597.

5. David Thomson, *A Biographical Dictionary of Films* (New York: Knopf, 1994), p. 597.

6. *New York Times*, February 6, 1988, p. 10.

7. Powell, *A Life in Movies*, p. 514.

8. *Films and Filming*, October 1986, p. 23.

9. *Film Quarterly*, Summer 1988, p. 28.

10. *Times* (London), February 25, 1990, p. E4.

11. *Films in Review*, May 1990, p. 270.

Bibliography

This book could not have been written without Ian Christie and Kevin Gough-Yates having laid the groundwork in their early interviews and assessments of Powell's career. Gough-Yates's interviews with Powell remain, along with Powell's own autobiographies, the richest source of information on how the director assessed his own films. As Emeric Pressburger granted few interviews, Kevin MacDonald's biography *Emeric Pressburger: The Life and Death of a Screenwriter* is a strong attempt to fill in the many gaps of his life. These sources also helped in preparing the filmography that follows, but all credits were checked against the original film if possible and against other sources related to the English cinema.

QUOTA QUICKIES

AR. "The Phantom Light." *Monthly Film Bulletin*, July 1935, p. 89.

"Born Lucky." *Picturegoer*, April 1, 1933.

Brown, Geoff. "Red Ensign." *Monthly Film Bulletin*, September 1981, p. 184.

Chap. "Two Crowded Hours." *Variety*, July 21, 1931.

Combs, Richard. "Something Always Happens." *Monthly Film Bulletin*, September 1981, pp. 184–85.

"Crown vs. Stevens." *Kine Weekly*, April 2, 1936.

Drek. "The Love Test." *Variety*, December 10, 1990, p. 81.

Durgnat, Raymond. "The Prewar B's Rewards and Fairies." *Film Comment*, May 1990, pp. 28–30.

EP. "The Love Test." *Monthly Film Bulletin*, January 1935, p. 116.

"Girl in the Crowd." *Kine Weekly*, December 6, 1934.

Greene, Graham. "Rynox." *Everyman*, December 10, 1931.

———. "The Star Reporter." *Everyman*, February 11, 1932.

"Her Last Affaire." *Kine Weekly*, October 24, 1935.

"His Lordship." *Picturegoer*, December 3, 1932.

"Hotel Splendide." *Biograph*, March 30, 1932.

Jolo. "Her Last Affaire." *Variety*, October 23, 1925.

———. "The Phantom Light," *Variety*, July 17, 1935.

MA. "Lazybones." *Monthly Film Bulletin*, January 1935, p. 116.

"My Friend the King." *Picturegoer*, March 13, 1932.

H. du P. "The Man behind the Mask." *Monthly Film Bulletin*, April 30, 1936, p. 62.

"Price of a Song," *Kine Weekly*, May 30, 1935.

RB. "The Brown Wallet." *Monthly Film Bulletin*, March 20, 1936, p. 126.

———. "Her Last Affaire." *Monthly Film Bulletin*, October 1935, p. 145.

———. "Red Ensign." *Monthly Film Bulletin*, April 1934, p. 29.

———. "Red Ensign." *Times* (London), March 8, 1934, p. 15.

———. "Red Ensign." *Variety*, February 20, 1934.

"Rynox." *Picturegoer*, March 5, 1932.

"Something Always Happens." *Kine Weekly*, June 28, 1934.

"The Fire Raisers." *Picturegoer*, January 22, 1934.

———. *Times* (London), September 18, 1933 p. 10.

"The Love Test." *Kine Weekly*, January 10, 1935.

"The Night of the Party." *Kine Weekly*, February 8, 1934.

———. *Variety*, February 13, 1934.

"The Phantom Light." *Spectator*, July 12, 1935.

"The Star Reporter." *Picturegoer*, May 7, 1932.

———. "Two Crowded Hours." *Times* (London), August 12, 1931, p. 8.

The Edge of the World

Buchanan, Andrew. "The Edge of the World." *Sight and Sound*, Autumn 1937, pp. 120–21.

Char. "The Edge of the World." *Variety*, September 14, 1938, p. 15.

EP. "Edge of the World." *Monthly Film Bulletin*, July 21, 1937, p. 13.

Hartung, Philip T. "Gifts from Abroad." *Commonweal*, September 30, 1938, p. 590.

MM. "Film Note." *Nation*, September 17, 1938, p. 278.

Nugent, Frank. "'Edge of the World,' the Story of a Doomed Island." *New York Times*, September 12, 1938, p. 13.

"Pictures from England." *New Republic*, September 14, 1938, p. 160.

"Screen Openings." *Newsweek*, September 26, 1938, p. 23.

"The Edge of The World." *Boxoffice*, September 17, 1938, p. 37.

———. *Time*, September 19, 1938, p. 26.

———. *Times* (London), September 13, 1937 p. 10.

———. *New Statesman and Nation*, September 18, 1937, p. 407.

The Spy In Black

Aaronson, Charles S. "U-Boat 29." *Motion Picture Daily*, October 9, 1939, p. 6.

Ames, Richard Sheridan. "U-Boat 29." *Rob Wagner's Script*, October 28, 1939, p. 17.

Crisler, Ben R. "Four Films in Review." *New York Times*, October 6, 1939, p. 31.

EP. "Spy in Black." *Monthly Film Bulletin*, March 31, 1939, p. 41.

Ferguson, Otis. "Another Language." *New Republic*, December 20, 1939, p. 260.

Jolo. "The Spy In Black." *Variety*, October 11, 1939, p. 13.

"Screen Openings." *Newsweek*, October 16, 1939, p. 44.

"The Spy In Black." *New Statesman and Nation*, August 12, 1939, p. 244.

———. *Times* (London), July 31, 1939, p. 10.

"U-Boat 29." *Boxoffice*, September 28, 1939, p. 41.

———. *Film Bulletin*, October 7, 1939, p. 6.

———. *Film Daily*, October 11, 1939, p. 6.

Zunser, Jesse. "U-Boat 29." *Cue,* Oct 14, 1939 p. 47.

Contraband

"Contraband." *Variety*, April 24, 1940

Hartung, Philip T. "Blackout." *Commonweal*, December 13, 1940, p. 210.

Sterne, Herb. "Blackout." *Rob Wagner's Script*, January 23, 1941, pp. 16–17.

Strauss, Theodore. "Blackout." *New York Times*, December 2, 1940, p. 19.

————. "The Return of the Somnambulist." *New York Times*, May 12, 1940.

VGS. "Contraband." *Monthly Film Bulletin*, April 30, 1940, p. 53.

The Lion Has Wings

"Air Lion." *Time*, November 20, 1939, p. 80.

Hartung, Philip T. "All of the People All of the Time." *Commonweal*, December 22, 1939, p. 206.

HGF. "Happy Landings." *Sight and Sound*, Spring 1940, p. 8.

Hobe. "The Lion Has Wings." *Variety*, January 24, 1940, p. 14.

Nugent, Frank. "The Lion Has Wings." *New York Times*, January 22, 1940, p. 11.

"Plays and Pictures." *New Statesman and Nation*, November 4, 1939, p. 644.

"R.A.F. on the Screen." *Times* (London), October 31, 1939.

RWD. "The Lion Has Wings." *Monthly Film Bulletin*, October 30, 1939, p. 201.

"The Lion Has Wings." *Documentary News Letter*, January 1, 1940, p. 8.

————. *Life*, December 11, 1939, pp. 69–72.

————. *Spectator*, November 3, 1939.

The Thief of Bagdad

Crowther, Bosley. "The Thief of Bagdad." *New York Times*, December 6, 1940, p. 28.

EO. "The Thief of Bagdad." *Monthly Film Bulletin*, January 31, 1941, p. 2.

Ferguson, Otis. "The Thief of Bagdad." *New Republic*, October 21, 1940, p. 870.

Hartung, Philip T. "England Expects Every Cinemagoer." *Commonweal*, December 13, 1940, pp. 209–210.

"Korda Opens Stops On Trick Camera Effects For His `Thief of Bagdad." *Life*, October 14, 1940, pp. 39–40.

Lejeune, CA. "An Old British Tradition." *New York Times*, July 9, 1939.

RSB. "The Thief of Bagdad." *High Fidelity Magazine*, September 1977, p. 116.

"The Thief of Bagdad." *Newsweek*, October 28, 1940, p. 58.

———. *Time*, November 4, 1940, pp. 76, 78.

Walt. "The Thief of Bagdad." *Variety*, October 16, 1940, p. 16.

49th Parallel

"11,012,000 to 6." *Newsweek*, March 16, 1942, pp. 72–73.

"49th Parallel." *Documentary News Letter*, November 1941, p. 215.

ER. "49th Parallel." *Monthly Film Bulletin*, October 31, 1941, pp. 129–130.

Farber, Manny. "With Camera and Gun." *New Republic*, March 23, 1942, p. 399.

"Filming The Invaders." *New York Times*, March 15, 1942.

Fleischmann, Mark. "49th Parallel." *Video*, May 1991, p. 62.

Hartung, Philip T. "Patriots Without Uniforms." *Commonweal*, March 20, 1942, p. 536.

"The Invaders," *Motion Picture Herald Digest*, November 8, 1941, p. 349

Jolo. "49th Parallel." *Variety*, November 5, 1941, p. 8.

Montagnes, James. "Camera Over Canada." *New York Times*, September 15, 1940.

Rayns, Tony. "49th Parallel." *Monthly Film Bulletin*, November 1984, pp. 356–358.

Rye, P. H. "Films." *Nation*, March 14, 1942, p. 320.

"Six Nazis Try To Invade Canada." *Life*, March 23, 1942, pp. 57–58.

"The New Pictures." *Time*, March 16, 1942, pp. 90–91.

Whitebait, William. "The Movies." *New Statesman and Nation*, October 18, 1941.

One of Our Aircraft Is Missing

Farber, Manny. "The Journey, Cont." *New Republic*, November 16, 1942, p. 641.

Hartung, Philip T. "One of Our Movies Is Missing." *Commonweal*, October 9, 1942, p. 594.

Hogue, Peter. "One of Our Aircraft Is Missing." *Film Comment*, May 1990, pp. 30–32.

"Invaders in Reverse English." *Newsweek*, September 21, 1942, pp. 80, 82.

Jolo. "One of Our Aircraft Is Missing." *Variety*, April 29, 1942, p. 8.

"One of Our Aircraft Is Missing." *Monthly Film Bulletin*, April 30, 1942, p. 42.

———. *Time*, September 28, 1942, p. 85.

TS. "One of Our Aircraft Is Missing." *New York Times*, November 2, 1942, p. 17.

The Life and Death of Colonel Blimp

Agee, James. "Colonel Blimp." *Nation*, March 31, 1945, p. 370.

Baxter, Brian. "The Life And Death of Colonel Blimp." *Films and Filming*, August 1985, pp. 40–41.

Chapman, James. "Life and Death of Colonel Blimp." *Historical Journal of Film, Radio and Television*, March 1995, pp. 19–54.

Christie, Ian. "The Colonel Blimp File." *Sight and Sound*, Winter 1978–79.

Combs, Richard. "The Life and Death of Colonel Blimp." *Monthly Film Bulletin*, August 1985, pp. 256–257.

EO. "The Life and Death of Colonel Blimp." *Monthly Film Bulletin*, June 30, 1943

Farber, Manny. "Sweet and Low." *New Republic*, April 30, 1945, p. 587.

"Forty Years of Blimpism." *Newsweek*, March 26, 1945, pp. 114–115.

"Gad Sir, He Had To Die." *Time*, June 21, 1943, p. 31.

Hartung, Philip T. "Lo! The English Man." *Commonweal*, March 30, 1945, pp. 590–591.

Jolo. "The Life and Death of Colonel Blimp." *Variety*, June 23, 1943, p. 24.

Lejeune, C.A. "The Life and Death of Colonel Blimp." *The Observer* (London), June 13, 1943.

"The Life and Death of Colonel Blimp." *Documentary News Letter* n 5, (1943) p. 219.

"The New Pictures." *Time*, April 2, 1945, p. 90.

Sarris, Andrew. "The Life and Death of Colonel Blimp." *Film Comment*, May 1990, pp. 32–33.

Sterne, Herb. "Colonel Blimp." *Rob Wagner's Script*, November 17, 1945, p. 14.

TMP. "The Life and Death of Colonel Blimp." *New York Times*, March 30, 1945, p. 18.

WG. "The Sun Never Sets." *New Yorker*, April 7, 1945, p. 65.

An Airman's Letter To His Mother

"Film Interpretation." *The Times*, June 12, 1941, p. 6.

The Volunteer

KFB. "The Volunteer." *Monthly Film Bulletin*, November 30, 1943, p. 122.

"New Films in London," *Times* (London), November 1, 1943 p. 8.

A Canterbury Tale

"A Canterbury Tale." *Fortnight*, July 22, 1949, p. 31.

———. *New York Times*, January 24, 1949, p. 16.

———. *Times* (London), May 10, 1944, p. 6.

———. *Variety*, May 31, 1944.

Fuller, Graham. "A Canterbury Tale." *Film Comment*, March 1995, pp. 33–36.

KFB. "A Canterbury Tale." *Monthly Film Bulletin*, June 30, 1944, p. 67.

McVay, Douglas. "A Canterbury Tale." *Films and Filming*, January 1982, pp. 18–19.

Wicking, Chris. "A Canterbury Tale." *Monthly Film Bulletin*, November 1984, pp. 355–356.

Winnington, Richard. "A Canterbury Tale." *News Chronicle*, May 13, 1944.

I Know Where I'm Going

Agee, James. "Films." *Nation*, September 13, 1947, p. 264.

Buford, K. Lee. "Reaching Kiloran." *Film Comment*, September 1991, pp. 75–76.

EHL. "I Know Where I'm Going." *Monthly Film Bulletin*, December 3, 1945, p. 147.

Hartung, Philip T. "Bonny Lassies and Braw Lads." *Commonweal*, September 5, 1947, pp. 501–502.

"I Know Where I'm Going." *Time*, September 15, 1947, pp. 102–104.

McNulty, John. "American Classic, British Ephemera." *New Yorker*, August 23, 1947, pp. 42–43.

O'Hara, Shirley. "I Know Where I'm Going." *New Republic*, September 22, 1947, p. 39.

Olson, Greg. "I Know Where I'm Going." *Film Comment*, May 1990, pp. 33-36.

"Pygmalion In the Hebrides." *Newsweek*, September 1, 1947, p. 79.

Richards, Jeffrey. "I Know Where I'm Going." *Monthly Film Bulletin*, October 1984, pp. 317-318.

Stal. "I Know Where I'm Going." *Variety*, September 26, 1946, p. 3.

Talb. "I Know Where I'm Going." *Variety*, November 14, 1945, pp. 12.

TMP. "I Know Where I'm Going." *New York Times*, August 20, 1947, p. 25.

A Matter of Life and Death

"British Heaven." *Newsweek*, January 6, 1947, p. 69.

Cane. "A Matter of Life and Death." *Variety*, November 20, 1946, p. 16.

Crowther, Bosley. "A Matter of Life And Death." *New York Times*, December 26, 1946, p. 28.

Hartung, Philip T. "Treat for Discriminators." *Commonweal*, January 3, 1947, p. 305.

Horton, Robert. "A Matter of Life and Death." *Film Comment*, May 1990, pp. 36-37.

HRI. "Between Two Years." *Theatre Arts*, February 17, 1947, pp. 34-38.

Lightman, Herb A. "Two Worlds in Technicolor." *American Cinematographer*, July 1947, p. 236-237.

McCarten, John. "Mostly Spooks." *New Yorker*, January 11, 1947, p. 64.

O'Hara, Shirley. "Two From Overseas." *New Republic*, January 13, 1947, p. 37.

Powell, Dilys. "Films of the Week." *Times* (London), November 3, 1946.

RWD. "A Matter of Life And Death." *Monthly Film Bulletin*, November 30, 1946, p. 148.

"Stairway To Heaven." *Life*, December 9, 1946, pp. 123-124.

"The New Pictures." *Time*, December 30, 1946, p. 66.

Turan, Kenneth. "Powell's Stairway Still Leads Somewhere." *Los Angeles Times*, April 14, 1995 p. 1F.

Vesselo, Arthur. "British Films of the Quarter." *Sight and Sound*, Winter 1946-47, pp. 155-156.

Winnington, Richard. "A Matter of Life and Death." *News Chronicle*, November 22, 1946.

Black Narcissus

Agee, James. "Films." *Nation*, August 30, 1947, p. 209.

"Black Narcissus." *Life*, September 1, 1947, pp. 55-56.

————. *Time*, August 25, 1947, pp. 88-89.

Cane. "Black Narcissus." *Variety*, May 7, 1947, p. 18.

Durgnat, Raymond. "Black Narcissus." *Monthly Film Bulletin*, October 1984, pp. 313-314.

————. ". . . and in Theory: Towards a Superficial Structuralism." *Monthly Film Bulletin*, October 1984, pp. 314-316.

Hartung, Philip T. "A For Color." *Commonweal*, August 22, 1947, p. 455.

Isaacs, Hermine Rich. "What's a Heaven For?" *Theater Arts*, October 1947, pp. 50-52.

K.F.B. "Black Narcissus." *Monthly Film Bulletin*, May 31, 1946, p. 60.

McNutty, John. "American Classic, British Ephemera." *New Yorker*, August 23, 1947, p. 42.

McVay, Douglas. "Black Narcissus." *Films and Filming*, January 1982, pp. 20-21.

O'Hara, Shirley. "Black Narcissus." *New Republic*, September 15, 1947, pp. 37-38.

Pulleine, Tim. "Black Narcissus." *Films and Filming*, February 1986, p. 31.

Rodrig, Antonio. "Black Narcissus." *Cinematographe*, April 1985, p. 5.

Sheehan, Henry. "Black Narcissus." *Film Comment*, May 1990, pp. 37-39.

"Storm Beaten Narcissus." *Newsweek*, August 18, 1947, pp. 77-78.

TMP. "Black Narcissus, British Study of Missionary Nuns." *New York Times*, August 14, 1947, p. 29.

Walker, Michael. "Black Narcissus." *Framework*, Winter 1978-1979, pp. 9-13.

The Red Shoes

Affron, Charles. "Reading as Performance: Danced by The Red Shoes." *North Dakota Quarterly* 51, (3), 1983, pp. 46-58.

Anderson, Jack. "The Red Shoes Can Still Prompt Sighs From Modern Moviegoers." *New York Times*, September 27, 1984, p. 21C.

Benson, Sheila. "The Red Shoes." *Film Comment*, May 1990, pp. 39-41.

Bower, Anthony. "Films." *The Nation*, November 6, 1948, pp. 529-530.

Carson, Saul. "Movies: Things Are Looking Up." *New Republic*, October 25, 1948, p. 26.

Como, William. "In Search of the Red Shoes." *Dancemagazine*, September 1983, pp. 58-65.

Comuzio, Ermanno. "La Musica e il balletto." *Cineforum*, June 1988, pp. 72-74.

Crowther, Bosley. "The Red Shoes." *New York Times*, October 23, 1948, p. 9.

"Dancers and Gangsters." *New Yorker*, October 23, 1948, p. 107.

Eames, Marian. "Gray Thoughts on Red Shoes." *Films In Review*, December 1950, pp. 20-24.

Fraser, Peter. "The Musical Mode: Putting on the Red Shoes." *Cinema Journal*, Spring 1987, pp. 44-54.

Gruen, John. "Moira Shearer: Still Chased by Red Shoes." *New York Times*, January 10, 1988, p. 22.

Hopkins, Arthur. "Red Shoes." *Theatre Arts*, January 1949, p. 52.

Jacobs, Laura. "The Red Shoes Revisited: An Appreciation of the Balletomane's Class Film." *Atlantic Monthly*, December 1993, pp. 129-134.

Lejeune, C. A. "British Movie Memos." *New York Times*, July 27, 1947, p. 3.

———. "Communiques From The London Film Front." *New York Times*, June 29, 1947, p. 5.

———. "London Begins a Busy Summer Film Schedule." *New York Times*, June 1, 1947, p. 5.

———. "The Red Shoes." *The Observer*, July 25, 1948.

Martini, Emanuela. "Scarpette rosse di Michael Powell e Emeric Pressburger." *Cineforum*, June 1988 pp. 67-74.

McLean, Adrienne L. "The Red Shoes Revisited." *Dance Chronicle*, Spring 1988, pp. 31-81.

Powell, Michael. "Dance Girl Dance." *American Film*, March 1987, pp. 39-44, 57.

St. Chernez, Casey. "Dancing Feats." *American Film*, July 1990, pp. 54-56.

"The Red Shoes." *Fortnight*, December 31, 1948, p. 29

———. *Monthly Film Bulletin*, August 1948, pp. 108-109.

———. *Newsweek*, October 25, 1948, p. 101.

———. *School and Society*, December 4, 1948, p. 386.

———. *Time*, October 25, 1948, p. 102.

———. *Variety*, August 11, 1948, p. 11.

The Small Back Room

HHT. "The Small Back Room." *New York Times*, February 2, 1962, p. 11.

Milne, Tom. "The Small Back Room." *Monthly Film Bulletin*, November 1984, pp. 358-359.

Myro. "The Small Back Room." *Variety*, January 26, 1949.

"The Small Back Room." *Monthly Film Bulletin*, March 31, 1948, p. 40.

Gone To Earth

Bergan, Ronald. "Gone To Earth." *Films and Filming*, November 1986, pp. 34-35.

Boyd-Bowman, Susan. "Heavy Breathing in Shropshire." *Screen*, November 1986, pp. 44-53.

Cahoon, Herbert. "The Wild Heart." *Library Journal*, June 15, 1952, p. 1071.

Cook, Pam. "Gone To Earth." *Monthly Film Bulletin*, December 1986, pp. 353-354.

Hartung, Philip T. "Sweeney Among Nightingales." *Commonweal*, June 20, 1952, p. 268.

Knight, Arthur. "Hail Britannia!" *Saturday Review*, June 28, 1952, p. 27.

Lambert, Gavin. "Gone to Earth." *Monthly Film Bulletin*, October 1950, p. 149.

McVay, Douglas. "Gone To Earth." *Films and Filming*, January 1982, pp. 23-25.

Myro. "Gone To Earth." *Variety*, September 27, 1950, p. 8.

"The Wild Heart." *Newsweek*, June 9, 1952, pp. 90-91.

———. *Time*, June 9, 1952, pp. 102-104.

———. *Variety*, June 4, 1952, p. 6.

Thompson, Howard. "Presenting the Lady Called Jones." *New York Times*, May 25, 1952, p. 5.

Williamson, Judith. "Male Order." *New Statesman*, October 31, 1986, pp. 24-25.

The Elusive Pimpernel

Myro. "The Elusive Pimpernel." *Variety*, November 22, 1950, p. 18.

P.H. "The Elusive Pimpernel." *Monthly Film Bulletin*, December 1950, p. 184.

"They Seek Him Here." *Times* (London), November 6, 1950.

The Tales of Hoffmann

Alpert, Hollis. "Strictly For The Art House." *Saturday Review*, April 28, 1951, pp. 27-28.

Bauer, Leda. "Twice Told Tales." *Theatre Arts*, June 1951, pp. 39-41.

Bron. "The Tales of Hoffmann." *Variety*, April 4, 1951, p. 6.

Challis, Christopher. "Hoffmann Sets New Pattern in Film Making Technique." *American Cinematographer*, May 1951, pp. 176-177.

Crowther, Bosley. "The Tales of Hoffmann." *New York Times*, April 5, 1951, p. 34.

de la Roche, Catherine. "The Tales of Hoffmann." *Sight and Sound*, May 1951, pp. 17-18.

Elsaesser, Thomas. "The Tales of Hoffmann." *Brighton Film Review*, 1968, n. 1.

Greenfield, Amy. "Tales of Hoffmann." *Film Comment*, March 1995, pp. 26-31.

Hartung, Philip T. "Delectable Bundles From Britain." *Commonweal*, April 20, 1951, p. 38.

"Import." *Time*, April 23, 1951, p. 108.

Kenny, Glenn. "The Tales of Hoffmann." *Video*, November 1992.

Kolodin, Irving. "Music To My Ears." *Saturday Review*, April 7, 1951, pp. 32-33.

Lambert, Gavin. "The Tales of Hoffmann." *Monthly Film Bulletin*, May 1951, pp. 277-278.

McCarten, John. "Culture by the Carload." *New Yorker*, April 14, 1951, p. 127.

Pascaud, Fabienne. "Les Contes d'Hoffmann." *Telerama*, June 6, 1984, p. 29.

Peltz, Mary Ellis. "The Tales of Hoffmann." *Films in Review*, May 1951, pp. 44-46.

Roller, Howard. "The Tales of Hoffmann." *The Perfect Vision*, Summer 1993, pp. 116-118.

Sabin, Robert. "The Tales of Hoffmann In British Film Version." *America*, March 1951, p. 9.

"The Tales of Hoffmann." *Life*, March 5, 1951, pp. 95-97.

———. *Newsweek*, April 16, 1951, pp. 106-107.

Whitebait, William. "The Movies." *New Statesman*, April 28, 1951, pp. 476-477.

The Sorcerer's Apprentice

"The Sorcerer's Apprentice." *Monthly Film Bulletin*, August 1945, pp. 142-143.

Oh Rosalinda!!

Clem. "Oh, Rosalinda." *Variety*, November 30, 1955.

"Die Fledermaus On the Screen." *Times* (London), November 21, 1955.

DR. "Oh Rosalinda." *Monthly Film Bulletin*, December 1955, p. 4.

Everson, William K. "Rediscovery." *Films In Review*, October 1985, pp. 477-480.

"Oh Rosalinda." *Films and Filming*, January 1956, p. 21.

The Battle of the River Plate

Baker, Peter. "Battle of the River Plate." *Films and Filming*, December 1956, p. 22.

Combs, Richard. "The Battle of The River Plate." *Film Comment*, March 1995, pp. 20-25.

Coultass, Clive. "The Battle of the River Plate." *History Today*, August 1996, pp. 23-27.

Crowther, Bosley. "Screen: Pursuit of the Graf Spree." *New York Times*, December 27, 1957, p. 23.

"Death of A Tiger." *Newsweek*, January 13, 1958, p. 88.

Finley, James Fenlon. "The Pursuit of the Graf Spree." *Catholic World*, July 1957, p. 304.

Hartung, Philip T. "Briny." *Commonweal*, January 24, 1958, p. 432.

Hatch, Robert. "Films." *Nation*, January 11, 1958, pp. 38-39.

HH. "The Pursuit of the Graf Spree." *Films In Review*, December 1957, pp. 524-525.

Kaufman, Stanley. "Arms and The Man." *New Republic*, March 3, 1958, p. 21.

Knight, Arthur. "The Pursuit of the Graf Spree." *Saturday Review*, September 14, 1957, p. 30.

McCarten, John. "From Here, There, and Everywhere." *New Yorker*, January 11, 1958, p. 102.

Myro. "The Battle of The River Plate." *Variety*, November 21,1956.

PH. "Battle of the River Plate." *Monthly Film Bulletin*, December 1956, p. 148.

"Royal Film Show." *Times* (London), October 30, 1956.

Walsh, Moira. "Films," *America*, November 16, 1957, p. 227.

"The New Pictures." *Time*, January 27, 1958, p. 90.

Ill Met By Moonlight

"Exciting British War Film Based On Fact." *Times* (London), February 4, 1957.

Myro. "Ill Met by Moonlight." *Variety*, March 20, 1957.

PJD. "Ill Met By Moonlight." *Monthly Film Bulletin*, December 1956, p. 63.

Richards, Peter. "Ill Met By Moonlight." *Film Comment*, March 1995, pp. 37-40.

Thompson, Howard. "Night Ambush." *New York Times*, April 25, 1958, p. 32.

Luna Del Miel

Arkadin. "Film Clips." *Sight and Sound*, Winter 1962, pp 34-35.

J. G. "Luna Del Miel." *Monthly Film Bulletin*, February 1962, pp. 32-33.

Peeping Tom

Baker, Peter. "Peeping Tom." *Films and Filming*, May 1960, p. 26.

Canby, Vincent. "Film: Michael Powell's Peeping Tom." *New York Times*, October 14, 1979, p. 65.

Chamerlin, Phillip. "Peeping Tom." *Film Society Review*, January 1966, p. 13

DR. "Peeping Tom." *Monthly Film Bulletin*, April 1960, pp. 65-66.

d'Allones, Fabrice Revault. "Le Cinema Au Stade Du Miroir." *Cahiers du Cinema*, January 1984, pp. 52-53.

Dubois, P. "Voir, la mort, ou l'effet-Meduse de la photographie au cinema." *Review Belge du Cinema*, Summer 1983, p. 63.

Dumont, Pascal. "Le Voyeur." *Cinema*, January 1984, pp. 44-45.

Durgnat, Raymond. "Movie Crazy, The Man(iac) With The Movie Camera." *Framework*, Winter 1978-79, pp. 3-9.

Findley, Janice. "Peeping Tom." *Film Comment*, May 1990, pp. 41-43.

Gough-Yates, Kevin. "Private Madness and Public Lunacy." *Films and Filming*, February 1972, pp. 27-33.

Humphries, Reynold. "Peeping Tom, Voyeurism, the Camera and the Spectator." *Film Reader* 4 (1979), pp. 193-200.

Johnson, Ian. "A Pin To See The Peep Show." *Motion*, February 1963, pp. 36-39.

Johnson, William. "Peeping Tom: A Second Look." *Film Quarterly*, Spring 1980, pp. 2-10.

Kelley, Bill. "Peeping Tom." *Cinefantastique*, Spring 1980, p. 4.

Lefevre, Raymond. "Du Voyeurisme a l'infini." *Midi-Minuit Fantastique*, October 1968, pp. 14-18.

McDonaght, Maitland. "The Ambiguities of Seeing and Knowing In Michael Powell's Peeping Tom." *Film Psychology Review*, Summer 1980, pp. 207-220.

MD. "Beau sujet gache." *Cahiers du Cinema*, December 1960, p. 61.

Morris, N.A. "Reflections on Peeping Tom." *Movie* 34/35 (Winter 1990), pp. 82-97.

PGB. "Peeping Tom." *Films and Filming*, May 1960, p. 26.

Philbert, Bertrand. "Le Voyeur." *Cinematographe*, December 1983, p. 55.

Renaud, Tristan. "Le Voyeur." *Cinema*, October 1976, pp. 120-122.

Rich. "Peeping Tom." *Variety*, April 20, 1960, p. 8.

Romer, Jean Claude. "Le Voyeur." *Ecran*, July 1973, p. 20.

———. "Lady Godiva Et Peeping Tom." *Midi-Minuit Fantastique*, January 1964, pp. 1-2.

Sarris, Andrew. "Vintage Voyeurism." *Village Voice*, October 15, 1979, pp. 45-47.

Sayre, Nora. "Films." *The Nation*, November 10, 1979, p. 473.

Stein, Elliot. "A Very Tender Film, A Very Nice One: Michael Powell's Peeping Tom." *Film Comment*, September 1979, pp. 57-59.

Thomson, David. "The Mark of the Red Death." *Sight and Sound*, Autumn 1980, pp. 258-262.

Torok, Jean-Paul. "Look At The Sea, Le Voyeur." *Positif*, November 1960, pp. 57-59.

Walker, John. "Peeping Tom." *Video*, June 1994, pp. 66-67.

Whitebait, William. "Hold the Nose." *New Statesman*, April 9, 1960, p. 520.

Wollen, Peter. "Dying For Art." *Sight and Sound*, December 1984, pp. 19-21.

The Queen's Guards

"Mr. Michael Powell's Latest Film." *Times* (London), October 15, 1961.

"Queen's Guards." *Monthly Film Bulletin*, November 1961, pp. 171-172.

Rich. "The Queen's Guards." *Variety*, October 25, 1961.

They're A Weird Mob

"Carnival Time Out of War." *Times* (London), October 20, 1966, p. 17b.

Stan. "They're A Weird Mob." *Variety*, September 14, 1966.

"They're A Weird Mob." *Monthly Film Bulletin*, November 1966, p. 56.

Age of Consent

Austen, David. "Age of Consent." *Films and Filming*, Jan 1970, p. 50.

Combs, Richard. "Age of Consent." *Monthly Film Bulletin*, December 1969, p. 256.

Stan. "Age of Consent." *Variety*, May 14, 1969.

Taylor, John Russell. "Age of Consent." *Times* (London), November 13, 1969.

Boy Who Turned Yellow

Combs, Richard. "The Boy Who Turned Yellow." *Monthly Film Bulletin*, October 1972, p. 208.

Articles on Michael Powell

"An Overrated Braggart." *Economist*, September 26, 1992, pp. 103-105.

Andrews, Nigel and Harlan Kennedy. "Peerless Powell." *Film Comment*, May 1970, pp. 50-55.

Assayas, Olivier. "Entretien Avec Michael Powell." *Cahiers du Cinema*, March 1981, pp. 20-21.

———. "Redecouvrir Michael Powell." *Cahiers du Cinema*, January 1981, pp. 7-9.

———. "Redecouvrir Michael Powell, L'Espirit Du Temps." *Cahiers du Cinema*, March 1981, pp. 10-19.

Azzopardi, John. "The Frenzied Art of Michael Powell." *Thousand Eyes Magazine*, February 7, 1976, p. 9.

Badder, David. "Powell and Pressburger, The War Years." *Sight and Sound*, Spring 1978, pp. 8-12.

Bassan, Raphael. "Michael Powell, Un Orfevre De L'objectif." *La Revue du Cinema*, May 1981, pp. 65-78.

"Bio-biblio-filmographie de Michael Powell." *Positif*, April 1981, pp. 32-45.

Brennan, M. "Powell and Pressburger At the NFT." *Films and Filming*, October 1985, p. 27.

Brunette, Peter. "A Life In Movies." *New York Times Book Review*, April 19, 1987, p. 17.

Carcasonne, Philippe, and Jacques Fieschi. "Entretien Avec Michael Powell." *Cinematographe*, May 1981, pp. 60-64.

Christie, Ian. "Michael Powell: After and Before the Archers." *Sight and Sound*, Spring 1990, p. 79.

———. "Powell and Pressburger: Putting Back the Pieces." *Monthly Film Bulletin*, December 1984, p. 611.

Codelli, Lorenzo. "The Edge of the World." (book review), *Positif*, November 1990, p. 79.

Cohn, Lawrence. "British Filmmaker Michael Powell Dies." *Variety*, February 28, 1990, p. 9, 18.

Collins, R., and Ian Christie. "Interview with Michael Powell, the Expense of Naturalism." *Monogram*, 3 (1972), pp. 32-38.

Cowie, Peter. "Million Dollar Movie." *Variety*, October 19, 1992, p. 178.

Derobert, Eric, and Philippe Rouyer. "Powell, Pressburger, Pat O'Conner et pas grand-chose d'autre . . ." *Positif*, January 1988, pp. 18-19.

"The Director's Tale." *Economist*, February 24, 1990, p. 91.

Dowd, Maureen. "The Impact On Scorsese Of a British Film Team." *New York Times*, May 18, 1991, pp. 11, 16.

Durgnat, Raymond. "Aiming at the Archers, sur Michael Powell." *Positif*, February 1981, pp. 22-33.

———. "Remembering Michael Powell." *Sight and Sound*, October 1992 pp. 22–25.

Eisenschitz, Bernard. "Cannes 65." *Midi Minuit Fantastique* 13 (1965), pp. 38-40.

Erens, Patricia Brett. "A Life in Movies." *Film Quarterly*, Summer 1988, pp. 28-29.

Everson, William K. "A Meeting of Two Great Visual Stylists." *Films In Review*, November 1977, pp. 546-549.

———. "Book Reviews." *Films In Review*, February 1987, pp. 113-15.

———. "Michael Powell." *Films In Review*, August 1980, pp. 415-17.

———. "Michael Powell: 1905-1990." *Films in Review*, May 1990, pp. 265-70.

"Flamboyant Film Maker of Idiosyncratic Brilliance." *Times* (London), February 21, 1990 p. 16.

French, Sean. "Age of Contempt." *New Statesman and Society*, October 2, 1992, p. 46.

Fuller, Graham. "Isn't It Romantic." *Village Voice*, July 19, 1988, p. 60.

———. "Memoirs of the Man Who Made Peeping Tom." *Interview*, October 1992, p. 34.

———. "Odd Man Out." *Village Voice*, April 21, 1987, p. 46.

Giammatteo, Fernaldo di. "I Registri: Powell e Pressburger nella Presitoria del Film a Colori." *Cinema* 20 (1949), pp. 79-81.

Gonzalez, Pierrett, and Claude Guiguet. "Bio-biblio-filmographie de Michael Powell, Enrichie de commentaries inedits du realisateur et de ses collaborateurs: Emeric Pressburger, Deborah Kerr, Brian Easdale, Kathleen Byron." *Positif*, March 1981, pp. 19-45.

Green, OO. [pseudonym of Raymond Durgnat]. "Michael Powell." *Movie*, Autumn 1965, pp. 17-20.

Grivel, Daniele and Bertrand Borie. "Le voleur de Bagdad, la genese du film. Le decoupage." *l'Ecran Fantastique*, (18) 1981, pp. 14-23.

Grosoli, Fabrizio. "P&P: L'occhio che anticipa." *Cineforum*, October 1982, pp. 39-47.

Hardy, Forsyth. "Lettera dalla Gran Bretagna: Il cinema inglese e gli esperimenti di Powell." *Cinema*, April 1950, pp. 210-11.

Hunter, Allan. "Powell's Life." *Films and Filming*, October 1986, pp. 23-25.

Huntley, John. "The Sound Track." *Sight and Sound*, January 1951, p. 381.

James, Caryn. "A Passion For Movies." *New York Times Book Review*, April 16, 1995, pp. 11-12.

Kaufmann, Stanley. "Successes." *New Republic*, May 11, 1987, pp. 24-26.

Kennedy, Harlan. "A Modest Magician." *American Film*, July 1990, pp. 32-36.

Lacourbe, Roland. "Introduction a l'oeuvre de Michael Powell." *Image et Son*, June 1971 pp. 23-70.

———. "Redecouvrir Michael Powell." *Ecran*, January 15, 1979, pp. 24-40.

———. "Redecouvrir Michael Powell." *Ecran*, February 15,1979, pp. 34-40.

Lambert, Gavin. "British Films 1947: Survey and Prospects." *Sequence*, Winter 1947, pp. 9-14.

Lefevre, Raymond, and Roland Lacourbe. "Londres, recontre avec Michael Powell." *Cinema 76*, December 1976, pp. 83-86.

Magney, Joel. "Michael Powell." *Cahiers du Cinema*, April 1990, p. 84.

McVay, Douglas. "Cinema of Enchantment." *Films and Filming*, December 1981, pp. 14-19.

Millar, Gavin. "Cox's Orange Pippin." *Sight and Sound*, Summer 1990, pp. 180-82.

Mose, Karl S. "Behind the Eyelid, Macrocosm and Microcosm in the Work of Michael Powell." *Aspern Review of Filmology*, March 1979, pp. 18, 27.

Nolan, Jack Edmund. "Films on TV." *Films In Review*, May 1968, pp. 303-305

O'Brien, Geoffrey. "Grand Illusions." *New York Review of Books*, August 13, 1987, pp. 14-16.

Powell, Dilys. "The Man Who Took Our Cinema On A Great Adventure." *Times* (London), February 25, 1990, p. E4.

Raphael, Frederic. "The Life and Death of Peeping Mike." *Spectator* (London), October 10, 1992, p. 37.

Rodrig, Antonio. "Michael Powell." *Cinematographe*, July 1984, pp. 38-39.

Sarris, Andrew. "The Life and Death of Colonel Blimp/Black Narcissus." *Video Review*, March 1989, pp. 60-61.

———. "Powell and Pressburger: A Matter of Life and Death." *Village Voice*, April 19, 1988, p. 68.

———. "Powell and Pressburger: Let Us Now Praise British Films," *Village Voice*, December 17-23, 1980, p. 92.

Sarris, Andrew, and Tom Allen. "Revivals." *Village Voice*, July 19, 1988, p. 66.

Sayre, Nora. "Michael Powell—At 75, A British Director Receives a Tribute." *New York Times*, November 30, 1980, pp. 17, 24.

Schidlow, Joshka. "Michael Powell: Le gentleman bricoleur." *Telerama*, June 6, 1984, pp. 28–29.

Secchi, Cesare, and Paolo Vecchi. "Mitopoiesi e voyeurismo nel cinema di Michael Powell." *Cineforum*, May 1989, pp. 40–48.

St. Charnez, Casey. "Dancing Feats." *American Film*, July 1990, pp. 54–56.

Tanner, Louise. "Accents and Umlauts." *Films in Review*, March 1995, pp. 28–31.

Tavernier, Bertrand. "Blimp, Powell, Pressburger . . . et la poesie deguisee." *Positif*, April 1981, pp. 22–26.

Tavernier, Bertrand and Jacques Prayer. "Entretien avec Michael Powell." *Midi Minuit Fantastique*, October 1968.

Taylor, John Russell. "Nine Lives of Michael Powell." *Sight and Sound*, Autumn 1986, pp. 243-244.

———. "Michael Powell, Myths and Supermen." *Sight and Sound*, Autumn 1978, pp 226-229.

Taylor-Corbett, Lynn. "Michael Powell: A Remembrance." *Dance Magazine*, February 1991, p. 28.

"The Red Faces." *Economist*, November 1, 1986, pp. 92, 96. (Review of Powell's autobiography.)

Thomson, David. "The Films of Michael Powell: A Romantic Sensibility." *American Film*, November 1980, pp. 47-52.

———. "Michael Powell: 1905–1990." *Film Comment*, May 1990, pp. 27–28.

Tobin, Yann. "Les Chaussons rouges Les Contes d'Hoffman." *Positif*, March 1985, pp. 63–66.

———. "Post-scriptum: le point du jour et les horizons perdus." *Positif*, April 1981, pp. 27–31.

"Une table ronde sur la notion d'auteur." *Journal des Cahiers*, November 1982.

Walker, Alexander. "Daddy of the Brats: Million Dollar Movie." *Times Literary Supplement*, October 2, 1992, p. 19.

Williams, Tony. "Michael Powell." *Films and Filming*, November 1981, pp. 10–16.

Wilson, Harry. "Michael Powell and His Pictures, The Story of a Man and His Work." *Film Monthly*, September 1947, pp. 4–5.

Yarrow, Andrew L. "Michael Powell Is Dead at 84; Film Career Spanned 50 Years." *New York Times*, February 20, 1990, p. 23.

Zimmer, Jacques. "Michael Powell (1905–1990): La deuxieme mort de Peeping Tom." *Revue du Cinema*, March 1990, p. 7.

Articles by Michael Powell

Powell, Michael. "Four Powers in Waltz Time." *Sight and Sound*, November 1955, p. 5.

———. "Leo Marks et Mark Lewis." *Cinema*, December 1984, pp. 56–57.

———. "Martin Scorsese." *Positif*, April 1981, pp. 46–47.

———. "Michael Powell's Guilty Pleasures." *Film Comment*, July 1981, pp. 28–31.

———. "Mr. Powell Replies." *Picturegoer*, December 30, 1950, p. 12.

———. "On The World's Edge." *New York Times*, September 4, 1938.

———. "Solus Rex." *Film Comment*, January 1981, p. 72.

———. "What's In It for Me." *AIP*, December 1985, p. 9.

———. "Your Questions Answered," *Penguin Film Review* 1 (1946), pp. 102–111.

Powell, Michael, and Hein Heckroth. "Making Colour Talk." *Kinematograph Weekly*, November 9, 1950.

Articles on Emeric Pressburger

Christie, Ian. "Alienation Effects." *Monthly Film Bulletin*, October 1984, pp. 318–320.

Cunningham, John. "From Imre To Emeric." *Hungarian Quarterly*, Autumn 1995.

Ellis, John. "Alien Insight." *New Statesman and Society*, May 27, 1994, pp. 46–47. (Review of Kevin MacDonald's biography.)

Gough-Yates, Kevin. "Pressburger: England and Exile." *Sight and Sound*, December 1995, pp. 30–34.

Heffer, Simon. "The Hungarian Half of an English Team." *Spectator* (London), August 13, 1994, pp. 27–28. (Review of Kevin MacDonald's biography.)

McCarthy, Todd. "Emeric Pressburger, Scenarist Partner of Michael Powell, Dies." *Variety*, February 10, 1988, p. 4.

Yarrow, Andrew L. "Emeric Pressburger Is Dead at 85; The Screenwriter for the Red Shoes." *New York Times*, February 6, 1988, p. 10.

Books

Aldgate, Anthony, and Jeffrey Richards. *Britain Can Take It*. Cambridge: Blackwell, 1986.

———. *Best of British Cinema and Society 1930–1970*. London: Oxford, 1983.

Armes, Roy. *A Critical History of the British Cinema*. London: Secker & Warburg, 1978.

Britton, Eric. *I Know Where I'm Going: The Book of the Film*. London: World Film Publications, 1946.

Christie, Ian. *Arrows of Desire*. London: Faber & Faber, 1994.

———. *Powell, Pressburger and Others*. London: British Film Institute, 1978.

Clover, Carol J. *Men, Women and Chainsaws: Gender in the Modern Horror Film*. Princeton, NJ: Princeton University Press, 1992.

Coultass, Clive. *Images for Battle*. London: Associated University Press, 1993.

Durgnat, Raymond. *A Mirror for England: British Movies from Austerity to Affluence*. London: Faber & Faber, 1970.

Eyles, Allen, and David Meeker. *Missing Believed Lost*. London: British Film Institute, 1994.

Forman, Denis. *Films 1945–1950*. London: Longmans Green, 1952.

Gibbon, Monk. *The Red Shoes Ballet: A Critical Study*. London: Saturn, 1948.

———. *The Tales of Hoffmann: A Study of the Film*. London: Saturn, 1951.

Godden, Rumer. *Black Narcissus*. London: World Film Publications, 1947.

Gottler, Franz, ed. *Living Cinema: Powell and Pressburger*. Munich: Kino Kontexte, 1982.

Gough-Yates, Kevin. *Michael Powell*. Brussels: Film Museum, 1973.

———. *Michael Powell, in Collaboration with Emeric Pressburger*. London: British Film Institute, 1971.

Hardy, Forsyth. *Scotland In Film*. Edinburgh: Edinburgh University Press, 1990.

Howard, James. *Michael Powell*. London: Batsford Press, 1996.

Huntley, John. *British Technicolor Films*. London: Skelton Robinson, 1949.

Kelly, Mary Pat. *Martin Scorsese: The First Decade*. New York: Redgrave, 1980. (Introduction by Powell).

Kulik, Karol. *Alexander Korda: The Man Who Could Work Miracles*. London: Allen, 1975.

MacDonald, Kevin. *Emeric Pressburger: The Life and Death of a Screenwriter*. London: Faber & Faber, 1994.

Manvell, Roger. *Films and the Second World War*. New York: Barnes, 1974.

Martini, Emanuela, ed. *Powell and Pressburger*. Bergamo: Bergamo Film Meeting, 1986.

McFarlane, Brian. *Sixty Voices*. London: British Film Institute, 1992.

Murphy, Robert. *Sixties British Cinema*. London: British Film Institute, 1992.

O'Leary, Liam. *Rex Ingram: Master of the Silent Screen*. Dublin: Academy Press, 1980.

Noble, Peter, ed. *The British Film Yearbook*. London: Skelton Robinson, 1949.

Oumano, Ellen, ed. *Film Forum: Thirty-five Top Filmmakers Discuss Their Careers*. New York: St. Martin's Press, 1985.

Perry, George. *The Great British Picture Show*. London: MacGibbon, 1974.

Pike, Andrew, and Ross Parker. *Australian Film 1900–1977*. Melbourne: Oxford University Press, 1980.

Powell, Michael. *200,000 Feet on Foula*. London: Faber and Faber, 1938.

———. *Death in the Atlantic*. London: Hodder & Stoughton, 1956.

———. *The Waiting Game*. London: Michael Joseph, 1975.

Powell, Michael and Emeric Pressburger. *The Red Shoes*. New York: Avon, 1978.

Pressburger, Emeric. *Killing a Mouse on Sunday*. London: Collins, 1961.

———. *The Glass Pearls*. London: Heinemann, 1966.

Robson, M. M. *The Shame and Disgrace of Colonel Blimp*. London: Sidneyan Society, 1944.

Roud, Richard, ed. *Cinema A Critical Dictionary: Vol. 2*. New York: Viking, 1980.

Rubenstein, Leonard. *The Great Spy Films: A Pictorial History*. Secaucus, NJ: Citadel, 1979.

Shirley, Graham, and Brian Adams. *Australian Cinema: The First Eighty Years*. Sydney: Currency, 1985

Silverman, Kaja. *The Acoustic Mirror: The Female Voice in Psychoanalysis and Cinema*. Bloomington: Indiana University Press, 1988.

Steinbrunner, Chris, and Burt Goldblatt. *Cinema of the Fantastic*. New York: Saturday Review Press, 1972.

Thomson, David. *A Biographical Dictionary of Film*. New York: Knopf, 1994.

Vermilye, Jerry. *The Great British Films*. Secaucus, NJ: Citadel Press, 1971.

Wakemann, John, ed. *World Film Directors: Vol. 1, 1890–1945*. New York: H. W. Wilson Company 1987.

Warman, Eric. *A Matter of Life and Death: The Book of the Film*. London: World Film Publications, 1946.

Laser Discs Available on the Archers

These discs, produced by the Criterion Company, contain additional material that makes them of interest to anyone looking to view the Archers' films.

Black Narcissus: The second audio track contains commentary by Powell and Martin Scorsese.

49th Parallel: The second track contains an audio commentary by Bruce Eders.

I Know Where I'm Going: The second track is by Ian Christie, but the attraction of the disc is the documentary on the film, containing not only reminiscences of some of the cast, but also the story of Nancy Franklin, who was so taken with the film that she traveled to the island of Kiloran to visit its sights.

The Life and Death of Colonel Blimp: The second track of the film contains reminiscences by Powell and commentary by Martin Scorsese.

Peeping Tom: This disc contains an audio commentary by critic Laura Mulvey.

The Red Shoes: In addition to containing a stunning transfer of the film, this disc also has an audio track with commentary by Ian Christie and interviews with Marius Goring, Moira Shearer, Brian Easdale, and Martin Scorsese. A second track contains excerpts from Powell and Pressburger's adaptation of *The Red Shoes*, read by Jeremy Irons. Additional features include a collection of stills from Scorsese's collection, the original trailer and a videography of the Archers.

The Tales of Hoffmann: The commentary is by Martin Scorsese and Bruce Eder.

Filmography

Written, Produced, and Directed by
Michael Powell and Emeric Pressburger

One Of Our Aircraft Is Missing

Production: British National. *Co-producer*: John Corfield. *Director of photography*: Ronald Neame. *Editor*: David Lean. *Art director*: David Rawnsley. *Sound*: C. C. Stevens. *Running time*: 102 minutes. *Released*: June 17, 1942. *Cast*: Godfrey Tearle (Sir George Corbett), Eric Portman (Tom Earnshaw), Hugh Williams (Frank Shelley), Bernard Miles (Geoff Hickman), Hugh Burden (John Glyn Haggard), Emrys Jones (Bob Ashley), Pamela Brown (Els Meertens), Joyce Redman (Jet Van Dieren), Googie Withers (Jo de Vries), Hay Petrie (Piet Van Dieren, the Burgomaster), Selma van Dias (Burgomaster's wife), Arnold Marle (Pieter Shys), Robert Helpmann (Julius De Jong), Peter Ustinov (the Priest), Alec Clunes (organist), Hector Abbas (driver), James Carson (Louis), Bill Akkerman (Willem), Joan Akkerman (Maartie), Peter Schenke (Hendrik), Valerie Moon (Jannie), John Salew (sentry), William D'Arcy (German officer), David Ward (first airman), Robert Duncan (second airman), Roland Culver (naval Officer), Robert Beatty (Hopkins), MICHAEL POWELL (dispatching officer), Stewart Rome (Commander Reynold), David Evans (Len Martin), John Longden (man), Gerry Wilmott (announcer), John Arnold, James Donald, John England, Gordon Jackson.

The Life and Death of Colonel Blimp
(U.S.: *Colonel Blimp*)

Production: Archers/Independent Producers. *Director of photography*: Georges Perinal. *Editor*: John Seabourne. *Production designer*: Alfred Junge. *Music*: Allan Gray. *Sound*: C. C. Stevens. *Military advisor*: Lt. General Sir Douglas Brownrigg. *Running time*: 163 minutes. *Released*: July 26, 1943. *Cast*: Anton Walbrook (Theo Kretschmar-Schuldorff), Roger Livesey (Clive Candy), Deborah Kerr (Edith Hunter/Barbara Wynne/Angela "Johnny" Cannon), Roland Culver (Colonel Betteridge), James McKechnie (Lieutenant Spud Wilson), Albert Lieven (von Ritter), Arthur Wontner (Counsellor), David Hutcheson (Hoppy), Ursula Jeans (Frau von Kalteneck), John Laurie (John Montgomery Murdoch), Harry Welchman (Major John E. Davies), Reginald Tate (Van Ziji), A. E. Matthews (President of Tribunal), Carl Jaffe (Von Reumann), Valentine Dyall (von Schonbron), Muriel Aked (Aunt Margaret Hamilton), Felix Aylmer (Bishop), Frith Banbury (Babyface Fitzroy), Neville Mapp (Stuffy Graves), Vincent Holman (club porter, 1942), Spencer Trevor (period Blimp), Dennis Arundell (cafe orchestra leader), James Knight (club porter, 1902), David Ward (Kaunitz), Jan van Loewen (indignant citizen), Eric Maturin (Colonel Goodhead), Robert Harris (embassy secretary), Count Zichy (Colonel Borg), Jane Millican (Nurse Erna), Phyllis Morris (Pebble), Diana Marshall (Sybil), Captain W. H. Barrett (Texan), Corporal Thomas Palmer (sergeant), Yvonne Andree (nun), Marjorie Greasley (matron), Helen Debroy (Mrs. Wynne), Norman Pierce (Mr. Wynne), Edward Cooper (BBC official), Joan Swinstead (secretary), Wally Patch (sergeant clearing debris), Ferdy Mayne (Prussian student), John Boxer (soldier), John Varley, Patrick Macnee.

The Volunteer

Production: Archers. *Production manager*: Sydney Streeter. *Director of photography*: Freddie Ford. *Editor*: John Seabourne. *Music*: Allan Gray. *Running time*: 46 minutes. *Released*: January 10, 1944. *Cast*: Ralph Richardson (himself), Pat McGrath

(Fred Davey), Laurence Olivier, MICHAEL POWELL, Anna Neagle, Herbert Wilcox, Tommy Woodroofe, Joan Richardson (?).

A Canterbury Tale

Production: Archers. *Director of Photography*: Erwin Hillier. *Editor*: John Seabourne. *Production designer*: Alfred Junge. *Music*: Allan Gray, conducted by Walter Goehr. *Assistant director*: George Busby. *Period advisor*: Herbert Norris. *Sound*: C. C. Stevens and Desmond Dew. *Running time*: 124 minutes. *Released*: August 21, 1944. *Cast*: Eric Portman (Thomas Colpepper, JP), Sheila Sim (Alison Smith), Sergeant John Sweet (Sergeant Bob Johnson), Dennis Price (Sergeant Peter Gibbs), Esmond Knight (narrator/Seven-Sisters soldier/village idiot), Charles Hawtrey (Thomas Duckett), Hay Petrie (Woodcock), George Merrit (Ned Horton), Edward Rigby (Jim Horton), Freda Jackson (Prudence Honeywood), Betty Jardine (Fee Baker), Eliot Makeham (organist), Harvey Golden (Sgt. Roczinsky), Leonard Smith (Leslie), James Tamsitt (Terry Holmes), David Todd (David), Beresford Egan (PC Overden), Antony Holles (Sergeant Bassett), Maude Lambert (Miss Grainger), Wally Bosco (ARP warden), Charles Paton (Ernie Brooks), Jane Millican (Susanna Foster), John Slater (Sergeant Len), Michael Golden (Sergeant Smale), Charles Moffatt (Sergeant "Stuffy"), Esma Cannon (Agnes), Mary Line (Leslie's mother), Winifred Swaffer (Mrs. Horton), Michael Howard (Archie), Judith Furse (Dorothy Bird), Barbara Waring (Polly Finn), Jean Shepeard (Gwladys Swinton), Margaret Scudamore (Mrs. Colpepper), Joss Ambler (police inspector), Jessie James (waitress), Kathleen Lucas (passerby), H. F. Maltby (Mr. Portal), Eric Maturin (Geoffrey's father), Parry Jones Jr. (Arthur).

I Know Where I'm Going

Production: Archers. *Associate producer*: George R. Busby. *Director of photography*: Erwin Hillier. *Editor*: John Seabourne. *Art director*: Alfred Junge. *Music*: Allan Gray, conducted by Walter Goehr. *Assistant director*: John Tunstall. *Sound*: C. C. Stevens. *Technical advisor*: John Laurie. *Running time*: 92 minutes. *Released*: December 17, 1945. *Cast*: Wendy Hiller (Joan Webster), Roger Livesey (Torquil MacNeil), George Carney (Mr.

Webster), Pamela Brown (Catriona Potts), Walter Hudd (Hunter), Capt. Duncanc MacKechnie (Captain "Lochinvar"), Ian Sadler (Iain), Finlay Currie (Ruairidh Mhor), Murdo Morrison (Kenny), Margot Fitzsimmons (Bridie), Capt. C. W. R. Knight (Colonel Barnstaple), Donald Strachan (shepherd), John Rae (old shepherd), Duncan MacIntyre (his son), Jean Cadell (postmistress), Norman Shelley (Sir Robert Bellinger), Ivy Milton (Peigi), Anthony Eustrel (Hooper), Petula Clark (Cheril), Alec Faversham (Martin), Catherine Lacey (Mrs. Robinson), Valentine Dyall (Mr. Robinson), Nancy Price (Rebecca Crozier), Herbert Lomas (Mr. Campbell), Kitty Kirwan (Mrs. Campbell), John Laurie (John Campbell), Graham Moffat (RAF Sergeant), Boyd Stevens, Maxwell Kennedy, Jean Houston (singers in Ceildhe), Arthur Chesney (harmonica player), Mr. Ramshaw (Torquil, the eagle).

A Matter of Life and Death
(U.S.: *Stairway to Heaven*)

Production: Archers. *Associate producer*: George R. Busby. *Director of photography*: Jack Cardiff. *Assistant director*: Parry Jones, Jr. *Production designer*: Alfred Junge. *Editor*: Reginald Mills. *Music*: Allan Gray. *Conductor*: W. L. Williamson. *Costumes*: Hein Heckroth. *Sound*: C. C. Stevens. *Running Time*: 104 minutes. *Released*: March 1947. Cast: David Niven (Peter Carter), Kim Hunter (June), Marius Goring (Conductor 71), Roger Livesey (Dr. Frank Reeves), Robert Coote (Bob Trumpshaw), Kathleen Byron (angel), Richard Attenborough (English pilot), Bonar Colleano (American pilot), Joan Maude (chief recorder), Edwin Max (Dr. McEwen), Abraham Sofaer (Judge/chief surgeon), Raymond Massey (Abraham Farlan), Robert Atkins (vicar), Betty Potter (Mrs. Tucker), Bob Roberts (Dr. Gaertler), Tommy Duggan (American policeman), Roger Snowden (Irishman), Robert Arden (GI), Joan Verney (girl), Wendy Thompson (nurse), Wally Patch (ARP warden).

Black Narcissus

Production: Archers. *Associate Producer*: George R. Busby. Screenplay from Rumer Godden's novel. *Director of photography*: Jack Cardiff. *Assistant director*: Sydney Streeter. *Editing*:

Reginald Mills. *Costumes*: Hein Heckroth. *Music*: Brian Easdale. *Sound*: Stanley Lambourne. *Running time*: 100 minutes. *Released*: May 26, 1947. *Cast*: Deborah Kerr (Sister Clodagh), Sabu (General Dulip Rai), David Farrar (Mr. Dean), Flora Robson (Sister Philippa), Esmond Knight (Old General), Kathleen Byron (Sister Ruth), Jenny Laird (Sister "Honey" Blanche), Judith Furse (Sister Briony), May Hallatt (Angu Ayah), Shaun Noble (Con), Eddie Whaley, Jr. (Joseph Anthony), Nancy Roberts (Mother Dorothea), Jean Simmons (Kanchi), Ley On (Phuba).

The Red Shoes

Production: Archers. *Assistant producer*: George Busby. *Director of photography*: Jack Cardiff. *Assistant director*: Sydney Streeter. *Special effects*: F. George Dunn, D. Hague. *Editor*: Reginald Mills. *Production designer*: Hein Heckroth. *Art director*: Arthur Lawson. *Music*: Brian Easdale, Sir Thomas Beecham. *Singer*: Margherita Grandi. *Dancer*: Alan Carter. *Sound*: Charles Poulton. *Choreographer*: Robert Helpmann. *Running time*: 133 minutes. *Released*: September 6, 1948. *Cast*: Marius Goring (Julian Craster), Anton Walbrook (Boris Lermontov), Moira Shearer (Victoria Page), Leonid Massine (Grischa Ljubov), Austin Trevor (Professor Palmer), Esmond Knight (Livingstone "Livy" Montague), Eric Berry (Dimitri), Irene Browne (Lady Neston), Ludmilla Tcherina (Boronskaja), Jerry Verno (George), Robert Helpmann (Ivan Boleslawsky), Albert Basserman (Ratov), Derek Elphinstone (Lord Oldham), Madame Rambert (herself), Joy Rawlins (Gladys), Jean Short (Terry), Gordon Littman (Ike), Julia Lang (Balletomane), Bill Shine (her companion), Marcel Poncin (M. Boudin), Michel Bazalgette (M. Rideaut), Yvonne Andre (Victoria's dresser), Hay Petrie (Boisson), George Woodbridge or Richard George (doorman).

The Small Back Room (U.S.: *Hour of Glory*)

Production: London Film Productions/The Archers. *Screenplay*: MICHAEL POWELL, Emeric Pressburger, Nigel Balchin. *Assistant Director*: Sydney Streeter. *Director of photography*: Christopher Challis. *Editor*: Reginald Mills, Clifford Turner. *Production designer*: Hein Heckroth. *Art director*: John Hoesli. *Music*: Brian

Easdale. *Sound*: Alan Allen. *Running time*: 108 minutes. *Released*: February 21, 1949. *Cast*: David Farrar (Sammy Rice), Kathleen Byron (Susan), Jack Hawkins (R. B. Waring), Leslie Banks (Colonel A. K. Holland), Michael Gough (Captain Dick Stuart), Cyril Cusack (Corporal Taylor), Milton Rosmer (Professor Mair), Walter Fitzgerald (Brine), Emrys Jones (Joe), Michael Goodliffe (Till), Renee Asherson (ATS corporal), Anthony Bushell (Major Strang), Henry Caine (Sergeant-Major Rose), Elwyn Brook-Jones (Gladwin), James Dale (Brigadier), Sam Kydd (Crowhurst), June Elvin (Gillian), David Hutcheson (Norval), Sidney James (Knucksie), Roderick Lovell (Bob Pearson), James Carney (Sergeant Groves), Roddy Hughes (Welsh doctor), Geoffrey Keene (Pinker), Bryan Forbes (dying gunner), Robert Morley (the minister), MICHAEL POWELL (gunnery officer).

Gone To Earth

Production: London Film Productions/Vanguard Productions. *Producer*: David O. Selznick. *Associate producer*: George R. Busby. Screenplay based on the novel by Mary Webb. *Assistant director*: Sydney Streeter. *Director of photography*: Christopher Challis. *Production designer*: Hein Heckroth. *Art director*: Arthur Lawson. *Editor*: Reginald Mills. *Music*: Brian Easdale. *Sound*: Charles Poulton. *Running time*: 110 minutes. *Released*: November 6, 1950. *Cast*: Jennifer Jones (Hazel Woodus), David Farrar (Jack Reddin), Cyril Cusack (Edward Marston), Sybil Thorndyke (Mrs. Marston), Edward Chapman (Mr. James), Esmond Knight (Abel Woodus), Hugh Griffith (Andrew Vessons), George Cole (Albert), Beatrice Varley (Aunt Prowde), Frances Clare (Amelia Clomber), Raymond Rollett (landlord, Hunter's Arms), Gerald Lawson (roadmender), Barlett Mullins, Arthur Reynolds (chapel elders), Ann Tetheradge (Miss James), Peter Dunlop (Cornet Player), Louis Phillip (policeman), Valentine Dunn (Martha), Richmond Nairne (Mathias Brooker), Owen Holder (Brother minister).

The Elusive Pimpernel (U.S.: The Fighting Pimpernel)

Production: The Archers for London Film Productions. *Producers*: Samuel Goldwyn, Alexander Korda. *Associate producer*:

George R. Busby. Screenplay from the novel by Baroness Orc-
zy. *Director of photography*: Christopher Challis. *Special effects*:
W. Percy Day. *Production Designer*: Hein Heckroth. *Art directors*: Arthur Lawson, Joseph Bato. *Editor*: Reginald Mills. *Music*: Brian Easdale. *Sound*: Charles Poulton, Red Law. *Running
time*: 109 minutes. *Released*: January 1, 1951. *Cast*: David
Niven (Sir Percy Blakeney), Margaret Leighton (Marguerite Blak-
eney), Jack Hawkins (Prince of Wales), Cyril Cusack (Chauvelin), Robert Coote (Sir Andrew Ffoulkes), Edmond Audran
(Armand St. Juste), Danielle Godet (Suzanne de Tournai),
Charles Victor (Colonel Winterbottom), David Hutcheson (Lord
Anthony Dewhurst), Arlette Marchal (Countess de Tournai),
Gerard Nery (Phillipe de Tournai), Eugene Deckers (Captain
Merieres), John Longden (Abbot), Arthur Wontner (Lord Gren-
ville), David Oxley (Captain Duroc), Raymond Rollett (Bibot),
Philip Stainton (Jellyband), Robert Griffiths (Trubshaw), George
de Warfaz (Baron), Jane Gill Davies (Lady Grenville), Richard
George (Sir John Coke), Cherry Cottrell (Lady Coke), John
Fitzgerald (Sir Michael Travers), Patrick MacNee (John Bristow),
Terence Alexander (Duke of Dorset), Tommy Duggan (Earl of
Sligo), John Fitchen (Nigel Seymour), John Hewitt (Major Pret-
ty), Hugh Kelly (Mr. Fitzdrummond), Richard Nairne (Beau Pep-
ys), Peter Copley (tailor), Howard Vernon (Comte de Tournai),
Peter Gawthorne (Chauvelin's servant), Archie Duncan, James
Lomas (men in bath), Sally Newland.

The Tales of Hoffmann

Production: The Archers for London Film Productions. *Associate producer*: George R. Busby. *Screenplay*: Dennis Arundell's
adaptation of the opera by Offenbach; libretto by Jules Barbi-
er. *Director of photography*: Christopher Challis. *Production designer*: Hein Heckroth. *Costumes*: Hein Heckroth. *Art director*:
Arthur Lawson. *Editor*: Reginald Mills. *Music*: Jacques Offenbach, directed by Sir Thomas Beecham. *Choreography*: Frederick Ashton. *Singers*: Robert Rounseville, Owen Brannigan,
Monica Sinclair, Rene Soames, Bruce Dargavel, Dorothy Bond,
Margherita Grandi, Grahame Clifford, Joan Alexander. *Running
time*: 127 minutes. *Released*: November 26, 1951. *Cast*: Prologue and Epilogue: Moira Shearer (Stella), Robert Rounseville
(E. T. A. Hoffman), Robert Helpmann (Councilor Lindorff), Pam-

ela Brown (Nicklaus), Frederick Ashton (Kleinzack), Meinhart Maur (Luther), Edmond Audran (Cancer), John Ford (Nathaniel), Richard Golding (Hermann), Philip Leaver (Andreas); "Tale of Olympia": Moira Shearer (Olympia), Robert Helpmann (Coppelius), Leonid Massine (Spalanzani), Frederick Ashton (Coshenille); "Tale of Giulietta": Ludmilla Tcherina (Giulietta), Robert Helpmann (Dr. Dapertutto), Leonide Massine (Schlemil), Lionel Harris (Pitichinaccio); "Tale of Antonia": Ann Ayars (Antonia), Robert Helpmann (Dr. Miracle), Mogens Wieth (Crespel), Leonid Massine (Franz).

The Wild Heart

Shortened version of *Gone To Earth* that was released in the United States with additional direction by Roubin Mamoulian and narration by Joseph Cotten. *Running Time*: 82 minutes. *Released*: July 1952.

Oh Rosalinda!!

Production: MICHAEL POWELL, Emeric Pressburger. *Associate producer*: Sydney Streeter. *Assistant director*: John Pellatt. Screenplay based on Johann Strauss' operetta *Die Fledermaus*, lyrics by Dennis Arundell. *Director of photography*: Christopher Challis. *Editor*: Reginald Mills. *Production designer*: Hein Heckroth. *Music*: Johann Strauss, directed by Frederick Lewis. *Choreography*: Alfred Rogriques. *Singers*: Sari Barabas (Rosalinda), Alexander Young (Alfred), Dennis Dowling (Frank), Walter Berry (Falke). *Running Time*: 102 minutes. *Release*: January 12, 1956. *Cast*: Anthony Quayle (General Orlovsky), Anton Walbrook (Dr. Falke), Dennis Price (Major Frank), Ludmilla Tcherina (Rosalinda), Michael Redgrave (Colonel Eisenstein), Mel Ferrer (Captain Alfred Westerman), Anneliese Rothenberger (Adele), Oska Sima (Frosh), Richard Marner (Colonel Lebotov), Nicholas Bruce (hotel receptionist), Barbara Archer, Betty Ash, Yvonne Barnes, Joyce Blair, Hildy Christian, Pamela Foster, Jill Ireland, Patricia Garnett, Annette Gibson, Eileen Gourley, Jean Graystone, Carol Gunn, Griselda Hervey, Maya Joumani, Olga Lowe, Sara Luzita, Ingrid Marshall, Alicia Massey-Beresford, Eileen Sands, Herta Seydel, Anna Steele, Jennifer Walmsley,

Dorothy Whitney, Prudence Hyman (the ladies), Michael Anthony, Igor Barczinsky, Cecil Bates, Richard Bennett, Nicholas Bruce, Ray Buckingham, Denis Carey, Rolf Carston, Terence Cooper, Robert Crewsdon, Peter Darrell, Edward Forsyth, Roger Gage, David Gilbert, Robert Harrold, Jan Lawski, Raymond Lloyd, William Martin, Kenneth Melville, Orest Orioff, Robert Ross, John Schlesinger, Frederick Schrecker, Maurice Metliss, Kenneth Smith, Richard Marner (the gentlemen), Arthur Mullard (Russian guard), Roy Kinear.

The Battle of the River Plate
(U.S.: *Pursuit of the Graf Spree*)

Production: The Archers/J. Arthur Rank. *Associate producer*: Sydney Streeter. *Assistant director*: Charles Orme. *Director of photography*: Christopher Challis. *Editor*: Reginald Mills. *Production designer*: Arthur Lawson. *Artistic advisor*: Hein Heckroth. *Music*: Brian Easdale, directed by Frederick Lewis. *Sound*: C. C. Stevens, Gordon K. McCallum. *Running Time*: 119 minutes. *Released*: December 24, 1956. *Cast*: John Gregson (Captain F. S. Bell), Anthony Quayle (Commodore Henry Harwood), Peter Finch (Captain Langsdorff), Ian Hunter (Captain Woodhouse), Jack Gwillim (Captain Perry), Bernard Lee (Captain Patrick Dove), Lionel Murton (Mike Fowler), Anthony Bushell (Mr. Millington-Drake), Peter Illing (Dr. Guani), Michael Goodliffe (Captain McCall), Patrick MacNee (Lt. Commander Medley), John Chandos (Dr. Langmann), Douglas Wilmer (Mr. Desmoulins), William Squire (Ray Martin), Roger Delgado (Captain Varela), Andrew Cruickshank (Captain Stubs), Christopher Lee (Manola), Edward Atienza (Pop), April Olrich (Dolores), Donald Moffat (Swanston), Maria Mercedes (Madame X), John Schles-inger (German officer), John Le Mesurier (Padre), Anthony Newley, Nigel Stock (British officers aboard *Graf Spree*), Richard Beale (Captain Pottinger), Brian Worth, Ronald Clarke.

Ill Met By Moonlight (U.S.: *Night Ambush*)

Production: Archers/J. Arthur Rank. *Associate Producer*: Sydney Streeter. *Screenplay*: based on the novel by W. Stanley

Moss. *Director of photography*: Christopher Challis. *Editor*: Arthur Stevens. *Art director*: Alex Vetchinsky. *Music*: Mikis Theodorakis, directed by Frederick Lewis. *Sound*: Charles Knott, Gordon K. McCallum. *Running time*: 104 minutes. *Release*: January 29, 1957. *Cast*: Dirk Bogarde (Major Paddy Leigh-Fermor), Marius Goring (Major General Karl Kreipe), David Oxley (Captain W. Stanley Moss), Cyril Cusack (Sandy), Laurence Payne (Manoli), Wolfe Morris (George), Michael Gough (Andoni Zoidakis), Rowland Bartrop (Micky Akoumianakis), Brian Worth (Stratis Saviolkis), Paul Stassino (Yani Katsias), Adeeb Assaly (Zahari), John Cairney (Elias), George Egeniou (Charis Zographakis), Demitri Andreas (Nikko), Theo Moreas (village priest), Takis Frangofinos (Michali), Christopher Lee (German officer at dentist), Peter Augustine, John Houseman, Phyllia Houseman, Andrea Maladrinos, Christopher Rhodes.

Michael Powell's Filmography

Two Crowded Hours

Production: Film Engineering. *Producer*: Jerome Jackson, Henry Cohen. *Screenplay*: J Jefferson Farjeon. *Director of photography*: Geoffrey Faithfull. *Editor*: A Seabourne. *Art director*: C Saunders. *Running time*: 43 minutes. *Release*: December 28, 1931. *Cast*: John Longden (Harry Fielding), Jane Welsh (Joyce Danton), Jerry Verno (Jim), Michael Hogan (Scammell), Edward Barber (Tom Murrray).

My Friend The King

Production: Film Engineering. *Producer*: Jerome Jackson. *Screenplay*: J. Jefferson Farjeon, from his own story. *Director of photography*: Geoffrey Faithfull. *Editor*: A Seabourne. *Art Director*: C Saunders. *Running time*: 47 minutes. *Release*: April 4, 1932. *Cast*: Jerry Verno (Jim), Robert Holmes (Captain Felz), Tracey Holmes (Count Huelin), Eric Pavitt (King Ludwig), Phyllis Loring (Princess Helma), Luli Hohenberg (Countess Zena), H Saxon Snell (Karl), Victor Fairlie (Josef).

Rynox

Production: Film Engineering, for Ideal Films. *Producer*: Jerome Jackson. *Screenplay*: Jerome Jackson, MICHAEL POWELL, Philip MacDonald, from MacDonald's novel. *Director of photography*: Geoffrey Faithfull. *Editor*: A Seabourne. *Running time*: 48 minutes. *Release*: May 7, 1932. *Cast*: Stewart Rome (Boswell Marsh/ F X Benedik), Dorothy Boyd (Peter), John Longden (Tony Benedik), Edward Willard (Captain James), Charles Paton (Samuel Richforth), Fletcher Lightfoot (Prout), Sybil Grove (secretary), Leslie Mitchell (Woolrich).

The Rasp

Production: Film Engineering. *Producer*: Jerome Jackson. *Screenplay*: Philip MacDonald, from his own story. *Director of Photography*: Geoffrey Faithfull. *Art director*: Frank Wells. *Running time*: 44 minutes. *Release*: April 11, 1932. *Cast*: Claude Horton (Anthony Gethryn), Phyllis Loring (Lucia Masterson), C. M. Hallard (Sir Arthur Coates), James Raglan (Alan Deacon), Thomas Weguelin (Inspector Boyd), Carol Coombe (Dora Masterson), Leonard Brett (Jimmy Masterson).

The Star Reporter

Production: Film Engineering. *Producer*: Jerome Jackson. *Screenplay*: Ralph Smart, Philip MacDonald, from a story by MacDonald. *Director of photography*: Geoffrey Faithfull. *Additional photography*: MICHAEL POWELL. *Art director*: Frank Wells. *Running time*: 44 minutes. *Release*: May 9, 1932. *Cast*: Harold French (Major Starr), Isla Bevan (Lady Susan Loman), Garry Marsh (Mandel), Spencer Trevor (Lord Longbourne), Anthony Holles (Bonzo), Noel Dainton (Colonel), Elsa Graves (Oliver), Philip Morant (Jeff).

Hotel Splendide

Production: Gaumont-British. *Producer*: Jerome Jackson. *Screenplay*: Ralph Smart, from a story by Philip MacDonald. *Director of photography*: Geoffrey Faithfull, Arthur Grant. *Art director*: C. Saunders. *Running time*: 53 minutes. *Release*: March 23, 1932. *Cast*: Jerry Verno (Jerry Mason), Anthony Holles (Mrs. Le Grange), Edgar Norfolk ("Gentleman Charlie"), Philip Morant (Mr. Meek), Sybil Grove (Mrs. Harkness), Vera Sherborne (Joyce Dacre), Paddy Browne (Miss Meek), MICHAEL POWELL (eavesdropping device operator).

C.O.D.

Production: Westminster Films. *Producer*: Jerome Jackson. *Screenplay*: Ralph Smart, from a story by Philip MacDonald. *Director of photography*: Geoffrey Faithfull. *Art Director*: Frank Wells. *Running time*: 66 minutes. *Release*: August 22, 1932. *Cast*: Garry Marsh (Peter Cowen), Hope Davy (Frances), Arthur Stratton (Briggs), Sybil Grove (Mrs. Briggs), Roland Culver (Edward), Peter Gawthorne (detective), Cecil Ramage (Vyner), Bruce Belfrage (Philip).

His Lordship

Production: Westminster Films. *Producer*: Jerome Jackson. *Screenplay*: Ralph Smart, based on the novel *The Right Honorable*, by Oliver Madox Heuffer. *Director of photography*: Geoffrey Faithfull. *Art director*: Frank Wells. *Music*: V. C. Clinton-Baddeley, Eric Maschwitz. *Running Time*: 77 minutes. *Release*: December 5, 1932. *Cast*: Jerry Verno (Bert Gibbs), Janet McGrew (Ilya Myona), Ben Weldon (Washington Lincoln), Polly Ward (Leninia), Peter Gawthorne (Ferguson), Muriel George (Mrs. Gibbs), Michael Hogan (Comrade Curzon), V. C. Clinton-Baddeley (Comrade Howard), Patric Ludlow (Honorable Grimsthwaite).

Born Lucky

Production: Westminster Films. *Producer*: Jerome Jackson. *Screenplay*: Ralph Smart, from the novel *Mops*, by Oliver Sandys. *Art director*: Ian Campbell-Gray. *Running time*: 78 minutes. *Release*: April 6, 1933. *Cast*: Talbot O'Farrell (Turnips), Renee Ray (Mops), John Longden (Frank Dale), Ben Welden (Harriman), Helen Ferrers (Lady Chard), Barbara Gott (Cook), Paddy Browne (Patty), Roland Gillett (John Chard).

The Fire Raisers

Production: Gaumont-British. *Producer*: Jerome Jackson. *Screenplay*: MICHAEL POWELL, Jerome Jackson, from an original story. *Director of photography*: Leslie Rowson. *Editor*: D. N. Twist. *Art director*: Alfred Junge. *Costume designer*: Cordon Conway. *Sound*: A. F. Birch. *Running time*: 77 minutes. *Released*: January 22, 1934. *Cast*: Leslie Banks (Jim Bronson), Anne Grey (Arden Brent), Carol Goodner (Helen Vaughan), Frank Cellier (Brent), Francis L. Sullivan (Stedman), Laurence Anderson (Twist), Harry Caine (Bates), Joyce Kirby (Polly), George Merritt (Sonners), MICHAEL POWELL (radio operator).

The Night of the Party
(U.S.: *The Murder Party*)

Production: Gaumont-British. *Producer*: Jerome Jackson. *Screenplay*: Ralph Smart. *Dialogue*: Roland Pertwee, John Hastings Turner, from their own play. *Director of photography*: Glen MacWilliams. *Art director*: Alfred Junge. *Running time*: 61 minutes. *Release*: July 16, 1935. *Cast*: Leslie Banks (Sir John Holland), Ian Hunter (Guy Kennion), Jane Baxter (Peggy Studholme), Ernest Thesiger (Chiddiatt), Viola Keats (Joan Holland), Malcolm Keen (Lord Studholme), Jane Millican (Anna Chiddiatt), Muriel Aked (Princess Amelta of Corsova), John Turnbull (Ramage), Laurence Anderson (Defence Counsel), W. Graham Brown (General Piddinghoe), Louis Goodrich (Judge), Cecil Ramage (Howard Vernon), Disney Roebuck (Butler), Gerald Barry (Baron Cziatch), Gordon Begg (Miles).

Red Ensign (U.S.: *Strike!*)

Production: Gaumont-British. *Executive producer*: Michael Balcon. *Producer*: Jerome Jackson. *Screenplay*: MICHAEL POWELL, Jerome Jackson. *Additional dialogue*: L. du Garde Peach. *Director of photography*: Leslie Rowson. *Art director*: Alfred Junge. *Editor*: Geoffrey Barkas. *Running time*: 69 minutes. *Release*: June 4, 1935. *Cast*: Leslie Banks (David Barr), Carol Goodner (June MacKinnon), Frank Vosper (Lord Dean), Alfred Drayton (Manning), Donald Calthrop (MacLeod), Allan Jeayes (Emerson—"Grierson"), Campbell Gullan (Hannay), Percy Parsons (Casey), Fewlass Llewellyn (Sir Gregory), Henry Oscar (Raglan), Henry Caine (Bassett), John Laurie (worker), Frederick Piper (bowler-hatted man in bar).

Something Always Happens

Production: Warner Bros.-First National. *Executive producer*: Irving Asher. *Screenplay*: Brock Williams. *Director of photography*: Basil Emmott. *Art director*: Peter Proud. *Editor*: Bert Bates. *Running time*: 69 minutes. *Release*: December 10, 1934. *Cast*: Ian Hunter (Peter Middleton), Nancy O'Neil (Cynthia Hatch), John Singer (Billy), Peter Gawthorne (Ben Hatch), Muriel George (Mrs. Badger), Barry Livesey (George Hamlin), Millicent Wolf (Glenda), Louie Emery (Mrs. Tremlett), Reg Marcus ("Coster"), George Zucco (proprietor of the Cafe de Paris).

The Girl In The Crowd

Production: First National. *Executive producer*: Irving Asher. *Screenplay*: Brock Williams. *Director of photography*: Basil Emmott. *Editor*: Bert Bates. *Running time*: 52 minutes. *Release*: May 20, 1935. *Cast*: Barry Clifton (David Gordon), Patricia Hilliard (Marian), Googie Withers (Sally), Harold French (Bob), Clarence Blakiston (Mr. Peabody), Margaret Gunn (Joyce), Richard Littledale (Bill Manners), Phyllis Morris (Mrs. Lewis), Patric Knowles (Tom Burrows), Marjorie Corbett (secretary), Brenda Lawless (policewoman), Barbara Waring (mannequin), Eve Lister (Ruby), Betty Lyne (Phyllis), Melita Bell (assistant manager), John Wood (Harry).

Lazybones

Production: Real Art. *Executive producer*: Julius Hagen. *Screenplay*: Gerald Fairlie, from a play by Ernest Denny. *Director of photography*: Arthur Crabtree. *Editor*: Frank Harris. *Running time*: 65 minutes. *Release*: June 24, 1935. *Cast*: Claire Luce (Kitty McCarthy), Ian Hunter (Sir Reginald Ford), Sara Allgood (Bridget), Bernard Nedell (Mike McCarthy), Michael Shepley (Hildebrand Pope), Bobbie Comber (Kemp), Denys Blakelock (Hugh Ford), Marjorie Gaskell (Marjory Ford), Pamela Carne

(Lottie Pope), Harold Warrender (Lord Melton), Miles Malleson (pessimist), Fred Withers (Richards), Frank Morgan (Tom), Fewlass Llewellyn (Lord Brockley), Paul Blake (Viscount Woodland).

The Love Test

Production: Leslie Landau for Fox British. *Producer*: Leslie Landau. *Screenplay*: Selwyn Jepson, from a story by Jack Celestin. *Director of photography*: Arthur Crabtree. *Running time*: 65 minutes. *Release*: July 1, 1935. *Cast*: Judy Gunn (Mary Lee), Louis Hayward (John Gregg), Dave Hutcheson (Thompson), Googie Withers (Minnie), Morris Harvey (Company president), Aubrey Dexter (Vice-President), Eve Turner (Kathleen), Bernard Miles (Allan), Jack Knight (managing director), Gilbert Davis (Hosiah Smith), Shayle Gardner (night watchman), James Craig (boiler man), Thorley Walters, Ian Wilson (chemists).

The Phantom Light

Production: Gaumont-British. *Producer*: Jerome Jackson. *Screenplay*: Ralph Smart, from the play *Haunted Light*, by Evadne Price, Joan Ray Byford. *Additional dialogue*: J. Jefferson Farjeon, Austin Melford. *Director of photography*: Roy Kellino. *Editor*: Derek Twist. *Art director*: Alex Vetchinsky. *Music*: Louis Levy. *Running time*: 76 minutes. *Release*: August 5, 1935. *Cast*: Binnie Hale (Alice Bright), Gordon Harker (Sam Higgins), Ian Hunter (Jim Pierce), Donald Calthrop (David Owen), Milton Rosmer (Dr. Carey), Reginald Tate (Tom Evans), Mickey Brantford (Bob Peters), Herbert Lomas (Cleff Owen), Fewlass Llewellyn (Griffith Owen), Alice O'Day (Mrs. Owen), Barry O'Neill (Captain Pierce), Edgar K. Bruce (Sergeant Owen), Louie Emery (station mistress), John Singer (cabin boy).

The Price of a Song

Production: Fox British. *Screenplay*: Anthony Gittens. *Director of photography*: Jimmy Wilson. *Running time*: 67 minutes. *Release*: October 7, 1935. *Cast*: Campbell Gullan (Arnold Grierson), Marjorie Corbett (Margaret Nevern), Gerald Fielding (Michael Hardwicke), Dora Barton (Letty Grierson), Charles

Mortimer (Oliver Broom), Oriel Ross (Elsie), Henry Caine (String-
er), Sybil Grove (Mrs. Bancroft), Eric Maturin (Nevern), Felix
Aylmer (Graham), Cynthia Stock (Mrs. Bush), Mavis Clair
(Maudie Bancroft).

Someday

Production: Warner British. *Producer*: Irving Asher. *Screenplay*:
Brock Williams, from the novel *Young Nowhere* by J. A. R.
Wylie. *Director of photography*: Basil Emmott, Monty Berman.
Editor: Bert Bates. *Art director*: Ian Campbell-Gray. *Running
time*: 68 minutes. *Release*: November 18, 1935. Cast: Esmond
Knight (Curley Blake), Margaret Lockwood (Emily), Henry Mol-
lison (Canley), Sunday Wilshin (Betty), Raymond Lovell (Carr),
Ivor Bernard (Hope), George Pughe (milkman), Jane Cornell
(nurse).

Her Last Affaire

Production: New Ideal. *Producer*: Simon Rowson, Geoffrey Row-
son. *Screenplay*: Ian Dalyrmple, from the play *S.O.S.* by Walter
Ellis. *Director of photography*: Geoffrey Faithfull. *Sound*: George
Burgess. *Running time*: 78 minutes. *Release*: May 25, 1936.
Cast: Hugh Williams (Alan Heriot), Viola Keats (Lady Avril Wey-
re), Francis L. Sullivan (Sir Julian Weyre), Sophie Stewart (Judy
Weyre), Felix Aylmer (Lord Carnforth), Cecil Parker (Sir Arthur
Harding), Shayle Gardner (Boxall), Henry Caine (Inspector
Marsh), Gerrard Tyrell (Martin), John Laurie (Robb), Eliot Make-
ham (Dr. Rudd), Googie Withers (Effie).

The Brown Wallet

Producer: Warner Bros.-First National. *Executive producer*: Irv-
ing Asher. *Screenplay*: Ian Dalyrmple, from a story by Stacy
Aumonier. *Director of photography*: Basil Emmott. *Running time*:
68 minutes. *Release*: July 20, 1936. *Cast*: Partic Knowles (John
Gillespie), Nancy O'Neill (Eleanor), Henry Caine (Simmonds),
Henrietta Watson (Aunt Mary), Charlotte Leigh (Miss Barton),
Shayle Gardner (Wotherspoone), Edward Dalby (Minting), Eliot

Makeham (Hobday), Bruce Winston (Julian Thorpe), Jane Millican (Miss Bloxham), Louis Goodrich (coroner), Dick Francis,
George Mills (detectives).

Crown v. Stevens

Production: Warner Bros.-First National. *Executive producer*: Irv-
ing Asher. *Screenplay*: Brook Williams, from the novel *Third
Time Unlucky* by Laurence Maynell. *Director of photography*:
Basil Emmott. *Editor*: Bert Bates. *Running time*: 66 minutes.
Release: August 3, 1936. *Cast*: Beatrix Thomson (Doris
Stevens), Patric Knowles (Chris Jansen), Reginald Purdell (Alf),
Glennis Lorimer (Molly Hobbs), Allan Jeayes (Inspector Carter),
Frederick Piper (Arthur Stevens), Googie Withers (Ella Levine),
Mabel Poulton (Mamie), Morris Harvey (Julius Bayleck), Billy
Watts (Joe Andrews), Davina Craig (Maggie), Bernard Miles (de-
tective).

The Man Behind the Mask

Production: Joe Rock Studios. *Producer*: Joe Rock. *Screenplay*:
Ian Hay, Sidney Courtenay, from the novel *The Chase of the
Golden Plate* by Jacques Futrelle. *Adaptation*: Jack Byrd. *Di-
rector of photography*: Ernest Palmer. *Running time*: 79 min-
utes. *Release*: August 24, 1936. *Cast*: Hugh Williams (Nick
Barclay), Jane Baxter (June Slade), Maurice Schwartz (the Mas-
ter), Donald Calthrop (Dr. Walpole), Henry Oscar (officer), Peter
Gawthorne (Lord Slade), Kitty Kelly (Miss Weeks), Ronald Ward
(Jimmy Slade), George Merritt (Mallory), Reginald Tate (Hayden),
Ivor Bernard (Hewitt), Hal Gordon (Sergeant), Gerald Fielding
(Harah), Barbara Everest (Lady Slade), Wilf Caithness (butler),
Moyra Fagan (Nora), Sid Crossley (postman).

The Edge of the World

Production: Rock Studios. *Producer*: Joe Rock. *Screenplay*:
MICHAEL POWELL. *Director of photography*: Ernest Palmer,
Skeets Kelly, Monty Berman. *Editor*: Derek Twist. *Music*: Cyril
Ray, orchestra directed by W. L. Williamson. *Chorus*: Women

of the Glasgow Orpheus Choir. *Sound*: L. K. Tregallas. *Running time*: 81 minutes. *Release*: January 10, 1938. *Cast*: John Laurie (Peter Manson), Belle Chrystall (Ruth Manson), Eric Berry (Robbie Manson), Kitty Kirwan (Jean Manson), Finlay Currie (James Gray), Niall MacGinnis (Andrew Gray), Grant Sutherland (John, the Catechist), Campbell Robson Dunbar, the Laird), George Summers (skipper), Margaret Grieg (Baby), MICHAEL POWELL (Mr. Graham), Frances Reidy (woman on boat), Sydney Streeter (man at dance).

Smith

Production: Embankment Fellowship Co. *Length*: 1000 feet. *Release*: June 1939. *Cast*: Ralph Richardson, Flora Robson, Allan Jeayes, Wally Patch.

The Spy In Black (U.S.: U Boat 29)

Production: Harefield. *Producer*: Irving Asher. *Screenplay*: EMERIC PRESSBURGER, from a novel by J. Storer Clouston. *Adaptation*: Roland Pertwee. *Director of photography*: Bernard Browne. *Supervising editor*: William Hornbeck. *Editor*: Hugh Stewart. *Production designer*: Vincent Korda. *Art director*: Frederick Pusey. *Music*: Miklos Rozsa, directed by Muir Mathieson. *Sound*: A. W. Watkins. *Running time*: 62 minutes. *Release*: August 12, 1939. *Cast*: Conrad Veidt (Captain Ernst Hardt), Valerie Hobson (Frau Tiel, actually Joan Blacklock), Sebastian Shaw (Lieutenant Ashington, but actually Captain Davis Blacklock), Marius Goring (Lieutenant Schuster), June Duprez (Anne Burnett), Athole Stewart (Reverend Hector Matthews), Agnes Laughlin (Mrs. Matthews), Helen Haye (Mrs. Sedley), Cyril Raymond (Reverand John Harris), Hay Petrie (engineer), Grant Sutherland (Bob Bratt), Robert Rendel (Admiral), Mary Morris (Edwars, the chauffeuse), George Summers (Captain Ratter), Margaret Moffatt (Kate), Kenneth Warrington (Commander Denis), Torin Thatcher (submarine officer), Bernard Miles (Hans), Skelton Knaggs (German orderly), Diana Sinclair-Hall, Esma Cannon.

The Lion Has Wings

Production: London Film Productions. *Producer*: Alexander Korda. *Associate producer*: Ian Dalrymple. *Codirectors*: Brian Desmond Hurst, Adrian Brunel. *Screenplay*: Adrian Brunel, E.V.H. Emmett, from a story by Ian Dalrymple. *Director of photography*: Harry Stradling. *Art director*: Vincent Korda. *Editor*: William Hornbeck. *Music*: Richard Addinsell, directed by Muir Mathieson. *Sound*: A. W. Watkins. *Running time*: 76 minutes. *Release*: November 3, 1939. *Cast*: Merle Oberon (Mrs. Richardson), Ralph Richardson (Wing Commander Richardson), June Duprez (June), Robert Douglas (briefing officer), Anthony Bushell (pilot), Derrick de Marney (Bill), Brian Worth (Bobby), Austin Trevor (Schulemburg), Ivan Brandt (officer), G. H. Mulcaster (controller), Herbert Lomas (Holveg), Milton Rosmer (head of Observer Corps), Robert Rendel (chief of air staff), E. V. H. Emmett (narrator, English version), Lowell Thomas (narrator, U.S. version), Archibald Batty (Air Officer), Ronald Adam (bomber chief), Bernard Miles (observer), John Longden, Ian Fleming, Miles Malleson, Charles Garson, John Penrose, Frank Tickle, Torin Thatcher.

Contraband (U.S.: *Blackout*)

Production: British National. *Producer*: John Corfield. *Associate producer*: Roland Gillett. *Production manager*: Anthony Nelson Keys. *Screenplay*: Brock Williams, MICHAEL POWELL, from an original story by EMERIC PRESSBURGER. *Director of photography*: F. A. Young. *Editor*: John Seabourne. *Art director*: Alfred Junge. *Music*: Richard Addinsell, directed by Muir Mathieson. *Sound*: C. C. Stevens. *Running time*: 92 minutes. *Release*: November 29, 1940. *Cast*: Conrad Veidt (Captain Anderson), Valerie Hobson (Mrs. Sorensen), Hay Petrie (Mate Skold/Chef Skold), Esmond Knight (Mr. Pidgeon), Raymond Lovell (Van Dyne), Charles Victor (Hendrick), Henry Wolston (first Danish waiter), Julian Vedey (second Danish waiter), Sydney Moncton (third Danish waiter), Hamilton Keen (fourth Danish waiter), Phoebe Kershaw (Miss Lang), Leo Genn (first Brother Grimm), Stuart Latham (second Brother Grimm), Peter Bull (third Brother Grimm), Dennis Arundell (Lieman), Harold

Warrender (Lt. Commander Ellis RN), Joss Ambler (Lt. Commander Ashton RNR), Molly Hamley Clifford (Baroness Hekla), Eric Berry (Mr. Abo), Olga Edwards (Mrs. Abo), Tony Gable (Mrs. Karoly), Desmond Jeans (first Karoly), Eric Hales (second Karoly), John Roberts (Hanson), Manning Whiley (manager of "Mousetrap"), Eric Maturin, John Longden (passport officers), Paddy Brown (singer), Bernard Miles (man lighting pipe), Torin Thatcher (sailor), Mark Daly (taxi driver), Frank Allenby, John England, Haddon Mason, Johnnie Schofield, Townsend Whitling, Ross Duncan, Albert Chevalier.

The Thief of Bagdad

Production: London Film Productions. *Producer*: Alexander Korda. *Associate producer*: William Cameron Menzies, Zoltan Korda. *Codirectors*: Ludwig Berger, Tim Whelan (Zoltan Korda, William Cameron Menzies, Alexander Korda-uncredited). *Screenplay*: Lajos Biro. *Adaptation*: Miles Malleson. *Assistant director*: Geoffrey Boothby, Charles David. *Director of photography*: Georges Perinal. *Special effects*: Lawrence Butler. *Editor*: William Hornbeck. *Art director*: Vincent Kalmus, assisted by W. Percy Day, William Cameron Menzies, Frederick Pusey, Ferdinand Bellan. *Music*: Miklos Rozsa, directed by Muir Mathieson. *Costume designer*: Oliver Messel, John Armstrong, Marcel Vertes. *Sound*: A. W. Watkins. *Running time*: 106 minutes. *Release*: December 25, 1940. *Cast*: Conrad Veidt (Jaffar), Sabu (Abu), June Duprez (Princess), John Justin (Ahmad), Rex Ingram (Djinni), Miles Malleson (Sultan), Morton Selten (King), Mary Morris (Halima), Bruce Winston (merchant), Hay Petrie (astrologer), Roy Emmerton (jailer), Allan Jeayes (storyteller), Adelaide Hall (singer), Viscount (the dog), Glynis Johns, John Salew, Norman Pierce, Frederick Burtwell, Otto Wallen, Henry Hallett, Cleo Laine.

An Airman's Letter To His Mother

Producer: MICHAEL POWELL. *Screenplay*: MICHAEL POWELL. *Director of photography*: MICHAEL POWELL. *Narrator*: John Gielgud. *Running time*: 5 minutes. *Release*: July 1941.

49th Parallel (U.S.: The Invaders)

Production: Ortus Films/ Ministry of Information. Producer: MICHAEL POWELL. Associate producer: Roland Gillett, George Brown. Screenplay: EMERIC PRESSBURGER. Dialogue: Rodney Ackland. Director of photography: Frederick Young. Assistant director: A. Seabourne. Editor: David Lean. Art director: David Rawnsley. Music: Ralph Vaughan Williams, directed by Muir Mathieson. Sound: C. C. Stevens. Running time: 123 minutes. Release: November 24, 1941. Cast: Eric Portman (Lieutenant Ernst Hirth), Richard George (Captain Bernsdorff), Raymond Lovell (Lieutenant Kuhnecker), Niall MacGinnis (Vogel), Peter Moore (Kranz), John Chandos (Lohrmann), Basil Appleby (Jahner), Laurence Olivier (Johnnie Barras), Finlay Currie (Albert, the factor), Ley On (Nick the Eskimo), Anton Walbrook (Peter), Glynis Johns (Anna), Charles Victor (Andreas), Frederick Piper (David), Leslie Howard (Philip Armstrong Scott), Tawera Moana (George the Indian), Eric Clavering (Art), Charles Rolfe (Bob), Raymond Massey (Andy Brock), Theodore Salt, O. W. Fonger (U.S. customs officer), Robert Beatty, Lionel Grose.

The Sorcerer's Apprentice

Production: 20th Century-Fox/Norddeutscher Rundfunk. English text: Dennis Arundell, from a story by Goethe. Director of photography: Christopher Challis. Editor: Reginald Mills. Production designer: Hein Heckroth. Sets: K. H. Joksch. Running time: 13 minutes. Release: July 14, 1953. Cast: Sonia Arova (dancer).

Luna De Miel (England: Honeymoon)

Production: Suevia Films/Cesario Gonsalez/Everdene. Producer: Cesario Gonsalez, MICHAEL POWELL. Associate producer: Sydney Streeter, Judith Coxhead, William J. Paton. Screenplay: MICHAEL POWELL, Luis Escobar. Director of photography: Georges Perinal. Editor: Peter Taylor, John V. Smith. Art director: Ivor Beddoes. Music: Mikis Theodorakis. Sound: John Cox, Fernando Bernaldes, Janet Davidson. Ballets: "El Amor Brujo," written by Gregorio Martinez Sierra. Music: Manuel de Falla.

Sets: Rafael Durancamps. "Los Amantes De Teruel," music by Mikis Theodorakis, conducted by Sir Thomas Beecham. *Running time*: 109 minutes. *Release*: March 28, 1961 France. *Cast*: Anthony Steel (Kit Kelly), Ludmilla Tcherina (Anna), Antonio (himself), Rosita Segovia (Rosita Candelas), Carmen Rojas (Lucia), Maria Gamez, Diego Hurtado, Juan Carmona (Pepe Nieto), Leonide Massine (Der Geist), Antonio Spanish Ballet Troupe (themselves).

Peeping Tom

Production: MICHAEL POWELL. *Producer*: MICHAEL POWELL. *Associate producer*: Albert Fennell. *Screenplay*: Leo Marks. *Director of photography*: Otto Heller. *Editing*: Noreen Ackland. *Art director*: Arthur Lawson. *Music*: Brian Easdale, Wally Scott. *Sound*: C. C. Stevens, Gordon K. McCallum. *Running time*: 109 minutes. *Release*: March 31, 1960. *Cast*: Carl Boehm (Mark Lewis), Anna Massey (Helen Stephens), Maxine Audley (Mrs. Stephens), Moira Shearer (Vivian), Esmond Knight (Arthur Baden), Michael Goodliffe (Don Jarvis), Shirley Anne Field (Diane Ashley), Bartlett Mullins (Mr. Peters), Jack Watson (Inspector Gregg), Nigel Davenport (Sergeant Miller), Pamela Green (Milly), Martin Miller (Dr. Rosen), Brian Wallace (Tony), Brenda Bruce (Dora), Miles Malleson (elderly gentleman), Susan Travers (Lorraine), Maurice Durant (publicity chief), Brian Worth (assistant director), Veronica Hurst (Miss Simpson), Alan Rolfe (store detective), MICHAEL POWELL (A. N. Lewis), Columba Powell (Mark as a child), John Dunbar (police doctor), Guy Kingsley-Poynter (P. Tate), Keith Baxter (Baxter), Peggy Thorpe-Bates (Mrs. Partridge), John Barrand (small man), Roland Curran (young extra), John Chappell (clapper boy), Paddy Edwardes (girl electrician), Margaret Neal (stepmother).

The Queen's Guards

Production: Imperial. *Producers*: MICHAEL POWELL, Sydney Streeter. *Associate producer*: Simon Harcourt-Smith. *Screenplay*: Roger Milner, from an idea by Simon Harcourt-Smith. *Director of photography*: Gerry Turpin. *Editor*: Noreen Ackland. *Art director*: Wilfred Shingleton. *Music*: Brian Easdale. *Sound*: James

Shields. *Running time*: 110 minutes. *Release*: October 23, 1961. *Cast*: Daniel Massey (John Fellowes), Robert Stephens (Harry Wynne Walton), Raymond Massey (Captain Fellowes), Ursula Jeans (Mrs. Fellowes), Judith Stott (Ruth Dobbie), Elizabeth Shepherd (Susan), Duncan Lamont (Wilkes), Peter Myers (Gordon Davidson), Ian Hunter (George Dobbie), Jess Conrad (Dankworth), Patrick Conner (Brewer), William Young (Williams), Jack Allen (Brigadier Cummings), Jack Watling (Captain Shergold), Andrew Crawford (Biggs), Cornel Lucas (photographer), Nigel Green (Abu Sibdar), Rene Cutforth (commentator), Jack Watson (Sergeant Johnson), Laurence Payne (Farinda), Frank Lawton (Commander Hewson), Anthony Bushell (Major Cole), Eileen Peel (Mrs. Wynne-Walton), Jack Conrad (Dankworth), William Fox (Mr. Walters), Roland Curran (Kenyon), Anthony Selby (Kishu), John Chappell (Private Walls).

Herzog Blaubert's Burg/Bluebeard's Castle

Production: Norman Foster Productions/Suddeutscher Rundfunk. *Producer*: Norman Foster. *Screenplay*: Bela Bartok from his opera, libretto by Bela Balazs. *Director of photography*: Hannes Staudinger. *Production designer*: Hein Heckroth. *Running time*: 60 minutes. *Release*: 1964, West Germany. *Cast*: Norman Foster (Bluebeard), Anna Raquel Sartre (Judit).

They're A Weird Mob

Production: Williamson/Powell International. *Producer*: MICHAEL POWELL. *Associate producer*: John Pellatt. *Screenplay*: Richard Imrie (pseudonym of EMERIC PRESSBURGER) from a novel by Nino Culotta (pseud. of John O'Grady). *Director of photography*: Arthur Grant. *Assistant director*: Claude Watson. *Editor*: G. Turney-Smith. *Art director*: Dennis Gentle. *Music*: Laurence Leonard, Alan Boustead, directed by Leonard. *Songs*: "Big Country," "In This Man's Country," by Reen Devereaux; "I Kiss You, You Kiss Me," by Walter Chiari. *Sound*: Don Saunders, Bill Creed. *Running time*: 112 minutes. *Release*: October 13, 1966. *Cast*: Walter Chiari (Nino Culotta), Clare Dunne (Kay Kelly), Chips Rafferty (Harry Kelly), Alida Chelli (Guiliana), Ed Devereaux (Joe Kennedy), Slim De Grey (Pat), John Meillon

(Dennis), Charles Little (Jimmy), Anne Haddy (barmaid), Jack Allen (fat man in bar), Red Moore (texture man), Ray Hartley (newsboy), Tony Bonner (lifesaver), Alan Lander (Charlie), Judith Arthy (Dixie), Keith Peterson (drunk man on ferry), Muriel Steinbeck (Mrs. Kelly), Gloria Dawn (Mrs. Chapman), Jeanne Dryman (Betty), Gita Rivera (Maria), Doreen Warburton (Edit), Jeannie Diamond (Jeannie), Barry Creyton, Noel Brophy, Graham Kennedy.

Age of Consent

Production: Nautilus Productions. *Producers*: James Mason, MICHAEL POWELL. *Associate producer*: Michael Pate. *Screenplay*: Peter Yeldham, from Norman Lindsay's novel. *Assistant director*: David Crocker. *Director of photography*: Hannes Staudinger. *Editor*: Anthony Buckley. *Art director*: Dennis Gentle. *Music*: Stanley Myers. *Sound*: Paul Ennis, Lloyd Colman. *Running time*: 98 minutes. *Release*: November 15, 1969. *Cast*: James Mason (Bradley Moraham), Helen Mirren (Cora), Jack MacGowran (Nat Kelly), Neva Carr-Glyn (Ma Ryan), Andonia Katsaros (Isabel Marley), Michael Boddy (Hendricks), Harold Hopkins (Ted Farrell), Slim de Gray (Cooley), Max Moldrum (T.V. Interviewer), Frank Thring (Godfrey), Dora Hing (receptionist), Clarissa Kaye (Meg), Judy McGrath (Grace), Lenore Katon (Edna), Diane Strachan (Susie), Roberta Grant (Ivy), Prince Nial (Jasper), Hudson Fausset (New Yorker), Peggy Cass (New Yorker's wife), Eric Reuman (art lover), Tommy Hanlon Jr. (Levi-Strauss), Geoff Cartwright (newsboy), Lonsdale (Godfrey).

The Boy Who Turned Yellow

Production: Roger Cherrill. *Production Manager*: Gus Angus. *Screenplay*: EMERIC PRESSBURGER. *Director of photography*: Christopher Challis. *Assistant director*: Neil Vine-Miller. *Editor*: Peter Boita. *Art director*: Bernard Sarron. *Music*: Patrick Gowers, David Vorhaus. *Sound*: Bob Jones, Ken Barber. *Running time*: 55 minutes. *Release*: September 16, 1972. *Cast*: Mark Digham (John Saunders), Robert Eddison (Nick), Helen Weir (Mrs. Saunders), Brian Worth (Mr. Saunders), Esmond Knight (doctor), Laurence Carter (schoolteacher), Patrick McAlinney (Supreme Beefeater), Lem Kitaj (Munro).

Return to the Edge of the World

Production: BBC Television. *Producer*: Sydney Streeter. *Premiere*: October 3, 1978. *Running Time*: 85 minutes, incorporating the film *The Edge of the World*. *Cast*: MICHAEL POWELL, John Laurie, Grant Sutherland, Frankie Reidy, Sydney Streeter.

Television Work

Espionage: "Never Turn Your Back on a Friend"

Production: Herbert Brodkin Ltd. *Executive producer*: Herbert Hirschman. *Producer*: George Justin. *Associate producer*: John Pellatt. *Assistant director*: Bruce Sherman. *Screenplay*: Mel Davenport. *Director of photography*: Ken Hodges. *Editor*: John Victor Smith. *Production designer*: Wilfred Shingleton. *Art director*: Tony Woollard. *Music*: Malcolm Arnold. *Sound*: David Bowen. *Titles*: Maurice Binder. *Running Time*: 48 minutes. *Airdate*: January 1, 1964. *Cast*: George Voskovek (Professor Kuhn), Donald Madden (Anaconda), Mark Eden (Wicket), Julian Glover (Tovarich), Pamela Brown (Miss Jensen).

Espionage: "A Free Agent"

Production: Herbert Brodkin/MGM. *Producer*: Herbert Hirschman. *Producer*: George Justin. *Associate producer*: John Pellatt. *Screenplay*: Leo Marks. *Director of photography*: Geoffrey Faithfull. *Editor*: John Victor Smith. *Production designer*: Wilfred Shingleton. *Art director*: Anthony Woollard. *Music*: Benjamin Frankel. *Sound*: Cyril Smith. *Running time*: 48 minutes. *Airdate*: March 25, 1964. *Cast*: Anthony Quayle (Philip), Sian Phillips (Anna), Norman Foster (Max), Goerge Mikell (Peter), John Wood (Douglas), John Abineri (town clerk), Ernst Waldner (watch factory mechanic), Gertan Klauber (innkeeper), Vivienne Drummond (Miss Weiss).

Espionage: "The Frantik Rebel"

Production: Herbert Brodkin/MGM. *Producer*: Herbert Hirschman. *Producer*: George Justin. *Associate producer*: John Pellatt. *Airdate*: February 12, 1964. *Cast*: Stanley Baxter, Roger Livesey, Jill Bennett.

Defenders: "The Sworn Twelve"

Production: Magnificent Herbert Brodkin-Reginald Rose. *Screenplay*: Edward DeBlasio. *Running time*: 50 minutes. *Airdate*: 1965. *Cast*: E. G. Marshall (Lawrence Preston), Robert Reed (Kenneth Preston), Murray Hamilton, King Donovan, Ruby Dee, Jerry Orbach, Ossie Davis, Brenda Vaccaro.

The Doctor and the Nurses: "A 38846"

Production: Herbert Brodkin. *Producer*: Arthur Lewis. *Screenplay*: George Bellak. *Running time*: 50 minutes. *Airdate*: April 4, 1965. *Cast*: Michael Tolan (Dr. Alex Tazinski), Shirl Conway (Liz Thorpe), Joseph Campanella (Dr. Ted Steffen), Zina Bethune (Gail Lucas), Jean-Pierre Aumont, Kermit Murdock, Louise Sorel, Thomas Carlin, Ted Von Griethuysen, Frank Campanella.

Additional Film Work by Michael Powell

Mare Nostrum (Rex Ingram; grip), 1925
The Magician (Rex Ingram; assistant; actor), 1926
The Garden of Allah (Rex Ingram; assistant; actor), 1927
Camels to Cannibal (short; actor), 1927
Riviera Revels (short; actor), 1928
Champagne (Alfred Hitchcock; still photographer), 1928
Compulsory Husbands (Harry Lachmann; still photographer), 1928
A Knight In London (Lupu Pick; editing), 1928
Blackmail (Alfred Hitchcock; co-screenplay—uncredited), 1929
Caste (Campbell Gullan; screenplay), 1930
77 Park Lane (Albert de Courville; co-screenplay), 1931
Perfect Misunderstanding (Cyril Gardner; screenplay, from a story by Miles Malleson), 1933
End of the River (Derek Twist; coproducer with Emeric Pressburger), 1947

Silver Fleet (Vernon C. Sewell, Gordon Wellesley; coproducer with Emeric Pressburger), 1943

Sebastian (David Green, co-producer), 1968

Pavlova - A Woman For All Time (Emil Lotianou; Western Version Supervisor), 1983

Additional Film Work by Emeric Pressburger

The films listed are English unless otherwise noted.

Abschied (Germany, Robert Siodmak; co-script), 1930

Das Ekel (Germany, Franz Wenzler, Eugen Schufftan; screenplay), 1931

Dann Schon Lieber Liebertran (Germany, Max Ophuls; co-screenplay), 1931

Der Kleine Seitensprung (Germany, Reinhold Schunzel; co-screenplay), 1931.

Le Petit Ecart (Germany, French version of *Der Kleine Seitensprung*, Reinhold Schunzel and Henri Chomette; co-story), 1931

Emil Und Die Detektives (Germany, Gerhard Lamprecht; co-screenplay uncredited), 1931

Ronny (Germany, Reinhold Schunzel; co-screenplay), 1931

Ronny (Germany, French version of *Ronny* Reinhold Schunzel; co-story), 1931

Das Schone Abenteuer (Germany, Reinhold Schunzel; co-screenplay), 1932

La Belle Aventure (Germany, French version of *Das Schone Abenteuer*, Reinhold Schunzel and Roger LeBon; co-screenplay), 1932

Wer Zahlt Heute Noch? (Germany, Heinz Hille; screenplay), 1932

Lumpenkavaliere (Germany, Carl Boese; editor), 1932

Sehnsucht 202 (Germany, Max Neufeld; co-screenplay), 1932

Une Jeune Fille Et Un Million (France-Germany, Max Neufeld and Fred Ellis; French version of *Sehnsucht 202*), 1932

Eine Von Uns (Germany, Johannes Meyer; co-screenplay uncredited), 1932

. . . Und Es Leuchtet Die Puszta (Germany-Hungary, Heinze Hille; screenplay), 1933

A Ven Gazenber (Germany-Hungary, Heinze Hille; Hungarian version of *Und es Leuchtet Die Puszta*), 1933

Incognito (France, Kurt Gerron; screenplay), 1933

Une Femme Au Volant (France, Kurt Gerron and Pierre Billon; screenplay), 1933

Mon Coeur Tappelle (France-Germany, Carmine Gallone and Serge Veber; co-screenplay uncredited), 1934

Mein Herz Ruft Nach (Germany, Carmine Gallone and Serge Veber; German version of *Mon Coeur T'appelle*), 1934

My Heart Is Calling (Great Britain, Germany, Carmine Gallone; English version of *Mon Coeur Tappelle*), 1934

Monsieur Sans-Gene (France, Karl Anton; co-screenplay), 1935

Emil and the Detectives (Milton Rosmer; English version of *Emil Und Die Detektives*), 1935

One Rainy Afternoon (U.S.A., Roland V. Lee; American version of *Monsieur Sans-Gene*), 1936

La Vie Parisienne (France, Robert Siodmak; screenplay), 1936

Parisienne Life (U.S.A., Robert Siodmak; co-screenplay, American version of *La Vie Parisienne*), 1936

The Challenge (Milton Rosner and Luis Trenker; co-screenplay), 1938

Spy For A Day (Mario Zampi; an adaptation of a script Pressburger co-wrote), 1939

Atlantic Ferry (Walter Forde; adaptation), 1941

Breach of Promise (Harold Hulth and Roland Pertwee; story), 1941

Squadron Leader X (Lance Comfort; story), 1943

Wanted for Murder (Lawrence Huntington; co-screenplay), 1946

Twice Upon A Time (Pressburger; production and screenplay), 1953

Miracle In Soho (Julian Amyes; production and screenplay), 1957

Operation Crossbow (Michael Anderson; co-screenplay), 1964

Behold A Pale Horse (Fred Zinnemann; based on Pressburger's novel), 1964

Michael Powell's Theatrical Work

Jan de Hartog's *Skipper Next to God* (Theatre Royal, Windsor, 1944)

Ernest Hemingway's *The Fifth Column* (Theatre Royal, Glasgow, 1944)

James Forsyth's *Heloise* (Golders Green, London, 1951)

Raymond Massey's *Hanging Judge* from the novel by Bruce Hamilton (New Theatre, London, 1952)

Index

About the Author

Scott Salwolke is a freelance writer for a variety of publications and a regular film critic for the *Dubuque Telegraph Herald* newspaper. He is also the author of *Nicolas Roeg: Film by Film* (1993).